A Moment o

Singapore in Malaysia and the Politics of Disengagement

Albert Lau

TIMES ACADEMIC PRESS

PHOTOGRAPH CREDITS
Front cover photographs reproduced by courtesy of the National Archives of
Singapore and the Straits Times.

CONTENTS

ABBREVIATIONS

AMD	Anglo-Malaysian Defence Agreement
BS	Barisan Sosialis
CEC	Central Executive Committee
CRO	Commonwealth Relations Office
FRU	Federal Reserve Unit
ISC	Internal Security Council
MCA	Malayan Chinese Association
MCP	Malayan Communist Party
MDU	Malayan Democratic Union
MIC	Malayan Indian Congress
MNP	Malayan Nationalist Party
MSC	Malaysian Solidarity Convention
MSCC	Malaysia Solidarity Consultative Committee
NTUC	National Trades Union Congress
PAP	People's Action Party
PMCJA	Pan-Malayan Council of Joint Action
PMIP	Pan-Malayan Islamic Party
PMU	Peninsular Malay Union
PPP	People's Progressive Party
SA	Singapore Alliance
SANAP	Sabah National Party
SATU	Singapore Association of Trade Unions
SEATO	South East Asia Treaty Organization
SF	Socialist Front
SLF	Singapore Labour Front
SMAC	Singapore Malays Action Committee
SMCA	Singapore Malayan Chinese Association
SMIC	Singapore Malayan Indian Congress
SPA	Singapore People's Alliance
SPP	Singapore Progressive Party
SUMNO	Singapore United Malays National Organization
SUPP	Sarawak United People's Party
UAR	United Arab Republic
UDP	United Democratic Party
UMNO	United Malays National Organization
UN	United Nations
UNKO	United National Kadazan Organization
UPKO	United Pasok-Momogun Kadazan Organization
UPP	United People's Party
USNO	United Sabah National Organization

S ingapore was part of the Federation of Malaysia for less than 23 months — from 16 September 1963 to 9 August 1965, yet that period stood out as one of the most critical periods in its recent history. Ever since Singapore's separation from the Malayan Union in 1946, it had been the goal of most of the Island's political parties to seek reunification with Malaya. The establishment of Malaysia on 16 September 1963 represented, therefore, the logical reintegration of Singapore into the Malay Peninsula with which it was connected by innumerable geographical, historical, economic and political ties. It was also through Malaysia that Singapore finally achieved full independence from Britain. The Malaysia years were also significant in giving birth to the new nation of Malaysia and also, after 9 August 1965, to the separate sovereign state of Singapore. It was the achievement of a new independence Singapore did not seek.

This study is an attempt to understand the circumstances, during the short but tumultuous period when Singapore was part of Malaysia, that precipitated Singapore's separation from Malaysia in August 1965. It is a continuation of my own research interests in the post-war history of Singapore and Malaysia. In embarking on this task, as in writing about contemporary history, I am aware that the field is open to controversy, not least, in this instance, because of the possibly still sensitive nature of the subject.[1] That the topic is one that has attracted widespread interest among scholars, however, is not in doubt.[2] Malaysian writers, like Mohamed Noordin Sopiee and Abdullah Ahmad, have also presented their perspectives on the episode.[3] So did a participant like Tunku Abdul Rahman.[4] One other major drawback for the historian who writes about contemporary events has always been the unavailability of primary sources. As Wee Shoo Soon observed, "Given the dearth of official documents, academics have relied almost exclusively on public sources, such as news reports and public speeches, as the bases of their studies".[5] Recent archival sources made available in Singapore and also in Britain, Australia and the United States, however, permit a more comprehensive study of the subject that was not possible in earlier works. In Singapore, the Special Branch and police reports kept at the Internal Security Department, Ministry of Home Affairs, have proven extremely useful in providing a perspective on the race riots in July and September 1964 as seen from the viewpoint of the security services. So were certain files from the Prime Minister's Office made available at the National Archives of Singapore. In the course of research, I have also benefited from recently declassified material from the Public Record Office in London, the Australian Archives in Canberra, and the National Archives and Record Administration in Washington. They have proven extremely valuable in providing a third-party perspective on the various issues and controversies that engulfed relations between Kuala Lumpur and Singapore during this period in Malaysia.

Though no longer in charge of the day-to-day running of Malaya from 1957, and the affairs of Malaysia after September 1963, Britain nevertheless retained an important measure of influence because of its involvement in the defence of the Malaysian-Singapore region, provided for within the legal framework of the Anglo-Malaysian Defence Agreement (AMDA), and its commitment to the defence of Malaysia after the outbreak of Indonesia's *Konfrontasi.*[6] Like London, Canberra and Wellington, too, took a lively interest in internal political developments within the two territories because of Australia and New Zealand's participation in the defence of Malaysia as part of AMDA. Confidential reports and telegrams from their men-on-the-spot both in Kuala Lumpur and Singapore consequently provided often detailed and valuable insights into the political happenings in the two territories. Of value, too, are the observations and assessments of equally keen observers like the Americans reporting from their embassy in Kuala Lumpur and consulate in Singapore. The key British, Australian, New Zealand and American diplomats who reported on events were men who had access to top government leaders in Kuala Lumpur and Singapore and often had good insights into their thinking. Depending on whether they wrote from the vantage point of either Kuala Lumpur or Singapore, shades of difference in emphasis would sometimes surface. Taken together, however, their views provide a useful foil to the perspectives offered by the local participants. The present study is an attempt, using these newly available sources, to shed some more light on the story of Singapore's separation from Malaysia. Given the significance of the episode in Singapore and Malaysian history, it is inevitable that the historiography on the subject will continue to be augmented, especially when more records become available from the archives in both Singapore and Malaysia — as well as from accounts of the period by the key participants themselves.

In the course of this work, I have received invaluable assistance from a number of quarters. Vimala Nambiar, Head of the Reprographics Services Department, National University of Singapore Central Library, has been most obliging in accommodating my requests. I am particularly indebted to Mrs Lily Tan, Senior Director of the National Archives of Singapore (NAS), for the support she had given to the project and also for permission to use the photographs from the NAS collection for this book. I would also like to extend my thanks to Pitt Kuan Wah, Deputy Director (NAS) and Jason Lim and Chong Ching Liang. I am especially grateful to the Internal Security Department, Ministry of Home Affairs, Singapore, for special permission to use and cite Special Branch sources in the work. In London, I benefited immensely from the exemplary services provided by the Public Record Office. In both Canberra and Washington, the staff of, respectively, the Australian Archives and the National Archives and Records Administration have shown me much courtesy and offered me considerable help. I would also like to express my gratitude, in particular, to Kate Cumming and Elyse Boutcher of the Australian Archives. To my research assistant, Chua Ai Lin, I am especially grateful. She has been excellent in ferreting out huge quantities of research material and in accommodating my numerous requests with efficiency and good cheer. The editorial and production team in Federal Publications Singapore has also shown me much patience and provided me with a thoroughly professional structure of support from the beginning. I need hardly say, however, that the responsibility for interpretation and errors in this study remains with the author and that the views expressed do not reflect those of the National University of Singapore or of the other institutions or individuals who have kindly and graciously facilitated my research.

Albert Lau
June 1998

Notes

1. On 7 June 1996, for instance, responding to a question regarding the possibility of a remerger with Malaysia at the Foreign Correspondents' Club in Singapore, Singapore's Senior Minister, Lee Kuan Yew, said that such an arrangement was,

indeed, possible if certain conditions were met. These were if Malaysia adopted the same policy of meritocracy as Singapore did, and if Malaysia pursued, as successfully, the same goals as Singapore, to bring maximum economic benefit to its people. Lee's remarks provoked a political storm from across the Causeway. Malaysian leaders thought he was opening old wounds and that Singapore was deliberately playing down Malaysia's achievements and casting the country in a negative light by suggesting that its ethnic groups were not treated equally. See *The Straits Times*, 8, 11, 12, 15, 22, 29 June 1996.

2. See, for instance, Willard Hanna, *The Separation of Singapore from Malaysia* (New York: American Universities Field Staff, 1965); Norman J. Parmer, "Malaysia 1965: Challenging the Terms of 1957", *Asian Survey*, 6, 2 (February 1966), pp. 111–18; R.S. Milne, "Singapore's Exit from Malaysia: The Consequences of Ambiguity", *Asian Survey*, 6, 3 (March 1966), pp. 175–84; Jean Grossholtz, "An Exploration of Malaysian Meanings", *Asian Survey*, 6, 4 (April 1966), pp. 227–40; R. Catley, "Malaysia: The Lost Battle for Merger", *The Australian Outlook*, 21, 1 (1967), pp. 44–60; Robert O. Tilman, "Malaysia and Singapore: The Failure of a Federation", in Robert O. Tilman (ed.), *Man, State and Society in Contemporary Southeast Asia* (New York: Praegar Publishers, 1969); Nancy McHenry Fletcher, *The Separation of Singapore from Malaysia* (Ithaca: Cornell University Southeast Asia Program Data Paper no. 73, 1969); Charles Richard Ostrom, "A Core Interest Analysis of the Formation of Malaysia and the Separation of Singapore" (Unpublished PhD dissertation submitted to the Claremont Graduate School, 1971); Robert Allen Anderson, "The Separation of Singapore from Malaysia: A Study in Political Involution" (Unpublished PhD dissertation submitted to The American University, 1973); Tae Yul Nam, "Malaysia and Singapore: The Failure of a Political Experiment" (Unpublished PhD dissertation submitted to Georgetown University, 1975); John Drysdale, *Singapore: Struggle for Success* (Singapore: Times Books International, 1984); Michael Barr, "Lee Kuan Yew in Malaysia: A Reappraisal of Lee Kuan Yew's Role in the Separation of Singapore from Malaysia", *Asian Studies Review*, 21, 1 (July 1997), pp. 1–17.

3. See Mohamed Noordin Sopiee, *From Malayan Union to Singapore Separation: Political Unification in the Malaysia Region 1945–65* (Kuala Lumpur: Penerbit Universiti Malaya, 1974); Abdullah Ahmad, *Tengku Abdul Rahman and Malaysia's Foreign Policy 1963–1970* (Kuala Lumpur: Berita Publishing, 1985).

4. See Tunku Abdul Rahman, *Looking Back* (Kuala Lumpur: Pustaka Antara, 1977).

5. Wee Shoo Soon, "The Separation of Singapore from Malaysia: Approaches and Issues" (Unpublished Academic Exercise submitted to the Department of History, National University of Singapore, 1998), p. 9.

6. See Chin Kin Wah, *The Defence of Malaysia and Singapore: The Transformation of a Security System 1957–1971* (Cambridge: Cambridge University Press, 1983).

CHAPTER 1

THE BATTLE FOR MERGER

Separation of Singapore, 1946

With the capitulation of British Malaya during the Second World War, the fate of the British Empire had reached its wartime nadir. In a campaign lasting a mere 70 days,[1] invading Japanese forces had inflicted what Churchill called the "greatest disaster to British arms which our history records"[2] — the capture of Britain's "impregnable fortress" in Singapore on 15 February 1942. The magnitude and ease of military defeat had profoundly humiliated Britain in Asian eyes, and precipitated strong demands in Britain for a reappraisal of British colonial policy. In Whitehall, officials of the Colonial Office accepted that a new deal was required for Malaya. The stresses of war had exposed the fragility of the old order, and made a return to the *status quo ante* impossible. The break in imperial continuity, at the same time, offered British planners a unique opportunity "to clear up all the country's troubles".[3] It was in such circumstances of change that the Malayan Union plan was devised by officials in the Colonial Office, and Singapore's severance from Malaya envisaged at the same time — with such far-reaching repercussions for the Island's future relationship with Malaya.[4]

The task of rebuilding a new Malaya necessitated, in the first instance, the creation of a united Malaya. Despite the efforts of numerous British officials before the war to bring about a semblance of administrative order to the patchwork of nine autonomous Malay states and three British settlements, a united Malaya remained an elusive goal of British policy. Also in urgent need was a policy for managing the rising aspirations of

Malaya's non-Malay, largely Chinese community for political rights and status so far denied them in the Malay states. In view of their numerical strength, economic power and wartime exertions on behalf of Malaya, the legitimate claims of the Malayan Chinese for political recognition could not be as easily dismissed, or ignored. The war, in its own way, had lent a greater urgency to the resolution of these pre-war concerns. For one, the new requirements of imperial security in the post-war world demanded a Malaya united under Britain, able and willing to fulfil its role in the envisaged security system for the region. For another, the spectre of a resurgent China after the war actively backing, and exerting pressure on behalf of, the Malayan Chinese in their quest for political recognition necessitated a pre-emptive British initiative to formulate an equitable scheme for granting reasonable political rights to at least a portion of the Chinese population in Malaya.[5] The Malayan Union scheme was designed with these considerations in mind. Under the plan, a peninsular union was to be created, comprising the nine Malay states and the settlements of Penang and Malacca, but not Singapore. There was also envisaged a common citizenship for all who regarded Malaya as their home. Fresh treaties would be negotiated with the Malay rulers whereby the British Crown would acquire the full powers necessary to effect these changes.[6]

The Malayan Union plan was as revolutionary as it was controversial, for it amounted no less to a new imperialism[7] foisted on the Malay states. Not only were the unwilling Malay kingdoms to suffer the ignominy of annexation, and forced into a single unitary constitutional mould for Britain's sake, they were also now asked to surrender their sovereignty and acquiesce meekly to British plans to lay the foundations for a multiracial Malaya for the benefit of all Malayans — at the expense of the Malays. Left unsaid was the implied abandonment of the pro-Malay policy that had underpinned Anglo-Malay relations since 1874. The price for this new initiative was also controversial — Singapore's exclusion from the Malayan Union, itself a tacit recognition that the Island's inclusion could only create obstacles to Malay acceptance of the scheme.

Rationalizations for Singapore's separate treatment were justified on economic, political and racial grounds. There was, first of all, the divergence of economic interest[8] between the mainland and Singapore:

> Economically, Singapore has special interests distinct from those of the Malayan mainland. The prosperity of the Peninsula depends on primary

production; that of Singapore depends upon its entrepot trade. Moreover, 90% of this entrepot is connected with the outside world … and only 10% with the Malayan mainland. It might be felt that this diversity of economic interest is an argument for including Singapore in the Union, since it would broaden the economic basis of the Union as a whole; but the fact is rather that the economic interests and outlook of Singapore and [the] mainland are so divergent as to be likely to create friction if the two entities are combined at this stage in a single political grouping.[9]

There was the additional fear of "Government from Singapore",[10] which historically stemmed from the fact that the High Commissioner of the Malay states was also the same person as the Governor of the Straits Settlements with his seat of power in Singapore:

> The more important point is a psychological one. If Singapore is included in the Union from the outset … it will establish itself as the centre of Union affairs … The Malays would have the sensation, which they have felt and resented in the past, of being governed from an alien city. If, however, Singapore is in the early stages excluded from the Malayan Union, and if the centre of the Union is placed at Kuala Lumpur in the Malay States, the cooperation of the Malays in making the Union a reality will be much easier to obtain.[11]

But the "strongest argument"[12] that sealed Singapore's fate was the racial factor. By 1941, the Malays were already outnumbered in their own country: 1.9 million Malays to 2 million non-Malays (Chinese and Indians). The inclusion of the Straits Settlements of Penang, Malacca and Singapore would cause the disparity to rise significantly: 3.1 million non-Malays to 2.2. million Malays. If only Penang and Malacca were included, non-Malays on the whole would still predominate at 2.4 million, but the Chinese, numbering 1.7 million, would be less than the 2.1 million Malays. Singapore's addition, however, would make the Chinese at 2.3 million the dominant race, with the Malays at 2.2 million relegated to second place.[13] As H.T. Bourdillon, an official in the Colonial Office, remarked:

> Singapore, with its 700,000 inhabitants, is almost entirely a Chinese city. The aggregate of the population of Malaya is made up in almost equal proportions of Malays and Chinese, but the population just tips the balance in favour of the latter … Our new policy for Malaya means the opening to the Chinese of many doors which have hitherto been closed to them. They are to be admitted to citizenship on equal terms

> with the Malays ... This policy will in any case cause anxiety amongst
> the Malays ... We must [therefore] be careful not to create a situation
> in which the Malays are dispirited and antagonized, and it can readily
> be seen how fundamental a difference the inclusion or exclusion of
> Singapore may make in their attitude.[14]

At the end of the war, Sir Harold MacMichael was despatched as the British government's Special Representative to secure the rulers' signatures to the new treaties, a task he accomplished amidst an "undercurrent of antagonism"[15] from a number of the Malay rulers between October and December 1945. The Malayan Union was formally inaugurated on 1 April 1946. At the same time, Singapore began its existence as a separate British colony.

Singapore's separation was not meant to be permanent. Britain recognized that "there were and will be close ties between Singapore and the mainland" and it was "no part of the policy of His Majesty's Government to preclude in any way the fusion of Singapore and the Malayan Union in a wider union at a later date should it be considered that such a course was desirable".[16] But separation created its own paradox. Once detached, it was not easy to re-attach the Island to the mainland. In the aftermath of the war, both Singapore and Malaya charted their own constitutional paths in the anti-colonial struggle for independence. Their roads crossed briefly in 1963, when Singapore was reunited with the mainland, only to experience the anguish of separation again in 1965.

Drifting Apart

Malaya's road to independence began with a constitutional bang. The Malayan Union so struck at the core of the Malays' consciousness of Malaya being primarily a Malay country that not even Singapore's tactical exclusion was sufficient to soothe their revulsion at British bad faith and betrayal. The constitutional uproar it provoked was impassioned and threatened to undermine the very basis of British rule in Malaya. Their fears heightened, the Malays rallied behind their traditional rulers and the newly formed United Malays National Organization (UMNO),[17] formed in March 1946 and led by Johore aristocrat Onn bin Ja'afar, to protest against the Malayan Union. Mass demonstrations, boycotts, and non-cooperation followed. Such was the intensity of Malay opposition — which contrasted sharply with the lukewarm response the scheme evoked among non-Malays who would have gained most from it — that British officials scrapped the scheme barely three months after it was introduced, and started talks with UMNO and the rulers to ascertain the features of the Malayan Union's constitutional successor, the Federation of Malaya. A belated attempt by largely non-Malay opinion through the Pan-Malayan Council of Joint Action (PMCJA) — later renamed the All Malaya Council of Joint Action — to oppose the Federation scheme and its more stringent citizenship provisions, from December 1946, came to naught as the British refused to sanction another volte-face so late in the day.[18] When the Federation of Malaya finally displaced the Malayan Union on 1 February 1948, it represented a major Malay victory in overturning a significant British initiative to put Malaya on a more Malayan footing. But it was not a total victory for Malay nationalism either. In accepting the Federation agreement, they had also tacitly accepted the principle of common citizenship — and the need for Malaya to develop into a multiracial state. Unification "under one name or another"[19] had also been achieved. The significance of the Malayan Union episode lay in its impact on future political change in Malaya. By beating off a dangerous threat to their political primacy, the Malays had set the tenor and established the framework for the future constitutional and political evolution of Malaya.

After the Malayan Union fracas, the Colonial Office fought shy of entanglement in further controversy with the Malays and their rulers over the vexed issues of their sovereignty and status.[20] In need of mustering Malay support in the battle against the largely Chinese communist insurgents after the outbreak of the Emergency[21] from June 1948, the British continued to uphold their pro-Malay policy. Confronted by an armed challenge from the Chinese-led communist movement, the Malays, in turn, closed ranks behind UMNO. These developments were to have significant ramifications for the future structure of politics in Malaya. First, given UMNO's refusal to open its ranks to non-Malays[22] and the lack of grassroot Malay support for multiracial parties, politics in the Federation of Malaya invariably gravitated towards the pattern of communal alignments, with the Malays, Chinese and Indians broadly represented by separate communal parties like UMNO, the Malayan Chinese Association (MCA), and the Malayan Indian Congress (MIC) respectively. It was through such a conglomeration of communally-based parties that UMNO, now led by Tunku Abdul Rahman, won the first Federal elections in July 1955 with an overwhelming majority. The success of the Alliance formula — UMNO, the MCA and MIC making up the Alliance Party of independence — thus established the pattern of communally-based politics in Malaya for many years to come. Second, the years of fighting a determined communist-armed insurrection had given rise to an Alliance government that was staunchly anti-communist, autocratic and rightwing.

The underlying principle of Malay political dominance, now underpinned by UMNO's hegemonic position within the Alliance, was to be jealously guarded in the negotiations for a new constitution in the run-up to independence. The formal terms of the 1957 constitution of independent Malaya thus gave the preponderance of political power to the Malays by granting them citizenship on a more liberal basis than other communities. While Malays born in the Federation were automatically citizens, non-Malays were not, unless born after Merdeka Day (or unless born in the former British settlements of Penang and Malacca). Apart from making Islam the official religion, Malay the sole official language from 1967, and a Malay ruler the Yang di-Pertuan Agong, the supreme head of state, Article 153 also assured Malays of "special privileges" in respect to education, positions in the public service, and the issuance of business permits and licenses. When a new group of leaders in the MCA, led by Lim Chong Eu, sought to modify the terms of the constitution to the advantage of the Chinese, and demanded a greater number of seats in the forthcoming elections of 1959, Malay reaction was swift and decisive. The Tunku threatened to contest the elections without the MCA, forcing the latter to back down.[23] Lim eventually left the party and was replaced by Tan Siew Sin. The Alliance went on to win the 1959 elections with the basic agreements intact.

If Malaya's constitutional road began with a bang, that of Singapore started with a whimper. While the change in the status of the Malay states had provoked an impassioned constitutional uproar in Malaya, and launched UMNO onto the forefront of the Malayan political stage, Singapore, whose status as a British colony had remained unchanged, was spared a tumultuous constitutional controversy. Singapore's exclusion from the Malayan Union evoked only subdued criticism from newspapers, like *The Straits Times*, *Malayan Tribune* and *Singapore Free Press*, and "feeble moves"[24] from newly formed and still struggling political parties, like the Malay Nationalist Party (MNP)[25] and the Malayan Democratic Union (MDU).[26] Singapore's severance had evinced little interest from the Malayan Communist Party (MCP) initially, whose priority then was on organizing an anti-colonial labour movement[27] rather than on discussing constitutional issues. The MCP probably calculated that once the British were removed, merger was inevitable, for its goal had always been a united communist Malaya. Only from December 1946, did agitation for merger begin in earnest after the MDU-led PMCJA launched its anti-Federation campaign. Included in one of its objectives was that of a united Malaya inclusive of Singapore.[28] But with its failure to make any headway, the initial efforts to achieve political unification collapsed.

British efforts to quicken the pace of political progressivism through the holding of early elections on 20 March 1948 also failed to elicit much interest from Singapore's majority Chinese population. Introduced mainly to stimulate interest and confidence in the Island's political future after the trauma[29] of its abrupt constitutional severance from the mainland, the 1948 elections were a rather placid affair with election fever "bringing no rise in temperature".[30] The limited franchise was not calculated to enthuse, and it did not. Out of an estimated potential electorate of 200,000 persons, only 22,395 bothered to register to vote, of whom only 5,627 or 25 per cent were Chinese, the majority of the other voters being either Indians or Europeans to whom elections were no novelty.[31] No single party emerged to dominate the political landscape, as UMNO did in Malaya, before 1959. The MDU had boycotted the 1948 election, finding it not democratic enough. Probably only the MCP came nearest to centre stage in Singapore, in view of its appeal among the Chinese masses as a consequence of its role in spearheading the anti-Japanese resistance movement during the war. But the MCP was outlawed after the outbreak of its armed insurrection in 1948 and was never to operate openly again. The MDU had also voluntarily ceased to operate under the hostile Emergency regulations. Winning three out of the six elected seats in 1948, and increasing its lead to six seats out of nine in the 1951 elections, the newly registered Singapore Progressive Party (SPP)[32] emerged as a potential contender when it was thrust into the forefront of the political stage. But the SPP was essentially a right-wing, elitist party of Anglicized and English-educated professionals, with no mass base.[33] Committed to a gradualist approach to independence in collaboration with the colonial power, the SPP appealed to the limited electorate of British subjects, and few others. Its political demise was inevitable, for the SPP was a right-wing party operating within a left-wing environment. It was to meet its Waterloo in the 1955 elections.

From 1955 the pace of political evolution changed suddenly. Beginning with the elections on 2 April that year to elect the government under the new Rendel constitution, Singapore accelerated rapidly to achieve self-government by 1959. Encouraged by the failure of the communist armed struggle in Malaya, and partly motivated by the desire to counter the attractions of communism to Singapore's urban Chinese, the British removed the lid that the Emergency had imposed on political activities and sought greater political participation. Accordingly, in 1953, a commission, headed by Sir George Rendel, was appointed to review the constitution. Published in February 1954, the Rendel Commission's report envisaged Singapore taking what Sopiee called a "leap towards self-rule".[34] The commission recommended a significant jump in the number of elected seats from 9 to 25, giving an elected majority in the Legislative Assembly. It also proposed that voters be automatically registered, thereby enlarging the electorate to about 300,000 voters,[35] the majority of whom were non-English speaking Chinese residents, and thus ushering Singapore into the era of mass politics.[36] The scope for anti-colonial mass agitation prompted left-wing parties to make a comeback. One such party was the Singapore Labour Front (SLF),[37] led by David Marshall, a prominent lawyer. Another was the People's Action Party (PAP) headed by Lee Kuan Yew.[38]

In the 1955 elections, left-wing parties were the ones that made the most gains,the SLF having won 10 seats and the PAP, in its token participation, took three of the four seats it contested. What the surprising left-wing victories showed was that the electorate would support parties that were stridently left-wing, anti-colonial and socialist in orientation over those that were right-wing, anti-colonial and capitalist.[39] Henceforth, the significant political parties in Singapore were left-wing ones: in 1955, it was the SLF that led the government; in 1959, it was the turn of the PAP. The right-wing SPP was totally eclipsed. Fielding 22 candidates, it won only 4 seats. The 1955 elections also highlighted another feature of Singapore politics: the electoral attractions of multiracial parties. Given the Island's large Chinese majority, the scope for communally-based parties was more limited, unlike in Malaya, where the numerical strengths of the various communities were less decisive. In the Singapore 1955 polls, the right-wing Democratic Party, which drew its appeal from Chinese chauvinism, was almost completely routed. Contesting 20 seats, it won only two.[40] In subsequent elections, other communal parties, offshoots of their parent bodies in Malaya, namely, the UMNO, MCA and MIC, also made their appearance, but they were never able to dominate the political scene in Singapore. Finally, after 1955, attracted by the potential for mass agitation under the Rendel constitution, and the failure of its rural insurrection in Malaya, the MCP also increased its subversion of political, educational and labour groups in Singapore, further radicalizing the Island's political atmosphere. The return of the MCP to urban subversion in Singapore was to result in a further heightening of the left-wing influence in Singapore and create the circumstances that would propel the PAP into the forefront of Singapore's political stage.

The new era of mass politics from 1955 necessitated a reorientation of political style and strategy in order to win the hearts and minds of the largely Chinese-educated, economically discontented, and communist-infiltrated electorate. The SLF government of Marshall and his successor, Lim Yew Hock, proved inept at mass mobilization because they failed to appreciate that, unlike in Malaya, where Anglo-Malay collaboration was necessary to stem the armed communist tide, collaboration with the colonial power to crush the largely Chinese-dominated communist movement in Singapore, without first isolating them from the Chinese community, spelled the death knell of political parties. Lim's anti-communist purges, while praised by the British, alienated his government from the Chinese masses who saw him as a puppet of the colonial power. The PAP's commitment to a mass-based anti-colonial united front, on the other hand, required the party to collaborate with the MCP to bridge the gap to the Chinese-educated world. Collaboration was fraught with danger, not only from subversion within, but also suppression from without. Through its exposition of political and economic issues, the intellectual content of its arguments, its resilience and skill in isolating and defeating the communists constitutionally, assisted by opportune SLF purges, the PAP was to emerge as a political force of significance by 1959. The election in May that year to bring into operation a self-governing constitution saw the PAP contesting all 51 seats and winning 43. Lim Yew Hock, who had gathered the remnants of the SLF into a new Singapore People's Alliance (SPA) contested 39 seats but won only 4. The communal Singapore UMNO won 3 seats while its MCA counterpart, failed to win even one. With its victory, the PAP emerged as the dominant political force on the Singapore stage. But the attainment of internal self-government marked only the close of a phase in Singapore's anti-colonial struggle. The final phase of the fight to gain full independence through merger with the Federation of Malaya was about to start.[41]

But, by then, 13 years of drifting apart had resulted in further political and ideological differentiation between the two territories. The government in power in Malaya had become characteristically right-wing, anti-communist and communal in its orientation with a distinctly pro-Malay bias. Singapore, on the other hand, had developed into a predominantly Chinese state administered by a government that was left-wing, non-communist and non-communal in outlook. There seemed no reason to assume that the rationalizations for Singapore's separation in 1946 might not be as relevant now as they appeared then.

The Formation of Malaysia

Since its inception, the PAP had always stood for a united Malaya inclusive of Singapore. After the PAP was voted into power in May 1959, it began to work assiduously to bring about merger with Malaya. Lee Kuan Yew had already started the process long before that, as he revealed in a speech in 1962: "I spent a great deal of time and effort between 1955 and 1959, when I assumed office, trying to convince him [the Tunku] that in the long run he had to reckon with Singapore, and that it was easier if he included us in his overall calculations."[42] To Lee, Singapore's exclusion from Malaya was the result of a "freak man-made frontier". "Had the British heeded the history of the peoples of Malaya and geography and economic realities," he said, "they would have put Singapore into the Malayan Union, just like Penang and Malacca."[43]

For Singapore, merger was urgent. Without it, the prospects of the Island surviving either economically or politically as an independent state, were grim. Devoid of natural resources and confronted by a declining entrepot trade and a growing population requiring jobs, Singapore needed the Federation "hinterland" to provide a bigger common market for its manufactured goods. "Without this economic base Singapore would not survive," Lee had argued.[44] Nor was it likely that Britain would agree to an independent Singapore state that was not economically viable. The inability to achieve independence for Singapore, on the other hand, would put the PAP's own political survival at risk, since the 1959 self-governing constitution was due for review in 1963, with independence as the next logical step. Merger was politically beneficial to the PAP for another reason: its erstwhile left-wing communist opponents would be politically neutralized in a Malaya headed by a right-wing and anti-communist government. For Lee, merger was, therefore, "as inevitable as the rising and setting of the sun."[45]

The problem, however, lay across the Causeway. Absorbed with fighting the communists in the jungle war, Kuala Lumpur showed little interest in constitutional experimentation. As far as the Tunku was concerned, independence must be achieved first before merger could be considered. "The question of merger," the Tunku said in January 1955, "is still a very long way off and nothing much can be done about it until Singapore and the Federation achieve independence."[46] The Tunku apparently feared that merger would have retarded and complicated the Federation's move towards independence.[47] He was to subsequently blow hot and cold on the matter, raising hopes in January 1956 about the possibility of Singapore joining the Federation as a "subordinate unit", so that "we could have control in the affairs of Singapore, especially subversive activities now being carried on there",[48] only to burst the bubble a year later when he declared in January 1957 that he would not accept Singapore "even as a unit".[49] The fact was, for Kuala Lumpur, merger with Singapore spelt big trouble. The differences in outlook of the people of the Federation and Singapore were so pronounced that "for me a merger was out of the question," the Tunku was to say later. He noted that the overwhelmingly Chinese population in Singapore was unlikely to want to pay homage to a Malay monarch as head of state, promote Malay as the national language or accept Islam as the state religion.[50] The real fears, however, were more demographic and ideological. In its own assessment of why Kuala Lumpur was anti-merger in 1958, the PAP had this to say: "The Alliance leaders have put out different reasons at different times, but we can summarize them into two: First, Singapore has about one million Chinese ... The inclusion of this one million into the Federation will upset the racial balance of power in the Federation. Second, Singapore has too many 'leftists' who are supported by the one million Chinese in Singapore."[51] In 1960, the Malays in the Federation numbered 3.1 million compared to 2.3 million Chinese and 700,000 Indians. If Singapore was included, the combined Chinese population of 3.6 million would outnumber the Malays at 3.4 million.[52] Merger was, therefore, unpalatable to the Malays because of the risk that it would bring Chinese predominance for, ultimately, the majority of the electorate would be non-Malays.[53] For UMNO, any significant increase in the number of Chinese voters would prejudice its political dominance in Malayan politics, its position in the Alliance and relations with the MCA.[54]

But the alternative risk of Singapore achieving separate independence outside the Federation was even greater. So long as Singapore remained a British colony, and Malaya's security concerns safeguarded by its casting vote in the Internal Security Council (ISC),[55] the possibility of the communists usurping power in Singapore was slim. Prolonging Singapore's status as a British colony, however, was unrealistic, for in the Tunku's mind,

11

"a time would come when Singapore would ask for and be given independence, and that time is not far off for new talks on the Constitution are to be held in 1963."[56] If Singapore were kept as a separate political entity, the Tunku foresaw that it must eventually emerge as a separate independent state, in which case it could not possibly consent to having its sovereignty compromised by the continued existence of the ISC.[57] The other alternative — whereby Britain refused to support either the abolition of the ISC or independence for Singapore — was equally problematic, for the likely outcome would be the fall of the moderate PAP government, and its replacement by one more radical, further to the left and unwilling to contemplate merger on terms acceptable to the Tunku. That the PAP was having difficulty holding its ground in Singapore was already evident in its defeat in the Hong Lim by-election on 29 April 1961, when Ong Eng Guan defeated the PAP candidate with a startling 73.3 per cent of the vote, followed closely by another by-election loss in Anson on 15 July 1961, when the PAP lost narrowly to David Marshall. Cracks had also appeared in the PAP's internal cohesion when 13 PAP assemblymen from its left-wing were expelled from the party after they refused to support a vote of confidence Lee demanded from the Legislative Assembly on 20 July 1961. This dissenting group, who retained their seats in the Assembly, went on to form the Barisan Sosialis (BS) with Lee Siew Choh as chairman and Lim Chin Siong as secretary-general. It did not take Alliance leaders long to realize that unless Singapore merged with a larger anti-communist Malaysia, it would become an ideological base from which the Malayan communists could subvert the mainland, a situation "quite unacceptable to us", said the Tunku.[58] However dangerous Singapore might be inside the Federation of Malaya, it could be even more dangerous outside it.

Both the demographic and ideological threats that Singapore posed to the Federation had to be contained if merger was to be acceptable to Kuala Lumpur and to UMNO. The problem of Chinese numbers could be resolved, so the Tunku assumed, by bringing the Borneo territories to act as a racial counterweight to Singapore's Chinese population. If the Borneo territories were added to the association, the total 3.7 million Chinese would be outnumbered by some 4 million Malays and the indigenous people. Apart from the 3 million Malays from the Federation, and another 200,000 from Singapore, the addition of the Borneo territories would add another 176,000 Malays, mainly from Sarawak and Brunei, and 700,000 indigenous people from the latter two states and North Borneo.[59] The ideological threat could be blunted by negotiating special terms for

Singapore's entry into Malaysia that would insulate the Federation from the robust politics of the state.

Thus, on 27 May 1961, in a speech made at the lunch hosted by the Foreign Correspondents' Association of Southeast Asia, the Tunku made his historic announcement that "sooner or later" Singapore, together with the Borneo territories, should be brought closer together in political and economic cooperation.[60] Lee Kuan Yew responded on 3 June affirming his support for the Tunku's proposal. After discussions between the two leaders, agreement on broad terms for merger was reached in principle on 23 August between Malaya and Singapore. On 16 October the Dewan Ra'ayat (House of Representatives) approved the Malaysia agreement which was subsequently published on 15 November.[61] Discussions between the Malayan and British governments were held in London from 20 to 22 November, and in December, the Singapore Legislative Assembly passed a motion supporting Malaysia in principle. The merger plans, however, were opposed by the BS. A referendum bill was introduced on 27 November and bitterly debated in the Assembly. The referendum was subsequently held on 1 September 1962, after almost a year long campaign to win popular support for the scheme. Arguing that all political parties had accepted merger in one form or another, the PAP government asked the people to choose the type of merger they favoured, and not whether they accepted or rejected merger. The result was an overwhelming 71 per cent of the electorate voting for the merger arrangements put forward by the PAP.

Meanwhile, the battle for Malaysia was also set in motion in the Borneo territories. While the British were prepared to allow the Borneo territories to merge with the Federation if Singapore was also included, the Borneo territories, on their part, viewed the Malaysia proposal with some suspicion. They feared that Malaysia might lead to domination by a pro-Malay Kuala Lumpur government. To assuage their suspicions, the North Borneo and Sarawak leaders were invited to the Commonwealth Parliamentary Association Conference in Singapore on 23 July 1961, where a Malaysia Solidarity Consultative Committee (MSCC), under the chairmanship of Donald A. Stephens, a leading North Borneo unofficial, was formed. The committee would facilitate discussions on the Malaysia proposal to identify the concerns of the Borneans. Brunei, disinclined to join Malaysia because of strong anti-Federation feelings among its government officials, was not represented at the first meeting and sent only observers to the remaining three meetings of the MSCC held in Kuching, Kuala Lumpur and Singapore. In the discussions, Lee

Kuan Yew apparently worked hard to establish rapport with, and allay the fears of, the Bornean leaders.[62] Both London and Kuala Lumpur consequently agreed at the London talks in November 1961 to despatch a commission of enquiry to ascertain the views of the Borneo territories towards Malaysia. Appointed on 16 January 1962, the Cobbold Commission, led by its chairman, Lord Cobbold, toured North Borneo and Sarawak between 19 February and 17 April 1962. It held 50 hearings at 35 different centres, interviewed over 4,000 persons in some 690 groups, and received nearly 600 letters and memoranda in Sabah and over 1,600 in Sarawak.[63] The Cobbold Commission's assessment was that about one-third of the population in each territory was strongly in favour of Malaysia, one-third was favourable but wanting certain safeguards, while the remaining third preferred independence without Malaysia or the continuation of British rule.[64] In further discussions in London between Britain and Malaya in July 1962, the Cobbold Report was accepted and the decision was made to set up an Inter-governmental Committee under Lord Lansdowne's chairmanship to work out detailed arrangements and safeguards for North Borneo and Sarawak. It was also agreed that Malaysia would be established by 31 August 1963. Only the oil-rich state of Brunei opted out because of differences over its terms of entry. On 9 July 1963, the Malaysia Agreement was signed in London by Britain, Malaya, Singapore, Sarawak and North Borneo. It was agreed that Malaysia would come into being on 31 August 1963.

In negotiating the terms for Singapore's entry into Malaysia, what the Tunku had in mind was for Singapore to have virtual autonomy in running its own affairs so that it would be possible to contain political exuberance within the Island. The broad principles agreed on 23 August 1961 envisaged Kuala Lumpur bearing responsibility for defence, external affairs and security while Singapore "laid particular stress" on the necessity of it retaining local autonomy, especially on matters of education and labour.[65] Placing control of internal security in the hands of the Federation was one of the "essential concessions"[66] Singapore had to make to ensure merger. Another concerned its representation in the Dewan Ra'ayat and the nature of its population's citizenship within the new Federation. When the full terms for merger, with the exception of the financial arrangements, were made public on 15 November 1961, following the joint meetings of Malayan and Singapore officials, what was revealed was that, in return for autonomy in education and labour, Singapore agreed to a more limited number of seats than its population warranted, 15 instead of possibly 24 on a proportionate basis. By contrast, Sarawak and Sabah were apportioned 24 and 16 seats, instead of meriting only 11 and 7 respectively on a strictly population basis.[67] As Ostrom put it, "not only were the Borneo territories brought in as a counterbalance to Chinese Singapore but also, by the special terms of merger, the political weight of the Borneo territories was greatly increased and that of Singapore was significantly decreased."[68] The provision for special Singapore citizenship rather than a unitary Malaysian citizenship also reflected Kuala Lumpur's desire to insulate the Federation politically from Singapore. In order that some 624,000 Singapore citizens, who were born outside of Singapore, would not be disenfranchised under the Federation's more stringent citizenship requirements for non-Malays, it was proposed that all Singapore citizens would continue to retain their Singapore citizenship while automatically becoming "nationals" of the larger Federation. But Singapore citizens could run as candidates for a legislative seat and vote only in Singapore. Federal citizens, in turn, could run for a legislative seat or vote only in Malaya.[69] In short, these provisions were designed to reduce the danger of Singapore's Chinese threatening the political dominance of the Malay-dominated Alliance in Malaya. At the same time, the "special position" of Singapore's Malay community was also safeguarded in the constitutional proposals, although Kuala Lumpur accepted that the "special privileges" accorded to their kith and kin in Malaya would not apply in Singapore.[70]

In view of Singapore's greater local autonomy, it was agreed that Singapore would "retain a very large proportion" of its state revenue to discharge its responsibility in education, labour and other state responsibilities. But because the Federal Minister of Finance, Tan Siew Sin, later insisted on obtaining various financial powers that he considered necessary, the negotiations over the economic terms of merger proved particularly tendentious. The difficulties arose because they affected the MCA, which had interests of its own to protect. Tan had wanted ultimate control over revenue matters, and a specified percentage of the Singapore revenue as payment for Federal services, whilst Singapore felt that unless it had sufficient control over its financial revenues, it could not bring about its own social and economic development. It, therefore, proposed that Singapore should collect and keep its revenue, and hand over a specified sum for payment of Federal services. Singapore, in turn, wanted a common market agreement written into the new constitution, while the Federation wanted only agreement in principle, leaving the details to be settled after Malaysia. Kuala Lumpur had little interest in such a proposal as it had its

15

own industries to protect. In the end, in exchange for Malaya's acceptance of a common market agreement, Singapore gave up 40 per cent of the total revenue it collected to the central government. Connected with the common market issue was the granting of pioneer status to industries. It was agreed that after Malaysia, the Federal Minister of Finance had to approve the pioneer status certificates issued by the Singapore government. Kuala Lumpur also demanded an outright gift of $50 million for the development of the Borneo states. After hard negotiations, it was finally agreed that Singapore would provide a loan of $150 million on attractive terms, provided that 50 per cent of the labour for projects financed from the loan came from Singapore.[71] The hard negotiations were to have ramifications for later Kuala Lumpur–Singapore ties, as the Tunku commented:

> What he [Tan Siew Sin] succeeded in getting went far beyond my idea, for not only did the Central Government exercise important powers in the State's administration, but Singapore found itself committed to financial development in the Borneo States on a very substantial scale. I felt that once we were enmeshed in Singapore's day to day life and administration, and controlling the finance of the State, the inevitable consequence would be that the Singapore Government would want to take a full share in the Malaysian administration; and if we were not prepared to give Singapore the right, then Mr Lee Kuan Yew's attack on Malaysia was justified.[72]

Meanwhile, the inclusion of the Borneo territories was opposed by Indonesia[73] and the Philippines, both of whom had interest in the area. The Tunku agreed to meet with the Indonesian President, Sukarno, and his Filipino counterpart, D. Macapagal, for a summit conference at Manila from 30 July to 5 August 1963, the upshot of which was Kuala Lumpur's agreement to postpone Malaysia Day in order to give the United Nations (UN) time to ascertain popular will in the Borneo territories on its formation. The Manila summit alarmed the PAP leaders who felt that any delay in inaugurating Malaysia would only encourage the anti-Malaysia forces to revive their internal agitation. "We are not partners to the Manila Agreement and therefore, as far as we are concerned, 31 August is still our Malaysia Day," Lee Kuan Yew declared.[74] Lee flew to Jesselton and Kuching to meet with Donald Stephens and Stephen Kalong Ningkan, the chief ministers designate of Sabah and Sarawak respectively. The result was a united front calling on the Tunku to set up Malaysia as agreed on 31 August 1963. The new date for Malaysia Day was subsequently postponed to 16 September 1963.[75] On 31

August 1963, Lee Kuan Yew declared Singapore's *de facto* independence, to Kuala Lumpur's chagrin.[76] As Drysdale commented, "It was an ominous beginning to a relationship which was not yet robust enough to face with equanimity the continuation of acerbic quarrels."[77] The PAP government, Lee said, would hold Singapore in trust until the formation of Malaysia. "This proclamation today is an assertion of our right to freedom," Lee declared.[78] In the meantime, from 16 August to 5 September, the nine-member UN team conducted its survey and its report, which was released on 14 September, confirmed that a sizeable majority of the people of both territories wished to join the new political group. Two days later, on 16 September, Singapore, together with Sabah and Sarawak, joined Malaya to form the new Federation of Malaysia.

In his speech to the people of Singapore, Lee called for unity and pledged the state's loyalty to the central government: "It is a loyalty which transcends party rivalries and petty personal differences. It is an unswerving loyalty to an unalterable principle of unity for the prosperity of Malaysia." In return, Lee asked for "an honourable relationship between the states and the Central Government, a relationship between brothers ... not a relationship between masters and servants."[79]

Notes

1. S.L. Falk, *Seventy Days to Singapore: The Malayan Campaign, 1941–1942* (London: Robert Hale, 1975).

2. See B. Montgomery, *Shenton of Singapore, Governor and Prisoner of War* (Singapore: Leo Cooper, 1984), p. 189.

3. Sir Roland Braddell to Sir Edward Gent, 27 November 1942, CO 865/1/M101/1, cited in A.J. Stockwell, *British Policy and Malay Politics during the Malayan Union Experiment, 1942–1948* (Kuala Lumpur: Malaysian Branch of the Royal Asiatic Society Monograph No. 8, 1979), p. 17.

4. Albert Lau, *The Malayan Union Controversy 1942–1948* (Singapore: Oxford University Press, 1991), pp. 276–79.

5. Lau, pp. 75–76.

6. See also J. de V. Allen, *The Malayan Union* (New Haven: Yale University Southeast Asia Studies, 1967); Mohamed Noordin Sopiee, *From Malayan Union to Singapore Separation: Political Unification in the Malaysia Region 1945–65* (Kuala Lumpur: Penerbit Universiti Malaya, 1974); M.R. Stenson, "The Malayan Union and the Historians", *Journal of Southeast Asian History*, 10, 2 (September 1969), pp. 344–54; Wong Lin Ken, "The Malayan Union: A Historical Retrospect", *Journal of Southeast Asian Studies*, 13, 1 (March 1982), pp. 184–91.

7. A.J. Stockwell (ed.), *British Documents on the End of Empire, Series B Volume 3: Malaya. Part I: The Malayan Union Experiment 1942–1948* (London: HMSO, 1995), p. lv.

8. Ibid.

9. Minutes by H.T. Bourdillon, n.d. (possibly August 1945), CO 825/42 no. 55104, cited in Lau, p. 283.

10. Memorandum by P.A.B. McKerron, 17 August 1943, CO 825/35 no. 55104/1, cited in ibid., p. 283.

11. Minutes by H.T. Bourdillon, n.d. (possibly August 1945), CO 825/42 no. 55104, cited in ibid., pp. 283–84.

12. Memorandum by Lord Hailey, 19 April 1943, CO 825/35 no. 55104/1, cited in ibid., p. 284.

13. See Appendix 2, Victor Purcell, *The Chinese in Malaya* (Kuala Lumpur: Oxford University Press, 1967).

14. Minutes by H.T. Bourdillon, n.d. (possibly August 1945), CO 825/42 no. 55104, cited in Lau, p. 284.

15. Ibid., p. 116.

16. *Malayan Union and Singapore: Statement of Policy on Future Constitution*, Cmd. 6724 (London: HMSO, 1946), p. 3.

17. The decision to form UMNO was taken at the first Pan-Malayan Malay Congress on 1 March 1946. UMNO was formally inaugurated on 11 May 1946. See Stockwell, *British Policy and Malay Politics*, pp. 69–70.

18. See Sopiee, pp. 38–55; Lau, pp. 212–19, 240–48; Yeo Kim Wah, "The Anti-Federation Movement in Malaya, 1946–48", *Journal of Southeast Asian Studies*, 4, 1 (March 1973), pp. 31–51.

19. MacMichael Papers, File No. 6, cited in C.M. Turnbull, "The Post-War Decade in Malaya: The Settling Dust of Political Controversy", *Journal of the Malaysian Branch of the Royal Asiatic Society*, 60, 1 (June 1987), p. 16.

20. See Simon C. Smith, *British Relations with the Malay Rulers from Decentralization to Malayan Independence 1930–1957* (Kuala Lumpur: Oxford University Press, 1995).

21. See Richard Stubbs, *Hearts and Minds in Guerrilla Warfare: The Malayan Emergency 1948–1960* (Singapore: Oxford University Press, 1989); Anthony Short, *The Communist Insurrection in Malaya 1948–60* (London: Frederick Muller Ltd, 1975).

22. Onn bin Ja'afar's efforts to open UMNO's ranks to non-Malays met with such stiff resistance that he eventually left the party to found his own non-communal Independence of Malaya Party (IMP) which was launched on 16 September 1951. Onn's experiment in non-communal politics failed, however, as the IMP, rejected by the Malays, and distrusted by the non-Malays, never became a strong electoral force. See Gordon P. Means, *Malaysian Politics* (London: Hodder and Stoughton, 1976), pp. 124–27.

23. Margaret Roff, "The Malayan Chinese Association, 1948–65", *Journal of Southeast Asian History*, 6, 2 (September 1965), pp. 50–51.

24. Sopiee, p. 92.

25. The pro-Indonesia MNP was formed in Ipoh in October 1945. See Means, p. 96.

26. The MDU was the first political party to be established in post-war Singapore. For a study of the MDU, see Cheah Boon Kheng, *The Masked Comrades: A Study of the Communist United Front in Malaya, 1945–1948* (Singapore: Times Books International, 1979).

27. On 25 October 1945, the MCP revived, for instance, the General Labour Union, later renamed the Singapore Federation of Trade Unions, to spearhead the anti-colonial struggle on the labour front. See Yeo and Lau, p. 119.

28. Its other objectives included responsible self-government through a fully elected central legislature for the whole of Malaya and equal citizenship rights for those who made Malaya their permanent home and the object of their undivided loyalty. See Sopiee, p. 93.

29. Memorandum by P.A.B. McKerron and W. Bartley, March 1945, CO 273/675 no. 50823/17, cited in Lau, p. 92.
30. Report by G. Hawkins (Supervisor of Elections), 16 April 1948, CO 953/1/7 no. 50034/4; and Report by G. Hawkins, "Electoral Registration in Singapore: Factors Affecting Response of Voters", n.d., CO 537/2137 no. 50823/40. See Lau, p. 263.
31. Ibid., p. 262.
32. Yeo Kim Wah, *Political Development in Singapore 1945–1955* (Singapore: Singapore University Press, 1973) pp. 98–105.
33. Yeo Kim Wah and Albert Lau, "From Colonialism to Independence, 1945–1965", in *A History of Singapore*, Ernest C.T. Chew and Edwin Lee (eds.) (Singapore: Oxford University Press, 1991), p. 132.
34. Sopiee, p. 103.
35. C.M. Turnbull, *A History of Singapore 1819–1975* (Singapore: Oxford University Press, 1977) p. 258.
36. Yeo and Lau, p. 129.
37. For a study of the origins of the SLF, see Yeo, pp. 113–17.
38. Ibid., pp. 117–30.
39. The SLF won 10 seats; the PAP secured 3 of the 4 seats it contested, see Yeo and Lau, p. 132.
40. See Yeo and Lau, p. 132.
41. Ibid., pp. 136–39, 148.
42. Speech by Lee Kuan Yew to the Royal Society of International Affairs in London, May 1962, cited in Han Fook Kwang, Warren Fernandez, and Sumiko Tan, *Lee Kuan Yew: The Man and His Ideas* (Singapore: Times Edition, 1998), p. 69.
43. Speech by Lee Kuan Yew to the Guild of Nanyang University Graduates, 6 November 1960, cited in Han *et al.*, p. 67.
44. Lee Kuan Yew, *The Battle for Merger* (Singapore: Government Printing office, 1961), p. 5.
45. Ibid., p. 4.
46. *The Straits Times*, 26 January 1955, cited in Sopiee, p. 111.
47. Ibid., p. 109.
48. *The Straits Times*, 24 January 1956; see also Ibid., p. 114.
49. *The Straits Times*, 18 January 1957, cited in Ibid., p. 116.
50. Lee, p. 125.
51. People's Action Party, "The New Phase After Merdeka — Our Tasks and Policy", 1958, printed in Lee, p. 149.
52. Han *et al.*, p. 68.
53. Colonial Office memorandum "Malaysia Bill: Singapore Political Situation", 17 July 1963, DO 169/329 no. 131/143/2.
54. Sopiee, p. 108.
55. Both Britain and Singapore had equal representatives on the ISC. The Malayan representative had the casting vote. See Yeo and Lau, p. 137.
56. Speech by Tunku in the Dewan Ra'ayat on 16 October 1961, printed in Lee, p. 126.
57. Ibid., p. 127. In fact, as Lee revealed, the "Plen" — the plenipotentiary of the MCP in Singapore — had urged him in their talks on 11 May 1961 to agree to the abolition of the ISC as the immediate target for the 1963 constitutional talks with Britain while deferring the question of independence for Singapore either alone or through merger. On 2 June, Lim Chin Siong, Fong Swee Suan, Sydney Woodhull, Dominic Puthucheary, S.T. Bani and Jamit Singh, in a statement called on the PAP "as a left-wing, anti-colonial party in power" to fight for "genuinely full internal self-government in

Singapore", including the aboliton of the ISC. See Lee, pp. 37, 175–76; *The Straits Times*, 4 June 1961.

58.   Speech by the Tunku in the Dewan Ra'ayat on 16 October 1961, printed in Lee, p. 127.

59.   See Appendix A in Memorandum "Closer Association of Singapore, the Federation of Malaya and the Borneo Territories", 30 June 1961, A1838/280 no. 3027/2/1 Part 1.

60.   Possibly the inclusion of the Borneo territories would also enable Kuala Lumpur to stake a claim over the Borneo territories, or it would not accept merger with Singapore without the Borneo territories. See Sopiee, pp. 125–27.

61.   Singapore, *Memorandum Setting Out Heads of Agreement for a Merger between the Federation of Malaya and Singapore*, Cmd. 33 of 1961 (15 November 1961).

62.   James P. Ongkili, *Nation-building in Malaysia 1946–1974* (Singapore: Oxford University Press, 1985), pp. 163–64.

63.   Ibid., p. 165.

64.   Colony of Sarawak, *Report of the Commission of Enquiry, North Borneo and Sarawak, 1962* (Kuching, 1962), p. vi; cited in Ongkili, pp. 165–66.

65.   Singapore, *Memorandum Setting Out Heads of Agreement for a Merger between the Federation of Malaya and Singapore*, Cmd. 33 of 1961 (15 November 1961).

66.   Milton E. Osborne, *Singapore and Malaysia* (Ithaca: Cornell University Data Paper No. 53, 1964), p. 19.

67.   C. Ostrom, "A Core Interest Analysis of the Formation of Malaysia and the Separation of Singapore" (Unpublished PhD dissertation submitted to the Faculty of Claremont Graduate School, 1970), pp. 132–35.

68.   Ibid., pp. 134–35.

69.   See *Memorandum Setting Out Heads of Agreement*, articles 14 and 15.

70.   Ibid., article 7.

71.   Colonial Office, Brief No. 13, "Negotiations for the merger of Singapore and Malaya", 17 July 1963, DO 169/329 no. 131/143/2.

72.   Tengku Abdul Rahman, *Looking Back* (Kuala Lumpur: Pustaka Antara, 1977), pp. 115–16.

73.   On 10 July 1963, Indonesian President Sukarno announced Indonesia's opposition to the Malaysia scheme. See *The Straits Times*, 11 July 1963; also *The Straits Times*, 12 and 18 July 1963.

74.   *The Straits Times*, 9 August 1963.

75.   Ibid., 30 August 1963.

76.   Ibid., 3 September 1963.

77.   John Drysdale, *Singapore: Struggle for Success* (Singapore: Times Books International, 1984), p. 337.

78.   *The SundayTimes*, 1 September 1963.

79.   *The Straits Times*, 17 September 1963.

CHAPTER 2

THE SNAP ELECTION

F ive days after the inauguration of Malaysia, Singapore went to the polls. The September 1963 election was to be one of the "most severely fought in the history of elections in Singapore".[1] It was a crucial election for the votes cast would decide the state government that would control Singapore for the first five years of Malaysia and during this period lay the basis for the island's relationship with Kuala Lumpur.[2] It was also an election the ruling People's Action Party (PAP) government had been preparing to fight for some time.

The Setting

Since the 1959 election, which brought the PAP into power, a series of intra-party intrigues, defections, electoral reverses, and two deaths, had reduced its strength in the Assembly from 43 to only 25 out of 51 seats.[3] As Toh Chin Chye, the then deputy premier, recalled, "It was a struggle, because every other day, the opposition including the Barisan, David Marshall, and Lim Yew Hock would move a motion of no confidence. So the government was on the verge of being toppled!"[4] As the absence of a majority made "the passing of certain important policies and bills troublesome … our Party had to face facts and pick a good time to dissolve the Assembly and hold another General Election."[5]

The facts were compelling enough. Without a majority, the PAP was literally at the mercy of the four votes from Lim Yew Hock's Singapore People's Alliance (SPA) and another three votes[6] from the Singapore United Malays National Organization (SUMNO)–Singapore Malayan Chinese Association (SMCA) alliance for its survival in the Assembly.

After Tunku Abdul Rahman's historic speech in May 1961, signalling his intention to bring about a closer association of the region's British territories with the Federation, both the SPA and the SUMNO–SMCA, on 1 June 1961, drew closer in an informal alliance "on the basis of the Alliance in the Federation of Malaya".[7] By July 1961, the Singapore Alliance (SA),[8] as the partnership came to be known, was expanded to include the Singapore Malayan Indian Congress (SMIC). The SPA–SUMNO–SMCA–SMIC partnership was finally formalized on 24 June 1963 with a view to contesting the forthcoming elections as an "integral member of the Grand Alliance[9] of Malaysia" which would be inaugurated when Malaysia came into being.[10] Like the Federation Alliance, the SA was favourably disposed towards Malaysia and, therefore, supportive of the PAP's merger proposals. It belonged, however, to the political right,[11] and could be differentiated politically and ideologically from the PAP's left-wing and socialist leanings.

The predicament of having to depend on the seven votes from these right-wing opposition parties was what Lee Kuan Yew clearly did not relish. First, it was politically inopportune for the PAP to suffer the "indignity of Lim Yew Hock calling the tune on the business of the Assembly"[12] and, in the event of the SA voting with the opposition on any significant issue, the Assembly would be deadlocked at 25 to 25, and the government would be under strong pressure to resign. As Toh Chin Chye pointed out: "If we had been defeated on any decisive Bill ... we would have no alternative but to resign."[13] Second, it also exposed the party to the more serious threat of Kuala Lumpur pursuing its own political agenda in Singapore through the SA. With the PAP lacking a moral majority, the danger of a right-wing plot backed by Kuala Lumpur to bring about the collapse of the left-wing Singapore government was considered seriously by the party.

The belief that Kuala Lumpur was "secretly conniving"[14] with Lim Yew Hock to "put the screws" on Singapore in order to "bring the PAP Government down"[15] was a concern the Singapore premier had expressed on numerous occasions to the British. "[W]hile he (Lee) did not doubt our sincerity in saying that we had no thoughts about an alternative government to the PAP he could not say the same about the Tunku", reported Lord Selkirk, the United Kingdom Commissioner, to London. The Tunku, Lee had suspected, was working "hand in glove with Lim Yew Hock",[16] Selkirk added. The Singapore premier's disquietude about Kuala Lumpur's intentions had also been noted by T.K. Critchley, the Australian High Commissioner in Kuala Lumpur, who reported that the

Tunku's relationship with the Singapore premier had not been good: "[Lee] has always been suspicious of the Alliance government's attitude towards himself and Singapore."[17]

Lee's fears were not without basis. In the Tunku's mind, Lim Yew Hock was the "favoured alternative"[18] to Lee Kuan Yew in Singapore. Not surprisingly, Lim Yew Hock "believes he is playing a shrewd political game from a position of some strength," wrote G.A. Jockel, the Australian High Commissioner in Singapore, reporting on his conversation with the former Chief Minister. He continued, "The picture of friendly intimacy which he claims to exist between him and the Tengku was put across well."[19]

Past initiatives by Kuala Lumpur to forge a united front between the PAP and the SPA–SMCA against the pro-communists, and to "find a place for Tun Lim Yew Hock" had all been spurned by the PAP, mainly because Lee "made it clear that the SPA and the MCA in Singapore were spent forces and that if the PAP were to successfully contain and conscribe the communists, it could not afford to be associated with leaders and elements who were known to be feeble".[20] After the death of Ahmad bin Ibrahim, the Minister for Labour and PAP member for Sembawang, in August 1962, the Tunku made a further overture to get the PAP to join the SA. As Philip Moore, the Deputy United Kingdom Commissioner in Singapore, reported of his conversation with the Singapore premier, the Tunku "stressed to Lee that he was not prepared to ask Lim Yew Hock to withdraw from the Sembawang by-election and suggested that Lee should himself discuss the question with the Alliance in Singapore" in order to prevent the communists winning on split votes. Not wishing to offend the Tunku by refusing to meet with Lim Yew Hock and his associates, Lee invited them for talks towards the end of 1962 and told the SA leaders that "it would help the PAP if the Alliance did not put up a candidate". Lee, however, also stressed that he did not want "active Alliance support ... since he thought this would harm the PAP." Moore surmised — accurately — that "Lee did not take all this very seriously ... [He] apparently has no plans for holding the Sembawang by-election in the near future".[21] A subsequent invitation to send observers to the Grand Alliance convention in Kuala Lumpur in March 1963 was also turned down by the PAP which maintained that "if the Grand Alliance was for the purpose of jointly contesting elections in Malaysia, then it could not participate even as observers".[22] Two months later, the Tunku had again sought to influence an electoral pact, which Lee rejected, between the SA and the PAP for the "apportionment" of seats in the forthcoming Singapore elections. The

Tunku had wanted the PAP to give the SA "a clear run in certain constituencies", reported Selkirk, referring to his conversation with the Singapore premier, but Lee "told the Tunku this was quite unrealistic since the MCA and SPA were 'empty vessels' who could in no circumstances be expected to win seats". In any case, as Selkirk noted, Lee "would not trust the Tunku to stand by any such arrangements once merger was achieved".[23]

Lee's refusal to to be associated with the SPA and MCA was not without its political costs — or dangers. W.K. Flanagan, First Secretary in the Australian High Commission in Singapore, recalling a conversation with the Deputy United Kingdom Commissioner, recorded, for instance, that "Lee is convinced that the Tengku is preparing to throw him over completely, once merger is accomplished, and Moore says that their best information confirms this ... After first denying that there was any intention of getting rid of Lee, the Malayans had finally admitted that, while this was the story they were giving out in Kuala Lumpur, they in fact would like to replace him".[24] As progress towards merger became more assured, Federation leaders were also beginning to display even fewer inhibitions in interfering in the Singapore political arena, particularly in their efforts to reorganize and revitalize the Singapore UMNO and MCA.[25] Since January 1961, a Federation minister had already been appointed to oversee the reorganization of SUMNO, and the intention to revitalize the SMCA was announced in November 1962 by the MCA leader, Tan Siew Sin.[26] A reorganization committee was eventually set up, chaired by Yap Pheng Geck, a local banker. In May 1963, in a direct challenge to the PAP, Tan further declared that his party "[had] a duty to perform in Singapore", as it was Singapore's "only hope" and "only alternative" to chaos and instability in the state.[27] On 15 May, the Tunku's deputy, Tun Abdul Razak, had also spoken confidentially to the British about the possibility of "elections producing an alternative government to replace Lee",[28] although, in this instance, Selkirk was quick to dismiss Tun Razak's assertion as unrealistic: "Unless the Federation want to install a Barisan Sosialis government they will be obliged after elections to come to some new arrangement with Lee and he would be the dominant partner."[29]

For Lee, there was, therefore, a political need to "inflict a decisive defeat on the Alliance and to show the Tunku that there was no effective moderate alternative to the PAP in Singapore".[30] He asserted that as long as the Alliance Party in Singapore believed that it could win the election, there would be friction between Singapore and Kuala Lumpur.[31]

An early election before the establishment of Malaysia, however, carried the undesirable risk of voting in the Barisan Sosialis (BS) with a majority ("quite possible" in British reckoning), in which case "merger would be off".[32] British assessment had initially put the PAP's chances in a general election if held in April 1963 at no higher than "fifty-fifty".[33] Although two months later a more upbeat appraisal had suggested that the PAP "might well get an overall majority",[34] by July, the British had put their earlier evaluation of a Barisan victory ("a real risk"[35]) back on the burner. Whilst Lee was more confident of victory, he also saw, as the British did, few tactical advantages in holding the general election before the formation of Malaysia. But the government's strategy to stave off opposition pressure for an early general election worked only so long as the SA was prepared to continue playing the political game that had kept the PAP afloat in the Assembly. When the SA finally mustered the opposition votes to defeat a crucial government motion, as it did on 25 July over the Singapore (Elections to the Federal House of Representatives) Bill, when it felt its interests were compromised, the PAP found it harder to fend off pressures for the dissolution of the Assembly.[36]

The bill had been presented on a certificate of urgency to the Assembly on 24 July 1963 and debated over two days. Although, under the Malaysia Agreement, Singapore was to elect 15 representatives to the Federal Parliament, there was no necessity for the elections to be held before Malaysia Day. The PAP's motive for introducing the bill was, therefore, perceived by the opposition as an attempt to "test the market". As Lim Yew Hock declared, "If they win in this election, they will straightaway have the Assembly dissolved and call for general elections."[37] The Minister of Culture, S. Rajaratnam, however, argued that its purpose was to circumscribe the BS politically in its "last-minute attempt to wreck merger and Malaysia".[38] And by paralyzing the communists politically, they would be able to ensure that the communists would not be in a position to capture state power when the elections for the 51 seats were held.[39] "[If] they win they get nothing; if they lose, they lose everything," he said.[40] In the unlikely event of the BS winning all the 15 seats, Rajaratnam argued, "they are not capturing any power because in an Assembly of well over 100 seats, 15 seats do not give them effective political power".[41] On the other hand, the defeat of the PAP government would only galvanize the pro-Malaysia parties to adjust their strategies to defeat the BS in the coming state election. But if the BS were defeated, that would "bury them completely".[42]

What was less explicitly stated, and which drew loud protests from the opposition, was that holding the elections to the Federal legislature before Malaysia Day also afforded the PAP another advantage: it would permit the government to redefine the electoral boundaries of the 51 constituencies in order for them to be regrouped into 15 Federal divisions for elections to the Federal legislature.[43] That the PAP government was "going to draw the wards in the way they could, the way they wanted", and not by an "impartial body"[44] like the Federal Elections Commission in Kuala Lumpur after Malaysia Day, was unacceptable to the SA, looking beyond the 15 Federal seats, as it did, to the 51 seats in the Singapore general election. Not wanting the PAP to profit from this unfair advantage, the SA voted with the opposition "in a concerted effort"[45] to block the bill, resulting in an impasse, with voting tied at 23 to 23. Two PAP members, Lee Kuan Yew and Goh Keng Swee, accompanied by two assembly members, Mohd Ali bin Alwi and A.P. Rajah, did not vote as they were in Kuala Lumpur on official business.

Bitterly upset by the defeat, Lee almost conceded to an early election — probably out of "anger and pique", reported Selkirk — but was brought round to accept the United Kingdom Commissioner's tactical recommendation not to make the decision until after the outcome of the Assembly debate on the Malaysia Agreement scheduled for the following week.[46] In the meantime, while Lee sought to regain tactical ground, publicly challenging the SA to topple his government by voting against the Malaysia Agreement,[47] the British, working behind the scenes, used their influence to rein in SA's ambitions and to ensure no further "slip up over this". Selkirk's stratagem worked. After a four-day debate,[48] the government's motion was eventually carried 25 to 17, with eight abstentions, including the seven from the SA.[49] Summing up, Selkirk was visibly not pleased: "Quite enough damage has already been done by this foolhardy action by the Alliance in thwarting Lee on a major piece of legislation at this stage in the game".[50]

But if an early election was risky, so was one withheld for too long after Malaysia's birth. There can be little doubt that a post-Malaysia election was politically more expedient, for "if by chance the Barisan won the election, they would find themselves already trapped inside an anti-communist Federation run by Kuala Lumpur".[51] Lee Kuan Yew had also wanted polling day immediately after Malaysia so that he could defeat the BS electorally before the communists had a chance to "all dive for cover". "I think we will do a disservice to Singapore if we let the symbol of the Barisan Sosialis remain forever a myth," he said.[52] Notwithstanding these tactical advantages, the PAP could not afford to wait too long before calling for an election. Constitutionally, the election only had to be held before 31 March 1964. But, as the PAP was well aware, once Malaysia was established, the SA's "truce" would be off, and Kuala Lumpur's ability to influence Singapore's electoral process on behalf of the SA, and to consolidate its own power in the state, would also significantly increase. Whilst the SA had assured the British confidentially that it had "absolutely no intention of attempting to bring the PAP down" before Malaysia was formed, it had also given notice that the "position would of course be different" after its establishment.[53] Lee clearly could not afford to wait too long after Malaysia to consolidate his power in an election since efforts were already underway in the Federation, as Critchley noted, to "revitalize and reorganize" the SA. "[If] the Alliance with the backing of the Federation were to gain enough support", he added, "Lee feared ... [this] could split the moderate vote in Singapore to the disadvantage of the PAP" and produce a situation in which BS would emerge "as the most powerful single party in Singapore".[54] That possibility, and the worry that the central government, when given enough time, would be in a position "to take over and exercise firm power over the police [and] to have [a] significant influence on the conduct of the elections"[55] were compelling enough reasons for elections to be held sooner, rather than later, *after* merger.

Choosing the appropriate moment to hold the battle for votes was a tactical prerogative the PAP exploited expertly. After the defeat of the government's Singapore Federal Elections Bill, Toh Chin Chye announced in the House on 25 July that the challenge by the Opposition to hold state elections before the Federal elections was accepted and that the Assembly would be adjourned *sine die* after the Malaysia debate scheduled to start on 29 July. "In the national interest," he said, "we will see this motion through so that the security of Malaysia is not put in jeopardy."[56] The significance of Toh's announcement was not missed by *The Straits Times*, which headlined its report: "S'pore general elections after Malaysia".[57] Lee Kuan Yew later hinted that it would be held "before the end of the year".[58] But pressed in the Assembly for the exact date, Toh stonewalled: "I have made it very clear that we will hold elections," he said, "[at] our own choosing and on our own grounds".[59]

On 3 September, five days after Kuala Lumpur declared 16 September as the new date for Malaysia Day,[60] the suspense was finally broken. The PAP government started its electoral clock. The Assembly was prorogued; writs for a general election were issued; and nomination day was set for

Thursday, 12 September.[61] The latter date was carefully chosen to afford the opposition parties "the minimum time to select their candidates for the election"[62] under the law, which was nine days after the dissolution of the Assembly. Polling day itself was a well-kept secret. Lee would only reveal that it would come "after" 16 September.[63] *The Straits Times* forecasted it would be "in mid-October"[64] — wrongly, as it turned out. In fact, six hours after nominations closed, the government stunned everyone by calling for a snap election to be held just nine days later — on Saturday, 21 September — again the minimum notice under the law.[65] Since no campaigning was allowed on polling day, there were in effect only eight days for canvassing, out of which three and a half days were public holidays, coinciding with the Malaysia Day festivities,[66] and therefore, affording precious little time for transacting essential business in this period.[67] "The PAP," observed Philip Moore, "felt it was to their advantage to catch the other parties napping with a snap election whilst the State was still gay with Malaysia celebrations".[68]

The Contending Political Forces

By September 1963, the PAP was well positioned to fight the elections it had prepared for — on their own grounds. In fact, since November 1962, the PAP had already initiated a "well prepared campaign"[69] to win votes, with the inauguration of the Prime Minister's widely publicized trek to all the 51 constituencies, ostensibly on government business, but with the intention of rallying political support for the anticipated election. While a majority of Singaporeans had endorsed the PAP's version of merger in the September 1962 Referendum, there were still 25 per cent, the results showed, who had heeded the BS's call to cast blank votes, with most of these coming from the poorer rural constituencies dominated by the BS and where the PAP machinery was weak. These same hostile constituencies were the ones the Prime Minister sought vigorously to influence during his tour. Largesse was extended deliberately, despite loud opposition protests,[70] for rural projects to ensure that the people "got what they wanted — a surfaced road, street lights, standpipes, drains, and above all the community centres that were to be the focus of their support".[71] So for 10 months, Lee Kuan Yew, in the words of Dennis Bloodworth, "worked like a man possessed", stomping indefatigably from ward to ward, "with a TV[72] team in tow", three to five days a week by July 1963, conducting "a one-man election campaign ... in the thinnest of disguises".[73] When the election was announced in September, Lee had already completed a tour of all the 51 constituencies, and as the BS leader, Lee Siew Choh, conceded, "had [already] many months of electioneering well ahead of other parties".[74]

Moreover, the PAP's standing as "a defender of Singapore's state rights"[75] was also high after it "won a number of notable battles in support of Singapore's state interests *vis-à-vis* the Central Government in Kuala Lumpur".[76] Ever since Singapore's entry into Malaysia was canvassed, and negotiations begun on the terms of merger, Lee shrewdly adopted a tough bargaining posture, not only to protect Singapore's interests but also to guard against the charge that he was "selling out" to Kuala Lumpur — an accusation the BS had repeatedly heaped on the government.[77]

Whilst agreement was more easily reached on the political terms of merger, where the convergence of interests — especially the containment of the left-wing threat — was greater, no such coincidence existed on the economic terms, and hard bargaining ensued. On no issue was perhaps more heat generated than over the extent of Kuala Lumpur's control of Singapore's finances. If the resultant acerbic exchanges ominously soured ties between Kuala Lumpur and Singapore, they afforded the PAP government, nonetheless, a unique opportunity to derive "excellent domestic political value from this controversy",[78] which it exploited by portraying the financial obstacles as MCA attempts to rob Singapore of its surplus, undermine the confidence of the business community, provoke a "collision"[79] between the Singapore premier and the Tunku, and further the party's political ambitions in Singapore.[80] As Selkirk noted, "[Lee] has deliberately played this up in the press so as to appear as the defender of State rights against the sinister attempt of corrupt MCA figures to get a Federal stranglehold on Singapore's money and commerce".[81] His deputy could not agree more: "Almost every time Tan opens his mouth he gives support to the impression that Singapore ministers are fighting a battle for the economic future of Singapore against financial interests in Kuala Lumpur."[82] Admittedly, there was "a good deal of ballyhoo in this", Selkirk added, but "Lee has done himself no political harm in Singapore in showing how tough he is in standing up for State rights."[83]

By the time the election was called, the PAP government had also shown itself firmly in the saddle and not afraid to govern with conviction.[84] According to Australian and British assessments, the incumbent government could lay claim to an excellent record[85]: not only had the PAP leaders been completely successful in achieving their aim of merger and Malaysia, they had also made "considerable progress with an excellent economic development programme", including the "outstanding achievements in the Jurong industrial site".[86] Additionally, apart from having successfully built up a climate of business confidence, the government could also boast of "a good record in slum clearance and housing projects".[87] What was also impressive was the PAP government's "fairly unique" position in Southeast Asia — "in being untainted by corruption".[88] Its image as "a progressive, corruption-free government with a firm but moderate and intelligent leader"[89] was further enhanced through its control over radio and television. In short, observed the British High Commission in Singapore, "The strength of the PAP seems to lie in the highly effective strong Government which they have exercised in Singapore over the last 18 months".[90]

Its nearest rival, the left-wing BS, fared less well. Seven months before, on 3 February 1963, the BS suffered a severe setback when 24 of its ablest non-parliamentary leaders,[91] including Lim Chin Siong and Fong Swee Suan, were detained after the launch of Operation Cold Store, a major pre-emptive security operation ordered by the Internal Security Council (ISC) to foil a suspected communist conspiracy of violence against the birth of Malaysia. A hundred and thirteen arrests were made. Apart from leading BS figures, other pro-BS and anti-Malaysia activists, including trade union leaders, university students, journalists and members of rural associations, were also locked up. That the arrests crippled much of the BS electoral apparatus — and benefited the PAP — was acknowledged retrospectively by Toh Chin Chye: "Well, those who were against us were under detention. ... The General Elections were held after Operation Cold Store, when their leaders were all in jail. That was the way it was."[92]

In fact, as members of the ISC, PAP government leaders[93] were interested participants[94] in the unanimous decision to order the arrests — and were also the main political beneficiary. Sensitive to the political ramifications that could rebound against him, Lee Kuan Yew, however, found it expedient, publicly at least, to distance himself from the arrests and thereby avoid being "charged with having picked up political opponents".[95] "If it were an action by the Singapore Government, we would never have contemplated it," Lee said, in response to a reporter's query upon his return from the Kuala Lumpur meeting of the ISC which sanctioned the arrests. "I think it is fair to say that for the Singapore Government it would have been easier to leave this action over till after August 31 this year," he added.[96] The Singapore premier's remarks brought a swift riposte from Lim Yew Hock who accused him of being "utterly irresponsible" in trying to shift the blame to the other members of the ISC: "If the Prime Minister and his Government feel that they cannot accept their responsibilities without squealing, then we call on them to resign".[97] Speaking confidentially to Moore later, Lee revealed that he was actually "trying to protect himself against any accusation of irresponsibility in having agreed to the arrests before the Tunku was finally and irrevocably committed to merger".[98] According to Moore, Lee still had doubts "whether he had been wise ... in playing his last card before merger was finally assured."[99]

What is less doubtful is that Operation Cold Store had dealt an unsettling blow to the BS's electoral machinery. This was not to be the end of the BS's troubles, however. Two months later, on 22 April,[100] after a belated BS protest march over the detention of its leaders turned into a riot outside City Hall, the police arrested 12 more BS leaders, including 10 assemblymen. Coming so soon after the Cold Store arrests, the tactical miscalculation on the part of the BS was, indeed, costly and one which the party could ill afford to make. The trial, which began on 7 August, was completed only on 29 August, barely two weeks before nomination day. Eight BS leaders, seven of them assemblymen,[101] were eventually convicted on a single charge of rioting, though its chairman, Lee Siew Choh, and three others were acquitted.[102] "The trial lasted nearly one month," remembered Lee Siew Choh, "And almost immediately ... General Elections! You see, we were completely occupied with the trial."[103]

Another crackdown was suddenly sprung on nomination day. Early in the morning on 12 September, Special Branch officers rounded up another 17 ex-detainees (who were potential opposition candidates) for questioning.[104] Held in custody until nomination closed at 12 o'clock, they were unable to file their papers *in person* at the nomination centres, as required by law, to be eligible to stand for the elections. One prospective BS candidate Tan Siew Chwee, for instance, claimed he was detained at the Joo Chiat Police Station from five in the morning to 12 noon. Tan was apparently questioned about his political activities and reminded that "as an ex-detainee, he had no right to be taking an active part in politics".[105] What the pre-emptive security operations and legal battles achieved was to make the timing and ground for an electoral campaign most unfavourable to the BS. As Lee Siew Choh ruminated, "Of course, they had the advantage over us. And I tell you it was quite difficult for us, at the last minute, to get enough members to stand for election. Ultimately, we managed to get 46. We put as many as we could."[106]

Despite its woes, the BS was still in possession of a far superior organizational network, one which the PAP lacked after the split of July 1961. Most of the mass organizations — farmers, hawkers, old boys, students and workers — were under BS control. All the BS needed to do to mobilize its mass organizations into action was a simple "telephone call", boasted one of its leaders — "easily done, no difficulty at all".[107] The dominant Singapore Association of Trade Unions (SATU), which controlled most of the unions — seven of its strongest unions had a total membership of over 60,000 — was also solidly aligned with the BS, a potent combination which the PAP government found necessary to neutralize before the elections. Six days before the Assembly was dissolved as a prelude to the polls, the government ordered seven SATU unions, including the largest three,[108] to "show cause" before 30 October why they should not be de-registered for engaging in "activities of a political nature outside the normal functions of genuine trade unions".[109] Ten days later, and three days before nomination day, the bank accounts of the three largest SATU unions were frozen to prevent funds from being withdrawn "for purposes not consistent with their constitutions".[110] Partly through government action, and partly by their own undoing, the BS and its backers found themselves on the defensive — just when electoral campaigning was about to commence.

The position of the PAP's right-wing rival, the SA, was not much better. Judging by the results of the 1959 elections, none of the partners in the coalition possessed much electoral appeal. Despite contesting 39 of the 51 seats in 1959, and active campaigning on its behalf by the leaders of the Malayan Alliance, the SPA, suffering from an anti-Chinese image, as well as financial scandals, secured only four seats. SUMNO won only three out of the eight seats it contested, with the victories coming mainly from the predominantly Malay enclaves of Geylang Serai, Kampong Kembangan and Southern Islands. Both the SMCA and SMIC, which fielded five and two candidates respectively, were completely routed.

Internal troubles further plagued the various partners in the SA. Since November 1961, the SPA was a house divided within itself, racked by bitter bickering over its "thorough reorganization" and "cleaning-up operations",[111] which saw the exodus of some 93 of its members by January 1962, including Lim Choon Mong, its Secretary-General, Tan Hai Tong, the deputy chairman of the organizing committee, and Tan Chor Yong, the chairman of the youth section. Although the resignations, more of which were to follow in June 1962, were being trumpeted as the outcome of SPA's own efforts to rid the party of "opportunists and internal saboteurs",[112] the truth was that these were the symptoms of a much deeper malaise afflicting the party, and one which it never was able to surmount completely. After the final selections of candidates on the eve of nomination day, more resignations followed. Leading the walk-out were Soh Ghee Soon and G.G. Samy, two central committee members who had not been nominated.[113]

The SPA's Malay partner, SUMNO, was also "in a mess",[114] after a series of disputes from April 1959 to July 1960 over the party leadership.[115] The prospects of direct affiliation[116] with UMNO Malaya had produced within the party "more rebels than loyalists"[117] and prompted Kuala Lumpur to appoint a Federation minister, Mohammed Khir Johari,[118] as its chairman in January 1961 to restore some semblance of order in SUMNO affairs. Despite the efforts at reorganization, internal stresses remained. Khir Johari's selection of Syed Esa Almenoar as Secretary-General, for instance, had given rise to "murmurs" within SUMNO because "he was not quite acceptable to some... [b]ecause of his Arab blood".[119] By June 1962, the chairman warned that factionalism had surfaced again and threatened to split the party.[120] Four months later, both the chairman and secretary of the SUMNO's east division, the party's largest with over 3,000 members, had to be suspended "indefinitely" over their refusal to submit a list of nominees for the forthcoming elections.[121] The east division's chairman, Darus Shariff, was finally expelled from SUMNO in December 1962.[122] In the 1963 general elections, Shariff made a comeback as an independent candidate in Geylang challenging the SUMNO's deputy chairman, Ahmad bin Haji Taff, on an anti-Malaysia platform.[123]

Inter-party strains further added to the woes of the troubled SA. SUMNO's association with the "politically bankrupt" SPA in June 1961 had never been popular with many younger Malays. The forging of the alliance was thus categorically condemned by Suyut Surmani, the secretary of SUMNO's city division, who warned that the link-up could only harm the party.[124] Opposition surfaced again in July 1963 when the youth wing of SUMNO's rebellious east division, looking ahead to the forthcoming elections, demanded the expulsion of the SPA from the SA.[125] More pressure to exclude the SPA was applied two days prior to nomination day when Hassan Yadi, the head of the east division's youth wing, publicly announced, but subsequently withdrew, his decision to contest as an independent candidate in Geylang Serai on a pro-Malaysia but definitely anti-SPA platform.[126] As *The Straits Times* warned, "[T]he rift has not been healed. The agitation against expulsion of the SPA by this younger group continues."[127]

Kuala Lumpur's efforts to forge the disparate partners into a credible electoral alliance only fuelled the PAP's charge that the SA was subservient to the former — an imputation the SA never was able to dispel. Instead, internal squabbling over the selection of candidates for the elections compelled its leaders to approach Kuala Lumpur for the final allocation, and unwittingly confirmed what the PAP had been saying all along — that the SA was a stooge of the Federation Alliance. Far from being the cohesive electoral partnership ready to "knock out the PAP if they dare come out for a general election", so boasted Lim Yew Hock in July 1963,[128] the SA was in truth the sorry picture of a party "bedevilled by divisions in their ranks"[129] by September 1963. Of all the political forces vying for power, the PAP was the best prepared for the elections. As Rajaratnam had earlier intimated, "We are surely not fools enough to fight an election at a time when we know we are going to lose".[130]

The Election Campaign

On nomination day, 210 candidates from eight political parties and independents filed their papers to contest the elections. Only four political parties, however, had put up enough candidates to be in the running for the control of the state. Apart from the PAP, which was contesting all the 51 constituencies, the BS was fielding 46 candidates, an acknowledgement that it stood no chance in the five predominantly Malay constituencies. The BS made way for its Malay ally, Partai Rakyat Singapura, in three wards and avoided altogether the solid Malay constituencies of Southern Islands and Geylang Serai. Also in the running were the left-wing United People's Party (UPP), led by the former PAP Minister of National Development, Ong Eng Guan[131], which put up the unexpectedly large field of 46 candidates, on par with the BS and the SA, which, after indicating its desire to contest every ward, fielded only 42. Putting a token appearance were three other parties — the Pan-Malayan Islamic Party (PMIP) with two candidates, the Workers' Party putting up three, and a solitary contestant from the United Democratic Party (UDP). There were 16 independents, including David Marshall, fighting to retain his Anson seat, who made up the rest of the candidates. Only in one ward — Southern Islands — was there a straight fight between two political parties. Multi-cornered contests were the salient feature in all the others. While eight constituencies had three candidates each wooing the voters, 14 wards saw five-cornered fights, and another 27 were hotly contested by four candidates each. One — Anson — was contested by six candidates.

The PAP's decision to have all its ministers stand in their 1959 constituencies was interpreted by *The Straits Times* as a sign of confidence.[132] "Whether it is a well-placed or a misplaced confidence, Sunday's results will reveal," opined *The Malay Mail*.[133] By contrast, the BS assemblymen, who defected from the PAP in 1961, were nearly all standing in new wards.[134] Lee Siew Choh, for instance, had moved from Queenstown to Rochore where he was pitted against the Deputy Prime Minister and PAP chairman, Toh Chin Chye. In Crawford, K.M. Bryne, the Minister of Health, Labour and Law, faced top BS unionist, S.T. Bani, who had contested Thomson in 1959. This was a deliberate BS strategy to match their top leaders against PAP ministers. Surprises were also in store in the SA's slate of candidates. Its intra-party machinations had produced two casualties. Dropped from its list of nominees was the controversial former SUMNO leader, Abdul Hamid bin Haji Jumat.[135] The other was Lim Yew Hock, who provided nomination day's biggest surprise by not standing for the election. Accusing the PAP of conducting a "malicious character assassination" campaign against him "obviously with a view to try and discredit the Alliance in the general elections", Lim announced that he had instructed his solicitors to issue a writ "to take the PAP to court to clear my name".[136] "The other parties in the Alliance ... feel he has become [an] embarrassment and he himself has wilted under Lee's continuing and bitter personal attack,"[137] was the Australian Acting High Commissioner's poignant comment on Lim's surprise exit.

Not surprisingly, opposition leaders were quick to denounce the snap election as a conspiracy against them. While the BS accused the PAP of foisting a "snap election — blitzkrieg style"[138] — and called the elections "the most unfair and undemocratic in the history of Singapore"[139] — the SPA's Lim Yew Hock lambasted the PAP's election time-table as a "dictatorial move"[140] and "unprecedented"[141] in the history of Singapore.

None of the rival parties, however, associated themselves with David Marshall's attempt to challenge the legality of the elections schedule in court, probably because the short run-up to polling day already permitted them little time for anything else but campaigning.[142] In his writ filed on 14 September 1963 against the returning officer, M. Ponnuduray, Marshall had argued that the earliest day in which polling could take place, by virtue of the fact that it must be "a Saturday not less than nine days" after nomination day, was 28 September, and not 21 September which was "only the ninth day after the notification". He contended, "That ninth day is a public holiday, and, therefore, an excluded day".[143] In dismissing Marshall's writ on 19 September, the Chief Justice, Wee Chong Jin, said in his oral judgment that the returning officer, as a servant of the Crown, could not be sued and that a private individual could not take action in his own name to vindicate public rights unless he had suffered damage. Wee, however, left open the interpretation of the term "not less than nine days".[144]

The PAP retorted that nine days after nomination was also "the minimum period for General Elections in Great Britain"[145] and reminded the opposition parties of their earlier boasts that they were all prepared to fight a general election any time, anywhere: "Now that the PAP has obliged by resigning and announcing fresh elections, the opposition parties complain that we have snapped a general elections on them".[146] *The Straits Times* commented in the same vein: "The hurt complaint of some of Singapore's party leaders that the Prime Minister has sprung a 'snap election' on them makes a nice contrast to the demand in the Assembly, less than six weeks ago, that he should resign and have an election".[147] Disagreeing also with the charge that the PAP had been "unfair" by holding the snap elections was the chairman of the Malaysian Election Commission, Haji Mustapha Albakri. Commenting on the PAP's tactics after the elections, he said, "They have observed all the rules in the game. There is undoubtedly nothing unfair. Any other ruling party would have done the same thing".[148]

Despite their public outbursts, the opposition parties were not as unprepared as they appeared. Noting that there had already been "fair warning", *The Straits Times* leader of 5 September 1963 opined: "They ought not to have been caught by surprise, and possibly they weren't".[149] Critchley noticed, for instance, that the opposition parties had "reacted quickly and generally mounted extensive campaigns".[150] The Deputy United Kingdom Commissioner, Moore, similarly reported: "[It] became clear that they, and particularly the Barisan, were much better prepared than had been expected and their meetings and posters were effective".[151] As far as PAP stalwart, Lee Gek Seng, was concerned, their outcry was "purely [an] election tactic ... to get sympathy from the masses. They [were] ready for the election."[152]

Indeed, as the BS boasted, its first election rally on 13 September 1963, to introduce its 46 candidates, drew "the largest crowd in the present election campaign of about 50,000 people":

> Shenton Way car park where the rally was held was packed from one end to the other. The roads along it were filled with people, so much so that traffic had to be diverted elsewhere ... Banners and placards attacking colonialism and imperialism, and the colonial stooge, the PAP, were displayed prominently. A large portrait of detained comrade, Lim Chin Siong, was also displayed.[153]

A Special Branch report showed that the BS claim had been grossly inflated. Only about 8,000 attended the Shenton Way rally, at least 7,000 of whom were either BS members or supporters who had been transported to the rally in 150 lorries and 30 buses:

> After the commencement of the rally at 7.25 p.m., lorries and buses carrying Barisan members and supporters were still coming. They alighted from the lorries and buses, lined up on the instructions of their leaders and marched to the site of the rally, singing on the way the song "Unity is strength" and shouting slogans and even firing crackers.[154]

The massive crowds swelling BS rallies, however, had the desired effect and, as Lee Kuan Yew acknowledged, led many people to fear that "we would lose to [the] Barisan Sosialis":

> Barisan election rallies drew huge crowds; their speakers were wildly cheered. Posters carrying the photographs of the leading detainees, Lim Chin Siong, Fong Swee Suan, and others, were part of their appeal to the voters. The huge crowds at Barisan rallies proved the communists were good at organizing big crowds to intimidate neutral onlookers. They were meant to demoralize and rout our supporters.[155]

Despite the earlier reverses, the BS electoral machinery was still very much intact. As one of its opponents observed, the BS "threw in everything they had ... They did not seem to have any handicap at all in conducting such a large-scale operation".[156] Funds were "readily forthcoming"[157] and their branch organizations, noted the Australian High Commission, were "cohesive and effective".[158] According to Lee Siew Choh, there were 300 to 400 campaign hands working indefatigably for the BS[159] in each of the BS's 46 contested constituencies. "As a result," reported the British High Commission in Singapore, "the Barisan Sosialis house-to-house campaign seems more effective".[160] Much of the BS manpower and resources, however, as one PAP contestant discerned, were "heavily concentrated in the ministerial and a number of downtown waterfront areas. They hoped to knock out the Ministers to deprive the Party of its leadership in Government even if we won the Elections".[161] Apart from the SATU unionists, there was also the large pool of Nanyang University supporters; 10 of its graduates, for instance, were contesting the elections on the BS slate, urged on by Tan Lark Sye, the multi-millionaire founder of Nanyang University and chairman of its Council, who openly exhorted Chinese voters to give their support to the Nanyang graduates. All these graduates were contesting the elections for the first time, so that there would be hope, Tan said, for Chinese education which had been neglected by previous governments.[162] "Since Nanyang University is supported by the people, I am sure that the electorate will also support its graduates," Tan said.[163] Tan apparently gave each Nanyang graduate entering the election $2,000 for their election funds.[164]

The BS's election manifesto,[165] unveiled on the eve of nomination day, called for the eradication of neo-colonialism, the expulsion of all foreign troops, the closure of the British bases, the revocation of repressive laws, and the release of all political detainees. On the labour front, the BS pledged to unify the trade union movement and to improve the employment terms of all workers, and replace the exploitative capitalist system with a socialist one. Advocating equal treatment for all streams of education, the BS promised free primary and secondary education, the promotion of Malay secondary education, and the recognition of Nanyang University degrees. The manifesto further pledged more and cheaper houses for the poor, more clinics and crèches, pitches and lower fines for hawkers and taxi drivers, and a better deal for farmers and fishermen.

Attacking the PAP's record in office, the BS charged that four and a half years of PAP "misrule" had "not basically improved the livelihood" of the poor, like the farmers and the fishermen, who were "completely neglected". The PAP's low-cost housing were still "all too expensive", its labour legislation "outmoded"; its industrialization programme, far from encouraging local capital had instead "done everything to facilitate exploitation by foreign capital".[166] Alleging further that the PAP was pro-English education, the BS corroborated Tan Lark Sye's claim that Nanyang University had received no official assistance since its opening in 1956, its graduates were usually discriminated against in the civil service,[167] and Nanyang degrees were not recognized.

Denouncing the PAP further for its "arrogance, bullying threats and intimidation",[168] the Barisan chairman accused the PAP of putting "all sorts of hindrances and obstructions" in the way of its rivals, like denying suitable sites for election rallies because most had been taken by the ruling party for its own rallies or for the celebration of Malaysia. The detention of the BS leaders and the PAP's "sell-out to Malaysia" were also made the "burning issues of the elections".[169] Condemning the "arbitrary arrest and detention of anti-colonialists without charge or trial" and denouncing the PAP for its inhuman and barbaric treatment of political detainees, the BS demanded their "unconditional release".[170] The Barisan campaign also attempted to depict Lee Kuan Yew as a neo-colonialist stooge, alternately selling out Singapore to the British and the central government in Kuala Lumpur. "Without the British behind him, Lee Kuan Yew would not have the courage to be tough",[171] the Barisan leader asserted. Vowing to "fight the PAP every inch of the way and defeat them",[172] Lee Siew Choh called on the electorate to "put the final nail in its coffin"[173] and "bury the PAP once and for all".[174]

From the outset, the SA campaign was handicapped by the knowledge that two of its top leaders were not contesting. Having stepped down from the election, Lim Yew Hock continued to canvass on behalf of the party but, as Moore noted, he "proceeded to become their chief and ineffectual spokesman".[175] Nor were the issues included in the SA election manifesto — published as a full page advertisement in *The Straits Times* on 13 September 1963 — sufficiently enthralling to evoke much appeal. Lacking ties with organized labour, the SA manifesto, nonetheless, promised reforms to promote industrial peace with justice, foster the growth of genuinely democratic trade unions, and increase the rate of interest of the Central Provident Fund for the benefit of workers. It also pledged to reduce the rental of public housing and facilitate the purchase of these flats "on easy terms"; restore pay cuts imposed on civil servants by the PAP in 1959; help those "unjustly victimized by the PAP"; ensure equality of treatment for all the four streams of education and increase support for higher education, including the Nanyang University — issues more or less already championed by the BS, but with greater conviction. Not surprisingly, SA rallies, as one commentator noted, were "poorly attended and marked by apathy".[176] "The Alliance campaign line is sober. And sobriety does not make for agitation and clamour," observed a *Malayan Times* journalist covering the election, who noted that in the "bustering political front in Singapore ... voters

... are often swayed by the oratory of dreamers and adventurers. It has a hard fight ahead," he predicted.[177]

The SA's appeal, however, lay elsewhere — in its claim that it could bring about political stability and security, and the certainty of harmonious cooperation with the central government of Malaysia, so vital, it argued, to the prosperity of Singapore. Expectedly, the PAP bore the main brunt of the SA's attacks, being its nemesis, and contesting, as it did, for the pro-Malaysia and moderate votes. Challenging the PAP's claim that it could provide a more effective state government within Malaysia, the party argued that only an SA government, by virtue of its close ties with Kuala Lumpur, could bring about greater stability for Singapore. Declaring that it was "closely linked with the Malayan Alliance that has fought and beaten the communists",[178] the SA warned that if the PAP was voted into power, given its past record for opportunistic fraternization with communism, it could again "fall over to the communist side"[179] and chaos and instability would prevail. Refuting the PAP's claim that it was the only party that could best meet the communist threat, Lim Yew Hock pointed out that, after Malaysia, the fight against subversion was now the responsibility of the Alliance Central Government: "We have not forgotten that when action was taken last February against the communists, Lee Kuan Yew said that the PAP Government on its own would not have taken this action. And yet he claims that he is a great fighter against the communists".[180]

The PAP was also taken to task by John Jacob, the president of the SMIC, for its record of "direct as well as indirect antagonism to the Federation".[181] "Electing a PAP government at odds with, and distrusted by, the central government would also result in the intrusion of a 'disruptive force' into the body politic of Malaysia, so warned Yap Pheng Geck, a local banker.[182] By accusing the SA of being a stooge of the Federation, for instance, the PAP was unwittingly agitating the Singapore ground against the central government, Yap argued, and doing a disservice to Malaysia. "The damage done will be aggravated if the PAP forms the next government,"[183] he added. Defending its close relationship with Kuala Lumpur as an asset, not a liability, the SA argued that, being more acceptable to the Federation, it could have obtained, in a way the PAP could not, an even better deal from the central government. If elected, the SA promised, for instance, to improve on the unsatisfactory features[184] of Singapore's representation in the Federal Parliament, better the "shameful"[185] Common Market terms negotiated by the PAP, and solve Singapore's water shortage problems wrought by a drought that year. Blaming PAP "misrule" for the people "suffering water rationing for many months",[186] Lim Yew Hock pledged that, if elected, the SA would undertake an immediate "crash project to terminate water rationing"[187] with the cooperation of the Alliance-controlled state of Johore: "If you vote for the Alliance, your water situation will be solved, because we have friends all over the Malaysian territories".[188] Yap Pheng Geck warned that should either the BS or UPP be elected into power, this would lead to the breaking up of Malaysia, with Singapore seceding.[189]

Federal leaders also threw their weight behind the SA campaign. On 19 September, the Malaysian Minister of Telecommunications and Works, V.T. Sambanthan, addressing a crowd of about 1,500 at the Canberra Padang, slammed the PAP for not "playing the game" by giving only nine days' notice for the elections. He said that if the people had faith in the "Father of Malaysia", then they must vote for the Alliance, which had ruled with justice and stability. At another meeting at Block 19, H.M. Naval Base, the secretary of the Johore Bahru MCA, Lai Lai Heng, urged the people to unite and vote for the Alliance and bring the downfall of the PAP.[190] The Menteri Besar of Malacca, Abdul Ghafar bin Baba, addressed another largely Malay crowd along Jalan Masjid.[191] A partial boost to the SA's flagging campaign was given two days before polling day when the Tunku, on his first visit to Singapore after Malaysia, supported the SA and asked voters to return it to power. Although the Tunku said that his visit was in no way connected with the elections, the Malaysian premier in fact campaigned on behalf of the SA. Speaking at an SA tea party at Federation House in Changi, the Tunku told the gathering that he knew they had little time to prepare for the election which had been "sprung upon you by surprise" and that there was not enough time "to gear your election machinery to the pitch of efficiency" but it was important to trust the voters "to give thoughts to getting the right party to run the state". Leaving no doubt as to which right party he had in mind, the Tunku added: "It is my prayer that the people of Singapore will give favourable consideration to the party of which I am the leader."[192] More significantly, the Tunku also refuted the Singapore premier's assertion that the Federation government would send troops across the Causeway if the BS was elected to power. "There is no question of revoking the constitution, even if an extremist Government comes into power," he said.[193] Although the PAP publicly ignored the Malaysian premier's remarks, privately, Lee Kuan Yew was "furious with the Tunku for having come down to Singapore [the day before] and intervened in the campaign," reported the British High Commissioner of his telephone conversation with the Singapore premier on the afternoon of 20 September. The latter, the High Commissioner added, "claimed this was part of an MCA plot to take away votes from the PAP so that the Barisan Sosialis would win the elections and the Federation Government would then be able to suspend the Singapore constitution and install Lim Yew Hock as Governor of Singapore".[194]

In the matter of organized electioneering, however, it was the PAP, in one *Malayan Times* journalist's opinion, which "tops the list of parties". The "normal advantages enjoyed by the ruling party," he added, "have been effectively utilized by the People's Action Party".[195] Radio and television facilities, after all, were owned by the government, and although these were offered on 16 September 1963 to the four main parties to present their views in a series of recorded forums and talks in the four main languages, to begin immediately on the following day. The short notice "put considerable strain on the opposition parties, who had to arrange for radio and television speakers in four different languages at this crucial time".[196] A 64-page Ministry of Culture booklet, *Democratic Socialism in Action June 1959–April 1963*, was also distributed before and during the campaign.[197] It publicized the government's achievements and contained pro-PAP excerpts like how it was "obvious to everyone" that "the PAP government is the only well-organized and coherent force which can give the leadership to this broad alliance of the nationalist elements of our people." Having the campaign period coincide with the Malaysia celebrations was also a tactical masterstroke for it "helped to give full publicity to the PAP's success in merger"[198] and, as V. Vythalingam (UPP) complained, also helped to "draw the crowd away from the opposition rallies".[199]

Still, despite the advantages of office and timing, the PAP campaign was a hard fought one, more so in the rural than downtown area.[200] Like the BS, the PAP depended heavily on outdoor rallies and intensive house-to-house canvassing to get its programmes to the voters. Although PAP rallies were generally "well attended", it was still a "tough campaign", admitted Fong Sip Chee.[201] Ng Kah Ting remembered, for instance, that Punggol constituency, where he stood as the PAP candidate, "was sparsely populated and covered an area of about 6.7 square miles, and to visit every household in the nine days was an impossible task". It was also "strongly pro-left because of the nature of its population — mostly farmers with a low income, large families and a low rate of literacy ... So the battle for votes was intensely fierce, mud slinging notwithstanding".[202] Toh Chin Chye, who lost his Rochore branch to the BS, recalled that while he had "a handful of faithful followers, who followed me around, personally canvassing door-to-door", he was "swamped by Nanyang University undergraduates, all paid for by Tan Lark Sye, campaigning for Lee Siew Choh. So I was outnumbered."[203]

The PAP campaigned on presenting itself as a democratic socialist party whose record demanded its return to power. Its record was an impressive one, as Finance Minister Goh Keng Swee pointed out: the construction of 24,000 public housing units, a new school "every three weeks", every child provided with free primary education, better business climate, infrastructural improvements, the development of the new Jurong industrial site, and a budgetary surplus of $400 million after four years of government.[204] "The four-year governing record has clearly manifested that only the PAP can honestly, uncorruptedly, efficiently, intelligently and constructively develop Singapore," its election manifesto, *New Tasks Ahead*, declared. Campaigning also as the architect of Singapore's independence through merger, the party asserted that it was the only party which could "guarantee Singapore's dignity and position in Malaysia",[205] having negotiated, after a firm defence of Singapore's state rights, the best possible agreement with the Federation on the terms of merger.

As far as the PAP was concerned, the election was a fight between the party and the BS. "The other parties were irrelevant," maintained Fong Sip Chee.[206] Dismissing Ong Eng Guan's "one man party" and the independents as "opportunists and not worthy to be mentioned", the PAP maintained that to vote these groups which could make "no useful contributions to Malaysia" would be a waste of time.[207] The SA, on its part, the PAP argued, could not safeguard Singapore's interests, not only because it was run by puppets who took orders from Kuala Lumpur but also because it consisted of "corrupt politicians, bank compradores, agents for the sale of aeroplanes and airport construction contractors, individuals interested in earning commission from social welfare lottery tickets and those who fraternize with notorious secret society members", who aimed only to deprive Singapore of its $400 million surplus. On the "various intimate relationships" the SA enjoyed with Federation politicians, the PAP warned that such connections would permit the latter to "secure from the Singapore Alliance Government the interests that the Federation Government have been unable to obtain from the PAP".[208] "Therefore," reasoned Goh Keng Swee in a radio and telecast talk on 19 September, "if you vote for the Alliance, you will be weakening Singapore's position against the centre. Many problems, some small, others important, are bound to crop up between centre and state and it would be foolish for us to weaken our own position in advance. This is what you would do if you vote for the Singapore branch of the Alliance." Goh said that voting SA presented a second danger: it would split the anti-BS vote.[209] Though it was unlikely that the BS had sufficient strength in itself to ensure victory, it was conceivable, the PAP argued, for the Barisan, and hence its communist backers, to capture power if the anti-communist vote were split, which would happen if the people voted for the SA.

That the ensuing electoral contest would be a "life and death struggle" between the party and the BS, few PAP stalwarts doubted. As Chor Yeok Eng recalled:

> [O]n nomination day when we finished filing our nomination papers at the nomination station, we were surrounded at the gates and threatened by supporters and members of the Barisan. They said they would pay any price to gain victory, and that when they gained power they would exterminate not only all their political enemies, but penalize me as well for being uncooperative. In our subsequent visits to voters, assaults, arguments and fights with Barisan supporters were not uncommon in areas which were influenced by them. As a result, there were many incidents where posters of our candidates were torn, banners ripped apart, and our supporters assaulted during the election campaigns.[210]

Accusations by the BS, bolstered by Tan Lark Sye's insinuations, of the PAP's alleged anti-Chinese education bias were already threatening to erode the ruling party's Chinese support, and put the party on the defensive early in the hustings. Much time was spent answering the Barisan's charges of discrimination. Insisting that Nanyang graduates were employed in the government and Nanyang degrees recognized, the PAP replied that the reason financial assistance was not given to Nanyang University was because the latter failed to raise its academic standards and comply with the government's accounting procedures.[211] Deploring what it saw as campaigning on Chinese chauvinist grounds, the PAP warned that such tactics would only "result in creating suspicion and hostility between the races and precipitating racial conflicts".[212]

The PAP's offensive against the Barisan capitalized largely on the voters' fear of the latter's anti-Malaysia and pro-communist connections. Charging that the Barisan was an instrumental part of a wider communist conspiracy whose mission was to destroy Malaysia, the PAP disclosed that the BS party symbol — the red star and blue circle — was the seal of a Chinese communist city.[213] Citing further the party's "intimate relations with the Indonesian Communist Party" and its advocacy of "a merger with Indonesia", the PAP accused the BS of being "at the service of anti-Singapore foreign elements. Therefore, a Barisan government will mean an immediate destruction of merger and Malaysia," it argued.[214] Warning that the central government would not allow a communist-controlled party to govern Singapore and that its reaction to this calamity would be "a very swift one", Lee charged in his final broadcast on the eve of election that there was already an MCA plot to take over Singapore by proclaiming an emergency. Having decided that the SA could not win, Lee alleged that the MCA wanted to split the anti-communist votes and "see the Barisan Sosialis win so that they can really take over Singapore, lock, stock and barrel and perhaps later to give a State Constitution like Penang and Kelantan, where the State Government has to go begging for money from the Central Government, where it can be controlled and emasculated from the centre".[215] A decisive defeat for the BS, on the other hand, "would convince alien confrontationists that they have no allies in Singapore,"[216] the PAP said. Calling on the voters to reject both the SA and the BS, Lee Kuan Yew declared: "Vote for corruption, vote for decadent government — vote for the Alliance. Vote for chaos and anarchy — vote for the Barisan Sosialis".[217]

No one was certain, however, if the majority of the voters would heed Lee's call to reject both the SA and BS on polling day. If the assessments of political observers provide any guide, the outlook for the PAP was not an entirely cheerful one. Whilst the Australian High Commission surmised on 14 September, at the beginning of the campaign, that the PAP would "win more seats than any other single party", including the "chance of winning the absolute majority", i.e. 26 seats, its evaluation of a PAP victory was less upbeat by 20 September, on the eve of polling day. "There is a general feeling that PAP prospects are not as good as they first appeared," the High Commission reported. While still adhering to its guess that the PAP would still obtain more seats than any other single party, the High Commission was no longer as confident of an absolute PAP majority, and reiterated the possibility of the PAP drawing the SUMNO into a coalition, and away from the SA, should it pick up two or three seats as part of the Alliance. Gloom also pervaded British appraisal of the outcome of the polls. "At the beginning of the week," reported the British High Commission on 20 September, "the general impression in Singapore was that the PAP would get a majority ... but the general view seems to be that

45

the PAP have been slipping in the last few days. There are very few independent observers now who will confidently predict an overall PAP majority in the Assembly".[218]

Both the Australian and British High Commissions, however, reckoned that the prospect of a Barisan victory "is now regarded as a distinct possibility"[219] and "cannot be ruled out".[220] The Barisan chairman himself had predicted that his party would win "hands down".[221] Privately, the Barisan had forecasted a majority win of 35 seats.[222] Speculating on the ramifications of such a Barisan victory, the British High Commissioner intimated:

> It is of course quite possible that the Federation Government would take drastic action and refuse to allow a Barisan Sosialis Government to come to power in Singapore. If, however, the Federation were to hold their hand for the time being I would guess the Barisan Sosialis will be fairly moderate to begin with and would adhere to their previous policy of taking a constitutional line and not exposing themselves unnecessarily to arrest. They would probably not seek secession from Malaysia but would press for what they call genuine and full merger, i.e. full proportionate representations in the Central Parliament. They would, however, denounce the inclusion of Sabah and Sarawak in Malaysia as neo-colonialism. They might also try to start labour trouble in the British bases.

Even if the BS pursued fairly moderate policies, he wondered how the central government could tolerate them in power in Singapore for very long. "We must, therefore, be prepared for a very difficult situation in Singapore if the Barisan Sosialis are successful in the elections," he warned.[223]

David Marshall was also in a "sombre mood".[224] On 19 September, the independent candidate for Anson asserted to R.A. Woolcott, the Australian Acting High Commissioner in Singapore, that the SA was simply a "lap dog of the Tengku" and was "finished". Lim Yew Hock's withdrawal, he said, was "an admission of bankruptcy and defeat" and had left the party "leaderless". Marshall saw the UPP's role as banking on getting enough votes to form a coalition with either the PAP or the BS. He doubted that the Barisan would be prepared to form a coalition with any party but believed the PAP might. He felt that lacking a majority, the PAP would "probably swallow their pride and turn to Ong Eng Guan for the necessary support" if it could not persuade SUMNO, should the latter win enough seats, to leave the SA and join its ranks. Woolcott remarked that Marshall, distraught at the PAP moving "in the direction of Fascism", was "unable to discuss rationally any merits the PAP might have". His estimate was that the PAP would probably win 18 or 20 seats, short of a majority. He suggested that a number of its ministers would be defeated, including Toh Chin Chye. Regarding a Barisan victory "as the start of a process which would lead to civil war in Malaysia", Marshall underlined that it was "madness" to blindly oppose Malaysia at that stage as the Barisan was doing. On his own chances, Marshall said with some emotion that he would not win Anson, which would probably be won by the BS candidate, Tan Chong Kim, the president of SATU. However, he could not simply run away like Lim Yew Hock, he said, and would rather fight and be defeated. He also would not mind leaving Singapore politics altogether, he added, partly because he felt the days of constitutional democracy "were as good as over" and also because he foresaw only the likelihood of civil war and dictatorship engulfing the state, with the central government unable or inexperienced enough to deal with the situation with which it would be confronted.[225]

Privately, both the SA and UPP leaders were also not optimistic about winning more than 15 seats each, a figure the Australian High Commission contested as "highly optimistic" and surmised that five seats was probably closer to reality.[226] "[N]ot likely to get more than half a dozen seats (three Malay and three middle-class constituencies),"[227] was the equally sober British forecast of the SA's chances. On UPP prospects, the Australians put the number of seats at possibly three[228]; the British were more dismissive: "not certain of any seats beyond that of Ong himself",[229] Notwithstanding their poor outlook, both the SA and UPP were still reckoned as pivotal players who could decisively affect the outcome of the elections by taking votes from the main contestants. Whilst the UPP was expected to draw Chinese-speaking votes from the Barisan, the SA "will everywhere take PAP votes and this could bring down the Government". The British High Commissioner warned: "[The] extent to which the Alliance and the UPP can draw votes away from the two main parties may be decisive."[230]

The PAP's own prediction was that it would win as many as 30 seats.[231] Reporting on his phone conversation with the PAP's Secretary-General in the afternoon of 20 September, the British High Commissioner noted, for instance, that Lee was "full of confidence" and said that he was "certain to get a majority". So sure was Lee of victory that he had "instructed his agents to put ten thousand dollars of his own money on the PAP". The High Commissioner's own prediction was that "the PAP will get an overall majority", adding, however, that "most of the people whose judgement I respect are less optimistic and do not give them more than 20–24".[232] Only the results on polling day would reveal who was right.

The PAP Victorious

On 21 September 1963, a record 587,948 (95 per cent) out of an electorate of 617,649 went to the polls.[233] Expected to lose its majority, the PAP won instead 37 seats — "a sweeping victory which exceeded even its most optimistic estimates," reported an ebullient Critchley.[234] Sharing his elation was Moore who hailed the resounding PAP victory as representing "an astonishing recovery from the brink of defeat".[235] The opposition was almost totally routed, with virtually only the BS left standing. The BS captured 13 seats while its ally, Partai Rakyat Singapura, lost all its three contested seats, although, like both the PAP and BS, it did well enough so that none of its candidates needed to part with his deposit. Both the SA and the UPP were virtually eliminated — 31 and 39 of their candidates respectively forfeited their deposits. Only Ong Eng Guan won the remaining seat, but with a greatly reduced majority. All 16 independents and the remaining six candidates from the other three minor parties were trounced. All forfeited their deposits.

Not only did the poll results confirm the BS as the PAP's strongest threat, and the former's appeal in the rural areas, but they also reflected more accurately the actual ground strength of the two parties. Except in Hong Lim, PAP and BS candidates, for instance, obtained the first and second highest votes in the 46 wards where they confronted each other. Out of the Barisan's 13 seats, 11 came from the rural wards.[236] And although the PAP captured 72.5 per cent of the seats, it secured only 272,924 votes, or 46.5 per cent of the total number of votes cast — down from the 53.4 per cent it won in 1959 — while the BS, which managed to secure only 25.5 per cent of the seats, received 193,301 votes, or 32.9 per cent of the total votes polled. If the UPP's 48,785 votes (8.3 per cent) were added to the Barisan's, representing the votes from the splinter groups from the 1959 PAP, they totalled 242,086 — or 41.6 per cent of all the votes cast, just about five percentage points short of parity with the PAP, although the number of seats won was only 14. Stated in a different way, much of the PAP's left-wing support in 1959 had gone to both these splinter groups. That the PAP surmounted the challenge from the Left to win by a comfortable majority was a testament not only of its superior political and tactical acumen, as we have seen, but was also a consequence of the splitting of the opposition votes and the gains it won at the expense of the right-wing parties.

In fact, only 20 PAP seats were secured by an outright majority.[237] It captured 17 others only because the opposition votes were split.[238] In seven wards, including those of four ministers — Toh Chin Chye, S. Rajaratnam, Ong Pang Boon and Yong Nyuk Lin — the PAP would almost certainly have been defeated had the UPP candidates not done well enough to deprive the BS of a win. "Four PAP ministers will have to thank the UPP for saving their skins by doing the dirty work of splitting the left-wing votes," charged the Barisan chairman,[239] who lost narrowly to deputy premier Toh Chin Chye in Rochore. "The people who voted for Ong Eng Guan were the labourers, hawkers, and rickshaw pullers. They were supporters of the Barisan. They would never have voted for the PAP!" he reiterated. Collaborating Lee's account, Toh acknowledged that his chances were indeed "very dicey":

> The Indonesian Confrontation had started. Rochore had high unemployment. Many of them were traders with the Rhio archipelago. So once you had an embargo from Indonesia, you could see the vessels lying in the harbour, doing nothing. No cargo was moving. The traders were losing money and this had a multiplier effect. Those who depended upon the flow of money, like trishaw riders, taxi drivers, lorry drivers, they also lost money.

Toh knew it was "useless" to attempt to win over such groups in his ward like the trishaw riders whom "Lee Siew Choh had ... going around carrying the Barisan logo" or the "lumpen-proletariat [who] were living in very old Singapore Improvement Trust flats, where you share the kitchen, toilet, and bathroom. ... Each time I went along to call on them, they just ignored me," Toh added, "I ended up with the slimmest majority of 89 votes over Lee Siew Choh. There were two recounts! Still, it was a win."[240] Of the eight PAP ministers, only Lee Kuan Yew (Tanjong Pagar) and Goh Keng Swee (Kreta Ayer) were returned with a convincing majority of 2,780 and 4,413 respectively. Both K.M. Byrne (Crawford), the Minister of Health and Law, and National Development Minister Tan Kia Gan (Paya Lebar) were defeated by the Barisan. Education Minister Yong Nyuk Lin, defeated his BS opponent in Geylang West with a majority of only 618; in Telok Ayer and Kampong Glam, Home Minister Ong Pang Boon and Culture Minister S. Rajaratnam retained their seats only with a slender majority of 403 and 220 respectively. In all the three latter wards, the UPP candidates polled 1,541, 1,484 and 1,224 votes respectively, whilst, in Rochore, the UPP took 1,067 votes. Potentially at least, UPP intervention in these wards held the balance between victory or defeat for half of the PAP cabinet. Notwithstanding this, even without the presence of the UPP, the BS would have gained, at best, only another seven seats, not enough to exert an influence on the overall outcome of the polls, which would point to the PAP winning at least 30 seats and the Barisan not more than 20, which still gave the government a clear majority.[241]

The PAP also owed much to the collapse of the Right, which saw its share of the votes dropping from 35.2 per cent in the 1959 polls to 8.3 per cent by the 1963 general elections. In 1959, the main right-wing vote came from the SPA (20.4 per cent of the votes), SUMNO/SMCA (6.3 per cent), SMIC (0.4 per cent), and the Liberal Socialist Party (8.1 per cent). By 1963, the latter had disappeared, having been dissolved on the eve of nomination day, leaving the field to the other right-wing parties, now under the new SA banner. The challenge of the SA, however, buckled in every constituency it contested. Of its 42 candidates only two — Ahmad bin Haji Taff (Geylang Serai) and Mohammed Ali bin Alwi (Kampong Kembangan) — got within striking distance of winning. Yap Pheng Geck, the SA's new leader, was trounced by the PAP in River Valley, and polled 1,512 votes fewer than the BS candidate. Its strongest candidate, A.P. Rajah, was defeated by the PAP and BS in Farrer Park who won 4,133 and 1,387 votes respectively. Vice-President Thio Chan Bee, shocked by his party's "unexpected and almost Dunkirk defeat",[242] put up a more credible performance, but failed to retain his Tanglin seat, losing to the PAP's E.W. Barker by 2,686 votes, and more narrowly to the Barisan candidate by 259 votes. Of the seven SPA–UMNO constituencies won in 1959, all had shifted their allegiance to the PAP. As Critchley commented, "When one considers that the Alliance parties gained a combined total of 143,000 votes (27 per cent of the total) in 1959, the extent of their failure becomes clear. Most of the former Alliance voters clearly switched to the PAP to an extent which even the latter had not anticipated".[243]

If the most striking aspect of the result, as the British High Commission saw it, was "the slaughter of all sections of the Alliance",[244] what was even more startling was the defeat of SUMNO candidates in their own strongholds of Geylang Serai, Kampong Kembangan and Southern Islands, which were won in 1959, and which SUMNO now lost to the PAP by a majority of 540, 1,703, and 3,435 votes respectively — a defeat even the PAP had not anticipated, as the Australian High Commissioner revealed: "I know from

PAP sources that they had assumed UMNO would win two or three predominantly Malay constituencies and that if they, the PAP, won 25 seats they would attempt to form a coalition government with UMNO."[245] Indeed, only in Southern Islands did the PAP receive 55.4 per cent of the votes cast in a two-cornered fight with SUMNO. In the other two constituencies, the PAP polled only 48 per cent. Be that as it may, the Malays did not vote *en bloc* for SUMNO. Not only had the Singapore electorate rejected communally-based political parties, but, especially among Malay voters, it had voted non-communally in favour of the non-communal socialist PAP against the traditional leadership of the UMNO. "Thus the Malays of Singapore deserted the Tunku in spite of the latter's ill-considered intervention in the elections when he visited Singapore on Thursday," observed the British High Commission.[246] In 1959, the Malays had voted UMNO candidates out of fear of the non-Malays in a competitive environment. But the PAP introduced a programme to demonstrate that the advancement of the Malays lay in correct socio-economic and educational policies and not in special Malay privileges. The 1963 election results vindicated the belief that the Malay outlook could be changed.

The magnitude of the PAP's win underlined the party's emergence as the dominant political force in Singapore. Compared to 1959, its victory in 1963 was much more decisive. Then the PAP had won with pro-communist support. In 1963, however, the party had fought the pro-communists openly and defeated them decisively. Of the major political contenders, only the BS remained, although, as Critchley noted, "Communist hopes of gaining power constitutionally by penetrating a Barisan Sosialis government have now dissipated".[247] Notwithstanding its electoral setback, the BS was still a political force to be reckoned with. Its 13 seats was only one less from its representation in the previous Assembly. And with the collapse of the UPP at the polls, the Barisan was now poised to consolidate and lead the still formidable anti-PAP Left. Having failed to gain power constitutionally, the BS was also expected to step up its subversive campaign.

Emboldened by the scale of its electoral success, the PAP, almost immediately, started its political consolidation — and cracked down hard on the Left. On 22 September 1963, the government began proceedings to strip Tan Lark Sye of his Singapore citizenship for having "actively and persistently collaborated with an active anti-national group of communists in Nanyang University".[248] Three days later, a security swoop led to the detention of 20 Nanyang University graduates with pro-communist affiliations, including three who had contested unsuccessfully in the elections as BS candidates.[249] On 3 October 1963, two pro-BS rural and three hawkers' associations were dissolved for being used as communist united front organizations.[250] Following an abortive strike by SATU unions on 8 October 1963, 14 of its leaders were arrested and detained, including three elected BS assemblymen, one of whom was S.T. Bani, its president.[251] And, on 31 October 1963, seven of SATU's strongest unions were finally deregistered.[252] Having recovered its own mass base, and with the Left crippled, the PAP, as Critchley noted, "has decisively consolidated [its] political power in Singapore".[253]

A strong PAP government in Singapore, for which its sweeping victory set the stage, was not without its virtues — or ramifications. As the British and Australian High Commissions saw it, the vote for the PAP could also be regarded as a "tremendous boost"[254] and a "further endorsement" of Malaysia. Both the PAP and the SA together polled some 56 per cent of the vote and "this should answer critics of merger referendum."[255] From the Australian security perspective, the return of a "friendly"[256] PAP government also "seems to offer the best prospect for the continuance of a stable, non-communist Singapore which will offer the British bases here security of tenure for the next five years".[257] Although welcoming the PAP win as the "best result for Singapore", the Australian High Commission also warned, as the British did, that the "decisive scope of it could create problems", especially in the extremely complex relations it shared with the central government in Kuala Lumpur.

The extent of the Alliance rout, as Critchley noted, had "effectively checked any movement towards an Alliance revival in Singapore by eliminating it for five years".[258] The PAP's sweeping victory, on the other hand, had considerably strengthened its hand *vis-à-vis* the central government, and consolidated the Singapore premier's position in Singapore. In Critchley's opinion, Lee Kuan Yew had emerged from the election "as a man of considerable stature" and Kuala Lumpur had little choice but "to accept him"[259] — a conclusion similarly reached by the British High Commission: "We have always said in Singapore that Lee Kuan Yew is the only man who can run this city and that the Malaysian Government would either have to do business with him or put him in jail. Latter is now unthinkable and we must hope that enough moderation will be shown on both sides to make a working partnership possible."[260] How that relationship could evolve would depend partly on the reactions from across the Causeway to the political ramifications of the total elimination of the SA in Singapore, and, perhaps more significantly, the rejection of the communal SUMNO by the Singapore Malay voters. As the British Deputy High Commissioner ruminated, "I hope the Malaysian Government will regard the PAP victory as a tremendous boost for Malaysia and will not take too badly the elimination of their party in Singapore".[261] "The Tunku must accept that the Alliance have no hope in Singapore and that he must do business with Lee. But equally important, Lee must show more tact and understanding towards Kuala Lumpur. Failure to work together," Moore warned, "could have [the] most serious consequences for Malaysia."[262]

Notes

1. Fong Sip Chee, The PAP Story — The Pioneering Years (Singapore: PAP, 1979), p. 135.
2. Critchley to Menzies, 13 October 1963, A1838/280 no. 3024/2/4 Part 1.
3. The shifting balance of power between the PAP and the opposition parties from May 1959 to August 1962 is indicated in the table below (adapted from Fong, pp. 120–21):

Date	Assembly Strength	Comments
30 May 1959	PAP 43/Opposition 8	The relative strength of the PAP and opposition parties in the Assembly after the general elections
27 July 1960	PAP 40/Opposition 11	Expulsion of Ong Eng Guan and 2 others who later formed the United Peoples Party (UPP)
15 July 1961	PAP 39/Opposition 12	PAP lost Anson by-election to David Marshall*
21 July 1961	PAP 26/Opposition 25	Expulsion of 13 dissidents who later formed the Barisan Sosialis (BS)
3 July 1962	PAP 25/Opposition 26	Resignation from PAP of Ho Puay Choo who remained as an independent
11 August 1962	PAP 25/Opposition 26	Ho Puay Choo defected to BS
16 August 1962	PAP 26/Opposition 25	S.V. Lingam defected from UPP and rejoined PAP**
21 August 1962	PAP 25/Opposition 25	Death of Ahmad bin Ibrahim (PAP Member of Sembawang)***

* The Anson by-election was precipitated by the death of the PAP member, Baharuddin bin Mohamed on 20 April 1961. The PAP candidate, Mahmud bin Awang lost narrowly to David Marshall, the leader of the Workers' Party.

** Lingam said that he had previously left the PAP not because of disagreement with the policies of the party but because of personal attachment to Ong Eng Guan, the UPP leader. He decided to leave the UPP because of growing differences and contradictions between his own political beliefs and Ong's handling of the UPP.

*** Another death, this time of the Minister for Labour, Ahmad bin Ibrahim, eliminated the PAP's absolute majority in the Assembly, which had been restored by the defection of S.V. Lingam from the UPP in August 1962, and his readmission to the PAP.

4. Cited in Melanie Chew, *Leaders of Singapore* (Singapore: Resource Press, 1996), p. 91.

5. Chor Yeok Eng, "Looking Back at the Early Activities of the PAP: The Rise of Nationalism", in *Petir: 25th Anniversary Issue. People's Action Party 1954–1979* (Singapore: PAP, 1979), p. 131.

6. The three votes came from the Singapore UMNO candidates in the 1959 general elections. The Singapore MCA candidates did not win a single seat.

7. *The People*, vol. 3, no. 5, June 1961, p. 1.

8. Ibid., vol. 3, no. 6, July 1961, p. 1.

9. The Grand Alliance, comprising 23 political parties from the Federation, Singapore, Sarawak, Sabah and Brunei (the Brunei Alliance subsequently withdrew in April 1963), was formed on 30 March 1963 in Kuala Lumpur. Modelled along the Federation Alliance, it was to be a united front of pro-Malaysia parties established to contest the forthcoming Federal and State elections within Malaysia. In his speech on behalf of the SA, Lim Yew Hock asserted that the Grand Alliance would be a "rallying point around which the various races in our territories will dedicate themselves to meet any threat or interference to Malaysia from any quarter" and that it was "unequivocally" anti-communist and would not "accept into our ranks pseudo-nationalists or parties ... who hide behind meaningless phrases like 'non-communists'" and who worked "hand-in-hand with communists and fellow-travellers to achieve their own selfish ends". *The People*, vol. 5, no. 2, 15 June 1963, p. 2.

10. *The People*, vol. 5, no. 3, 22 July 1963, p. 1.

11. The SPA's newsletter, *The People*, recorded its ideological position more ambivalently: "We do not whip ourselves into a frenzy by styling ourselves as leftists or rightists for, after all, the terms left and right are relative". *The People*, vol. 3, no. 6, July 1961, p. 2.

12. Telegram no. 224, Moore to Secretary of State, 4 April 1963, DO 169/248 no. 131/33/2 Part B.

13. *Singapore Legislative Assembly Debates*, 24 July 1963, Col. 86.

14. Telegram no. 108, Selkirk to Secretary of State for the Colonies, 13 February 1963, DO 169/248 no. 131/33/2 Part B.

15. Telegram no. 90, Selkirk to Secretary of State for the Colonies, 5 February 1963, DO 169/248 no. 131/33/2 Part B.

16. Ibid.

17. Critchley to Menzies, 13 October 1963, A1838/280 no. 3024/2/4 Part 1.

18. W.K. Flanagan to Secretary, Department of External Affairs, 14 January 1963, A1838/280 no. 3024/2/1 Part 11.

19. Record of conversation between G. Jockel and Lim Yew Hock, 17 January 1963, A1838/280 no. 3024/2/1 Part 11.

20. *The Straits Times*, 12 September 1963.

21. Telegram no. 5, Moore to Secretary of State for the Colonies, 3 January 1963, DO 169/19 no. 33/45/1.

22. *The Straits Times*, 12 September 1963.

23. Telegram no. 336, Selkirk to Secretary of State for the Colonies, 18 May 1963, DO 169/19 no. 33/45/1.

24. Flanagan to Secretary, Department of External Affairs, 1 December 1962, A1838/280 no. 3024/2/1 Part 11.
25. The Federation Minister for Agriculture and Co-operatives, Khir Johari, for instance, was in Singapore "tidying up the UMNO division" and "acquainting the Malays with UMNO leadership". Federation MCA leaders, like Finance Minister Tan Siew Sin, and Senators Khaw Khai Boh and T.H. Tan, were also involved in reorganizing the Singapore MCA and recruiting businessmen for support. On 24 June 1963, the Singapore Alliance (SA) was established as a regional branch of the Grand Alliance. See *The Malay Mail*, 9 October 1962, 13 March 1963; 20 September 1962, 1 May 1963, 18 May 1963, cited in Lee Kah Chuen, "The 1963 Singapore General Election" (Unpublished Academic Exercise, Department of History, University of Singapore, 1976), pp. 14–15.
26. *The Straits Times*, 11 November 1962.
27. Ibid., 23 May 1963.
28. Telegram no. 402, Selkirk to Secretary of State for the Colonies, 13 June 1963, DO 169/19 no. 33/45/1.
29. Ibid.
30. Telegram no. 5, Moore to Secretary of State for the Colonies, 3 January 1963, DO 169/19 no. 33/45/1.
31. *The Straits Times*, 12 September 1963.
32. Telegram no. 224, Moore to Secretary of State for the Colonies, 4 April 1963, DO 169/248 no. 131/33/2 Part B.
33. Ibid.
34. Telegram no. 402, Selkirk to Secretary of State for the Colonies, 13 June 1963, DO 169/19 no. 33/45/1.
35. Telegram no. 522, Selkirk to Secretary of State for the Colonies, 26 July 1963, DO 169/19 no. 33/45/1.
36. Both David Marshall and Ong Eng Guan had called on the government to resign. See *Singapore Legislative Assembly Debates*, 25 July 1963, Col. 175–78.
37. Ibid., 24 July 1963, Col. 77.
38. Ibid., 25 July 1963, Col. 140.
39. Ibid., Col. 143.
40. Ibid., Col. 141.
41. Ibid., Col. 141.
42. Ibid., Col. 140.
43. On 26 June 1963, the Minister of Home Affairs, Ong Pang Boon, had written to all the parties represented in the Assembly, including the two independents, inviting suggestions on how the existing 51 electoral divisions could be grouped together to form the 15 Federal electoral divisions. None of the political parties responded formally to the invitation. A reminder despatched on 8 July 1963, inviting the opposition parties to nominate a representative each to a meeting of all parties represented in the Assembly, elicited only a solitary response from the Singapore UMNO, informing Ong that the latter did not wish to participate. The reason for the poor response, argued Ong Eng Guan, the UPP leader, was because the opposition parties felt it was a "farce" to be invited to delineate boundaries "which have already been decided": "We send four, the Government sends five: first, the Government hopes that the four in the Opposition will give four different views... And if in case we do not fight and we agree among ourselves first before we meet... they will have five to outvote us four". See Ibid., 25 July 1963, Col. 171, 119.

44. Ibid., 31 July 1963, Col. 455.

45. Ibid., 24 July 1963, Col. 79.

46. Selkirk had argued that, as the vote in the Assembly had not been a vote of no confidence on Malaysia, there was no "tactical advantage" for the government to hold elections before the establishment of Malaysia. The Singapore government, he added, had a "perfectly sound moral right to take Singapore into Malaysia … provided the Malaysia Agreement was approved by the Singapore Assembly next week." Telegram no. 522, Selkirk to Secretary of State for the Colonies, 26 July 1963, DO 169/19 no. 33/45/1.

47. Lee issued the challenge during a televised press conference on 26 July 1963. *The Straits Times*, 27 July 1963.

48. *Singapore Legislative Assembly Debates*, 29 July–1 August 1963, Col. 297–422, 426–95, 496–572, 576–718.

49. Ibid., 1 August 1963, Col. 716–17.

50. Telegram no. 522, Selkirk to Secretary of State for the Colonies, 26 July 1963, DO 169/19 no. 33/45/1.

51. Dennis Bloodworth, *The Tiger and the Trojan Horse* (Singapore: Times Books International, 1986), p. 282.

52. *The Straits Times*, 19 September 1963.

53. Telegram no. 108, Selkirk to Secretary of State for the Colonies, 13 February 1963, DO 169/248 no. 131/33/2 Part B.

54. Critchley to Menzies, 13 October 1963, A1838/280 no. 3024/2/4 Part 1.

55. Lee Kuan Yew, "What of the Past is Relevant to the Future?", in *Petir: 25th*, p. 35.

56. *Singapore Legislative Assembly Debates*, 25 July 1963, Col. 176.

57. *The Straits Times*, 26 July 1963. [Emphasis mine.]

58. *Singapore Legislative Assembly Debates*, 30 July 1963, Col. 347.

59. Ibid., 25 July 1963, Col. 177.

60. The proclamation was signed by the Yang di-Pertuan Agong on 29 August 1963. Malaysia was originally to come into effect on 31 August 1963. It was postponed to 16 September 1963 to give the United Nations time to ascertain the wishes of peoples of the Borneo territories towards joining Malaysia. *The Straits Times*, 30 August 1963.

61. Under the law, nine days had to elapse between the dissolution of the Assembly and nomination day, and another nine before elections. See F.L. Starner, "The Singapore elections of 1963" in K.J. Ratnam and R.S. Milne, *The Malayan Parliamentary Election of 1964* (Singapore: University of Malaya Press, 1967), p. 323.

62. Critchley to Menzies, 13 October 1963, A1838/280 no. 3024/2/4 Part 1.

63. *The Straits Times*, 4 September 1963.

64. Ibid.

65. See Section 34(4) of *The Singapore Legislative Assembly Elections (Amendment) Ordinance, 1960*, Ordinance no. 23 of 1960 (Singapore, 1960).

66. As Thursday, 12 September 1963, was nomination day, the business of campaigning could only start from Friday, 13 September 1963. The period included a half-day Saturday (14 September), a Sunday public holiday (15 September), a Monday Malaysia Day (16 September), and a Tuesday proclaimed legal public holiday (17 September). Polling day (21 September) was also a public holiday. This left only four and a half working days for the transaction of essential businesses. See Lee, "The Singapore General Election", pp. 21–22; also Starner, pp. 323–24.

67. *The Straits Times*, 14 , 15 and 21 September 1963.

68. Telegram no. 4, Moore to British High Commissioner (Kuala Lumpur), 27 September 1963, DO 169/19 no. 33/45/1.

69. Critchley to Menzies, 13 October 1963, A1838/280 no. 3024/2/4 Part 1.
70. The BS chairman, Lee Siew Choh, for instance, accused the PAP of using "government machinery and public money for public purposes" in the Prime Minister's constituency visits. See *Plebeian*, vol. 2, no. 10, 16 September 1963, p. 1; the SA had also accused the Prime Minister of conducting "personal electioneering campaigns at public expense" under the guise of his constituency tours. *The Straits Times*, 12 August 1963.
71. Bloodworth, p. 280.
72. Television was introduced in Singapore on 15 February 1963. *The Straits Times*, 16 February 1963.
73. Bloodworth, p. 280.
74. *Plebeian*, vol. 2, no. 10, 16 September 1963, p. 1.
75. Telegram no. 40, Australian High Commission (Singapore) to Department of External Affairs, 27 September 1963, A1838/280 no. 3024/2/4 Part 1.
76. Telegram no. 4, Moore to Tory, 27 September 1963, DO 169/19 no. 33/45/1.
77. On 17 April 1963, in a statement on the financial talks, the BS accused Lee of having "already sold out the total rights of the people of Singapore" and putting "our head in the Federation noose". In the Assembly on 30 July 1963, Lee Siew Choh again harped on the "PAP sell-out". The following day, it was Ong Eng Guan of the UPP who denigrated the Malaysia Agreement as "a sell-out by the PAP minority Government". See *The Straits Times*, 18 April 1963; *Singapore Legislative Assembly Debates*, 30 July 1963, Col. 379, and 31 July 1963, Col. 479.
78. Telegram no. 290, Moore to Secretary of State for the Colonies, 29 April 1963, DO 169/220 no. 131/9.
79. *The Straits Times*, 18 May 1963.
80. Lee, "The 1963 Singapore General Election", p. 17.
81. Telegram no. 402, Selkirk to Secretary of State for the Colonies, 13 June 1963, DO 169/19 no. 33/45/1.
82. Telegram no. 290, Moore to Secretary of State for the Colonies, 29 April 1963, DO 169/220 no. 131/9.
83. Telegram no. 402, Selkirk to Secretary of State for the Colonies, 13 June 1963, DO 169/19 no. 33/45/1.
84. Telegram no. 7, Singapore to Kuala Lumpur, 20 September 1963, DO 169/19 no. 33/45/1.
85. Telegram no. 39, Woolcott to Department of External Affairs, 14 September 1963, A1838/280 no. 3024/2/4 Part 1.
86. Telegram no. 7, Singapore to Kuala Lumpur, 20 September 1963, DO 169/19 no. 33/45/1.
87. Critchley to Menzies, 13 October 1963, A1838/280 no. 3024/2/4 Part 1.
88. Telegram no. 39, Woolcott to Department of External Affairs, 14 September 1963, A1838/280 no. 3024/2/4 Part 1.
89. Critchley to Menzies, 13 October 1963, A1838/280 no. 3024/2/4 Part 1.
90. Telegram no. 7, Singapore to Kuala Lumpur, 20 September 1963, DO 169/19 no. 33/45/1.
91. The BS members included Lim Chin Siong, Secretary-General; Poh Soo Kai, Assistant Secretary-General; S. Woodhull, Vice-Chairman; J.J. Puthucheary, Adviser; Fong Swee Suan, Executive Committee Member; Lim Hock Siew, Executive Committee Member; Dominic Puthucheary, Executive Committee Member; Lee Tiow Meng, Executive Committee Member; Koh Lam Seng, Executive Committee Member; Chok Koh Thong, Executive Committee Member. *The Straits Times*, 6 February 1963.
92. Cited in Chew, *Leaders of Singapore*, p. 93.
93. Among those present at the meeting of the ISC on 2 February 1963 which ordered the arrests were: (from Singapore) Lee Kuan Yew (Prime Minister), Goh Keng Swee (Finance

Minister), and Ong Pang Boon (Minister for Home Affairs); (from Britain) Lord Selkirk (UK Commissioner), chairman, Major-General E.A.W. Williams (GOC, Singapore Base District), P.B.C. Moore (Deputy UK Commissioner, Singapore); (from Malaya) Dato Ismail bin Dato Abdul Rahman (Minister of Internal Security). *The Sunday Times*, 3 February 1963.

94. Moore reported that Lee "had been more anxious than we to make the arrests before Malaysia" and that he had also "insisted on the three UPP members being arrested" because he was "worried about Ong Eng Guan" in the coming elections. The Deputy UK Commissioner, however, managed to confirm Lee's report that another British official had mentioned to him that if the arrests were not agreed to then merger and Malaysia would fail. "It is true that I told Lee that in our view the Federation almost certainly would not see merger through unless the arrests were made," Moore said. Telegram nos. 108 and 109, Selkirk to Secretary of State for the Colonies, 13 February 1963, DO 169/ 248 no. 131/33/2 Part B; Telegram no. 100, Selkirk to Secretary of State for the Colonies, 9 February 1963, DO 169/248 no. 131/33/2 Part B.

95. *The Straits Times*, 4 February 1963.

96. Ibid.

97. Ibid.

98. Telegram no. 108, Selkirk to Secretary of State for the Colonies, 13 February 1963, DO 169/248 no. 131/33/2 Part B.

99. Ibid.

100. A BS procession, led by assemblymen Ong Chang Sam and about 100 relatives of detainees and party supporters marched from the party headquarters at Victoria Street and arrived at the City Hall steps at 2.10 p.m. on Monday, 22 April 1963. After the protesters failed to meet the Prime Minister, a scuffle broke out and rioting ensued. After order was restored, eight persons, including seven who were BS assemblymen, were charged. See *The Straits Times*, 23 April 1963; also Drysdale, pp. 325–26.

101. Apart from Soh Hwee Hong, the seven assemblymen were Fung Yin Ching, Lin You Eng, Ong Chang Sam, Hoe Puay Choo, Tee Kim Leng, Leong Keng Seng, and Tan Cheng Tong. *The Straits Times*, 30 August 1963.

102. Though Lee Siew Choh himself did not lead the protest march, he and the BS legal advisor, T.T. Rajah, had gone to the police station to bail out the other assemblymen when they were subsequently arrested and charged for having "abetted" the other six BS leaders who were charged with "being members of an unlawful assembly whose common object was to over-awe the executive Government of the State", and "rioting while members of an unlawful assembly" and "assaulting public servants who were discharging their duties in endeavouring to disperse an unlawful assembly". The principal charge, upon conviction, carried a maximum sentence of seven years' jail. Lee was subsequently defended by Elwyn Jones and acquitted. "This was not surprising," he said, "because there was no reason for us to be found guilty. None at all…. I was not there at all." See *The Straits Times*, 24 April 1963; and also interview with Lee in Chew, *Leaders of Singapore*, pp. 126–27.

103. Cited in Chew, *Leaders of Singapore*, p. 127.

104. Starner, p. 325; Lee, "The 1963 Singapore General Election", pp. 23–24.

105. *The Straits Times*, 13 September 1963.

106. Interview with Lee Siew Choh, in Chew, *Leaders of Singapore*, p. 127.

107. A quote by Ong Chang Sam, the BS administrative secretary, cited in Bloodworth, p. 250.

108. SATU's big three were the Singapore General Employees' Union, Singapore Business Houses Employees' Union and the Singapore Bus Workers' Union. The other four unions were the Singapore Brickmaking Workers Union, Singapore National Seamen's Union,

Singapore Machine and Engineering Employees Union, and the National Union of Building Construction Workers.

109. The immediate context concerned a mass rally organized by the Chinese Chamber of Commerce to agitate for Japanese reparation for wartime atrocities, which was to be held on Sunday, 25 August 1963. On 22 August and again on 24 August, the government had warned that it had information that the pro-communist trade unions and other anti-Malaysia elements were preparing to mobilize a large number of left-wing trade unionists and students to be present at the rally to "incite the people attending to acts of public disorder. They hoped to create an atmosphere of unrest and tension and, thereby, frustrate Malaysia." The organizers had already prepared anti-Malaysia banners "unconnected with the object of the rally" and had instructed their followers to shout anti-government and anti-Malaysia slogans. The government warned that it would "move swiftly" against the organizers should they continue with the intention to cause public disorder. On the night of the rally, *The Straits Times* reported that "a big group of masked youths disrupted proceedings for an hour with their booing and jeering" against the Prime Minister when he addressed the crowds. See Singapore Government Press Statement, 22, 24 and 29 August 1963; *The Straits Times*, 29 August 1963.

110. The government had received official information that a few of the top SATU leaders had met on 1 and 3 September 1963 and decided to withdraw funds from the bank accounts of the unions they controlled "in furtherance of their campaign to stir up political unrest to further the communist united front campaign against Malaysia". See Singapore Government Press Statement, 9 September 1963; *The Straits Times*, 10 September 1963.

111. *The Straits Times*, 12 June 1962.

112. Ibid., 8 January 1962.

113. Ibid., 12 September 1963.

114. Ibid., 19 July 1960.

115. Much of the earlier conflict centred around the election of Abdul Hamid bin Haji Jumat as chairman of Singapore UMNO. As the Minister of Local Government, Lands and Housing in Lim Yew Hock's government, Abdul Hamid was implicated in the corruption scandal involving the then Minister of Education, Chew Swee Kee. On 18 April 1959, he was dismissed as chairman by the executive committee of the Singapore UMNO "in order to maintain the good name of UMNO" in the run-up to the 1959 elections. In September 1959, when he was reelected as chairman of Singapore UMNO, 48 out of a total of 210 delegates staged a walk-out in protest. See *The Straits Times*, 22 April 1959; *The Sunday Times*, 20 September 1959 and *The Straits Times*, 21 September 1959.

116. To ensure greater control over the decentralized and faction-ridden state in UMNO, and to curb their development as separate power centres in their own right, the 13th UMNO General Assembly on 16 and 17 April 1960 agreed to a major amendment to the 1955 UMNO constitution, resulting in the concentration of power in the Supreme Executive Committee of UMNO in Kuala Lumpur. Singapore UMNO had asked to be independent of its Malayan counterpart, in view of the fact that both territories were by now different political entities and that the Societies Ordinance had made it legally impossible for direct affiliation with UMNO Malaya, since Singapore UMNO must exist as a separate entity with its own constitution before it could be registered. A new constitution was registered with the Singapore Registrar of Societies, giving control of the branches and members on the island to the Singapore UMNO rather than Kuala Lumpur. Under the new constitution, however, all five divisions of the Singapore UMNO would have to dissolve "and with them will go five snug corners of prestige". Four of the five divisions consequently broke away from Singapore UMNO to seek affiliation with UMNO Malaya. See B.H. Shafruddin, *The Federal Factor in the Government and Politics*

of *Peninsular Malaysia* (Singapore: Oxford University Press, 1987), pp. 282–89; S.S. Bedlington, "The Singapore Malay Community: The Politics of State Integration" (Unpublished PhD dissertation submitted to Cornell University, 1974), p. 118.; *The Straits Times*, 7 June 1960, 18 and 19 July 1960.

117. *The Straits Times*, 19 July 1960.

118. Khir Johari's appointment was proposed by the Tunku, who wanted a person from the peninsula to head the Singapore UMNO "in view of the importance of Singapore", and unanimously endorsed by the Supreme Executive Committee of UMNO Malaya. Transcript of interview with M. Khir Johari by the Oral History Centre, National Archives of Singapore.

119. Ibid.

120. *The Straits Times*, 18 June 1962.

121. The secretary of the east division was Zainuddin Talib. Ibid., 23 October 1962.

122. Ibid., 23 October 1962.

123. Ibid., 7 September 1963.

124. Ibid., 14 June 1961.

125. Ibid., 30 July 1963.

126. He withdrew on 11 September 1963, the day after he had announced his candidacy. Ibid., 11 and 12 September 1963; Lee, "The 1963 Singapore General Election", p. 25.

127. *The Straits Times*, 12 September 1963.

128. *Singapore Legislative Assembly Debates*, 24 July 1963, Col. 78.

129. Telegram no. 4, Moore to British High Commissioner (Kuala Lumpur), 27 September 1963, DO 169/19 no. 33/45/1.

130. *Singapore Legislative Assembly Debates*, 25 July 1963, Col. 155.

131. Ong was expelled from the PAP on 27 July 1960 after his abortive power struggle to seize control of the party. Joined by his two assembly supporters, S.V. Lingam and Ng Teng Kian, and emboldened by the crushing scale of his by-election victory at Hong Lim on 29 April 1961, which he won largely by the force of his personal charisma, Ong set up the UPP as a "new Party of the masses" to continue his political campaign against the PAP. Of Ong's public persona and popularity with the masses in Hong Lim, there can be little doubt, as R.A. Woolcott, the Acting Australian High Commissioner in Singapore, noted: "Ong himself is an articulate demagogue and, in Hokkien, is as good a rabble-rouser as Lim Chin Siong". See Gary Lee, "The Political Career of Ong Eng Guan" (Unpublished Academic Exercise, Department of History, National University of Singapore,1987); *Unity*, no. 1 (June 1963), p. 3; Woolcott to Department of External Affairs, 14 September 1963, A1838/280 no. 3024/2/4 Part 1.

132. *The Straits Times*, 13 September 1963.

133. *The Malay Mail*, 20 September 1963.

134. Only Tan Cheng Tong (Jalan Kayu) and Wong Soon Fong (Toa Payoh) remained in their old wards.

135. See note 117. Abdul Hamid had represented Geylang Serai in the last Assembly.

136. *Malayan Times*, 13 September 1963.

137. Woolcott to Department of External Affairs, 14 September 1963, A1838/280 no. 3024/2/4 Part 1.

138. *The Straits Times*, 4 September 1963.

139. *Plebeian*, vol. 2, no. 10, 16 September 1963, p. 1.

140. *Malayan Times*, 14 September 1963.

141. *The Straits Times*, 16 September 1963.

142. Starner, p. 324.

143. *Malayan Times*, 14 September 1963.
144. *The Straits Times*, 21 September 1963; *Malayan Times*, 21 September 1963.
145. *Malayan Times*, 13 September 1963.
146. *The Straits Times*, 5 September 1963.
147. Ibid.
148. *The Malay Mail*, 27 September 1963.
149. *The Straits Times*, 5 September 1963.
150. Critchley to Menzies, 13 October 1963, A1838/280 no. 3024/2/4 Part 1.
151. Telegram no. 4, Moore to British High Commissioner (Kuala Lumpur), 27 September 1963, DO 169/19 no. 33/45/1.
152. Transcript of interview with Lee Gek Seng by the Oral History Centre, National Archives of Singapore.
153. *Plebeian*, vol. 2, no. 10, 16 September 1963, p. 1.
154. "Special Branch Report on mass rally of Barisan Sosialis at Shenton Way car park on 13.9.63", 18 September 1963, ISD.
155. Lee, *Petir: 25th* , p. 35.
156. Fong, p. 135.
157. Ibid., p. 135.
158. Telegram no. 39, Australian High Commission (Singapore) to Department of External Affairs, 14 September 1963, A1838/280 no. 3024/2/4 Part 1.
159. Starner, p. 337.
160. Telegram no. 7, Singapore to Kuala Lumpur, 20 September 1963, DO 169 no. 33/45/1.
161. Fong, p. 137.
162. Starner, p. 343; *Nanyang Siang Pau*, 14 and 15 September 1963.
163. *The Straits Times*, 15 September 1963.
164. Special Branch report, 18 September 1963, ISD.
165. See Manifesto of Barisan Sosialis, 1963 Singapore General Elections, published in *Plebeian*, vol. 2, no. 10, 16 September 1963. The BS election manifesto was unveiled on the eve of nomination day.
166. See Ibid.
167. *Nanyang Siang Pau*, 16 September 1963, cited in Lee, "The 1963 Singapore General Election", p. 50.
168. *The Straits Times*, 5 September 1963; *Malayan Times*, 13 September 1963.
169. Lee, *Petir: 25th*, p. 35.
170. Manifesto of Barisan Sosialis, 1963 Singapore General Elections, in *Plebeian*, vol.2, no. 10, 16 September 1963.
171. *The Straits Times*, 14 September 1963.
172. *Plebeian*, vol. 2, no. 10, 16 September 1963, p. 1.
173. *The Straits Times*, 14 September 1963.
174. *Malayan Times*, 14 September 1963.
175. Telegram no. 4, Moore to British High Commissioner (Kuala Lumpur), 27 September 1963, DO 169/19 no. 33/45/1.
176. Starner, p. 336.
177. M. Sivaram, "The War of Slogans & Symbols: Who Will Win Polls?" *Malayan Times*, 19 September 1963.
178. *The Straits Times*, 13 September 1963.
179. Speech by Lee Kim Chuan on the eve of polling day, cited in Starner, p. 342.
180. *The Straits Times*, 21 September 1963.
181. *Malayan Times*, 18 September 1963.

182. Ibid., 19 September 1963.
183. *The Straits Times*, 16 September 1963.
184. *Malayan Times*, 20 September 1963.
185. *The Straits Times*, 19 September 1963.
186. Ibid., 21 September 1963. Water-rationing had been imposed since April 1963. Much of Singapore's water requirements came from Johore. "The PAP are to blame for this and no one else", declared SA candidate for Farrer Park, A.P. Rajah. "The PAP did not add a single drop of water to the water supply," he said, "although consumption had increased yearly at the rate of 3 million gallons a day." *Malayan Times*, 15 September 1963.
187. *The Straits Times*, 20 September 1963.
188. *Malayan Times*, 14 September 1963.
189. Ibid., 19 September 1963.
190. Naval Police Force (Singapore) Daily Security Intelligence Report, 20 September 1963, ISD.
191. Report on "Alliance Rally at Jalan Masjid", 19 September 1963, ISD.
192. *The Malay Mail*, 20 September 1973.
193. *Malayan Times*, 20 September 1963.
194. Telegram no. 7, Singapore to Kuala Lumpur, 20 September 1963, DO 169/19 no. 33/45/1.
195. *Malayan Times*, 19 September 1963.
196. Starner, p. 332.
197. Ministry of Culture, *Democratic Socialism in Action June 1959–April 1963* (Singapore, 1963); cited in Lee, "The 1963 Singapore General Election", p. 37.
198. Lee, "The 1963 Singapore General Election", p. 37.
199. *Malayan Times*, 18 September 1963.
200. Fong, p. 138.
201. Ibid., pp. 136–37.
202. Ng Kah Ting, "Punggol in the Old Days", pp. 146–48.
203. Cited in Chew, *Leaders of Singapore*, pp. 92–93.
204. *The Straits Times*, 21 September 1963.
205. Ibid.
206. Fong, p. 135.
207. *New Tasks Ahead* (Election Manifesto of the PAP), see Lee, "The 1963 Singapore General Election", pp. 68–69
208. Ibid.
209. *The Straits Times*, 21 September 1963.
210. Chor Yeok Eng, *Petir: 25th*, p. 131.
211. Starner, pp. 343–44.
212. *The Straits Times*, 15 September 1963.
213. Ibid., 19 September 1963.
214. *New Tasks Ahead*.
215. *The Straits Times*, 21 September 1963.
216. Ibid., 12 September 1963.
217. Ibid., 13 September 1963.
218. Telegram no. 7, Singapore to Kuala Lumpur, 20 September 1963, DO 169/19 no. 33/45/1.
219. Telegram no. 539, Australian High Commission (Singapore) to Department of External Affairs, 20 September 1963, A1838/280 no. 30254/2/4 Part 1.
220. Telegram no. 7, Singapore to Kuala Lumpur, 20 September 1963, DO 169/19 no. 33/45/1.
221. *The Sunday Mail*, 22 September 1963.

222. Telegram no. 539, Australian High Commission (Singapore) to Department of External Affairs, 20 September 1963, A1838/280 no. 30254/2/4 Part 1.

223. Telegram no. 7, Singapore to Kuala Lumpur, 20 September 1963, DO 169/19 no. 33/45/1.

224. Marshall had argued in his campaign that a vote for the PAP was "a vote for further enslavement" and a vote for the BS was "a vote for civil war". His election manifesto further criticized the PAP for allowing Singapore to enter Malaysia under "dreadful threatening disadvantages" and making the status of Singapore citizenship "inferior to all other Malaysian citizens". The PAP, he charged, had "put the rope round our throat and given the Federation the right to squeeze when they want". See *Malayan Times*, 18 September 1963; and *Light of Truth*, Marshall's election manifesto.

225. R. Woolcott to Secretary, Department of External Affairs, 20 September 1963, A1838/280 no. 3024/2/4 Part 1.

226. Telegram no. 539, Australian High Commission (Singapore) to Department of External Affairs, 20 September 1963, A1838/280 no. 30254/2/4 Part 1.

227. Telegram no. 7, Singapore to Kuala Lumpur, 20 September 1963, DO 169/19 no. 33/45/1.

228. Telegram no. 539, Australian High Commission (Singapore) to Department of External Affairs, 20 September 1963, A1838/280 no. 30254/2/4 Part 1.

229. Telegram no. 7, Singapore to Kuala Lumpur, 20 September 1963, DO 169/19 no. 33/45/1. Weak in terms of organizational support, and drawing little appeal outside Hong Lim where Ong was fielded, the UPP campaign focused largely on the image and personality of its secretary-general and, unwittingly gave credibility to its opponents' charge that the UPP was a one-man party. It also campaigned on a "Chinese chauvinist platform intended to appeal to the very poor", attacking the PAP for its arrogance, the BS for its opportunism and the SA for being a party of the rich and privileged class. *The Straits Times*, 17 and 18 September 1963; Critchley to Menzies, 13 October 1963, A1838/280 no. 3024/2/4 Part 1.

230. Telegram no. 7, Singapore to Kuala Lumpur, 20 September 1963, DO 169/19 no. 33/45/1.

231. Telegram no. 539, Australian High Commission (Singapore) to Department of External Affairs, 20 September 1963, A1838/280 no. 30254/2/4 Part 1.

232. Telegram no. 7, Singapore to Kuala Lumpur, 20 September 1963, DO 169/19 no. 33/45/1.

233. The population of Singapore was about 1.8 million. That there were not more voters was a reflection of the high proportion who were under the voting age of 21.

234. Critchley to Menzies, 13 October 1963, A1838/280 no. 3024/2/4 Part 1.

235. Telegram no. 4, Moore to British High Commissioner (Kuala Lumpur), 27 September 1963, DO 169/19 no. 33/45/1.

236. The 11 constituencies were: Bukit Merah, Bukit Panjang, Bukit Timah, Chua Chu Kang, Jalan Kayu, Jurong, Nee Soon, Paya Lebar, Tampines, Thomson, and Toa Payoh. The two "urban" wards it captured were Crawford and Havelock.

237. These were the wards of Aljunied, Anson, Bras Basah, Cairnhill, Farrer Park, Jalan Besar, Joo Chiat, Kallang, Kreta Ayer, Moulmein, Queenstown, River Valley, Sepoy Lines, Serangoon Gardens, Siglap, Southern Islands, Stamford, Tanglin, Tanjong Pagar and Upper Serangoon.

238. The 17 constituencies were: Changi, Delta, Geylang East, Geylang Serai, Geylang West, Kampong Glam, Kampong Kapor, Kampong Kembangan, Mountbatten, Pasir Panjang, Ponggol, Rochore, Sembawang, Telok Ayer, Telok Blangah, Tiong Bahru and Ulu Pandan.

239. *Malayan Times*, 23 September 1963.

240. Cited in Chew, *Leaders of Singapore*, pp. 92–93.

241. Telegram no. 15, Singapore to Kuala Lumpur, 22 September 1963, DO 169/19 no. 33/45/1.

242. Letter from Thio to (?), November 1963, Thio Chan Bee Papers, cited in Noel Ong, "A Bridge-Builder: Dr Thio Chan Bee (1904–1978)", in *Journal of the Malaysian Branch of the Royal Asiatic Society*, Vol. LXX, Part 1 (1997), p. 95.
243. Critchley to Menzies, 13 October 1963, A1838/280 no. 3024/2/4 Part 1.
244. Telegram no. 15, Singapore to Kuala Lumpur, 22 September 1963, DO 169/19 no. 33/45/1.
245. Telegram no. 40, Australian High Commission (Singapore) to Department of External Affairs, 27 September 1963, A1838/280 no. 3024/2/4 Part 1.
246. Telegram no. 15, Singapore to Kuala Lumpur, 22 September 1963, DO 169/19 no. 33/45/1.
247. Critchley to Menzies, 13 October 1963, A1838/280 no. 3024/2/4 Part 1.
248. *The Straits Times*, 23 September 1963.
249. Ibid., 27 September 1963. The three unsuccessful Nanyang University candidates were: Ong Hock Siang (Tanjong Pagar), Lim Chien Sen (Hong Lim), and Siek Shing Min (Changi).
250. Ibid., 4 October 1963. The two rural associations were the Singapore Rural Residents Association and the Singapore Country People's Association. The three hawkers' organizations were: the Singapore Hawkers' Union, the Singapore Itinerant Hawkers and Stall-Holders Association and the Association of Singapore Hawkers.
251. Ibid., 9 October 1963.
252. Ibid., 1 November 1963.
253. Critchley to Menzies, 13 October 1963, A1838/280 no. 3024/2/4 Part 1.
254. Telegram no. 4, Moore to British High Commissioner (Kuala Lumpur), 27 September 1963, DO 169/19 no. 33/45/1.
255. Telegram no. 40, Australian High Commission (Singapore) to Department of External Affairs, 27 September 1963, A1838/280 no. 3024/2/4 Part 1.
256. Critchley to Menzies, 13 October 1963, A1838/280 no. 3024/2/4 Part 1.
257. Telegram no. 39, Australian High Commission (Singapore) to Department of External Affairs, 27 September 1963, A1838/280 no. 3024/2/4 Part 1.
258. Critchley to Menzies, 13 October 1963, A1838/280 no. 3024/2/4 Part 1.
259. Ibid.
260. Telegram no. 15, Singapore to Kuala Lumpur, 22 September 1963, DO 169/19 no. 33/45/1.
261. Ibid.
262. Telegram no. 4, Moore to British High Commissioner (Kuala Lumpur), 27 September 1963, DO 169/19 no. 33/45/1.

CHAPTER 3

THE PAP AS "CROSS-BENCHERS"

C ontrary to what the British Deputy High Commissioner had hoped, the leaders of the United Malays National Organization (UMNO) did not view the People's Action Party's (PAP) victory positively — as a big boost for Malaysia. Their immediate reaction to the defeat of the Singapore Alliance (SA) — and the Singapore United Malays National Organization (SUMNO) — was one of shock and disbelief. Ghazali Jawi, UMNO's Secretary-General, who was in Singapore for two days to observe the election campaign, revealed to *The Straits Times* on 22 September that he had been really surprised by the scale of the defeat.[1] Tunku Abdul Rahman himself was shocked that the Malays in Singapore, who had always supported UMNO had turned their backs on the party and had voted instead for the PAP.[2] "I heard everything was all right when I came down," he said, "Therefore when I heard of the defeat of UMNO candidates, one after another, I couldn't sleep that night."[3]

UMNO Reacts to the Defeat

UMNO leaders took the defeat badly, and seemed, momentarily at least, unable to come to terms with the loss. So aghast was the Tunku by the complete annihilation of his party in Singapore that he blamed "traitors" within for SUMNO's debacle.[4] The Tunku's anger was explicable. He had assumed that, with the formation of Malaysia, the minority Malays in Singapore would become even stronger UMNO partisans and supporters. They did not. Instead, by repudiating SUMNO, they had also dealt a shattering blow to the Tunku's personal prestige, as the American Ambassador, Charles F. Baldwin, noted: "The Tunku had been warned by some Cabinet colleagues that he should not involve himself in [the] Singapore political arena. By campaigning there on behalf of the Alliance, he lent his prestige to a horse which stood little chance of winning."[5] Other UMNO stalwarts, stung by the rejection of SUMNO, offered a plethora of excuses to explain the party's ruin. Ghazali Jawi himself ascribed the party's thrashing to the shortness of the campaigning period,[6] while SUMNO's deputy chairman, Ahmad bin Haji Taff, who had stood as a candidate in Geylang Serai, blamed the SPA (Singapore People's Alliance) for SUMNO's failure and immediately led a drive to evict the SPA from the SA.[7]

By triumphing over the SUMNO candidates, the PAP also incurred UMNO's wrath. Bitterly disappointed by their party's total eclipse, and abetted by UMNO national leaders in Kuala Lumpur, SUMNO leaders, in the words of the American Consul, Arthur H. Rosen, immediately "orchestrated a campaign to recapture Malay popular support"[8] from the PAP government in Singapore. Partly to cushion the shock of defeat, and partly to agitate the Malay ground, the allegation was swiftly made that unruly PAP members had beaten up two SUMNO officials just prior to the elections and had thrown firecrackers indiscriminately into Malay homes and SUMNO branches during victory tours in the Geylang Serai and Changi constituencies. Two days after the Singapore election, on 23 September, a special meeting was convened by SUMNO at its Jalan Penggaga branch attended by over 300 persons to protest the alleged firecracker incident and to discuss the reasons for the defeat of the Alliance, which was eventually attributed to the inclusion of the SPA in the Alliance and the inactivity of the former SUMNO assemblymen.[9] An apology was demanded.

At another meeting held at the same place on 24 September, attended by some 500 members and supporters, it was agreed to ask Mohammed Khir Johari to come down to Singapore and explain to SUMNO members the causes of the party's defeat. The following night, another meeting was held with some 600 persons present.[10] Invited to speak at the meeting was noted UMNO extremist, Syed Ja'afar bin Hasan Albar. As UMNO's Chief Publicity Officer since 1953, Syed Ja'afar was particularly incensed at SUMNO's devastating defeat in the Singapore polls and took the dramatic step of announcing on 24 September his resignation from his position with effect from 1 October, a move with "far-reaching implications for UMNO solidarity," noted Baldwin. "It manifests split of opinion in party over Tunku's handling of Malaysia issue especially regarding Singapore's and Borneo's terms of entry which Malays regard as detrimental to their position in new Malaysia."[11] Known to the British as "one of [the] wild men of UMNO", Syed Ja'afar, speaking in Johore Bahru on 24 September *en route* to Singapore, admitted that he had been unhappy over the rout of the SA and vowed to "fix" Lee Kuan Yew when he shows up in the Malaysian Parliament. "We are prepared to use both words and fists to teach him a lesson in democracy," he thundered.[12] At the Singapore meeting, Syed Ja'afar made a fiery speech against the government and Lee Kuan Yew. The defeated SUMNO candidates made equally heated speeches and others followed with suggestions of holding a protest march to Lee's residence. At this meeting, an old man was assaulted with threats of "crush him" because a speaker had referred to the old man as one of those who had participated in the welcoming ceremony for Lee Kuan Yew when he visited Geylang Serai a few weeks before the election.[13] The allegations were investigated and no proof was found as to whether the incidents did take place or whether, indeed, PAP members were responsible. Nevertheless Lee Kuan Yew thought it prudent, in the interests of better relations with UMNO, to publicly apologize for the alleged incidents, which he did at a lunchtime rally at Fullerton Square on 25 September. But UMNO leaders were not satisfied and determined that the matter should not be laid to rest.

A follow-up protest rally was staged — this time with the Tunku himself in attendance — at the SUMNO's Kampong Ubi branch on the night of 27 September. Recounting his own distress upon hearing the news of SUMNO's defeat, the Tunku told the crowd, "We believed before that wherever there were Malays, UMNO would get their support. We got it in better times, but now we know differently." His duty was to safeguard UMNO and the Malay people wherever they were. Rehearsing his condemnation of the Malays who had betrayed the party, the Tunku asserted that, henceforth, SUMNO would be an integral part of the national UMNO and he would be personally directing the affairs of the party branch in Singapore. In an open and deliberate challenge to the PAP, the Tunku declared, "[I]n future, I will play an important part in the elections"[14] and asserted to his Malay crowd that the government of Singapore was not in the hands of the PAP nor Lee Kuan Yew. It was in the hands of the central government in Kuala Lumpur. To emphasize his point, the Tunku announced that he had ordered the closure of the South African Consulate General in Singapore. He also chided the PAP government for permitting the Bank of China and Bank Negara Indonesia to continue their operations in the state. Heated and angry speeches were made by the other speakers, and, reported Rosen, "passions were ... stirred by a violent anti-PAP speech with strong racist overtones by Ja'afar Albar". Some newspaper reporters were threatened, presumably on the suspicion that they were pro-PAP, and, as one Chinese reporter of *The Straits Times* told the American Consul, "it was perhaps the only time he had been in fear for his life." An effigy of Lee Kuan Yew was burned before the screaming crowd. The Tunku, who was on the platform, was "apparently surprised by this explosion but did nothing about it. ... The effigy burning was never reported in the local papers."[15]

Lee Kuan Yew, on his part, had tried hard to please. Speaking to a lunchtime crowd at Fullerton Square on 25 September 1963, and reiterating what he had said before in his Malaysia Day speech on 16 September[16] — that his immediate task was to rebuild good relations with Kuala Lumpur, Lee pledged to cooperate with the central government on a fair and equal basis, but not as master and servant. It was a theme he returned to when he addressed a night rally from the City Hall steps to introduce the new assemblymen on 28 September. Urging both sides to "get over this post-election phase and face up to the realities of life", the Singapore premier then repeated his government's intention to work together with the central government for the benefit of Singapore and Malaysia, but, as he again emphasized, "it must be a cooperation on equal terms, not that of master and servant", for Singapore would not accept Lee as a puppet of Kuala Lumpur.

Not wanting to strain his post-election ties with Federation leaders, Lee had refrained from reacting publicly to the Tunku's branding of Malays who voted for the PAP as "traitors". But the Malaysian premier's open assertion of Kuala Lumpur's paramountcy over the island in his speech of 27 September, and so soon after the PAP's landslide victory, was a more serious political challenge to his authority on his home ground — and one he could not ignore. It befitted a robust reply from Lee, which he obliged. Responding in his speech on 28 September, Lee contested the necessity of the central government saying they had ultimate authority: "[W]e understood that before we went into Malaysia; we understand that now."[17] Warning Kuala Lumpur, in turn, against wanting to lord it over Singapore, or worse, attempt a takeover of the island by force, Lee told his supporters, "[I]n the eventuality of stupidity taking over, do not believe — I hope the people in Kuala Lumpur will read this — do not believe you can keep Singapore down. It is not possible. If they could, the British would have stayed here and never given up this island fortress. They knew it cannot be, and I refused to keep it down for them."[18] And if the PAP had fought the communists and were no longer afraid of them, "How then can we be afraid of what the Central Government can do to Singapore?" Lee asked. He conceded that "Kuala Lumpur may be able to take over Singapore by force and throw away the constitution", but he warned that "Malaysia will be destroyed" in the end.[19] Lee urged Kuala Lumpur to let Singapore "resolve the problems which they in the Federal Capital could not understand".[20] In an oblique reminder to Kuala Lumpur of Singapore's "autonomy" in education and labour — terms which the Singapore premier had insisted, and which the Federation leaders had accepted, during the Malaysia negotiations — Lee asserted that these were "trouble points" which "[w]e understand how to deal with" and it was best that what the Federation "can't really resolve, leave to us to resolve".[21] Assuring Kuala Lumpur, in turn, of Singapore's "good faith", Lee revealed that he ordered the action against Tan Lark Sye immediately after the elections precisely to demonstrate that "we are not out under the guise of Chinese education, culture and language to protect the communists — that we are prepared to fight them provided we first expose them, as we did to Tan Lark Sye".[22]

Notwithstanding the ensuing "contest of 'one-upmanship'",[23] as the American Ambassador described it, the road ahead for Lee was clear. "I want to work with UMNO," the Singapore leader openly declared, "That's why on Wednesday at the rally in Fullerton Square, I apologized on account of some PAP supporters who were over-enthusiastic and threw crackers at UMNO branches in Geylang Serai." Presumably to allay UMNO's fears of PAP ambitions, Lee said he could concede the necessity of having a Malay as Prime Minister of Malaysia for the next two decades. "We are not out to capture power in Kuala Lumpur," Lee said, "We will not take part in the 1964 elections in the Federation".[24] What the PAP hoped to accomplish, together with UMNO, was the strengthening of the central government for the betterment of Malaysia through an "intelligent appraisal" of the urban Chinese problem which UMNO lacked. Singapore, Lee emphasized, was "really the hub of the overseas Chinese in Malaysia" and the PAP could help UMNO "understand what we fear sometimes they do not understand — the problem of the urban Chinese in the cities, in the towns, where over the last few years, the MCA [Malayan Chinese Association] and MIC [Malayan Indian Congress] have lost ground to a whole host of opposition parties in Malaya".[25] Criticizing MCA leaders for lacking such an intelligent approach, not only in understanding the urban Chinese problem but also in managing the last two elections, resulting in the defeat of all their candidates, Lee predicted that the Alliance would continue to lose support in the big towns if the MCA and MIC did not change their policy towards the people. He added that, while the PAP would want to cooperate with UMNO, it could not bring itself to associate with an Alliance in which there were "unclean" (i.e. MCA/MIC) people.[26]

The Singapore premier's diatribe against the MCA drew immediately a sharp rebuke from the Tunku the following day. Calling Lee's outburst unfair and deploring his attempt "to cause a rift in the Alliance", the Tunku rallied swiftly to the defence of his Alliance partners, stating, "I have found their leadership sound, honest, straightforward and absolutely trustworthy." Questioning the PAP's motive in attacking the MCA, the Malaysian leader reminded Lee that "[a]crimonious statements against political leaders on this side do not help to improve friendly relationships". He defended his Alliance partners as "friends and patriots" who never "lost sight of the national interest" and had "contributed much towards the success of the Alliance at the elections." The Tunku declared, "UMNO is certain to be with MCA as we have been for the last 10 years," and added in more conciliatory tones, "[I]n the same way, we will work closely with the Government of Singapore. But Singapore must appreciate that the political set-up of States on this side of the Causeway is not quite the same as Singapore's."[27] The message to Lee was unmistakably clear, as the American Ambassador, Baldwin, commented: "The Tunku is putting Lee on notice that he is willing to cooperate in the context of Singapore/Central Government affairs but he is not receptive to Lee's bid to have PAP replace the MCA in the Alliance."[28]

Welcoming the Tunku's 29 September statement as an "offer of cooperation", the Singapore premier immediately replied that he was also prepared to accept the conditions the Tunku had set out, which Lee assumed were that no more attacks would be made on the MCA. "I am sure if they are the only conditions, that I should not attack the leading personalities of the Malayan Chinese Association, there should be no trouble between us at all," Lee said. "It was they who started the dog fight and not me."[29] In another peace offering to UMNO, Lee reiterated, "I do not intend to start a branch in Kuala Lumpur and won't want to for quite a long time."[30] After a ten-day holiday in the Cameron Highlands with his wife,[31] Lee flew to Kuala Lumpur on 30 September, for talks with Malaysian leaders to "set the course for honourable cooperation".[32] Both leaders were anxious to defuse their public row — "to minimize differences instead of magnifying

The PAP as "Cross-Benchers"

them", as the Tunku put it.[33] Playing down the view that Kuala Lumpur wanted to control Singapore, the Malaysian premier opined that "The trouble with Singapore is that they cannot get rid of the idea of being under Britain and they think that they are now under us."[34]

By way of mollifying the Tunku over the defeat of SUMNO, Lee on his part had also suggested privately that the Malaysian leader should nominate a Malay member as one of the two Singapore representatives to the Federal Senate,[35] a proposal which pleased the Tunku, who subsequently selected SUMNO leader, Ahmad bin Haji Taff, as his nominee.[36] In return, Lee received the Tunku's promise that he would allow the Singapore-based Bank of China and Bank Negara of Indonesia to keep open, provided that they were not staffed by senior government officials[37] and grant the Singapore Chief Justice precedence over his Borneo counterpart. Describing his talks as "friendly", Lee was gratified that the Tunku was at pains to put over to the Chief Ministers that he was "fully acceptable as one of the team".[38] The Singapore premier was also pleased to learn from Ghazali Shafie, the Permanent Secretary in the Malaysian Ministry of External Affairs, that the possibility of having him join the Federal Cabinet was being considered. But, fearing a rebuff, the Singapore leader had decided to postpone discussing this with the Tunku until a more opportune time. Nevertheless, as Philip Moore reported, Lee was obviously "very keen on this and asked whether we could prepare the ground a little in Kuala Lumpur".[39]

Back from holiday, Lee immediately set about to position a strong PAP team to represent Singapore in the Federal Parliament. One of his first tasks was the announcement on 17 October of the new PAP Cabinet built around "experienced and able men of proven loyalty", ostensibly "to ensure against defections and frictions like those which almost caused his downfall in 1961".[40] Honouring his deal with the Tunku, Lee also proposed, during the first session of the new Legislative Assembly on 22 October, the election of Ahmad bin Haji Taff as one of the two Singapore senators to the Federal Senate, the other being Ko Teck Kin, the president of the Chinese Chamber of Commerce. Upon securing the election of the two senators, Lee moved swiftly to table, and facilitate the passage of, an urgent bill[41] for the election of the Singapore representatives to the Federal Parliament, after disposing the ineffectual Barisan Socialis' (BS) attempt to make two amendments to the bill.[42] Permitting the Barisan three members, the PAP claimed for itself 12 of the 15 representatives, even though this seemed, as the British pointed out, "one more than appears mathematically to be their share".[43] The PAP nominees, which included all the nine Cabinet members, two parliamentary secretaries, and the chairman of the pro-PAP National Trades Union Congress (NTUC)[44] constituted a "strong Federal team," noted Curtis, which "reflects Lee's recognition that the centre of political power has shifted to Kuala Lumpur and his intention to make Singapore's influence felt there."[45]

In a bid to smoothen ties with Kuala Lumpur in the run-up to the state's debut participation in the Federal Parliament, the Singapore government also spared no effort to emphasize the island's loyalty to Malaysia and the importance of mutual trust between state and Federal leaders. Thus, on 17 October, in his first press conference since his election victory, Lee Kuan Yew underlined Singapore's resolve to defend the sovereignty and integrity of Malaysia.[46] Speaking moments after the swearing in of his new Cabinet on 19 October, the Singapore leader again stressed that the island's fate was, indeed, "intertwined" with that of Malaysia, and repeated his hope to work together with the Federal government "in the higher interests of Malaysia".[47] And in a major policy speech to the Foreign Correspondents Association on 25 October, Lee further asserted that whatever their differences of approach, the long-term objectives of the Singapore and central governments were the same, namely, to build "a cohesive, strong and united nation with undivided loyalties to Malaysia".[48] Speaking to reporters on 30 October, just before his flight to Kuala Lumpur to attend the opening of the new Parliament building and the swearing in of the Singapore, Sabah and Sarawak representatives to the Federal Parliament on 2 November, Lee was also at pains to project an image of the PAP representatives in the central Parliament as "cross-benchers — friend, loyal opposition and critic" who would not rock the boat on important national issues. Contrasting the PAP's constructive role with that of the "destructive" tactics of the Socialist Front and Barisan Sosialis, Lee said: "They are the disloyal opposition. We are the loyal opposition, whose aim is to improve the working of the democratic system." To a question on whether the PAP had decided to sit with the Alliance government or with the opposition in the central Parliament, Lee replied tactfully, "We leave it to the discretion of the Speaker."[49]

Not unexpectedly, the anticipation of having the PAP as the loyal opposition in the Federal Parliament evinced little cheer from political circles across the Causeway, already sensitized, if Lee's adversaries were to be believed, that the Singapore leader was "a danger to Malaysia and should from now be controlled and placed where he should rightly be".[50] If anything, the Singapore premier's oblique overtures, coming after his public feud with the MCA and the Tunku, served only to feed their already existing suspicions about the PAP's — and Lee's — ultimate intentions. Replying to the Singapore Prime Minister's "uncalled for" remarks about its loyalty, the Socialist Front warned, for instance, that "Mr Lee and his PAP cross-benchers will be loyal to no one but to themselves".[51] The Malaysian Deputy Prime Minister, Tun Abdul Razak, had also asked Lee "how he could be both friendly and critical".[52] And on the placement of the PAP members in Parliament, there was no ambiguity as far as the Speaker, Mohamed Noah bin Omar, was concerned. "[T]here is no question as to where the PAP members will sit," he said, "They will be sitting with the Opposition."[53]

But, as it turned out, not all the PAP members sat with the Opposition during their swearing-in ceremony on 2 November. Four PAP leaders — Lee Kuan Yew, Toh Chin Chye, Goh Keng Swee and S. Rajaratnam — were seated in the four "vacant" seats on the government benches which, according to the Clerk of the House, "happened to remain unfilled after all the Alliance members had been assigned seats".[54] The truth of the matter was that Lee had thought it tactful beforehand to ask the Tunku where the PAP contingent should sit, a gesture which apparently pleased the Malaysian premier, and "the outcome had been that the twelve PAP representatives were sitting partly on the government side and partly on the Opposition side of the House".[55] Whatever his private reservations about the PAP, the Tunku apparently had no wish, at this stage, to close the door firmly to Lee's expressed wish to cooperate with the central government. Such a minor concession would also do the Alliance no harm, since the distinction between government and opposition seats had already been blurred after the spilling over of Alliance members to the opposite benches where the opposition members were seated.[56] As the First Secretary of the American Embassy, William B. Kelly, surmised: "The placing of the four PAP members on the Government side may have happened as casually as the Clerk suggests, however, it is also possible that this arrangement was contrived by the Alliance and PAP to emphasize a distinction between the latter party and the rest of the Opposition. In any case, the seating arrangements in the new House do not clearly define party alignments and these will probably only be discernible through the future pattern of voting".[57] Meanwhile, for the PAP at least, its seating arrangement on both sides of the House was also "useful ... in maintaining its announced policy of non-alignment".[58]

In Kuala Lumpur, Lee had also wanted to take advantage of the occasion to sound the Tunku out on the prospects of further strengthening their ties but, as he intimated to Moore later, he found the Malaysian leader preoccupied with other matters and was consequently unable to have any fruitful discussion on their general relationship. More engaging were his talks with Ghazali Shafie who informed Lee that the deputy premier Tun Razak "was thinking in terms of Lim Kim San, Singapore Minister of National Development, entering the Malaysian Cabinet". Pleased with the progress, Lee was in favour of this choice since Lim was a businessman on good terms with the Malays, having been made a *dato*. Once Lim had established a "better atmosphere", Lee hoped "it could be possible later for himself and Goh to enter the Cabinet". Ghazali cautioned Lee, however, against any premature optimism, stating that "Razak would have great difficulty in getting the MCA's agreement to this" and that the idea probably could not come to fruition until after the election in Malaya which he did not expect to take place until March or April 1964. To Ghazali's query as to whether the Singapore premier was "seriously expecting the Tunku to break with the MCA now", Lee denied any such suggestion.[59] If the Singapore leader had hoped for a more positive lead from Kuala Lumpur, he was disappointed. As Moore reported, Lee returned to Singapore "not very satisfied with his visit".[60]

For the two remaining months of the year, and probably sobered by Ghazali Shafie's damper, Lee realized that "he would have to play things fairly slowly,"[61] at least until after the Federal elections some time next year, if he hoped at all of getting Kuala Lumpur to consider more assiduously the PAP's bid to be represented in the Federal Cabinet. In the meantime, the PAP's strategy to win friends in Kuala Lumpur, and to convince the central government of Singapore's special role in building Malaysia and the need for the island to be consulted on matters of mutual concern, continued.

On the occasion of the Yang di-Pertuan Agong's first official visit to the island from 11 to 13 November, for instance, the PAP government went out of its way not only to accord the Malaysian paramount ruler the full honours and respect he deserved but also to provide the royal entourage with intensive media coverage.[62] Taking advantage of an address on 18 November, the Singapore premier again underlined his government's task "to see that Malaysia prospers" and the need "to establish rapport" with the central government. Similarly, in another major address, this time by the Yang di-Pertuan Negara on 29 November, the point that "loyalty to the new nation must transcend all other interests" and that Singapore's destiny was "irrevocably intertwined with that of the rest of Malaysia" was further underscored.[63] In acknowledging the central government's future role in determining "the order of our society", the Yang di-Pertuan Negara's address also asserted that while Kuala Lumpur must have pan-Malaysian support, Singapore, in turn, must be allowed to play its full part in Malaysia.[64] The Singapore premier also referred to this theme in his speech in the Assembly on 9 December.[65] And in his hour long maiden address to the Malaysian chamber on 21 December — listened to by a "[h]ushed, attentive House" — Lee was especially careful not to stray from the PAP's self-assigned role — that of "neither Opposition booster nor Government backbencher" but of a "friendly critic" of both.[66] While he took the Opposition to task for their irresponsible attacks on the government and used the occasion to chide his political opponent, Finance Minister and MCA chief, Tan Siew Sin, for presenting a budget that was "good for big business" but of doubtful benefit to the "have-nots", he shrewdly avoided any criticism that might reflect on the Tunku and backed his handling of relations with both the Philippines and Indonesia.[67] The PAP government's underlying plea for recognition, as Curtis observed, "reflects their concern that their pledges of loyalty to Malaysia and readiness to work out a cooperative relationship with Kuala Lumpur should evoke a positive response."[68] While the PAP's conciliatory overtures had so far been encouraging, as R.A. Woolcott, the Australian Acting High Commissioner in Singapore remarked, "it does not mean that we can count on Lee maintaining this attitude indefinitely It will be unfortunate," he warned, "if, because of suspicion and mistrust in Kuala Lumpur ... the Central Government were to mistake an olive branch for a cactus."[69]

The "Truth Mission" to Africa

The Tunku himself was not unamenable to Lee's offer of an olive branch, or to find some role to occupy the talents of the Singapore Prime Minister. By late December 1963, plans were already underway to despatch the Singapore premier on a "truth" tour of African countries to counter Indonesian "lies" about Malaysia being a neo-colonialist plot. Lee had proposed such a mission to Ghazali Shafie, when he was in Kuala Lumpur for the swearing-in ceremony. Doubtful at first whether the Tunku would welcome such an initiative, Ghazali suggested that Lee put it to him, which he did. The Malaysian premier readily agreed, to Lee's surprise.[70] So it was that a day after Christmas, the Malaysian Ministry of External Affairs announced that Lee, assisted by Sabah Chief Minister, Donald Stephens, would lead a 17-, later revised to 27-, member representative Malaysian delegation on a "truth mission" of African countries from the middle of January 1994.[71] Stephens subsequently withdrew from the trip reportedly because of the worsening security situation following the intensification of the Indonesian guerrilla activities in Kalabakan. Taking his place, and presumably to serve as deputy leader,[72] was Sarawak's new Chief Minister, Stephen Kalong Ningkan, who would join the mission midway through its more than month long tour.

The Tunku's choice of Lee to head the mission could not have been more appropriate. Besides the fact that it was Lee who had suggested the initiative, the Singapore premier had been one of the most ardent and effective spokesmen for Malaysia from the beginning. Prior to Malaysia's inauguration, Lee had already spearheaded missions to Burma, India, the United Arab Republic and Yugoslavia, between April and May 1962, to garner support from non-aligned countries for Malaysia's formation. In July that year, he had also defended successfully his government's position on merger at the United Nations, after several Singapore opposition parties sought to block Malaysia through the UN committee on colonial questions.[73] Lee's credentials as a staunch advocate of Afro-Asian solidarity would also have stood him in good stead in his forthcoming meetings with African leaders. And as "one of the most articulate of Malaysia's political leaders", observed *The Times*, Lee also "should not have any difficulty in persuading African leaders".[74]

For some time, concern about African uncertainty towards Malaysia had given rise to the need to establish a stronger Malaysian presence in the continent. "The Malaysian image is not all that bright in the Dark Continent," observed *The Malay Mail*.[75] According to Antony Head, the British High Commissioner in Kuala Lumpur, part of the blame must be borne by the Tunku who had a tendency to regard the principal Afro-Asian countries with "mistrust mingled with contempt. ... External relations for him," Head added, "comprises visits to England, America, Canada, Australia or New Zealand. Beyond that he is not interested. He has virtually no knowledge of the problems, policies, aims and aspirations of the numerous newly independent countries which form the bulk of the Afro-Asian group. The Tunku is flagrantly aligned and quite unashamed of the fact. He ... cannot understand why he is not more loved by the non-aligned Afro-Asians. ... It is not at all easy to get this into the Tunku's head," the High Commissioner continued, but "[s]ome of the younger Malays and Lee Kuan Yew... see it clearly."[76]

Apart from its solitary mission in Cairo, Malaysia had no other diplomatic post in Africa — putting it at a considerable disadvantage when countering Indonesian-Philippine misinformation about Malaysia. Already, Algeria and Mali appeared to have been swayed by Indonesia's reservations about Malaysia's United Nations credentials. African opinion could not be ignored, as Lee pointed out, not only because Malaysia would "lose by default" by failing to put its case to the newly emergent African states, which still kept an open mind on many issues, but also because they constituted a formidable bloc in the United Nations should the Malaysian-Indonesian dispute be brought to the vote before the international body: "I think an important aspect is that solidarity of the African states in the UN is much more pronounced than the solidarity of the Asian nations in the UN."[77] "It helps very much not to have them on the other side," quipped an official from the Ministry of External Affairs.[78] Apart from presenting Malaysia more effectively to the African states and nailing the lie of Indonesian accusations, the Truth Mission, as it was called, would also help Malaysia identify more closely with the Afro-Asian non-aligned movement. At the same time, it would provide a forum to explain why it was necessary for Malaysia to seek the assistance of "those big powers who for various and diverse reasons are prepared to help us".[79]

For Lee, however, there was a further, albeit more personal, reason for wanting to undertake such a mission: the chance to have friends in Afro-Asia was another useful lever against the uncertainty of his own political tenure in Malaysia. As Moore revealed, "Lee regards the trip as a further opportunity of enhancing his own international prestige so that the Tunku would have to pay the price if things ever came to a point where he wanted to lock Lee up".[80]

Already, the choice of Lee as leader of the delegation had been bitterly resented by his political foes in Kuala Lumpur. Voicing his dissent in the Dewan Ra'ayat (House of Representatives) on 3 January 1964 was Lee's UMNO antagonist, Syed Ja'afar Albar — now UMNO's Secretary-General.[81] Objecting vehemently to the selection of the Singapore leader as the person to sell Malaysia to the Africans, Syed Ja'afar warned, "He does not want to make Malaysia known, but only to make himself known to the African countries." A Malaysian Cabinet minister — and not Lee — should more appropriately head the mission, he charged. Further blasting Lee for his reported exchange of correspondence with the Chinese communist premier, Chou En Lai, Syed Ja'afar asked sarcastically why the government had not informed the House that Lee Kuan Yew was now directing the country's foreign affairs. Though "obviously discomfited"[82] by Syed Ja'afar's open criticisms of his government, the Tunku remained unflappable when he rose to reply. In fairness, the Singapore premier had sought his permission to "try and explain Malaysia to our friends in Africa", the Tunku said, and there was, therefore, "no wrong done in the intention ... to visit these countries". On Lee's correspondence with Chou En Lai, the Malaysian Prime Minister stated that, if the reports were true, then it was very wrong of him to have done so and he would "take it up with him". But his information was that the incident occurred before Malaysia's formation and, "if that was so, then it was the British responsibility and not ours". Adding a lighter touch, the Tunku said, to laughter, that if the mission was not a success, he might consider sending another headed by Syed Ja'afar![83] The Tunku's swift and deft intervention had helped to defuse the tense proceedings. But the UMNO Secretary-General's outburst against his party leaders in the House had also been unprecedented — "something he had not done before," observed the American Embassy's Second Secretary, Robert W. Drexler, and "indicates the forces working against any sort of accommodation between UMNO and Lee Kuan Yew's PAP".[84]

So it was that with the Tunku's blessings, the Truth Mission left Singapore on the night of 20 January 1964 for North Africa.[85] The following day it arrived at its first stop — Cairo, the capital of the United Arab Republic (UAR) and "the heart of political activity in Africa,"[86] where intense diplomatic "lobbying goes on without pause".[87] Lee had led a remarkably successful mission to Cairo before — in April 1962 — which resulted in a "fulsome endorsement of Malaysia"[88] by the UAR President, Gamal Abdul Nasser, a leading spokesman of the Afro-Asian bloc and "one of the giants of Africa" whose opinion invariably carried weight.[89] On this occasion, the UAR remained as supportive as ever of Malaysia's cause. The Singapore premier was "generally given red carpet treatment" and his interview with Nasser on 22 January lasted nearly two hours.[90]

Tunisia and Morocco, the next two Mediterranean-fronting African destinations on the itinerary, however, were less forthcoming in their support. Tunisia's President, Habib Bourguiba, while giving the delegation a polite and sympathetic hearing on 28 January, refused to be drawn into the dispute. No joint communiqué was issued at Tunis, although the President had "expressed the hope that the two parties will not fail to find a peaceful and just solution permitting a return to peace, stability and friendship between the two brother countries."[91] At Rabat, the reception was "less warm than elsewhere"[92] This was attributed to the Moroccan mission's unfruitful visit to Malaya on the Mauritania issue four years earlier[93] and the effectiveness of the anti-Malaysia Indonesian propaganda machine.[94] In any case, the Malaysian delegation failed to meet King Hassan II who was busy playing host to visiting United Nations Secretary-General, U Thant. On 29 January, the delegation finally held talks with the premier, Ahmed Bahnini, and the King's personal representative, M. Ahmed Belfrej, who, according to Lee, "had understood Malaysia and hoped it would arrive at a peaceful settlement of its problems".[95] However, no public statement on the Malaysian position was released.[96]

From Rabat, the Truth Mission flew to Algiers in the continuation of its tour of Muslim North Africa. The Algerian capital had not been included in the original itinerary, largely because Algiers' reservations about Malaysia's UN membership and its close friendship with Jakarta, forged after Sukarno's unreserved support for its independence struggle, had convinced Kuala Lumpur that no useful purpose would be served by a visit at this juncture. But Lee agreed to make the journey, after having been assured by the Algerian Ambassador, M. Brahimi, when in Cairo, that the delegation would be most welcome.

Lee himself was twice received by President Ahmed Ben Bella. Thinking that his friendly reception was purely personal, Lee had gone in "with his guns blazing" in his first interview with the President on 30 January. But, to his surprise, he found Bella "very ready to listen and even prepared to help", offering to send Brahimi on another visit to see Sukarno. Bella, not desiring to antagonize Sukarno, reacted less favourably to a proposal that he should make some public declaration of support for Malaysia. But he promised to consider this further and give his opinion at a second meeting, prompting Lee to put off his departure for 24 hours.[97] The subsequent talks turned out better than Lee expected and, in the joint communiqué that was published, the Algerian President informed Lee of his hope that peace would be established on a "definite and satisfactory" basis and his determination to support any effort likely to induce Malaysia and Indonesia to find a peaceful resolution of their dispute.[98] More significantly, Lee was also informed that Algeria's reservations about Malaysia's UN membership had been withdrawn. Algeria's more open attitude towards the Malaysia–Indonesia dispute was a significant breakthrough for the

Malaysian mission. That one of Indonesia's friends had not only received the Malaysian delegation but had also given the visit a good deal of publicity in the press, remarked the British Ambassador, "could not fail to have an effect on President Sukarno.[99]

Quite possibly, Algeria's example had a knock-on effect on Mali, the neighbouring sub-Saharan state at its southern frontier which was visited next. Like Algeria, Mali had reservations about Malaysia's UN credentials and had remained "mildly hostile to Malaysia largely because of the British military bases in that country".[100] Nevertheless, the Malian President, Modibo Keita's discussions with Lee on 2 February had given him a "better understanding of the meaning of this dispute" and, in this matter, he was prepared to be guided by Algeria's lead, and withdrew the reservations it had about Malaysia's UN credentials.

From Bamako, the Truth Mission journeyed to Monrovia, the capital of Liberia, and the first of the five west African coastal states on its itinerary. There, Lee found President William Tubman, whom he met on 3 February, "understanding and sympathetic".[101] The next state, Guinea, handled the Malaysian mission "with discretion and played down the importance of the visit," observed the American post at Conakry.[102] Privately, however, the Guinean President, Sekou Toure, who had a two-hour talk with Lee on 4 February, "listened carefully as the Malaysian team presented its views, then ... called in the Indonesian Ambassador to get the other side of the story. The next day he told Lee Kuan Yew that he was convinced Malaysia was in the right and assured the Malaysians of Guinea's moral support."[103]

An assurance of support from President Felix Houphouet-Boigny of the Ivory Coast, whom the delegation met on 5 February, was also significant, for, as Lee pointed out, "The Ivory Coast is a member of the Security Council, representing the African bloc." After his talks with the President, Lee declared that he was confident that, if the Malaysia–Indonesia dispute should end up before the Security Council, the Ivory Coast would take "a clear and unequivocal stand for non-interference in the internal affairs of another country and respect for its territorial integrity." Houphouet-Boigny, Lee added, was "forthright in his reaction to what I had to tell him."[104] Although the final communiqué mentioned only the President's "desire to contribute in whatever way he could" to resolve the conflict peacefully, and within the context of the principles of territorial integrity and non-interference in the internal affairs of the two states,[105] "[t]here is little doubt," concurred the American post at Abidjan, "that

Houphouet will support Malaysia rather than Indonesia if he has to take a stand on the dispute between the two."[106]

In Accra, Lee conferred with President Kwame Nkrumah, who also promised Ghana's help to achieve a peaceful settlement of the dispute so that "opportunity might not be given to imperialism and neo-colonialism of bigger powers to exploit the situation for their benefit" in a joint communiqué issued after hearing the Malaysian team on 8 February.[107] "If you had not come you would have lost by default, your fault," the anti-imperialist Ghanaian leader subsequently told Lee.[108]

But it was in the last of the five west African states visited — Nigeria — that the Truth Mission received its first unequivocal declaration of support, from an "old friend of Malaysia,"[109] Sir Abubakar Tafawa Balewa, the Nigerian premier, who assured the delegation on 11 February that while "we cannot promise you physical support like the great and powerful nations, you can count on our unqualified moral support."[110]

The team — now bolstered by the presence of the Chief Minister of Sarawak, Stephen Kalong Ningkan, who joined the delegation in Nigeria on 12 February — left Lagos the same night for East Africa to begin the final leg of its whirlwind tour. Northern Rhodesia, the mission's next stop, had been an integral part of the Central African Federation established in 1953, and which included two other states, Southern Rhodesia and Nyasaland. By the early 1960s, however, that federation had crumbled, wrecked by indigenous opposition to British rule, and while both Northern Rhodesia and Nyasaland were on the threshold of gaining independence, the large and deeply-entrenched population of white settlers of Southern Rhodesia opposed widening the franchise to the black majority. One of the mission's concerns in Northern Rhodesia was, therefore, to assure its leaders that Malaysia bore no resemblance to the Central African Federation that was being dismantled. In the absence of the Northern Rhodesian premier, Kenneth Kaunda, away on official business in Dar-es-Salaam, Tanzania, the Malaysian team held "frank and friendly" talks with other key leaders in Lusaka, not all of whom, however, were persuaded to embrace immediately Malaysia's cause in the dispute with Indonesia. Nor was much achieved in the team's brief visit to neighbouring Nyasaland, where Lee held "satisfactory" talks with its premier, Hastings Banda, on 15 February.[111] With independence still looming — Nyasaland was to become the independent state of Malawi only in July 1964 while Northern Rhodesia was to achieve its freedom as Zambia in October

— it was perhaps understandable why both Lilangwe and Lusaka still saw advantages in maintaining their friendship with "a vociferous anti-colonial power" like Indonesia.[112]

Across the channel, on 16 February, the delegation was warmly received in the island republic of Malagasy. Lee appeared to have had no difficulty in getting his message across to President Tsiranana with whom he conferred the following day. Tsiranana even offered "some fatherly advice about the right of appeal to friends for military help whenever the country is under attack".[113] "If one must be colonized, it is at least preferable that the colonizing be done by a higher rather than a lower civilization," the President told Lee.[114]

Continuing his airborne trek on the continent, in Dar-es-Salaam, Lee reported that Tanzanian President, Julius Nyerere, after discussions with the delegation on 19 February, had expressed his support for Malaysia in "unequivocal terms".[115] Less fruitful was the team's visit to Uganda from 20 to 21 February. The mission failed to meet the Prime Minister, Milton Obote. Nonetheless, Kampala gave the visit extensive publicity, "presumably for prestige".[116] Asked about Ugandan support for Malaysia, Lee replied less categorically, "I have not found anything to suggest the contrary".[117]

The team arrived in Kenya on 21 February. The Prime Minister, Jomo Kenyatta, met with Lee the following day. Facing similar threats to its territorial integrity from neighbouring Somalia, Kenyatta found much to sympathize with Malaysia and, in a joint communiqué, offered to do all he could to bring about a resolution of the differences between the two states. As Lee put it, "I think we can rely on Kenya to do the right thing in the United Nations and within the Afro-Asian organization."[118]

Winding up its extensive African tour, the Truth Mission arrived in Addis Ababa from Nairobi on 23 February and saw the Ethiopian Emperor, Haile Selassie, the following morning. Selassie "listened with sympathy" to the Malaysian delegation, probably because "the parallel between Malaysia and Ethiopia in their disputes with Indonesia and Somalia must have been evident to the Emperor in his talk with Lee", but the resultant communiqué "failed to give much support to the Malaysian case against Indonesia", being confined to an expression of hope for pacific settlement. As Robert H. Wenzel, the First Secretary of the American Embassy at Addis Ababa, observed, Selassie's "preoccupation with his own problems as well as the sheer distance to Malaysia probably limited the effectiveness of the Malaysian presentation."[119] Overall, however, there was no mistaking that "the group appears to have had considerable ... success in putting Malaysia's case before African leaders," remarked the American Consulate in Singapore.[120]

Its 35-day African safari accomplished, the Truth Mission returned home arriving in Kuala Lumpur on 26 February. Lee's own assessment was that the delegation had succeeded in presenting Malaysia's case to the Africans. All the African countries had shown "sympathy and understanding" for Malaysia, he told an airport press conference. "In all the 17 countries we visited," Lee said, "There was no question of them not recognizing Malaysia. … In North Africa, you cannot find anybody more radical than President Ahmed Ben Bella and President Nasser. They sympathize with us. They told us that we would have lost by default if we did not visit them."[121] For Lee, the triumphant African tour had also been a "personal propaganda harvest".[122] Not only had the Singapore premier's performance during the tour showcased his diplomatic acumen and enhanced his international stature, it had also confounded his critics and fully vindicated the Tunku's faith in having him head the mission. James Wong,[123] the Deputy Chief Minister of Sarawak and a member of the delegation, for instance, had only good things to say about the delegation leader. "Our case had been very ably put across to African leaders by Mr Lee and other mission members," he said. Praising the Tunku for his foresight in choosing Lee, Wong added that the Singapore premier had proved himself "an able diplomat of international standing".[124]

Indeed, gratified by the success of the African tour, the Tunku was already planning to despatch Lee on a second mission — to drum up support for Malaysia in the United States. That American policy makers needed to be goaded from their passivity and ambivalence Kuala Lumpur had known for some time. Although Washington did not question the fact of Indonesian aggression, it had been reluctant to openly support Malaysia's cause or to condemn the armed Indonesian incursions, largely because, as *The Straits Times* leader put it, "[o]n the broad canvas of the East-West struggle for the support of the uncommitted nations, 100 million Indonesians are worth more than 10 million Malaysians."[125] That Lee was up to the task there was not a doubt. As one officer of the Ministry of External Affairs remarked, "Everyone realizes, … including the Tunku himself, that Lee Kuan Yew is a more able debater and probably a more impressive figure than the Tunku."[126] Nor were American Embassy officials, whose duty it was to report home, unimpressed with the choice of Lee. Sam P. Gilstrap, the American Consul General in Singapore, for instance, immediately cabled Washington, upon being informed of Lee's impending visit: "I think it highly important that he, as a Western-educated but sensitive Asian, be received by top Washington personalities, hopefully including Secretary Rusk and the President."[127] Noting that Lee's "discretion and good taste can be depended upon", and that he would not "launch an intemperate attack on Sukarno but would support the Malaysia concept with reason and logic," Gilstrap further recommended that speaking engagements and appearances before scholarly university forums, press groups, and TV panel shows be arranged during the visit. "He can more than hold his own with sharp interrogators," he added, and "entertain as well as enlighten sophisticated audiences".[128] The new American Ambassador in Kuala Lumpur, James D. Bell,[137] concurred: "While Lee currently occupies what may appear relatively minor position of Prime Minister Singapore, he is very likely in next four to six years [to] become much more influential throughout Malaysia. ... We should see he gets best possible treatment and is received by highest officials, including if possible the Secretary and the President."[130]

Naturally, Lee welcomed the chance to contribute further to the consolidation of Malaysia, a cause to which he was irrevocably committed.[131] For that purpose, he had promised the Tunku on 26 February, upon his return from Africa, that, after a fortnight's rest, he would be "prepared to undertake whatever he wants me to do".[132] Still convalescing following a minor surgery on his left foot, Lee had planned to leave only on 20 March and remain in the US for about a fortnight.[133] On 12 March, Lee publicly announced that he had been authorized by the Malaysian government to visit the US to prepare the ground for Malaysia's case to be heard at the UN. Unbeknown to Lee, however, powerful political forces in Kuala Lumpur were already at work to torpedo his mission. The day after Lee's announcement, the Malaysian premier issued a coldly worded statement declaring that Lee's US trip was off. "In view of the fact that the PAP is contesting the elections against the Alliance," the Tunku's statement read, "it would be inconsistent politically for the PAP to represent this Government abroad."[134]

Notes

1. *The Straits Times*, 23 September 1963.
2. Ibid.
3. Ibid., 28 September 1963.
4. Ibid., 23 September 1963.

5. Airgram no. 188, American Embassy (Kuala Lumpur) to Department of State, 27 September 1963, RG 59 Box 3976 Pol 2.
6. *The Straits Times*, 23 September 1963.
7. *Ibid.*, 27 September 1963.
8. Airgram no. 60, American Consulate (Singapore) to Department of State, 27 August 1964, RG 59 Box 2457 Pol 23-8 1/1/64.
9. *Royal Malaysia Police (Singapore) Intelligence Journal*, no. 9, 30 September 1963, p. 114.
10. Ibid.
11. Airgram no. 188, American Embassy (Kuala Lumpur) to Department of State, 27 September 1963, RG 59, Box 3976, Pol 2.
12. *Malayan Times*, 25 September 1963.
13. "Memorandum Submitted by the Government of Singapore to the Commission of Inquiry into the Disturbances in Singapore in 1964" (March 1965), pp. 7–8.
14. *The Straits Times*, 28 September 1963.
15. Airgram no. 60, American Consulate (Singapore) to Department of State, 27 August 1964, RG 59 Box 2457 Pol 23-8 1/1/64.
16. In his speech on 16 September 1963, Lee pledged Singapore's "unswerving loyalty to an unalterable principle of unity for the prosperity of Malaysia" and the state's loyalty to the central government and "to bear our share of the burden that independence brings to us. In return, all we ask for is an honourable relationship between the states and the Central Government, a relationship between brothers ... not a relationship between masters and servants". *The Straits Times*, 17 September 1963.
17. Republic of Singapore, *Lee Kuan Yew. Prime Minister's Speeches, Press Conferences, Interviews, Statements, etc* (Singapore, 1962–63).
18. Ibid.
19. *Malayan Times*, 30 September 1963.
20. Ibid.
21. *The Sunday Times*, 29 September 1963.
22. Ibid.
23. Airgram no. 215, American Embassy (Kuala Lumpur) to Department of State, 4 October 1963, RG 59 Box 3975.
24. *The Sunday Times*, 29 September 1963.
25. Ibid.
26. Ibid.
27. *The Straits Times*, 30 September 1963.
28. Airgram no. 215, American Embassy (Kuala Lumpur) to Department of State, 4 October 1963, RG 59 Box 3975.
29. *Straits Echo*, 1 October 1963.
30. Ibid.
31. Ibid.
32. *The Straits Times*, 1 October 1963.
33. Ibid.
34. Ibid.
35. Minutes by Moore, "Notes of Conversation between Mr Lee Kuan Yew and Mr Moore held on 15th October, 1963", DO 169/20 no. 33/45/1.
36. *Singapore Legislative Assembly Debates*, 22 October 1963, Col. 7.
37. *The Straits Times*, 1 October 1963.
38. Minutes by Moore, "Notes of Conversation between Mr Lee Kuan Yew and Mr Moore held on 15th October, 1963", DO 169/20 no. 33/45/1.
39. Ibid.

40. Telegram no. 48, Australian High Commission (Singapore) to Department of External Affairs, 7 November 1963, A1838/280 no. 3024/2/1 Part 12.

41. This was the Singapore (Election to the House of Representatives) Bill, which was introduced on a certificate of urgency. See *Singapore Legislative Assembly Debates*, 22 October 1963, Col. 12.

42. On the opening day of the Legislative Assembly, the parliamentary opposition comprised only nine members. Apart from Ong Eng Guan, there were eight other BS members present, since three of its assemblymen who were implicated in the abortive SATU strike on 8 October had been detained, while two others, Chan Sun Wing (Nee Soon) and Wong Soon Fong (Toa Payoh), had gone underground, presumably to escape arrest and did not appear for the swearing in ceremony. One amendment which the BS made was to provide for nomination by the parties themselves instead of by the Assembly — the effect of which would have been to permit the BS to appoint as members persons who were not members of the Legislative Assembly, including the defeated but capable leaders like Lee Siew Choh and Low Por Tuck, or those who had been elected but had not been sworn in because they were under detention or in hiding. The second amendment was to increase the BS's representatives from 3 to 4. See Peter J. Curtis (First Secretary) to Secretary, Department of External Affairs, 24 October 1963, A1838/280 no. 3024/2/1 Part 12.

43. Telegram no. 71, Singapore to Kuala Lumpur, 21 October 1963, DO 169/20 no. 33/45/1. The BS member for Jurong, Chia Thye Poh, had sought, without success, to move an amendment to reduce the PAP's number of representatives to 11 and to increase the Barisan's to 4, on the basis that, mathematically, the PAP's 37 seats, which was only 72 per cent of the total of 51 seats, would only entitle the party to 10.8 representatives while the BS should have 3.8 members. See *Singapore Legislative Assembly Debates*, 22 October 1963, Col. 48.

44. The PAP team comprised Lee Kuan Yew (Prime Minister), Toh Chin Chye (Deputy Prime Minister), Goh Keng Swee (Finance Minister), S. Rajaratnam (Culture Minister), Ong Pang Boon (Education Minister), Yong Nyuk Lin (Health Minister), Lim Kim San (National Development Minister), Jek Yeun Thong (Labour Minister), Othman Wok (Home Affairs and Social Welfare Minister), Rahim Ishak (Parliamentary Secretary, Ministry of Education), Wee Too Boon (Parliamentary Secretary, Ministry of Labour), and Ho See Beng (Assemblyman and Chairman, NTUC). Ho was expected, in due course, to vacate his seat to make way for Devan Nair, Secretary-General of the NTUC, if he won a by-election in Moulmein (held by his wife) after qualifying for Singapore citizenship. The BS members were Chia Thye Poh (Jurong), Lim Huan Boon (Bukit Merah) and Kow Kee Seng (Paya Lebar). Both Chia and Lim were Nanyang University graduates while Kow was the former secretary of the Singapore Bus Workers' Union, and the only one of the three with a knowledge of Malay.

45. Telegram no. 48, Australian High Commission (Singapore) to Department of External Affairs, 7 November 1963, A1838/280 no. 3024/2/1 Part 12.

46. *The Straits Times*, 18 October 1963.

47. *The Sunday Times*, 20 October 1963.

48. *The Straits Times*, 26 October 1963.

49. Ibid., 31 October 1963.

50. *Utusan Melayu*, 30 September 1963; in Airgram no. 215, American Embassy (Kuala Lumpur) to Department of State, 4 October 1963, RG 59 Box 3975.

51. *The Straits Times*, 1 November 1963.

52. Minutes by Moore, "Notes of Conversation between Lee Kuan Yew and Mr Moore held on 5th November, 1963", DO 169/20 no. 33/45/1.

53. *The Straits Times*, 1 November 1963.

54. Airgram no. 272, American Embassy (Kuala Lumpur) to Department of State, 10 November 1963, RG 59 Box 3979 Pol 15.

55. Minutes by Moore, "Notes of Conversation between Lee Kuan Yew and Mr Moore held on 5th November, 1963", DO 169/20 no. 33/45/1.

56. The 159-seat House of Representatives included, from the government side, the associated Alliance parties of Malaya, Sabah and Sarawak which together hold a total of 107 seats, one more than a two-third majority. Additionally, the Alliance government had also the support of one independent and three PANAS representatives from Sarawak. The new chamber in which the House met had 160 places, 80 on each side. Partly because of the constraints of the seating capacity of the chamber, 76 Alliance members sat on the government side and the remaining Alliance members were accommodated on the opposite benches along with the opposition parties.

57. Airgram no. 272, American Embassy (Kuala Lumpur) to Department of State, 10 November 1963, RG 59 Box 3979 Pol 15.

58. Ibid.

59. Minutes by Moore, "Notes of Conversation between Lee Kuan Yew and Mr Moore held on 5th November, 1963", DO 169/20 no. 33/45/1.

60. Ibid.

61. Ibid.

62. Telegram no. 52, Australian High Commission (Singapore) to Department of External Affairs, 22 November 1963, A1838/280 no. 3024/2/1 Part 12.

63. *Singapore Legislative Assembly Debates*, 29 November 1963, Col. 116–17.

64. Ibid., Col. 118.

65. Ibid., 9 December 1963, Col. 139–42.

66. Airgram no. 370, American Embassy (Kuala Lumpur) to Department of State, 27 December 1963, RG 59 Box 3976 Pol 2.

67. *Malaysia Parliamentary Debates. Dewan Ra'ayat (House of Representatives) Official Report*, 21 December 1963, Col. 2938, 2953–54.

68. Peter J. Curtis to Secretary, Department of External Affairs, 4 December 1963, A1838/280 no. 3024/2/1 Part 12.

69. Telegram no. 49, Woolcott to Department of External Affairs, 14 November 1963, A1838/280 no. 3027/2/1 Part 18.

70. Minutes by Moore, "Notes of Conversation between Lee Kuan Yew and Mr Moore held on 5th November, 1963", DO 169/20 no. 33/45/1.

71. *The Straits Times*, 27 December 1963.

72. Airgram no. 175, American Consulate (Singapore) to Department of State, 14 January 1964, RG 59 Box 2452 Pol 7 1/1/64.

73. Abraham Joseph, "The 'Foreign Relations' of the People's Action Party, 1961–1965: The International Campaign for Malaysia" (Unpublished Academic Exercise submitted to the Department of History, University of Singapore, 1979), pp. 44–45.

74. *The Times*, 17 February 1964.

75. *The Malay Mail*, 29 December 1963.

76. Telegram no. 6, British High Commissioner to Secretary of State for Commonwealth Affairs, 15 October 1964, PREM 13/428.

77. *The Straits Times*, 21 January 1964.

78. Ibid., 28 February 1964.

79. Ibid., 18 January 1964.
80. Minutes by Moore, "Notes of Conversation between Lee Kuan Yew and Mr Moore held on 5th November, 1963", DO 169/20 no. 33/45/1.
81. Syed Ja'afar Albar replaced Ghazali bin Jawi who was appointed Assistant Minister of Rural Development on 15 October 1963. *The Straits Times*, 16 October 1963.
82. Airgram no. 391, American Embassy (Kuala Lumpur) to Department of State, 8 January 1964, RG 59 Box 2455, Pol 15-2, 1/1/64.
83. *Malaysia Parliamentary Debates. Dewan Ra'ayat (House of Representatives) Official Report*, 3 January 1964, Col. 3970–71.
84. Airgram no. 391, American Embassy (Kuala Lumpur) to Department of State, 8 January 1964, RG 59 Box 2455 Pol 15-2 1/1/64.
85. The official members of the delegation included the following: (from Singapore) Lee Kuan Yew, Prime Minister of Singapore and Personal Representative of the Malaysian Prime Minister; Abdul Rahim bin Ishak, Parliamentary Secretary; C.V. Devan Nair, Secretary-General (Singapore), Afro-Asian Solidarity Committee; Teo Yik Kwee, Personal Secretary to the Prime Minister; (from Sarawak) James Wong, Deputy Chief Minister of Sarawak; (from Sabah) Harris bin Mohamed Salleh, State Minister for Local Government; John Dusing, Personal Secretary to Sabah delegation; Ganie Gilong, Member of Federal Parliament; (from the Federation of Malaya) Tengku Ngah Mohamed, Deputy Secretary, Ministry of External Affairs; Zakaria bin Haji Mohammed Ali, Counsellor, Malaysian Permanent Mission to the United Nations; Zainal Abidin bin Sulong, Assistant Secretary, Ministry of External Affairs, also secretary to the delegation; Lim Chooi Sian, ADC to the Prime Minister of Singapore. Rex Ebert served as the French interpreter.
86. Joseph, "The 'Foreign Relations' of the People's Action Party, 1961–1965: The International Campaign for Malaysia", p. 83.
87. *The Straits Times*, 25 January 1964.
88. W.K. Flanagan, First Secretary, to Secretary, Department of External Affairs, 10 May 1962, A1838/280 no. 3024/7/1 Part 1.
89. *The Straits Times*, 28 January 1964.
90. Airgram no. 706, American Embassy (Jakarta) to Department of State, 5 February 1964, RG 59 Box 2452 Pol 7 1/1/64.
91. *The Straits Times*, 30 January 1964.
92. Ibid., 2 February 1964. See also the American Embassy (Rabat) to Department of State, 31 January 1964, RG 59 Box 2452 Pol 7 1/1/64.
93. *The Straits Times*, 2 February 1964. Indeed, as Devan Nair, a member of the delegation revealed later, the Moroccans had listened carefully to the Malaysian presentation but had "gone out of [their] way to note that Malaya had not supported Morocco's claims on Mauritania". Airgram no. 250, American Embassy (Abidjan) to Department of State, 12 February 1964, RG 59 Box 2452 Pol 7 1/1/64.
94. American Embassy (Rabat) to Department of State, 31 January 1964, RG 59 Box 2452 Pol 7 1/1/64.
95. Ibid.
96. Ibid.
97. T.E. Evans to R.A. Butler, 5 February 1964, FO 371/175058.
98. *The Straits Times*, 2 February 1964.
99. Ibid.
100. Airgram no. 182, American Embassy (Bamako) to Department of State, 5 February 1964, RG 59 Box 2452 Pol 7 1/1/64.

101. *The Straits Times*, 5 February 1964.
102. Airgram no. 199, American Embassy (Conakry) to Department of State, 14 February 1964, RG 59, Box 2458 Pol 1/1/64.
103. American Embassy (Abidjan) to Department of State, 12 February 1964, RG 59 Box 2452 Pol 7 1/1/64.
104. *The Straits Times*, 9 February 1964.
105. Ibid.
106. Airgram no. 250, American Embassy (Abidjan) to Department of State, 12 February 1964, RG 59 Box 2452 Pol 7 1/1/64.
107. *The Straits Times*, 12 February 1964.
108. Ibid., 13 February 1964.
109. Airgram no. 515, American Embassy (Lagos) to Department of State, 18 February 1964, RG 59 Box 2452 Pol 7 1/1/64.
110. *The Straits Times*, 14 February 1964.
111. *Malayan Times*, 17 February 1964.
112. Joseph, "The 'Foreign Relations' of the People's Action Party, 1961–1965: The International Campaign for Malaysia", p. 93.
113. Airgram no. 244, American Embassy (Tananarive) to Department of State, 29 February 1964, RG 59 Box 2452 Pol 7 1/1/64.
114. *The Straits Times*, 19 February 1964.
115. Ibid., 21 February 1964.
116. American Embassy (Kampala) to Department of State, 25 February 1964, RG 59 Box 2452 Pol 7 1/1/64.
117. Ibid.
118. Airgram no. 426, American Embassy (Nairobi) to Department of State, 29 February 1964, RG 59 Box 2452 Pol 7 1/1/64.
119. Airgram no. 454, American Embassy (Addis Ababa) to Department of State, 4 March 1964, RG 59 Box 2452 Pol 7 1/1/64.
120. Singapore to Washington, 27 February 1964, RG 59 Box 2450 Pol 2 1/1/65.
121. *The Straits Times*, 27 February 1964.
122. Singapore to Washington, 27 February 1964, RG 59 Box 2450 Pol 2 1/1/65.
123. Wong had left the delegation at Tanzania to attend the Sarawak Council Negri meeting in Sarawak on 24 February 1964.
124. *The Straits Times*, 22 February 1964.
125. Ibid., 13 March 1964.
126. Memorandum of conversation between Jerrod M. Dion and Khalil bin Ya'acob, 30 June 1964, RG 59 Box 2452 Pol 7 7/1/64. Khalil was the American desk officer at the Malaysian Ministry of External Affairs.
127. Telegram no. 601, American Consulate (Singapore) to Department of State, 11 March 1964, RG 59 Box 2452 Pol 7 1/1/64.
128. Ibid.
129. Bell succeeded Charles Baldwin who had served as ambassador for three years. Bell was Deputy Director of the Office of Philippine and Southeast Asian Affairs, Department of State, July 1955–March 1956; Director of the Office of Southwest Pacific Affairs, March 1956–April 1957; Counselor of the American Embassy in Indonesia, April–December 1957; Director, Office of Southwest Pacific Affairs, Bureau of Far Eastern Affairs, Department of State, until April 1962.
130. Telegram no. 830, American Embassy (Kuala Lumpur) to Department of State, 12 March 1964, RG 59 Box 2452 Pol 7 1/1/64.

131. Telegram no. 49, Australian High Commission (Singapore) to Department of External Affairs, 14 November 1963, A1838/280 no. 3027/2/1 Part 18.
132. *The Straits Times*, 13 March 1964.
133. Telegram no. 601, American Consulate (Singapore) to Department of State, 11 March 1964, RG 59 Box 2452 Pol 7 1/1/64.
134. *The Straits Times*, 14 March 1964.

CHAPTER 4

CROSSING THE RUBICON

The PAP Contests the Federal Elections

I t was Toh Chin Chye, the People's Action Party (PAP) chairman, who announced the decision to contest the mainland elections on the morning of 1 March 1964. Speaking at the opening ceremony for a new Tamil language newspaper, the *Tamil Malar*, Toh revealed that the PAP would field a very small number of candidates and play a token part in the forthcoming Federal elections. Coming close on the heels of Lee Kuan Yew's assurances[1] to Tunku Abdul Rahman just a few months before — that the PAP would stay away from the 1964 Federal elections — Toh's announcement amounted to a dramatic volte-face on the part of the PAP leadership and plunged the party immediately into the throes of controversy. As the Tunku's cancellation of Lee's US trip portended, the dire ramifications of the fateful decision on the state of Singapore–Kuala Lumpur relations within Malaysia were just beginning to unravel.

It was not that the PAP thrust had been unexpected. Amongst some diplomatic observers, the view that the PAP would eventually enter the political fray in the mainland had been much touted ever since the party's "smashing victory"[2] in the September 1963 Singapore elections. That the Singapore premier was "young, tough, ambitious, extremely talented"[3] and "determined to play a major role in Federal politics"[4] was already known. His desire to be Prime Minister of Malaysia was also "an open secret", they asserted.[5] Sam P. Gilstrap, the American Consul General, for instance, had cabled Washington in September 1963 shortly after the PAP's electoral success: "We believe he [Lee] would be prepared to work with Tunku and UMNO [United Malays National Organization] if they will accept him on reasonable terms. If not, we anticipate that before long he will move into the cities of the Federation, build up a competing organization and work against the Alliance."[6] Sharing his analysis was the then outgoing American Ambassador in Kuala Lumpur, Charles F. Baldwin, who commented in January 1964: "Lee is almost certainly determined to build up the strength of the PAP and extend its influence throughout Malaysia as rapidly as possible. He apparently believes that this could be done at the expense of the MCA [Malayan Chinese Association] and he may be right".[7] The Australian High Commissioner in Kuala Lumpur, T.K. Critchley, had also written in a similar vein in October 1963 of his suspicion that Lee harboured wider ambitions to be "the leader of the Malaysian Chinese — an objective that he knows must bring him into conflict with the MCA and its partners in the Alliance". Among Lee's other longer-term goals, Critchley maintained, were his plans to "replace the Alliance as the stabilizing force in Malaysian politics with a multiracial party along the lines of the PAP." He believed that "the Alliance in the Federation will have served its historical purpose in a decade or so." The High Commissioner predicted that, in keeping with the latter objective, Lee would not only want to build up the image of the PAP as a "forward looking, socialist and genuine multiracial [party] with a vigorous capacity for national leadership as demonstrated by its own achievements in Singapore" but he would also promote the view that support for a strong Malaysia "does not necessarily mean support for the Alliance and the Tunku and that a multiracial party with the vigour and imagination of the PAP could carry Malaysia faster and further than its present leadership. ... No doubt 'progressive' elements in other areas in Malaysia ... will be carefully cultivated", he said, leading eventually to the establishment of PAP branches throughout Malaysia, with Lee setting himself up as the leader of "Little Malaysia" (Singapore, Sarawak and Sabah). "Although he is inclined to deny it," Critchley wrote, "his ambitions almost certainly include becoming the first Chinese Prime Minister of Malaysia".[8]

How seriously Lee eyed the premiership of Malaysia is now a moot point. Lee himself had asserted matter-of-factly in August 1962 — shortly after the Tunku announced that a Malaysian Cabinet would include representatives from the Borneo territories but none from Singapore[9] — that although the PAP was not out for Cabinet seats, this did not mean that PAP members were not eligible for Cabinet appointments. Lee argued that the Malaysian constitutional process, entitled every elected representative to become "a Minister or even a Prime Minister if he could command a majority in the House".[10] But as he himself was acutely aware, realistically, the odds were stacked against a Chinese assuming the mantle of a Malaysian premier — at least in the foreseeable future. "He is a fool who believes that he can govern Malaysia without the support of the Malays," Lee had said in July 1963, "I can envisage the PAP working together with Malay leaders, but I can't see a Singapore-based party capturing the Malaysia Parliament. ... As long as the Tunku is there, he will be the leader of Malaysia."[11] Lee clarified his position again shortly after Malaysia Day, on 28 September 1963, this time conceding the necessity of having a Malay as Prime Minister of Malaysia "for the next two decades".[12] He was to say so a third time, on 9 April 1964, in the course of the Malayan election campaign. Questioned during a television interview, Lee replied that it was a "statement of fact" that there was no alternative leadership from the Malay mass base to the one provided by the Tunku and Tun Abdul Razak: "I think the Prime Minister or the Number One leader man must be preferably a Malay or a Dayak or a Dusun. Certainly not a Chinese because that raises a lot of fears, quite confounded fears, but fears which can be exploited."

> _Kajapathy_: So, you don't think a Chinese can be Prime Minister of Malaysia in the foreseeable future?
>
> _Lee Kuan Yew_: No, I am not saying a Chinese cannot — constitutionally he can. I think it is unwise — it is politically unwise, it will raise a lot of problems. In the next generation when you've bred people who think in terms of themselves as Malaysians, not as Malaysian Chinese, Malaysian Indians, Malaysian Malays, but the emphasis is on the first — Malaysians — then I say it makes no difference whether the Prime Minister is a Malay, Chinese, Indian, Dusun, Dayak, Murut or what have you. But for this present generation we have got to accept the fact that people react first in terms of their racial origins and then, next, in terms of their national interest. ... may take 20, 25 years — I think we have got to be realistic enough to see that.[13]

Of course, Lee's assurances, however well reasoned or intentioned, were never enough to satisfy his critics, as R.A. Woolcott, the Acting Australian High Commissioner in Singapore, acknowledged: "There ... seems to be a tendency to see Lee as **either** a scheming, unprincipled, ambitious opportunist, hell bent on the Prime Ministership of Malaysia (as some of his critics do) *or* as a man sincerely dedicated to the consolidation of Malaysia and prepared to subjugate his personal ambitions to this end (as some of his admirers do)." Woolcott himself saw no reason to doubt the Singapore premier's sincerity in wanting to avoid "rocking the Malaysian boat" by usurping the Tunku. "Whatever Lee's long-term personal ambitions may be — and I would agree that these probably encompass the Prime Ministership of Malaysia," Woolcott reported, "I believe he is at present sincere when he says that, given the present balance of racial and political forces, a Singapore Chinese could not become the Prime Minister of Malaysia within the next five to ten years." In private conversations, Woolcott added, "he tends to use the phrases 'two decades' or a 'generation'".[14]

This is not to say, however, that the PAP had no pan-Malaysian ambitions. While Lee had assured Kuala Lumpur openly on numerous occasions, as we have seen, both before and after merger, of the PAP's non-participation in the 1964 Federal elections, his public statements can only mean what they say, and did not preclude the possibility of the PAP fielding candidates to contest the polls in *subsequent* Malaysian elections. In the first place, the PAP never pretended it had no interest in extending its presence across the Causeway. Ever since its formation in 1954, the PAP had always intended to be at least a pan-Malayan party with Malaya-wide objectives. "Though … technically a political party operating in Singapore," its inaugural party manifesto had declared in 1954, "we shall in our approach to the problems of this country [Malaya] disregard the constitutional division." It added: "When Malayans in the Federation who agree with our aims join us we shall work throughout Malaya." Malaya — and not just Singapore — was the wider arena where the PAP said it would operate to fulfil its political and ideological mission. Merger through Malaysia had opened the door. However, it was the party's sweeping electoral performance in Singapore, five days after Malaysia Day, which showed the way. Not only had the victory vindicated the correctness of its socialist socio-economic and non-communal convictions but it had also given the party an urban political base and further convinced its leaders of the wider role the PAP could — and must — play in the building of a "united democratic and socialist Malaysia, based on the principles of social justice and non-communalism". To remain a Singapore-bound party was not an option the PAP could seriously acquiesce.

In fact, as its leaders saw it, the PAP's own long-term survival as a political party and as the state government would be in peril if it confined its activities to Singapore alone. The reason was to be found in the shift in the power axis which Malaysia wrought: in the new Malaysian setting, the Alliance government possessed sufficient powers under the merger terms to clip the wings of the PAP state government. This was hinted at during the Yang di-Pertuan Negara's address in the Singapore legislature on 29 November 1963: "The centre of gravity of political power is the Central Government of Malaysia," he noted. "In other words, it means that in the long run the order of our society will be determined by the Central Government." It was policy decided in Kuala Lumpur "that will decide our fate". For that reason, "any political movement that seeks to bring changes in our society must necessarily have pan-Malaysian support ... No political movement can be effective if it is localized and isolated either to Singapore or Kuala Lumpur."[15] The same point was echoed by Lee Kuan Yew in his parliamentary address slightly over a week later, on 9 December 1963: "[U]ltimate power is now vested in the Parliament of Malaysia, and any political movement or Party that wishes to re-order the state of our society will have to assume authority for all Malaysia":[16]

> Indeed, it is a truth, which has to be faced by whichever political movement that wishes to win authority and the right to reshape the structure of our economy and our society, that we must first win the majority of the number of seats in Parliament, the Parliament of Malaysia, and command a loyalty of the administration and the obedience of the Army and the Police.[17]

PAP leaders would not have failed to note that the Alliance, on its part, had reorganized itself to become a pan-Malaysian party even before merger and Malaysia. In Singapore, branches of UMNO, MCA and MIC (Malayan Indian Congress) had also been established from the early 1950s, and, through the formalization of their partnership in the Singapore Alliance (SA) in July 1961, recast again in June 1963 to include the Singapore People's Alliance (SPA), the SA had tried to duplicate the communally-based politics of the Federation on the island. While the Malaysian constitution had, indeed, prohibited Federation and Singapore voters from contesting in each other's elections — permitting them only to vote respectively, in the Federation and Singapore, their own members of Parliament to the Dewan Ra'ayat

(House of Representatives) — it did not prevent Malayan, or Singapore-based political parties, from expanding their political activities across the Causeway. The Alliance was the first to do so when it participated in the 1963 Singapore general elections through the Singapore Alliance, after it had contested, in a pre-Malaysia context, in the 1959 polls through the Singapore branches of UMNO, MCA and MIC. Although the SA was totally eclipsed in 1963, Alliance leaders had every intention — as the Tunku's remarks on 27 September 1963 indicated — of revitalizing the party to take on the PAP at the next election. With the backing and resources of the Alliance-led central government, the SA could, given time, become a more attractive alternative to the Singapore electorate. As W.B. Pritchett, the Australian Deputy High Commissioner, noted, "the mere fact that, with Malaysia, power in many fields has gone to, or is now shared with, the Federal government is a threat to the PAP's position: insofar as people wish to influence government it will be increasingly to the Alliance that they will have to turn in many fields."[18] It was a threat the PAP could not take lightly. Fong Sip Chee argued that if the PAP confined itself to operating only in Singapore, the party "would gradually fade out and eventually disintegrate" since it would be unable to "withstand the big hammer from the Central Government".[19] The demands of *realpolitik* necessitated the extension of the PAP's influence beyond Singapore. In Toh Chin Chye's words, spoken a day after his 1 March announcement, the PAP had no intention "of being cornered like a rat in Singapore".[20]

There was also a related economic dimension, as Lee Kuan Yew was to reveal later on 17 April 1964, when he spoke of his fear that the MCA might use their ministerial position in the Federal government to upset or obstruct the smooth implementation of Singapore's industrialization programme: "As long as the MCA believe that they can make a comeback in Singapore using their ministerial position in the Federal Government, they will be tempted to obstruct or interfere in Singapore. Such interference cannot succeed in blocking us. But it will inevitably lead to an unnecessary repetition of the sharp conflict that bedevilled the financial negotiations between Singapore and Kuala Lumpur." As Lee disclosed, one of the reasons for the PAP's participation in the Malayan elections was, therefore, to "demonstrate to the MCA that they do not even have a base in Malaya. To try and create one in Singapore when they cannot succeed and have not succeeded after nine years in power in Malaya is wishful thinking."[21]

One thing was clear: even if the PAP kept out of the 1964 Federal polls, it could not remain outside the fray forever. "We have opted out of the competition to form the next government of Malaysia by declaring that we have no intention of contesting the Federal general election," Lee said, "But it is not possible for us to opt out a second time (assuming that elections continue in 1968 or 1969)." He explained: "Having brought about the merger and Malaysia, if we leave the future of the country in the hands of merchant adventurers, then we will be held responsible for their misdeeds if we make no attempt to provide a better alternative."[22] Lee himself believed that "long before the next 5 years are up, they [UMNO] must come to terms with us as the acknowledged leadership of the urban inhabitants of Malaysia."[23] Indeed, as Moore intimated, Lee saw that, within the next two or three years, the "relationship between himself and the Tunku would have to come to a head. … There was about two years from the date of the Malayan elections in which to bring about a proper understanding. Positions would then have to be taken up for the next elections and the Tunku would have to decide either to drop the MCA and to work with the PAP or to fight the PAP for control of the towns in Malaya."[24] In the Singapore premier's own estimate, "This objective must be achieved at the latest in three years' time, for by the fourth year, if we have not moved into a position where UMNO leaders are thinking of the 1968 or 1969 elections working in conjunction with the PAP it must mean that they will have to face the problems of fighting the PAP with all that it means for them, and for us."[25]

That the PAP decided, in the end, not to wait out the 1964 polls but to send a token force represented a tactical reversal on the part of its leadership. The available evidence would suggest that, right up to early November 1963 at least, the party leadership was still undecided on the question of whether it should contest directly the Federal polls, even if it was hoping for some form of indirect participation. Reporting on his conversation with Lee on 15 October, the British Deputy High Commissioner, Philip Moore, remarked for instance that whilst the Singapore premier would "adhere to his undertaking not to intervene in these elections", he "hoped that perhaps the Tunku would allow the PAP to give support in Penang to Ramanathan, who had broken away from the Socialist Front [SF] and lost his seat on the City Council." Moore added: "If, as he [Lee] expected, Ramanathan could defeat the Socialist Front with PAP support, this would show the Tunku how much the PAP could help UMNO in the towns all over Malaya and Sarawak."[26] In Lee's mind, the inherent dangers of a premature thrust into the Malayan heartland would have to be weighed carefully. In a memorandum to members of the Publicity and Propaganda Coordinating Committee on 25 October 1963, he warned of the "difficulties [which] are bound to arise" should the Alliance leadership "believe that we are to challenge their authority" by intruding into their political field. "For urgent strategic reasons", Lee wrote, "I have stated that we have no intention of challenging the Alliance in the Federation in the next general elections. Had I not clarified this position, the chances were a great deal more acrimony and bitterness would have developed between us." He was dismayed that UMNO leaders, for various reasons, were "still not completely convinced that we know it to be in our interest that they should govern Malaysia for the next five years and that, in fact, there is no alternative government."[27] "How do we convince the Malay leadership that we are sincere in wanting to cooperate with them and not to overwhelm them?" Lee asked in his memorandum of 8 November. "How do we convince the Malay rural population that our policy in cooperating with their UMNO leaders is likely to bring them a better life and future for themselves and their children?"[28]

Statements by PAP leaders in early December did not suggest any change in the party's non-interventionist stance although, by the month's close, there emerged the first indications that a major reappraisal of the policy was underway. On 9 December, speaking in the Singapore Legislative Assembly, Lee hinted that the PAP would take stock of its position and make some crucial decisions after the 1964 Malayan elections.[29] "Our influence over the deliberations of Parliament in the policies of the Central Government has yet to be felt," he said, "Much will depend on what happens in the election in Malaya next year." As to what could happen, Lee offered this analysis:

> Everybody concedes that the UMNO side of the Alliance can and will win a clear majority. But everybody is waiting to see what happens to the vote in the urban areas and in all the main towns in Malaya, for arising out of that vote, some vital decisions will have to be made both by UMNO leaders and by us in Singapore.
>
> It is fairly obvious that if it were possible for the MCA to hold the towns in Malaya, then the present structure of the Central Government and the policies it pursues can go on unchanged.
>
> But if the towns decisively reject all MCA candidates, then there must be a reappraisal by UMNO leaders. They will then have to decide

whether they come to terms with the leadership that can command the loyalty of the sophisticated urban population — Chinese, Indians, Eurasians and others — or govern without the partnership of the towns.[30]

As Osborne pointed out, "The implication here was clear: if the MCA failed in the urban areas, the PAP would aim to fill the gap. But the implication also was that such a decision would come after the elections."[31]

By the end of the month, however, it was evident that the PAP's public position on non-intervention had shifted somewhat. On 23 December, the Singapore Minister of Culture, S. Rajaratnam, made explicit for the first time what had hitherto only been hinted: the PAP, he said, considered itself a pan-Malaysian party and was likely to extend its activities to the Malayan states. "When the time is opportune," he asserted, "we will move in".[32] The PAP's aim was to set up a non-communist and socialist society: "We have shown in Singapore that our aims can be achieved," he said. What about the PAP's undertaking not to participate in Federal elections? Rajaratnam argued that since the UMNO, the MCA, and the MIC had established branches in Singapore, the PAP was, therefore, entitled to "disreciprocity".[33] Making the same points again the following month, Rajaratnam reiterated on 17 January 1964 that the PAP must "start operating as a Pan-Malaysian Party on a Pan-Malaysian basis" to "exert an influence throughout Malaysia — to convince people that the socialist philosophy of the PAP can help to solve in a practical and peaceful way Malaysian problems as well".[34] He added: "We must think of how best to use this victory [the September 1963 Singapore elections] not only to make a better future but also to make certain that the PAP wins the next election five years from now".[35]

The question of the PAP's "token intervention" was discussed during a meeting of the Publicity and Propaganda Coordinating Committee chaired by Lee Kuan Yew on 20 January 1964 — on the day he was scheduled to leave with the Truth Mission for Africa. As the minutes of the meeting recorded: "The point that the PAP was a force in Malaya and not only in Singapore would have to be put across and it could openly be said that the PAP policies are the right ones. But the key point to be determined is whether it will make it better or worse for the PAP to put up token candidates in the forthcoming elections; whether such intervention would undermine the moderate English-speaking Malay leadership in Malaya?" The minutes noted that the "situation was now so serious that all previous assumptions had to be thrown overboard":

> While the PAP could not make a bid for power in Malaya because of Malay feelings, the Singapore Government's influence would have to be brought to bear on the Tengku and this could possibly be done by making a token show and contesting five or six seats in the forthcoming elections. The objective would be to gain influence over the Central Government and get them to adopt a correct attitude. So far the reasonable line had not been productive.

As Lee would be leaving for Africa later that evening, he had asked that no decision be taken on the question of the PAP's participation in the Federal elections in his absence. The minutes recorded that the issue which the Chairman "wished members of the Committee to consider while he was away in Africa but not to make any decision on was the desirability of the PAP intervening in the forthcoming elections in Malaya."[36] The evidence would suggest that, while the issue of a token intervention was considered by the PAP leadership in January, until the end of the month at least, no go-ahead decision had been taken. Reporting on its conversations with S. Rajaratnam and Toh Chin Chye, the Australian High Commission in Singapore noted, for instance:

> The Minister of Culture has twice recently indicated that the PAP was preparing to enter Malaysian Federal politics. However, in conversations with us, both the Minister and the Deputy Prime Minister have said that it was unlikely the PAP would move outside Singapore in the near future. They saw secure prospects of electoral support both in the Federation and the East Malaysian states, but they considered that relations with Malay political leaders would not at this stage bear the strain of a move outside Singapore by the PAP. At the same time they wanted it understood that the PAP could not stand aside once the MCA was discredited in Malaya.[37]

By February, however, "Reports multiplied that the PAP would contest the Federal Malay [sic] elections in April".[38] The Australian High Commission in Singapore observed: "[T]here was clearly eagerness for this in PAP circles. At the end of the month the official party line was that the PAP would not make such a move out of regard for UMNO feelings."[39] Until the final week of February, it appeared that the PAP had still not taken the decision to intervene. As late as 21 February, K.M. Byrne, the Minister for Health and Law in the previous PAP government and also a PAP Central Executive Committee member who had access to the "inner plans and policies of the PAP", had intimated to Critchley that, while the PAP "would have no trouble in winning an election in Malaya", it had chosen "not to contest the coming elections but it would run the elections that followed and would certainly win." As Critchley reported, Byrne was "very emphatic and confident about this". To a comment by Critchley on the need for the PAP to be careful in its relations with UMNO, Byrne replied, "We can wait … 5 years, 10 years. It doesn't matter." Conceding that the PAP might not get the Malay vote, Byrne said he was sure, however, of the Chinese and that "we can wipe out" the MCA as well as the Socialist Front "if we chose to contest the coming elections." "While the PAP would not contest the coming elections in Malaysia as a matter of tactics," Critchley was led to conclude prematurely, "it would enter the following elections and had plans to win them."[40]

By the last week of February, however, the PAP had decided to throw its hat into the Malayan ring. The final decision to go ahead was apparently made between 21 February — if Byrne's remarks to Critchley were accurate — and before Lee's return from Africa on 26 February. During his absence, members of the PAP's Central Executive Committee (CEC) — spearheaded by Toh Chin Chye and S. Rajaratnam — apparently took the momentous decision to contest the 1964 Malayan elections. As Lee Kuan Yew later recalled:

> When I came back I found that the CEC had decided to fight the Malaysian Federal Elections. I was not enthusiastic. There was a gentleman's understanding between the Tunku and me that we should stay out of each other's backyard. This was known to the CEC.
> But the Tunku had allowed Peninsula UMNO and MCA–MIC Alliance leaders to intervene in the Singapore General Elections in September 1963. So the CEC considered all bets off. Although I was not personally enamoured of the proposal, I abided by the decision.[41]

That Lee was not "personally enamoured" of the decision would seem to be corroborated by Critchley's own assessment:

> From my own talks with Lee and others I had the strong impression that although the idea of contesting the next election had been under consideration, Lee's own opinion tended to be against it. He was, however, wobbly on the issue and I suspect that the influence of people like Dr Toh was eventually decisive.[42]

Lee was not the only CEC member who was unenthusiastic. Lee Khoon Choy, another CEC member, had also opposed the move as "untimely", since the PAP had no branches or candidates in Malaya, and no funds. "I predicted that it would be extremely difficult for us to win," he wrote.[43] Three months before, Goh Keng Swee, like the rest of the CEC, had felt that the PAP's chances were good. As Moore noted in his interview with Lee in November 1963, "Goh Keng Swee, who had previously been doubtful of the PAP's prospects in Malaya, was now convinced that within a year or so they could rout both the Socialist Front and the MCA. According to Goh, the young Chinese in Kuala Lumpur were longing for Chinese leadership of the quality given by the PAP in Singapore."[44] It appeared that Goh later changed his mind, fearing its ramifications on Singapore's push for a Common Market. When the campaign started, Goh remained in Singapore and was not involved in the electioneering. The dissenters were apparently "overruled" by the rest of the CEC.[45]

What had prompted the CEC's sudden volte-face? Perhaps, as W.B. Pritchett, the Australian Deputy High Commissioner in Singapore surmised, it "stems to an important extent from the deep dissatisfaction of Toh and his colleagues from what they regard as Kuala Lumpur's failure to take them into its confidence and consult with them on National Policy and tactics on the confrontation issue. [T]hey feel that without a show of power by the PAP, Kuala Lumpur will continue this way." Lee's own explanation, as reported by Pritchett, was that the PAP wanted "to get a foot in the door": it was merely a gesture — to show power, but not to take power. Lee thought Malay reactions should not be too strong or lasting as the number of candidates were being kept to a few.[46]

A confidant of the Singapore premier, George Thomson, the Director of the Singapore Political Studies Centre, provided a different explanation for the PAP *putsch* to the American Consul, Arthur H. Rosen, who reported him as suggesting that what Lee had in mind was "to start a leavening process; to encourage the UMNO leadership to use more effective tactics against the communists". The Singapore leader, Rosen reported, "sees himself as the only politician in Asia who has engaged the communists in a straight parliamentary fight and won. And he believes he was able to win because he had learned in the days when he worked closely with the communists that their strength depended not on any intrinsic appeal of communist ideology, but rather on the communists' ability to appropriate non-communist slogans and ideals." There was no desire to usurp UMNO: "Malaysia's first and most pressing need ... is domestic political stability. Such stability, Mr Lee contends, can exist in a country only when there is an elite whose right to rule has been recognized by the people. In Malaysia that elite is the Malay leadership under Prime Minister Tunku Abdul Rahman and the UMNO. Any attempt by the PAP or a Chinese like Prime Minister Lee to challenge their pre-eminent political position would be irresponsible in the extreme, since it would jeopardize the fragile structure of political stability already established here".[47]

Lee Khoon Choy recalled that the CEC made the decision, partly "encouraged by its new-found Malay support in the recent General Elections" and also because his colleagues were "convinced that the pro-Malaysian parties must thwart the anti-Malaysian Socialist Front to ensure Malaysia's continued existence".[48] Why only a "token intervention"? Lee was later to disclose the very compelling reasons why the PAP had not fielded as many candidates as there were seats in the urban areas: "We believe that any massive intervention in the elections can easily be misinterpreted, and will be presented to the rural Malays as an attempt to challenge UMNO ... [and] encourage extremist Malay elements to work up feelings that with merger and Malaysia, the position of the Malays has been endangered and the Chinese in the towns are making a bid for power."[49]

On 27 February, the PAP formally applied for registration on Malayan soil.[50] The unmistakable hint of intention was correctly read by Critchley on 28 February, although his prediction of the PAP's timetable was off the mark: "PAP applied yesterday for registration as a political party in the Federation. I am satisfied that the PAP do not intend to contest the coming election but the one after."[51] What remained was for the PAP to inform Alliance leaders. Goh Keng Swee broke the news informally to Tun Razak "on the 15th hole", just a day before Toh's announcement, on 29 February.[52] Visibly upset, Tun Razak immediately urged Goh to call the whole thing off, but without success.[53] So it was that on 1 March 1964, Toh Chin Chye publicly unveiled the PAP's plans to contest the 1964 Federal elections — an announcement timed to coincide with the dissolution of the Malaysian Parliament on that day as a prelude to the calling of elections, a few months shy of its constitutional life of five years.[54]

Toh was at pains to stress that the PAP's intention was not to challenge the central government or UMNO: "Far from it. It is our purpose to cooperate with UMNO and the Central Government of Malaysia to help Malaysia succeed."[55] The PAP's objective, he said, was to fight the pro-Indonesia, pro-communist and anti-Malaysia parties — which he identified as the Socialist Front and the Pan-Malayan Islamic Party (PMIP) in the Federation and the Barisan Sosialis in Singapore — and ensure the triumph of the pro-Malaysia parties if Malaysia were to withstand Indonesian hostility: "This election must be won by the pro-Malaysia parties. It is a matter of life and death for us that the Federation of Malaysia should succeed."[56] Toh had also alluded to a second motive for the PAP's entry: its desire to play a larger role in the consolidation of Malaysia. As a party which had played a leading part in the struggle for the formation of Malaysia, Toh argued, it was essential that the PAP as a non-communal party should not remain a parochial Singapore party but must henceforth consider itself a national Malaysian party, "and it is vital for the PAP to take part in the affairs of Malaya".[57] If it remained a Singapore-bound party, Toh reasoned, the PAP's ability to give "added strength and lustre to Malaysia" would be severely restricted.[58] The PAP chairman's remarks the following evening, at the opening of a cultural bureau in the PAP headquarters, revealed a third motive: the token entry of a few candidates was also a first step in developing the party to be "a force to be reckoned with" by the time of the next elections in 1969, so that UMNO, by then realizing the PAP's strength, would cooperate with it in uniting the races of Malaysia.[59] Rajaratnam next disclosed on 2 March that the party would contest only in the urban areas.[60]

Caught off-guard, UMNO leaders tried initially to play down the significance of the PAP intervention — and claimed that they had anticipated the PAP thrust for some time. "If they want to join in the fight, they are welcome", shrugged Khir Johari.[61] "Let them come," was Syed Ja'afar Albar's blasé reply.[62] The UMNO Secretary-General disclosed that the Alliance leadership was "all along aware of the PAP's intentions as it had been sending its agents to the mainland to survey the election possibilities for some time."[63] Senu bin Abdul Rahman, the Alliance election campaign chief, conceded that the PAP had as much right as any other party.[64] The Tunku himself had apparently also "known in advance of the PAP decision to enter the elections", according to Rosen, citing Syed Esa Almenoar, SUMNO's Secretary-General, as his source.[64]

That may be so. But, as Critchley noted, "Privately, the comments of Alliance leaders are not so restrained."[66] As reported by Robert W. Moore (First Secretary, American Embassy) on a conversation with Abdul Khadir bin Talib (Secretary, Federal Elections Commission):

> Alliance realizes that if the PAP can demonstrate its appeal on the mainland by picking up several seats, the Alliance might face the prospect after the elections of the PAP working to woo away the

Alliance's Sabah and Sarawak seats, which together with its own and some from other mainland opposition parties, could produce a voting bloc in the House of sufficient size to challenge the Alliance's control.[67]

Kuala Lumpur's nervousness about PAP ambitions ran deep. Before Malaysia's formation, and during the talks leading to merger, signs of the Alliance leaders' distrust of the PAP were already manifest. Wanting to contain the political role of Singapore within Malaysia, Kuala Lumpur allocated Singapore only 15 seats in the Dewan Ra'ayat in return for autonomy in education and labour, although the island was entitled to more on a proportional basis. An undertaking was apparently secured from the PAP to settle for its 15-seat allotment and not to seek more seats by entering candidates in the Federal elections. At least, this was assumed by the Tunku who subsequently saw the PAP's "attempt to have a hand in the affairs of Malaysia" by contesting the 1964 elections as a violation of this understanding and "contrary to what we had agreed".[68] It was a charge Tan Siew Sin, the MCA chief, also levelled at the PAP. According to Tan, when Lee Kuan Yew "came to the Tengku pleading for help" against the Barisan Sosialis prior to merger, he had "pledged that he would never contest any elections on the mainland".[69]

Indeed, after the nightmare of the Alliance debacle in Singapore in September 1963, the spectre of a more self-assured, left-inclined, and non-communal PAP crossing the Straits of Johore and engaging the conservative and communally-oriented mainland Alliance in political combat for the mastery of Malaysia became a worrying concern for Alliance leaders. As the British observed, the PAP's "overwhelming victory in the recent Singapore elections has aroused fears that [it] is aiming to displace the present Malay leaders from power in the centre in the long term."[70] It was easy for the Alliance to see the latest PAP thrust as an outworking of what the SPA called the Singapore party's "sinister intentions".[71]

Alliance leaders had no trouble interpreting the PAP move as a direct political challenge to the MCA and indirectly to UMNO — confronting the latter with the choice of either accepting the PAP now or facing future consequences of a challenge by a potentially dangerous opponent. The MCA's own "instantaneous reading"[72] of the move was that the PAP was out to smash the party, even though Toh's announcement had not mentioned the MCA at all. Calling Toh's statement "a masterpiece of prevarication", the MCA chief, Tan Siew Sin, in his first public reaction on 2 March, bristled: "The PAP claims it wants to fight not the Alliance, not the Central Government and not UMNO. By a process of elimination, it leaves only the MCA and MIC and your guess is as good as mine". Tan declared that the PAP's intention was "absolutely clear": it wanted the destruction of the MCA although it did not have the "guts" to tell the truth. "We in the MCA accept this challenge because it is nothing less than a challenge to the MCA as to whether it is the PAP or the MCA that should represent the Chinese in Malaysia", he added.[73] UMNO's reading of the PAP's motives was not much different. "What the PAP really wants is to displace the MCA," the Tunku asserted.[74] "By trying to destroy the MCA which is a partner of the Alliance, they are in fact trying to destroy the Alliance," warned Abdul Rahman bin Talib, the Malaysian Minister of Health, "The PAP's motive is clear. They want to capture the Central Government by using the MCA as the scapegoat."[75] Its dark scheme, so the argument ran, was to "kill the MCA and later force UMNO to accept the PAP as a partner, or compel UMNO to work with it". And if the PAP succeeded in destroying the MCA, "it will no doubt later turn on UMNO itself".[76] For UMNO's Secretary-General, Syed Ja'afar Albar, the PAP move was tantamount to the declaration of "an open war".[77]

Tan's outburst brought a swift — and telling — riposte the following day from Rajaratnam: "If a token participation can destroy the MCA, the MCA must be shakier than we thought it was." Nor was it accurate to say that the PAP wanted to replace the MCA as the champion of the Chinese, as Tan had alleged. "Whether if this is the real choice … is a matter for debate," Rajaratnam asserted, "However, as a non-communal party, the PAP has not and never has, aspired for the leadership of any one community."[78] The Tunku's subsequent warning to the MCA two days later against taking a "chauvinistic line"[79] must have brought a cheer to the PAP, and prompted its chairman to press his plea for the need to remove communal thinking among political leaders. "We cannot depend forever upon communal parties playing a leading part in Malaysian politics because their influence will not unite the different races but constantly remind them of their racial separateness."[80] Elaborating on the PAP's reasons for contesting the elections, Toh expressed his hope that his party's entry would persuade the people to accept the PAP's non-communal doctrine:[81] "We have shown in Singapore that a non-communal party like the PAP can govern effectively in a multiracial society."[82]

The PAP lost no time in moving its gears into election mode. Adding urgency was the Election Commission's announcement on 2 March that nomination day had been fixed on 21 March and polling day on 25 April.[83]

Two days later, Toh himself spearheaded a PAP vanguard to Kuala Lumpur, comprising three other ministers — Rajaratnam, Ong Pang Boon and Othman Wok, all apparently closely associated with the interventionist wing of the PAP CEC — to set the PAP election machinery in motion. A strong hint that Lee might campaign personally for the PAP candidates in Malaya was dropped on 9 March when the PAP announced that it was postponing the Singapore premier's constituency tours of the island "until the election campaign is over".[84] With the notification of the party's official registration the following day, 10 March,[85] the way was finally clear for the PAP to establish branches throughout Malaya. Anxious at the same time to allay fresh fears of PAP political ambitions, and as an indication of how the PAP had Malaysian interests at heart, and was cooperating with Kuala Lumpur, Rajaratnam highlighted, as an example, Lee's impending trip to galvanize support for Malaysia in the United States and the United Nations at the request of the Tunku: "We need Mr Lee Kuan Yew for the coming General Elections, but he has been assigned for a very important task in the United States. The PAP is prepared to allow him to go on this tour in the interests of the nation."[86]

Rajaratnam's remarks had the opposite effect on Kuala Lumpur. Alliance leaders saw no reason to continue to let the PAP profit politically at the Alliance's expense. The Tunku promptly cancelled Lee's trip. Timed just a day after Lee had announced it, there was little doubt in Gilstrap's mind at least that the object was not only to "humiliate Lee" and "deny him [the] center stage he would have enjoyed at the UN and Washington, and which would have profited [the] PAP in [the] elections", but also to "serve to remind many Malay voters of his distrust of PAP".[87] American Ambassador James Bell's own reading was not much different. He saw the hand of other UMNO party leaders behind the Tunku's decision. They had possibly "brought pressure to bear on Tunku to call off sending Lee to [the] US". Recalling that Syed Ja'afar had earlier opposed Lee's appointment to lead the Truth Mission to Africa, Bell noted that "Lee was sent despite this protest and his subsequent triumphant return from [the] African mission no doubt proved galling for Ja'afar and others ... [It is] conceivable they have now convinced Tunku [that] it is not helping the Alliance any in the coming elections to add more to Lee's prestige by sending him to lay Malaysia's case before the US and the UN."[88] Unfazed, Lee accepted that, in foreign relations, he abided by the Tunku's instructions. In private, Lee confided more philosophically to Gilstrap that "such developments are perhaps to be expected in politics."[89] Up to that point, in view of his mission to the US, Lee had refrained from commenting publicly on the April elections. Now, he was under no such constraints.

"The Winds of Change"

It was the Tunku who fired the first shot, on the day after he had called off Lee's mission, when he launched the Alliance election campaign with a rally in Serdang Bahru. Accusing the PAP of trying to supplant the MCA and to align itself with UMNO, the Tunku declared, to loud cheers, "But we don't want them"[90] and pledged to stand solidly by the MCA "even if the MCA were left with only five members".[91]

The next day, Lee Kuan Yew broke his silence and, like the Tunku, he too set the tone for his party's campaign. "[I]f nothing else," Lee asserted, "our enlightened self-interest demands that we should do nothing to hinder or embarrass the present Malay leadership of the Tengku and Tun Razak" because the alternative Malay leadership represented in the PMIP and SF would "drag Malaysia into Indonesia". So while the Malay leadership of the Tunku and Tun Razak was "vital" to Malaysia, that of the Chinese leadership in the Alliance, represented by the MCA, was "replaceable".[92]

But barely had Lee warmed up when his electioneering plans were suddenly placed in jeopardy by a ruling on 18 March from the chairman of the Federal Elections Commission, Haji Mustapha Albakri, inspired by a comment from Mohammed Khir Johari, the Malaysian Minister of Agriculture and Cooperatives, earlier in the day, stating that it was "illegal" for any non-Federal citizen to campaign in the election.[93] Mustapha's decision would have excluded Lee and other PAP luminaries who were Singapore citizens from campaigning for the party's candidates and seriously affected the PAP's plans for its first major rally in Kuala Lumpur, in four days' time, featuring Lee as its keynote speaker. Recalling that Khir Johari himself had campaigned on behalf of the SA in the September 1963 elections in Singapore, Rajaratnam shot back, "The law on this matter is clear. It is that we can campaign in the Federation".[94] As the American Ambassador learned from a source in the Election Commission, the chairman's ruling was apparently challenged by the Federal Attorney-General who accepted that Singapore citizens were, indeed, disallowed by law from standing as mainland candidates but disagreed that they were also prohibited from engaging in electioneering activities. "As of late this morning," Bell cabled Washington on 19 March, "difference not resolved and EC officer said AG considering issuing public statement setting forth his contrary opinion re Commissioner's ruling".[95] As it turned out, Mustapha was in error and reversed his decision the day after he had made his remarks. Wanting to give him the benefit of a doubt, Bell surmised that Mustapha's interpretation was probably based on a genuine misreading of the law.[96] Lee, however, was not so sure: "It is one thing getting the election fever on the eve of nomination, but it is another thing altogether to start tinkering with the basic political rights of Malaysian citizens guaranteed in the constitution and the Malaysia Act."[97]

On 19 March, the PAP unveiled its election manifesto, which rehearsed the two reasons for its participation: first, a long-term objective to build a united, democratic, socialist, and non-communal Malaysia; second, a more immediate objective to ensure that the SF did not benefit from the "substantial protest votes" against the MCA, and inadvertently send the wrong signals to both Indonesia ("as support for Indonesia's 'crush Malaysia' policy") and the United States (as confirming the need to "sacrifice Malaysia's interests to placate President Sukarno and so save Indonesia from communism"). Given the ineffectiveness of the MCA in rallying the masses in the urban areas, so the argument ran, the PAP had to help in the battle against the SF. It, therefore, urged the people in the urban areas to vote for PAP candidates and, where there were no PAP candidates, to vote instead for "pro-Malaysia opposition party candidates".[98] The PAP's call immediately provoked the Alliance to reply with a fighting statement of its own the next day decrying the so-called protest votes as a "myth created by the PAP" and condemning the PAP's call to vote for pro-Malaysia opposition parties as clear proof that the PAP was an "anti-Alliance Party", whose real purpose was to "break the unity of the Alliance Party by attacking one partner ... and praising the other", a tactic which it asserted would not succeed: "UMNO regards any attack on any of its partners as an attack on itself".[99] As Critchley commented, "Almost all Alliance leaders, including those in UMNO, were angry with Lee for introducing what they regarded as a red herring into an election fought on the issue of 'national survival'."[100]

On nomination day, 21 March, only the Alliance contested all the 104 Parliament and 282 State Assembly seats at stake. The SF fielded candidates in most states but concentrated them mainly in the west coast urban areas. Most of the PMIP candidates contested in the predominantly Malay areas of Kelantan, Trengganu, Kedah, Perlis, and north Perak and parts of Pahang. The United Democratic Party (UDP), contesting the elections for the first time, focused on Penang and Perak, whilst the People's Progressive Party (PPP) in urban areas in Perak, and the Partai Negara (PN) confined itself to Trengganu. Despite rumours that the PAP would put up as many as 30 parliamentary candidates, the party chose only 11 parliamentary and 15 state seats to be contested by its 17 candidates, mostly on selected urban constituencies on the west coast, a "token" engagement, as the PAP earlier stated its intention to be.[101] Even so, after it was learnt that two of its men were running against UMNO instead of MCA candidates, the PAP immediately withdrew them from the contest, keeping faith with its promise not to challenge UMNO.[102] As Rajaratnam further assured the latter, "17 persons certainly cannot destroy any party in the election". He added: "The real reason we are coming here is to carry on the fight for Malaysia, which was started and completed as far as Singapore was concerned in the last general elections, where the anti-Malaysia forces have been defeated and contained."[103]

That there was a "grander design"[104] behind this new phase of the PAP's "fight for Malaysia" was revealed by Lee the next day. On the evening of 22 March, the PAP launched its campaign "in a blaze of publicity",[105] with its first mass rally at Suleiman Court in Kuala Lumpur "drawing some 20,000 people, said to be unprecedented for the mainland".[106] A three-minute standing ovation greeted Lee Kuan Yew when he rose to speak at 9 p.m. Lee's clarion call was for change — radical change to put into practice a "forward-looking social and economic policy" designed to "close the gaps between the 'have' and the 'have-nots'" and "blow out the growing evils of greed and graft". A victory for the nine PAP parliamentary candidates, Lee declared, would signal to UMNO that the people in the towns wanted "honest government with a dynamic social and economic policy" and propel UMNO leaders who "not unnaturally may prefer to carry on as before if all can be well" to make "inevitable adjustments" that would lead to a "social revolution" in Malaya. "[T]hen," Lee added, borrowing a phrase from Harold Macmillan[107] — "the winds of change will begin to sweep throughout Malaysia." And if the change began in 1964, Lee said that there would be less of a drastic upheaval than if the change was made in 1969: "Everybody knows that the election this year is really the preliminary of the elections in 1969. If it is possible to get the winds of change to blow in gently this year, so much less of an upset it will be all round in 1969".[108]

If Lee had expected to get a rational and stimulating debate on the merits of social and economic change as an intelligent means to combat communism in the towns, as he later said he had hoped, he was sorely disappointed.[109] His talk of change and social revolution had struck at the very heart of the conservative and communally-organized Alliance, and provoked instead a sharp response. No less prominent a leader than Tun Razak locked horns with Lee the next day, and declared that Malaya's "social evolution" was more desirable than Lee's social revolution. Under Alliance stewardship, as Tun Razak was wont to argue, the "terrific winds of change" had already been sweeping Malaya and only the Alliance could guarantee the present racial harmony in Malaya. But nervous, at the same time, about the impact of the PAP's populist appeals on his own Malay rural base, even Tun Razak was not averse to playing on their communal fears and dutifully warned the Malays of Lee's sincerity towards them.[110] Tun Razak's racially accented remarks were unacceptable to Lee — certainly not when the Malays in Singapore, from Lee's perspective, were convinced of the PAP's sincerity and had voted in PAP candidates in the last election. "Time alone will tell how sincere we are," the Singapore premier retorted, "It took us some time to convince the 200,000 Malays in Singapore of the PAP's sincerity." And in a more belligerent vein, he added: "I do not think it will be all that difficult to convince the three million Malays in Malaya. Even the most sceptical will take us for what we stand for — a united, democratic and socialist Malaysia, a society more just and more equal."[111] If Lee had not said so before, he had, at least in UMNO's reckoning, openly implied it now: in time, the PAP was also confident of winning over even the Malays in Malaya, as it had succeeded in Singapore, a prospect UMNO found totally unacceptable.

UMNO quite naturally read Lee's latest remarks as a veiled threat to undermine its own Malay power base, and confirmed what it had long presumed, that, notwithstanding the token nature of its challenge, the PAP was fast emerging as a serious potential political contender, if also a dangerous enemy, not only to the MCA but also to UMNO itself. Indeed, as an American Embassy assessment later revealed, "Significant numbers of Malays have turned out for the [PAP] rallies … and the young seem uniformly enthusiastic over Lee Kuan Yew."[112]

A vigorous response to nip the PAP challenge in the bud was called for, and the Alliance leaders left little doubt that it intended to go all out in its campaign against the PAP, even if that meant invoking the dangerous weapon of stoking communal passions to turn the Malay ground against the PAP, a stratagem which certain extremist UMNO campaigners, and "in particular the fiery Syed Ja'afar Albar", seemed all too eager to endorse. In the Australian

High Commissioner's words, "[They] played hard on Malay fears of this allegedly unknown and untrustworthy Chinese group from Singapore."[113] They were determined in particular to demolish the PAP's premise that it had the willing support of the Malays in Singapore. SUMNO's deputy chairman, Ahmad bin Haji Taff, for instance, was immediately enlisted to warn Malays not to be deceived by PAP promises. "There may be a few Malay Ministers and other officials of the PAP who are quite happy," Ahmad said on 25 March, "but the rest of the Malay community in Singapore are very much frustrated."[114] On the same day, UMNO's Secretary-General, Syed Ja'afar Albar, also slammed Lee's claim to Malay support, and insisted that the PAP's victorious Malay candidates in the last Singapore elections benefited more from non-Malay votes than from Malay ones. As proof of the defeated SUMNO candidates' widespread support from the Malay community, Syed Ja'afar pointed to the fact that none of them lost their deposits. After accusing the PAP of treating Malay civil servants in Singapore like "step-sons", he said that Lee was in fact "so contemptuous of the Malays that his Government refused to appoint any Malay to serve on statutory bodies in Singapore."[115] In a further attempt to blacken the populist attractions of the PAP's democratic socialism to Malays, Syed Ja'afar sarcastically questioned the Singapore premier's claim to be a socialist "just because he shouts socialist slogans and just because he builds a few Malay secondary schools which produced 100 per cent failures in the recent Malayan secondary schools' examination". Why would Lee not say he would nationalize factories and industries in Singapore? "[W]hile Lee talks glibly about winds of change in Malaya, in his own backyard he not only protects but also promotes capitalism," he charged. Questioning Lee's definition of social revolution, Syed Ja'afar next hinted that the PAP was actually out to get rid of the Sultans, something Lee later protested he had never said:[116] "Revolutionary manuals are very precise in defining social revolution and it implies direct confrontation with the established political, economic and cultural order. Does Lee, therefore, advocate the eventual disappearance of the Sultans of Malaysia?" He hoped that the Malays did not take Lee literally when he talked about revolution. The UMNO leader adumbrated, "Revolution is gory and bloody business. This is highly dangerous talk and the way he is talking now ... may spark off communal tension between Malays and Chinese".[117] Syed Ja'afar's remarks on Sino-Malay tensions were a warning — and a threat — to Lee to lay off UMNO's Malay preserve.

Not wishing to be baited to fight UMNO, Lee had refrained from replying, he scoffed instead at the "unthinking and unintelligent" MCA.

And in Malacca the following day, Lee hit out at Tan Siew Sin, "the man with the silver spoon", for proposing financial policies that favoured the haves rather than the have-nots.[118] But Lee's political foes made sure that controversy continued to stalk the Singapore premier, this time by attributing to him, falsely in the latter's own reckoning, certain disparaging remarks he allegedly made about the Tunku while campaigning in Seremban, during which he was supposed to have imputed in Chinese, as the Tunku disclosed at a rally at Suleiman Court in Kuala Lumpur on 28 March, "that I have not the calibre to lead the nation." "Should the Prime Minister of Singapore belong to a party opposed to Malaysia, I could understand his criticism," the Tunku said, sounding "very hurt".[119] If Lee's enemies had wanted to drive a wedge between the Tunku and Lee, they could not have succeeded more famously. The Tunku, reacting to Lee's alleged remarks, closed ranks with the MCA: "If we sink, we sink together," he said. His attitude towards Lee and the PAP hardened considerably. Calling Lee's social revolution a "real threat to us all", the Tunku angrily blurted: "Unless all his past attitudes and conduct demonstrating a desperate desire to join Malaysia were merely a screen behind which he has fondly been nurturing other ambitions, it is strange that on the very morrow of Malaysia he has found so much that his itching hands would like to pull down and rebuild."[120] Adding that the PAP had a record of stabbing its friends in the back, Tan Siew Sin, who spoke after the Tunku, opined that it was "far safer to be their enemy than their friend" and concluded that the PAP was "a grave security risk to this country".[121]

Lee, who had a useful exchange with the Tunku only two days before on the future of Malaysia, was saddened that the Malaysian premier should accuse him of running him down in Chinese, the implication being that, first, "we are a deceitful people who say one thing in Chinese and a different thing in English and Malay", and, that, second, "although I had said so often publicly that the UMNO leadership is irreplaceable, off the record in Chinese I have contradicted this by saying this leadership is not of the right calibre". Blaming the Tunku's so-called "friends" for falsely attributing to him words he did not say, Lee angrily retorted that MCA propagandists "should credit us with enough intelligence to know that taking two different lines in two different languages is the surest way to discredit ourselves".[122] His harshest words were reserved for the MCA leader: "[T]o project the PAP as a security threat to the country more grave than the threat from the communists in the SF shows an imbalance of judgment of a magnitude to qualify its author for admission to an asylum for the politically insane."[123]

With the gloves off, the ensuing battle was a bruising one for all, not least for the PAP, forced to fend off a series of racist allegations from both MCA and UMNO leaders. Not only did Tan Siew Sin repeat Lee's disparagement of the Tunku,[124] and added how the remarks blatantly revealed the Singapore premier's "not ... high opinion of the Malays or their leaders", but he also accused the PAP of now recklessly stirring the fires of racism by working on communal feelings,[125] championing the urban Chinese against the rural Malays and "gunning for the special position of the Malays":[126]

> In its attempt to woo the Chinese community, the PAP could well create the impression among the Malays that a large section of our community is not really sincere in its expressed desire to achieve cooperation and understanding with them. The Malays, from the Tengku downwards, feel strongly that the retention of this special position is their only hope of survival. The Tengku himself has stated repeatedly that he and his people regard agreement on this question as the acid test of our sincerity towards the Malays. Any erosion of this principle could make the Malays desperate and you know, as well as I do, what desperate people can resort to.[127]

Lee's alleged "thoughtless criticism" of the Tunku was also seized upon by Syed Ja'afar as further proof that the Singapore premier was "anything but a friend of the Tunku",[128] and by attempting to smash the MCA, the PAP was also threatening UMNO–MCA unity and putting at risk Sino-Malay friendship. He said: "I warn the PAP not to destroy this partnership and hence racial harmony and Sino-Malay friendship in Malaysia."[129] Disclosing that he had received many letters from Malays in Singapore complaining of their dismal plight under the PAP, Syed Ja'afar warned that, although the Malays were tolerant, there was a limit to their patience.[130] He advised the PAP to stop antagonizing the Malays, "Otherwise, the Malays will throw democracy overboard and start using fists to teach the PAP democracy."[131]

Even the more moderate UMNO leaders like Tun Razak and the Minister for Internal Security, Ismail bin Abdul Rahman, who had earlier stayed above the fray, closed ranks to attack the PAP. Repeating his doubts about the "sincerity of the PAP towards the Malays",[132] Tun Razak accused the PAP of being guilty of a new type of communalism when it tried to drive a wedge between the urban and rural peoples[133] and warned that should the PAP come into power it would only divide the country as it would not get the support of the Malays.[134] The PAP was not "helping the Tunku, me or the Malays or the State by participating in the 1964 polls", he emphasized: every vote against the Alliance was a vote for Sukarno.[135] Ismail, on his part, regretted that "so brilliant" a man as Lee should "make such mistakes as to disturb racial harmony, encourage anti-Malaysia parties and further Sukarno's policy of confrontation":

> If you have been persuaded by Mr Lee that he can bring the winds of change into this country as he has done in Singapore, then you must think again. The winds of change as promised by Mr Lee can't take place in this election for the simple reason that the PAP, with a token number of candidates, can never form a government, and UMNO, which Mr Lee says will win, has refused to form a coalition government. Let the winds of change come in 1969. It does not matter if in 1969, as Mr Lee predicted, they come with a drastic upheaval.[136]

The PAP deplored the "crudely communal"[137] nature of the attacks and hit back at the MCA for "striving to retrieve their waning political fortunes by spreading mischievous falsehood in order to create ill-will between the Malays and a non-communal PAP".[138] As Devan Nair, the PAP candidate contesting the constituency of Bungsar, put it: "We in the PAP are well aware that the desperate men of the MCA are getting certain Malay leaders to attack the PAP on their behalf, so that this election campaign would become a verbal slanging between the PAP and UMNO."[139] On the charge of Lee bad-mouthing the Tunku in Seremban, Rajaratnam challenged the MCA leaders, if they were politically honest, to "play back the recording" of Lee's speech and dispose of the matter once and for all.[140] Accusing the MCA instead of championing the communal line that "only Chinese should lead the Chinese", Rajaratnam stressed that the PAP's analysis of Malaysian society in terms of urban and rural population was a social and political one, transcending racial divisions: "The MCA has failed to realize this. It lays emphasis on the racial divisions and treats economic divisions as of secondary importance."[141] Brushing aside another Alliance insinuation, Lee Kuan Yew rebutted that the PAP had never questioned Malay rights in the Constitution in any rally.[142] "Whatever our faults," Lee said, "it is not communalism nor chauvinism … Our sin, it would appear, is to be able to muster a following in the urban areas which includes a large bulk of the Chinese."[143] And as far as the

PAP's record towards the Malays was concerned, Lee had this to say: "In Singapore, where the Malay vote is only 15 per cent, we have honoured Malay rights and given all Malays free education from primary to university level — something the Central Government cannot do."[144] That the PAP was confident of withstanding the challenge to its ideological integrity was clear from the remarks of the Deputy Director of the party's political bureau, Lee Khoon Choy: "We are content to let the three million Malays of Malaya take time over the next five years to judge the sincerity of the People's Action Party. We have done our duty to the people of Singapore, especially the Malay community. They are the final judges."[145]

Quite so. The PAP, in any case, expected to do well. Pritchett observed, for instance, that the PAP leaders "were delighted with their reception and more than ever convinced that there was a strong feeling of discontent and protest against the Alliance that was finding expression in support for the PAP."[146] In fact, so confident was Rajaratnam of the PAP's good showing that he summarily dismissed a boast by MCA leader Lee San Choon about how his party would thrash the PAP with the equally spirited riposte that Lee was entitled to his "share of famous last words — which is what his prophecy about the MCA thrashing the PAP amounts to".[147] Indeed, barely a week into the campaigning and Rajaratnam was already predicting that the MCA was "out of the running" and destined to be further "reduced to a side attraction" by the end of the campaigning period.[148] Lee Kuan Yew, on his part, had also suggested that, notwithstanding the fact that the Tunku had said "many unnecessary things" about the PAP out of pique, he believed that, after the heat of battle had worn off, the Tunku and the other UMNO leaders would review the situation and accept the PAP's sincerity in wanting to cooperate with them.[149] The fate of a country, Lee explained, did not depend on personal likes or dislikes, or upon statements made before or during elections, but upon basic political factors: "It does not matter whether I like the Tengku or if he likes me. The Tengku represents the mass of the Malay rural people. We have to deal with him politely and courteously and offer our help to build a prosperous and preferably equal Malaysia." If the MCA could not hold the urban population, Lee argued, "the choice before UMNO is to govern without the support of the towns or come to terms with groups which can."[150]

Lee was also not particularly perturbed by the communalist pressures that were building up, believing these to be, as reported by Pritchett, "either the work of extremists or a tactic of despair by those threatened with destruction" and with little effect either on the rural Malay mass, whose vote the PAP was not competing for, or on the urban Malay, who was "more sophisticated and not so easily taken in".[151] Lee believed that the communalist agitation could instead rebound to the PAP's advantage, as people were saying that "if this is the reaction when somebody stands up for us a bit, then let's get behind a good tough party that will know how to protect us". Lee expected communalism to lose its importance "with the play of other social forces as the new society took shape". In his mind, these social pressures had to be "canalized or there would be trouble". The PAP had "come in none too early," he felt. "Tremendous pressures have built up. It's frightening. Singapore in 1959 all over again." Like Lee, Goh Keng Swee also professed himself "undisturbed" by the communal politicking and dismissed the recent attacks by Tun Razak as "the heat of the battle", although he confided several times to Pritchett that "we could all go up in flames" and saw the importance of both sides working together.[152] The Singapore leaders' confidence, Pritchett noted, was reflected in "their expectations of office in the new government, which, I understand, had their basis also in approaches by Federal Ministers during the campaign." They were very confident of winning at least five of the seats they were contesting. Such a margin, confided PAP stalwart, E.W. Barker, would be regarded by party leaders as a "victory" for the PAP.[153]

At least five out of its nine token parliamentary seats were also what the American Embassy felt the PAP must win to "make a meaningful Malaysia-wide political impact" from its maiden venture.[154] Numerous sources had already attested to widespread potential support for the PAP on the mainland, noted Robert W. Moore, the embassy's First Secretary: "Lee Kuan Yew's attractiveness as a leader and the PAP's image as a dynamic, young, progressive yet not too radical party, have infected not only numerous young Chinese but a significant scattering of young Malays on the mainland as well."[155] The drawing power which the Singapore premier and the PAP demonstrated at rallies "can only be attributed in part to curiosity," added Arthur H. Rosen, the American Consul in Singapore: "The younger Chinese, who might be attracted to the Socialist Front in protest against the 'minority mentality' of the MCA which he feels is content to leave the Chinese 'a second class citizen', may well find the PAP combination of aggressiveness, self-confidence and youthful vigour highly appealing. This, at least, is what the PAP is counting on."[156] Heralding the PAP's entry as posing "the most significant new element in mainland politics", Moore also opined that a "sufficiently significant showing by the PAP in the elections, particularly if juxtaposed against a poor MCA performance as predicted by the PAP, could have far-reaching implications for Malaysia's future internal political power structure." But whilst predicting that the PAP would do well enough to establish its credibility, Moore did not think that the PAP would win as many House seats as people had expected, for three reasons: one, "as a last minute entry the PAP ha[d] not had time to build effective local party organizations"; two, the MCA was being "swiftly and unequivocally backed by its other Alliance partners", the Tunku in particular, against the PAP's challenge; and, three, the MCA was a wealthy and influential party and had demonstrated "unfathomable staying-power in past challenges and crises".[157]

The Alliance also expected to do well. Campaigning on the theme of safeguarding national unity, progress and racial harmony in the face of Indonesian aggression, the party warned of domestic chaos should the electorate fail to return the Alliance to power. It accused its two main opponents, the SF and the PMIP, against whom its aggressive campaign was largely directed, of working hand-in-glove with the Jakarta regime, and would sell Malaysia out to Sukarno.[158] At the same time, facing a divided opposition and with the token nature of the PAP challenge, Moore had little doubt that the latter would be "returned to power in ten of the eleven states and will win about the same number of Parliament seats it previously held, with an outside chance of picking up a few more seats due to vicissitudes associated with 'confrontation'".[159] Significantly, by the latter weeks of the campaign, as Moore noted, the Alliance directed but little of its effort against the PAP, concentrating almost entirely on the SF and the PMIP — "an indication perhaps that Alliance soundings showed then what was to come".[160]

The Brink of Defeat

Robert Moore's prognosis was not off the mark, as the balloting results on 25 April 1964 revealed. Over 77 per cent of the electorate went to the polls to return the ruling Alliance Party to power in a stunning landslide victory. Losing none of the House seats it held before Parliament was prorogued, the Alliance made a clean sweep of every one of the parliamentary seats at stake in Johore, Negri Sembilan, Malacca, Pahang, Kedah and Perlis, and achieved clear majorities in Penang, Perak, Selangor and Trengganu, winning altogether 89 out of the 104 seats, 15 more than in 1959. In the state elections, the Alliance, having taken 240 of the 282 seats, an increase of 75 over its 1959 record, retained control of 10 of the 11 states, winning all of the Assembly seats in Johore, Negri Sembilan, Pahang and Kedah, and more than two-thirds majorities in all of the other states, except Kelantan where it failed to unseat the PMIP although it increased its seats there from 2 to 9 out of the total of 30. The opposition parties, in contrast, fared dismally, winning only 15 of 182 parliamentary and 42 of 486 state seats contested, down from the 1959 figures of 30 and 75 seats respectively. The SF lost heavily. Rooting for 63 parliamentary and 167 state constituencies, it took only 2 parliamentary and 7 state seats, a "near-annihilation"[161] compared to the 8 and 16 respective seats it won in 1959. The PMIP thwarted the Alliance's all-out campaign to unseat it from power in Kelantan but suffered losses across the board elsewhere, and emerged with only 9 parliamentary seats (8 in Kelantan and 1 in Trengganu, 3 less than it previously held), from the 54 wards contested. Of the 158 state constituencies where its candidates fought, the party was victorious in only 25 (all but 4 of them in Kelantan), and lost control of the Trengganu state government which it had previously held. Losing 3 of its former seats to the Alliance, the PPP which fielded 9 parliamentary candidates, won only 2 seats in Ipoh — those of the two brothers who led the party, D.R. and S.P. Seenivasagam. Five of the 19 state seats it won were all in Perak. Neither the Partai Negara, fighting only in Trengganu, nor the independents won even a single seat. The UDP, which ran in 27 parliamentary and 65 state wards succeeded only in electing its Secretary-General and former MCA president, Lim Chong Eu, to the Dewan Ra'ayat, and Lim and three other candidates to Penang's State Assembly. As the Election Commissioner confided to the American ambassador, the UDP forfeited enough deposits to "underwrite [the] whole election's expenses".[162]

The PAP's own token venture was also, in Bell's words, an "unrelieved disaster",[163] its "almost complete rout"[164] hardly redeemed by the single win eked out by its Bungsar candidate, Devan Nair, who won narrowly by 808 votes. Worse still, 6 PAP parliamentary and 8 state candidates suffered the further humiliation of losing their deposits by failing to take more than one-eighth of the votes cast in their constituencies. "The rejection of the PAP was a surprise to many," wrote Critchley, not least to the PAP leaders themselves, who received the news with shock dismay.[165] Rajaratnam simply refused to believe the results:[166] how, for example, could the party poll 733 votes in Johore, where it had withdrawn its candidate and made not one campaign speech,[167] and only 778 in

Penang, where it had campaigned intensively and drawn large crowds? The rank and file were "incredulous", Goh Keng Swee confided to Pritchett.[168] Toh Chin Chye too was "disappointed".[169] So was Lee Kuan Yew but his consolation was that the results "could not have been better for international effect. No Government in the world can now doubt that Malaysia is the free will of its people".[170] Congratulating the Tunku on his resounding victory, Lee sought to patch up with the Alliance leader: "Whatever our party differences, you can count upon us to support you on all national issues."[171] But it was a forlorn gesture, coming, as it was, from the brink of defeat.

What happened to the PAP? Without doubt, the Alliance's success in making *Konfrontasi* (confrontation) the principal issue in the elections played no small part in the PAP's fall. In Critchley's view, "The main reason for MCA success can be given in one word — Indonesia."[172] *Konfrontasi* lent force to the Alliance presentation of the elections as a test of loyalty, especially to the non-Malays, and that a vote against the ruling party at the time of crisis was disloyalty to the nation. As the Minister for Internal Security, Ismail, revealed: "We scared the Chinese voters so much (with our heavy emphasis on Indonesian confrontation) that they did not dare vote for anyone except the MCA. If it had not been for confrontation, Lee Kuan Yew would have won all nine seats he contested".[173] Lee would probably not disagree. For both national (*Konfrontasi*) and party (PAP–UMNO relations) reasons, the PAP had sought to back the Tunku while simultaneously seeking to attract support from the MCA to itself, a tactic Lee regretted as being too subtle: "Since we said 'Back the Tengku' and since the Tengku said 'Back all my colleagues in the MCA and MIC', we had to accept this situation [failure] arising".[174] Indeed, if the voters were being urged to give a solid national vote, why should they vote for the few candidates from an "outsider" Singapore party, whose relations with the Alliance were at the very least doubtful, in a House likely to be dominated by the latter?[175] "Why not vote directly for the Tunku? Why vote for him *through* Lee Kuan Yew?" ran a typical query.[176] Even the PAP rank and file were confused. Pritchett reported that the PAP leaders saw that the main reasons for their failure were that they had been in the first place "their own destroyers".[177]

Another reason lay in the PAP's misjudgement of the character of the electorate, and its assessment of the level of its dissatisfaction with the MCA. The PAP, for one, as Rosen noted, had accepted without question the "major myth" that the MCA had lost its influence in the urban areas[178] and invariably also believed, as Critchley put it, "their own propaganda about the 'irreversible' trend against the MCA, about the support they would get from the allegedly sophisticated urban Malays, and — especially — about their urban 'social revolution'."[179] The truth was, as Robert Moore pointed out, the "young voters apparently did not flock to the PAP's banner in the numbers one might have expected from the consistently heavy turnout of young people at Lee Kuan Yew's rallies."[180] And while many of the older folks believed that what Lee said made sense, they preferred to "just stick with the Tunku and the Alliance". The opinion generally held was that Lee Kuan Yew was really just preparing for five years hence, when the real challenge for power would come.[181] Additionally, in Critchley's view, the pragmatic Chinese voter "may not have greatly admired the MCA, but he wanted a Chinese at the Tunku's side and the MCA provided the means of achieving this. If he did not particularly like voting for the MCA, he wanted to vote for the Tunku."[182] According to M.W.B. Smithies (Second Secretary, Australian High Commission, Kuala Lumpur), the sophisticated "intellectual" quality in Lee's campaign, which limited its appeal to a minority in the electorate, probably did not help either,[183] a point reinforced by PAP stalwart Jek Yeun Thong's comment that "something more simple might have been more effective".[184] As Moore observed, facing external threats and nervous about the ever present danger of internal racial disharmony, the electorate, revealing itself as inherently conservative in nature, "rallied massively to the banner of the status quo" instead.[185] Indeed, according to *The Times*, the results showed "that in Malaya, voters have preferred the Alliance for stability against the People's Action Party just as in Singapore they chose the People's Action Party against the Alliance for the same reason."[186] In Pritchett's report, Lee Kuan Yew's own post-mortem pointed to the possibility of having misjudged the character of the electorate, which was more lower-middle class than those in Singapore, and he had now become less certain about the "dissatisfaction … he was so emphatic during the election campaign [that] was carrying the PAP to victory". While Goh Keng Swee was "certainly now inclined to scepticism", other PAP leaders whom Pritchett interviewed, including Toh Chin Chye, Rajaratnam, and Jek Yeun Thong, however, took the view that discontent was certainly still there, though "only temporarily submerged" by the national spirit generated in the election campaign.[187]

In failing to read the ground accurately, the PAP leaders' certitude in their own ability to deliver the *coup de grace* to the MCA probably blinded them to a contrary prognosis. As Critchley commented: "Success in the Singapore elections against the MCA apparently gave the PAP a false sense of confidence. They appear to believe that they could move into urban areas of Malaya at — literally — the drop of a hat, and ... have the urban electors falling over each other in the rush to vote for the PAP".[188] In their post-mortem, party leaders admitted as much, and, as reported by Pritchett, had recognized that it would have been "a remarkable achievement to have walked into Malaya and simply picked up four or five seats almost solely on the strength of its Singapore reputation":

> The leaders I have spoken with believe that their lack of a party organization, their failure to prepare and distribute information about their views and programme and to start working for support for them much earlier, as well as their hasty and sometimes unfortunate selection of candidates all contributed to their failure.[189]

While funding was not a problem, with the bulk coming from Singapore so as "to avoid obligations and political embarrassment",[190] organizationally, the PAP was unprepared. It had no headquarters or branches in Malaya until the decision to contest the elections was made. In certain wards, branches were only found after nomination day. Most of its campaign workers had come from Singapore, with the drawback of their "unfamiliarity ... with local geography and communities, which handicapped canvassing."[191]

In defeat, nevertheless, the PAP claimed it "played no small part"[192] to "generating a tidal wave of patriotism"[193] behind the Tunku, leading to the Alliance's resounding victory[194] and its rout of the SF. "In the process, however, we ourselves were sacrificed," rationalized Toh Chin Chye.[195] By engaging the Alliance, and challenging it to debate the party's economic and social agenda, the PAP felt it had also made another important advance. At the very least, as both Rajaratnam and Barker intimated, the party was now launched as a national party and, in Devan Nair, their one successful candidate, the PAP had a "toehold".[196]

Useful as such rationalizations might be, by way of making the best of things, they did not conceal the fact that the PAP had, in Critchley's opinion, "made a big mistake in contesting these elections in the way they did."[197] As *The Times* leader put it, "Mr Lee Kuan Yew's People's Action Party might superficially reassure itself from these [election] figures that one candidate returned in nine was not bad. It was not good either."[198] Most damaging of all, the PAP's whole rationale for participating in the elections, and for its controversial foray into mainland politics (i.e. the Alliance needed PAP help), had been discredited. Not only had the MCA confounded its PAP detractors, it was also returned stronger than ever before, winning 27 of its allotted 33 parliamentary seats (an impressive 82 per cent win ratio over its 1959 performance of 61 per cent) and 65 of its 81 state wards, also improving its 1959 record considerably. And while UMNO increased its votes won by 43 per cent, the MCA topped it by a record 67 per cent, the biggest gain by any party in parliamentary elections.[200] Compared to the MCA's performance, the PAP's dismal failure, additionally, could only have further "reinforced UMNO's repudiation of any ties with Lee Kuan Yew's party in the foreseeable future."[199] As Pritchett commented, "Their hope, indicated clearly in several conversations, was to be offered Cabinet posts after the recent election and, by their victories at the polls and the prospect of more to come, to be in a position to bargain on this point. This hope has been dashed."[201] Worse still, having challenged and lost, the PAP now faced the ire of a politically-augmented, Alliance-dominated central government suitably placed to exercise its powers, should it desire to do so, to damage Singapore's interests. With its 89 parliamentary seats, the Alliance now controlled enough seats on the mainland alone to form an outright majority in the Dewan Ra'ayat. Together with the 37 from the allied parties in Sarawak and Sabah, the Alliance had a commanding 126 seats, 20 over a two-thirds majority, which would present no obstacle to the passage of either government legislation or constitutional amendments (requiring a two-thirds majority) presented by the latter. As Pritchett put it, "There is very extensive scope for the Federal government to work effectively against Singapore should it wish to." Citing one instance, the Australian Deputy High Commissioner reported how Tan Siew Sin, on the economic front, had, shortly after the elections, asserted privately that "the export levy on tin and other commodities would continue to apply to Singapore for many years — Singapore's industrialization had gone far enough."[202] On the "more dangerous" political front, the PAP was also "not free from worry on this score" as Kuala Lumpur was also well positioned to exert pressure by "seek[ing] to intervene in Singapore's state politics", after the PAP's own foray into the Federal fray, and threaten not only the PAP's ability to preserve its urban base in Singapore but also its political future and survival.[203] Already, John Jacob, the leader of the SMIC, was predicting that the Alliance's victory "will be reflected in the next general elections in Singapore":

[T]he Alliance is bound to score a mighty victory. I am certain of this because, unlike last time, the Alliance leaders in the Federation will not keep away from Singapore in the future. And when leaders like the Tunku campaign for the Alliance in Singapore, the Alliance's victory may be taken for granted.[204]

It was not a comforting thought, as the PAP pondered the future.

Notes

1. On 9 September 1963, Lee indicated that the PAP did not intend to enter the 1964 mainland elections but predicted MCA losses and the future necessity of UMNO and the PAP working together. A few weeks later, on 28 September 1963, Lee again declared: "We are not out to capture power in Kuala Lumpur. We will not take part in the 1964 elections in the Federation." Two days later, on 30 September 1963, in reply to a question of the PAP coming into the mainland, Lee replied: "I do not intend to start a branch in Kuala Lumpur and won't want to for quite a long time"; on 18 November 1963, Lee again "made clear that the PAP would not attempt to take part in the forthcoming federation elections in Malaya". See *The Straits Times*, 10 September 1963; *The Sunday Times*, 29 September 1963; *Straits Echo*, 1 October 1963; Telegram no. 52, Australian High Commission (Singapore) to Department of External Affairs, 22 November 1963, A1838/280 no. 3024/2/1 Part 12.
2. Telegram no. 291, Gilstrap to Secretary of State, 22 September 1963, RG 59 Box 3979 Pol 14.
3. Critchley to Menzies, 13 October 1963, A1838/280 no. 3024/2/4 Part 1.
4. Telegram no. 40, Australian High Commission (Singapore) to Department of External Affairs, 27 September 1963, A1838/280 no. 3024/2/4 Part 1.
5. Airgram no. 414, American Embassy (Kuala Lumpur) to Department of State, 17 January 1964, RG 59 Box 2456 Pol 16 1/1/64.
6. Telegram no. 291, Gilstrap to Secretary of State, 22 September 1963, RG 59 Box 3979 Pol 14.
7. Airgram no. 414, American Embassy (Kuala Lumpur) to Department of State, 17 January 1964, RG 59 Box 2456 Pol 16 1/1/64.
8. Critchley to Menzies, 13 October 1963, A1838/280 no. 3024/2/4 Part 1.
9. *The Straits Times*, 10 August 1962.
10. Ibid., 16 August 1962, cited in Charles Richard Ostrom, "A Core Interest Analysis of the Formation of Malaysia and the Separation of Singapore" (Unpublished PhD dissertation submitted to the Claremont Graduate School, 1970), p. 180.
11. *The Straits Times*, 31 July 1963.
12. *The Sunday Times*, 29 September 1963.
13. "Text of TV Interview by A. Kajapathy with Mr Lee Kuan Yew, Secretary General, People's Action Party", telecast on Channel 5 at 8 p.m., 9 April 1964, A1838/318 no. 3024/2/2/1 Part 1.
14. Telegram no. 49, Australian High Commission (Singapore) to Department of External Affairs, 14 November 1963, A1838/280 no. 3027/2/1 Part 18.
15. *Singapore Legislative Assembly Debates*, 29 November 1963, Col. 117–18.
16. Ibid., 9 December 1963, Col. 140.
17. Ibid., 9 December 1963, Col. 141.

18. W.B. Pritchett to Secretary, Department of External Affairs, 15 May 1964, A1838/280 no. 3027/2/1 Part 18.

19. Fong Sip Chee, _The PAP Story — The Pioneering Years_ (Singapore: PAP, 1979), p. 149.

20. _The Straits Times_, 3 March 1964.

21. Ibid., 18 April 1964.

22. Memorandum by Lee Kuan Yew to Publicity and Propaganda Coordinating Committee, 8 November 1963, PMO.

23. Memorandum by Lee Kuan Yew to Publicity and Propaganda Coordinating Committee, 25 October 1963, PMO.

24. Minutes by Moore, "Notes of Conversation between Lee Kuan Yew and Mr Moore held on 5th November, 1963", DO 169/20 no. 33/45/1.

25. Memorandum by Lee Kuan Yew to Publicity and Propaganda Coordinating Committee, 8 November 1963, PMO.

26. Minutes by Moore, "Notes of Conversation between Mr Lee Kuan Yew and Mr Moore held on 15th October, 1963", DO 169/20 no. 33/45/1.

27. Memorandum by Lee Kuan Yew to the Publicity and Propaganda Coordinating Committee, 25 October 1963, PMO.

28. Memorandum by Lee Kuan Yew to the Publicity and Propaganda Coordinating Committee, 8 November 1963, PMO.

29. Milton E. Osborne, _Singapore and Malaysia_. Data Paper No. 53 (Ithaca: Cornell University Southeast Asia Program Data Paper No. 53, 1964), p. 79.

30. _Singapore Legislative Assembly Debates_, 9 December 1963, Col. 141–42.

31. Osborne, _Singapore and Malaysia_, p. 79.

32. _The Malay Mail_, 24 December 1963.

33. _Straits Echo_, 24 December 1963.

34. _Malayan Times_, 18 January 1964.

35. _The Straits Times_, 18 January 1964.

36. "Minutes of the Meeting of the Publicity & Propaganda Coordinating Committee held on Monday, 20th January, 1964, at 12.15 p.m. in the Cabinet Room", PMO

37. Telegram no. 3, Australian High Commission (Singapore) to Department of External Affairs, 1 February 1964, A1838/280 no. 3024/2/1 Part 12.

38. Telegram no. 4, Australian High Commission (Singapore) to Department of External Affairs, 6 March 1964, A1838/280 no. 3024/2/1 Part 12.

39. Ibid.

40. T.K. Critchley to Secretary, Department of External Affairs, 11 March 1964, A1838/318 no. 3024/2/2/1 Part 1.

41. Speech by Lee Kuan Yew at the valedictory dinner on 22 August 1981 at the Istana, printed in _Petir_ (March 1982), p. 7.

42. T.K. Critchley to Secretary, Department of External Affairs, 11 March 1964, A1838/318 no. 3024/2/2/1 Part 1.

43. Lee Khoon Choy, _On the Beat to the Hustings: An Autobiography_ (Singapore: Times Books International, 1988), p. 75.

44. Minutes by Moore, "Notes of Conversation between Lee Kuan Yew and Mr Moore held on 5th November, 1963", DO 169/20 no. 33/45/1.

45. Pang Cheng Lian, _Singapore's People's Action Party: Its History, Organization and Leadership_ (Singapore: Oxford University Press, 1971), p. 18.

46. Telegram no. 172, Australian High Commission (Singapore) to Department of External Affairs, 2 March 1964, A1838/318 no. 3024/2/2/1 Part 1.

47. Airgram no. 276, American Consulate (Singapore) to Department of State, 16 April 1964, RG 59 Box 2453 Pol 12 1/1/64.

48. Lee, *On the Beat to the Hustings: An Autobiography*, p. 75.

49. *Malayan Times*, 18 March 1964.

50. Telegram no. 293, Australian High Commission (Kuala Lumpur) to Department of External Affairs, 28 February 1964, A1838/318 no. 3024/2/2/1 Part 1.

51. Ibid.

52. Telegram no. 172, Australian High Commission (Singapore) to Department of External Affairs, 2 March 1964, A1838/318 no. 3024/2/2/1 Part 1.

53. Ibid.

54. The Yang di-Pertuan Agong's declaration was carried in a Gazette Extraordinary published the day before stating that Parliament would be prorogued on 1 March 1964.

55. *The Straits Times*, 2 March 1964.

56. Ibid.

57. *Malayan Times*, 2 March 1964.

58. *The Straits Times*, 2 March 1964.

59. Ibid., 3 March 1964.

60. Ibid.

61. Ibid., 2 March 1964.

62. *Malayan Times*, 2 March 1964.

63. Ibid., 4 March 1964.

64. Ibid., 2 March 1964.

65. Airgram no. 236, American Consulate (Singapore) to Department of State, 8 March 1964, RG 59 Box 2453 Pol 12 1/1/64.

66. T.K. Critchley to Secretary, Department of External Affairs, 11 March 1964, A1838/318 no. 3024/2/2/1 Part 1.

67. Airgram no. 543, American Embassy (Kuala Lumpur) to Department of State, 18 March 1964, RG 59 Box 2454 Pol 14 1/1/64.

68. *The Straits Times*, 21 September 1964; Ostrom, "A Core Interest Analysis of the Formation of Malaysia and the Separation of Singapore", p. 194.

69. *The Straits Times*, 29 March 1964.

70. Telegram no. 30, Commonwealth Relations Office to British High Commission (Singapore), 17 December 1963, DO 169/233 no. 131/23.

71. *The Straits Times*, 4 March 1964.

72. Willard A. Hanna, *The Separation of Singapore from Malaysia* (American University Field Staff Reports Service, Southeast Asian Series, vol. 13 no. 21, 1965), p. 11.

73. *Malayan Times*, 3 March 1964; *The Straits Times*, 3 March 1964.

74. *The Straits Times*, 15 March 1964.

75. Ibid., 7 March 1964.

76. Ibid., 21 March 1964.

77. *Malayan Times*, 4 March 1964.

78. *The Straits Times*, 4 March 1964.

79. The Tunku had warned the MCA that it should not demand the allocation of all seats where Chinese voters were in the majority. "The MCA cannot go on any chauvinistic line because they must depend on the Malay votes to get the MCA candidates in and once the Malays feel the MCA is not toeing the Alliance line then they can only hope to get a few Chinese votes but will lose the Malay votes," he said. Ibid., 6 March 1964.

80. Ibid., 10 March 1964.

81. *Malayan Times*, 10 March 1964.

82. *The Straits Times*, 10 March 1964.

83. Ibid., 3 March 1964. The announcement was made by the Election Commission on 2 March 1964, a day after Toh unveiled the PAP's plans for a token intervention.

84. *Malayan Times*, 10 March 1964.
85. *The Straits Times*, 11 March 1964.
86. *Malayan Times*, 13 March 1964.
87. Telegram no. 606, American Consulate (Singapore) to Department of State, 14 March 1964, RG 59 Box 2452 Pol 7 1/1/64.
88. Telegram no. 843, American Embassy (Kuala Lumpur) to Department of State, 14 March 1964, RG 59 Box 2452 Pol 7 1/1/64.
89. Telegram no. 606, American Consulate (Singapore) to Department of State, 14 March 1964, RG 59 Box 2452 Pol 7 1/1/64.
90. *The Straits Times*, 15 March 1964.
91. *Malayan Times*, 15 March 1964.
92. *The Straits Times*, 16 March1964.
93. *Malayan Times*, 19 March 1964.
94. Ibid., 19 March 1964.
95. Telegram no. 861, American Embassy (Kuala Lumpur) to Department of State, 19 March 1964, RG 59 Box 2454 Pol 14 1/1/64.
96. Telegram no. 866, American Embassy (Kuala Lumpur) to Department of State, 20 March 1964, RG 59, 95900 Box 2454 Pol 14 1/1/64.
97. *Malayan Times*, 20 March 1964.
98. "Election Manifesto of the People's Action Party", in RG 59 Box 2454 Pol 14 1/1/64.
99. *Malayan Times*, 21 March 1964.
100. T.K. Critchley to Paul Hasluck, 25 May 1964, A1838/280 no. 3027/2/1 Part 18.
101. Airgram no. 578, American Embassy (Kuala Lumpur) to Department of State, 11 March 1964, RG 59 Box 2454 Pol 14 1/1/64.
102. The two were Mohamad Noor bin Jettey (Johore Bahru Timor) and Ling Teck Sum (Johore Bahru Barat).
103. *Malayan Times*, 22 March 1964.
104. John Drysdale, *Singapore: Struggle for Success* (Singapore: Times Books International 1984), p. 352.
105. T.K. Critchley to Paul Hasluck, 25 May 1964, A1838/280 no. 3027/2/1 Part 18.
106. Airgram no. 578, American Embassy (Kuala Lumpur) to Department of State, 1 April 1964, RG 59 Box 2454 Pol 14 1/1/64.
107. Harold Macmillan, *Winds of Change* (London: Macmillan, 1966).
108. *The Straits Times*, 23 March 1964.
109. Lee revealed that he had made an issue of economic and social change in his speech for that purpose. *The Malay Mail*, 7 April 1964.
110. *The Straits Times*, 24 March 1964.
111. Ibid., 25 March 1964.
112. Airgram no. 578, American Embassy (Kuala Lumpur) to Department of State, 1 April 1964, RG 59 Box 2454 Pol 14 1/1/64.
113. T.K. Critchley to Paul Hasluck, 25 May 1964, A1838/280 no. 3027/2/1 Part 18.
114. *Malayan Times*, 26 March 1964.
115. *The Straits Times*, 26 March 1964.
116. *The Malay Mail*, 7 April 1964.
117. *The Straits Times*, 26 March 1964.
118. Ibid., 28 March 1964.
119. Ibid., 29 March 1964.
120. Ibid.
121. Ibid.
122. Ibid., 30 March 1964.

123. Ibid.
124. Ibid.
125. *Malayan Times*, 2 April 1963.
126. Ibid., 7 April 1964.
127. *The Straits Times*, 1 April 1964.
128. *Malayan Times*, 31 March 1964.
129. Ibid., 4 March 1964.
130. *The Straits Times*, 31 March 1964.
131. *Malayan Times*, 4 March 1964.
132. "Text of TV Interview by A. Kajapathy with Tun Abdul Razak, Deputy National President of the United Malays National Organization", telecast on Channel 5 at 8 p.m., 9 April 1964, A1838/318 no. 3024/2/2/1 Part 1; *Malayan Times*, 10 April 1964.
133. *Malayan Times*, 4 April 1964.
134. *The Straits Times*, 24 April 1964.
135. *Malayan Times*, 6 April 1964.
136. *The Straits Times*, 10 April 1964.
137. *Malayan Times*, 3 April 1964.
138. Ibid.
139. Ibid.
140. Ibid.
141. *The Straits Times*, 13 April 1964.
142. *Malayan Times*, 6 April 1964.
143. *The Sunday Times*, 12 April 1964.
144. Ibid.
145. Cited in Drysdale, p. 471.
146. W.B. Pritchett to Secretary, Department of External Affairs, 15 May 1964, A1838/280 no. 3027/2/1 Part 18.
147. *The Straits Times*, 18 March 1964.
148. Ibid., 27 March 1964.
149. *The Sunday Times*, 12 April 1964.
150. *The Straits Times*, 25 March 1964.
151. W.B. Pritchett to Secretary, Department of External Affairs, 5 April 1964, A1838/1 No. 741/1 Part 1.
152. Ibid.
153. Memorandum of conversation between James Hahn (Southeast Asia Manager, Reuters) and Arthur H. Rosen, 10 April 1964, enclosed in Airgram no. 278, American Consulate (Singapore) to Department of State, 18 April 1964, RG 59 Box 2453 Pol 12, 1/1/64.
154. Airgram no. 578, American Embassy (Kuala Lumpur) to Department of State, 1 April 1964, RG 59 Box 2454 Pol 14 1/1/64.
155. Airgram no. 535, American Embassy (Kuala Lumpur) to Department of State, 11 March 1964, RG 59 Box 2454 Pol 14 1/1/64.
156. Airgram no. 276, American Consulate (Singapore) to Department of State, 16 April 1964, RG 59 Box 2453 Pol 12 1/1/64.
157. Airgram no. 535, American Embassy (Kuala Lumpur) to Department of State, 11 March 1964, RG 59 Box 2454 Pol 14 1/1/64.
158. T.K. Critchley to Paul Hasluck, 25 May 1964, A1838/280 no. 3027/2/1 Part 18.
159. Airgram no. 578, American Embassy (Kuala Lumpur) to Department of State, 1 April 1964, RG 59 Box 2454 Pol 14 1/1/64.
160. Airgram no. 641, American Embassy (Kuala Lumpur) to Department of State, 8 May 1964, RG 59 Box 2454 Pol 14 1/1/64.

161. T.K. Critchley to Paul Hasluck, 25 May 1964, A1838/280 no. 3027/2/1 Part 18.
162. Telegram no. 992, Bell to Department of State, 26 April 1964, RG 59 Box 2454 Pol 14 1/1/64.
163. Ibid.
164. Ibid.
165. W.B. Pritchett to Secretary, Department of External Affairs, 15 May 1964, A1838/280 no. 3027/2/1 Part 18.
166. Ibid.
167. Although both PAP candidates in Johore were withdrawn, their names, however, appeared on the ballot papers since their nomination had already been filed before the identity of their opponents were known. During the elections, the Alliance made play of this and accused the PAP of not honouring their promise to withdraw. *Malayan Times*, 26 March 1964.
168. W.B. Pritchett to Secretary, Department of External Affairs, 15 May 1964, A1838/280 no. 3027/2/1 Part 18.
169. *Malayan Times*, 28 April 1964.
170. Ibid., 27 April 1964.
171. Ibid.
172. T.K. Critchley to Paul Hasluck, 25 May 1964, A1838/280 no. 3027/2/1 Part 18.
173. M.W.B. Smithies (Second Secretary) to Secretary, Department of External Affairs, 14 May 1964, A1838/318 no. 3024/2/2/1 Part 1.
174. *The Straits Times*, 27 April 1964.
175. W.B. Pritchett to Secretary, Department of External Affairs, 15 May 1964, A1838/280 no. 3027/2/1 Part 18.
176. Airgram no. 641, American Embassy (Kuala Lumpur) to Department of State, 8 May 1964, RG 59 Box 2454 Pol 14 1/1/64.
177. W.B. Pritchett to Secretary, Department of External Affairs, 15 May 1964, A1838/280 no. 3027/2/1 Part 18.
178. Airgram no. 294, American Consulate (Singapore) to Department of State, 30 April 1964, RG 59 Box 2454 Pol 14 1/1/64.
179. T.K. Critchley to Paul Hasluck, 25 May 1964, A1838/280 no. 3027/2/1 Part 18.
180. Airgram no. 641, American Embassy (Kuala Lumpur) to Department of State, 8 May 1964, RG 59 Box 2454 Pol 14 1/1/64.
181. Airgram no. 578, American Embassy (Kuala Lumpur) to Department of State, 1 April 1964, RG 59 Box 2454 Pol 14 1/1/64.
182. T.K. Critchley to Paul Hasluck, 25 May 1964, A1838/280 no. 3027/2/1 Part 18.
183. M.W.B. Smithies to Secretary, Department of External Affairs, 14 May 1964, A1838/318 no. 3024/2/2/1 Part 1.
184. W.B. Pritchett to Secretary, Department of External Affairs, 15 May 1964, A1838/280 no. 3027/2/1 Part 18.
185. Airgram no. 641, American Embassy (Kuala Lumpur) to Department of State, 8 May 1964, RG 59 Box 2454 Pol 14 1/1/64.
186. *The Times*, 27 April 1964.
187. W.B. Pritchett to Secretary, Department of External Affairs, 15 May 1964, A1838/280 no. 3027/2/1 Part 18.
188. T.K. Critchley to Paul Hasluck, 25 May 1964, A1838/280 no. 3027/2/1 Part 18.
189. W.B. Pritchett to Secretary, Department of External Affairs, 15 May 1964, A1838/280 no. 3027/2/1 Part 18.
190. Ibid.
191. Ibid.

192. *Malayan Times*, 2 May 1964.
193. *The Straits Times*, 28 April 1964.
194. *Malayan Times*, 2 May 1964.
195. Ibid., 28 April 1964.
196. W.B. Pritchett to Secretary, Department of External Affairs, 15 May 1964, A1838/280 no. 3027/2/1 Part 18.
197. T.K. Critchley to Paul Hasluck, 25 May 1964, A1838/280 no. 3027/2/1 Part 18.
198. *The Times*, 27 April 1964.
199. Airgram no. 641, American Embassy (Kuala Lumpur) to Department of State, 8 May 1964, RG 59 Box 2454 Pol 14 1/1/64.
200. Ibid.
201. W.B. Pritchett to Secretary, Department of External Affairs, 15 May 1964, A1838/280 no. 3027/2/1 Part 18.
202. Ibid.
203. Ibid.
204. *Malayan Times*, 27 April 1964.

CHAPTER 5

THE ALLIANCE STRIKES BACK

The PAP in Opposition

B y virtue of its Bungsar win, the People's Action Party (PAP) had
become the largest opposition party in the Dewan Ra'ayat (House
of Representatives) with 13 seats, not enough to impact House
decisions, even if it succeeded in mustering the other pro-Malaysia
opposition seats behind its banner. Its cross-benching days, however, were
over, as far as Kuala Lumpur was concerned. Tunku Abdul Rahman made
it clear that the PAP would sit with the opposition benches when the
Dewan Ra'ayat convened on 18 May, bringing to an end its "twilight status
between friend and foe".[1] "It was understood that the PAP won't be taking
part in Malayan politics," the Tunku explained, "But they contested the
recent elections and have said they proposed to contest all future elections."
He said that it did not seem right that the PAP members continued to sit
with the government.[2] The fact that the Tunku had offered to make Lee
Kuan Yew the leader of the opposition was small consolation, for Lee did
not believe it would be good for the nation, and resisted it successfully: if
the PAP were forced to bat as the opposition, he argued, it would hit every
ball for six; but what good would that do to the cause of integration?[3] The
truth was, what good could the PAP do in any case, now that its maiden
venture fell so lamentably short of all expectations?

Party leaders who pondered the options were not sanguine about the
future. Goh Keng Swee much preferred to avoid further entanglement in
Federal politics and to concentrate on affairs in Singapore. But few of the
other top PAP leaders wanted to renege on the party's "national" mission,

seriously concerned as they were at the prospect of Malaysia continuing under the old regime and firmly believing at the same time in their own capacity to contribute to its betterment. Lee's initial reading of the election outcome was that "it means the old order will carry on, the same old economic and social policies in the same old way" — a "retrograde step" which had to be "prevented", he said. "Every analysis I have made of the basic political situation in Malaysia remains undemolished," the Singapore premier had boldly asserted, convinced that the "winds of change" would come back once *Konfrontasi* (confrontation) ended and that the way ahead during the transition lay in building up the party's organization and recruiting able and honest men "to help carry on the battle for a more equal and more just society".[4] Like Lee, Toh Chin Chye was also of the belief that, with better organization and political education, the PAP could still "grow to become a decisive force".[5] Another "pointer to the trend", as S. Rajaratnam disclosed, was the fact that the PAP had been approached by Malayan-based groups to move for certain legislation in the Federal Parliament like those enacted in Singapore.[6] Its leaders felt that there was not a doubt that there was clearly a potentially large audience interested in the democratic-socialist ideals of the PAP.[7] Having already launched the PAP as a Malaysian party, they saw no future in the party remaining as simply a parochial movement and envisaged continuing with its national role. Such a prospect, as they were well aware, carried risks, for it would invariably pit the PAP against the Alliance, with possibly serious consequences.

The hard reality was also that the variety of credible options available to the PAP in pursuit of its professed role were really few and far between. To W.B. Pritchett's suggestion of "if you can't beat them, join them", Toh stiffly reminded the Deputy Australian High Commissioner: "We are not gate crashers." The PAP would have to wait for an invitation, which, given its electoral debacle, was now unlikely to happen.[8] The alternative of "if you can't join them, fight them", a hard-hitting approach favoured by Rajaratnam, was also fraught with peril and conjured up consequences too dire for party leaders to contemplate. None of the top PAP leaders apparently shared Rajaratnam's enthusiasm for outright opposition, even if, as Toh commented ruefully, the "mantle of opposition has been placed upon us". Going about "as with a pea-shooter picking off corrupt officials and politicians" was one thing, argued Jek Yeun Thong, but the notion of militant opposition was different altogether. If the PAP had gone into the opposition, Goh Keng Swee warned, people would expect it to hit hard, and "he rolled his eyes and shook his head at the prospect".[9] Not only would UMNO's (United Malays National Organization) suspicion and hostility be provoked, all prospects of future cooperation with the party would also be jeopardized, including the PAP's hope of securing the Malay mass base with UMNO's help. The possibility of the Alliance using its superior resources and position to damage the PAP's and Singapore's interests in retaliation was another woeful consequence not easily dismissed, even though both Lee and Rajaratnam insisted that if Kuala Lumpur got tough, Singapore would fight back. Lee asserted that Singapore knew how to fight, having fought the British before and argued that if the situation deteriorated too far, Singapore could always turn to the British to make Kuala Lumpur hold back, but even he conceded that this would hardly be a Malayan solution.[10] Rajaratnam, on his part, boasted that Singapore was well positioned to react politically in Malaya, with "disastrous" results to the Alliance government should the latter decide to wield the big stick. Goh Keng Swee thought otherwise. His caustic riposte was that Rajaratnam was only "Minister for Talk". As Finance Minister, Goh "probably has a much more lively appreciation of the Federal government's powers of injury than his colleagues," surmised Pritchett.

Reprising the PAP's previous role as the loyal opposition seemed by far the more realistic option. But even this moderate role was less credible now that the Alliance, and Tun Abdul Razak in particular, no longer trusted the PAP ever since its venture into Malayan politics, and it was with the Malaysian Deputy Prime Minister that the political business in Malaysia would increasingly have to be done, even though relations with the ageing Tunku might still not be bad. Nonetheless, Lee Kuan Yew believed that there was still scope in raising issues in the Dewan Ra'ayat and "bring the government to talk his language and face the issues he put to it". But he acknowledged at the same time that here, too, he "always had to keep his eye cocked to see if he was frightening anybody", for the more outspoken he was, the more likely he would also prejudice the prospects of cooperation with UMNO and harm the interests he sought to promote. He was in "a most serious dilemma, and one to which he could see no solution".[11] Pritchett could only concur: "All I spoke with acknowledged this dilemma with profound gloom and none had an answer to it."[12]

The best that Toh could offer was that the PAP would have to steer a very careful course, while waiting for circumstances to change and offer the PAP its opportunities.[13] What that course entailed no one was yet certain, though Pritchett presumed that a possible line of action would be to "seek to persuade Razak that the next elections will not be so easy; that what the

PAP says about the MCA (Malayan Chinese Association) being finished is right and that the PAP is the party to which Tun Razak and the UMNO must ultimately look for cooperation". Such a policy would require "the Singapore base to be strongly held" and activity in the Federal field to be restricted, sufficient only to illustrate accusations of incompetence and corruption and to demonstrate the PAP's ability to attract support. There was little doubt in Pritchett's mind that the PAP faced a daunting task ahead: "To pursue a path of moderation and yet to succeed in convincing a reluctant UMNO that the PAP, after its recent debacle, is the party of the future will require tremendous political skill — and patience."[14]

The Anti-PAP Campaign

Lee Kuan Yew's first post-election speech in the newly convened Dewan Ra'ayat on 21 May 1964, reflected the PAP's desire to proceed with its national role as the "loyal opposition — loyal to Malaysia". Making the distinction, however, that a loyal opposition was not a "subservient Opposition", the Singapore premier said that criticisms, however unwelcome, about the dangers of government policies and the lapses of political leaders and bureaucrats, would continue to be "made seriously and in good faith", in the hope that they could "set off a change for the better". He foresaw possible differences with Kuala Lumpur arising over two politically difficult fields where the latter, in his view, had failed to give strong leadership: economic and social reform and communalism. *Konfrontasi* had submerged the economic and social pressures somewhat, Lee conceded, but feared that they would resurface by 1969 and the "mandate the next time against the broader canvass of Malaysia may not be so easy to come by". "[I]t leaves us with a deep anxiety," Lee stressed, "that all that is needed is a shift, between 10 to 15 per cent, of the mass base and in a fragmented Chamber, no coherent authority would be possible". Although Indonesian pressures had also acted as a catalyst for racial unity, Lee warned that "we cannot go on forever to play this game of communal checks and balances with impunity" for unless new values were instilled and attempts made to integrate the races, "then all we shall be doing would be living on borrowed time". Whilst the formation of Malaysia was inevitable, its success was not, and the PAP considered it "[their] duty to open up the windows for the 'winds of change'".[15]

It was no secret that Kuala Lumpur much preferred the windows shut, and the PAP contained. The Tunku had told Lee, in the presence of Tan

Siew Sin in their post-election meeting at Fraser's Hill on 28 April, that he wanted Singapore to become "the New York of South East Asia", the implication being that the PAP government should confine its role to Singapore and devote its energies to bringing about that suggested end. The Tunku assured him that the MCA would stay out of Singapore.[16] But as events soon demonstrated, the MCA was not yet the PAP's main worry; the extremists in UMNO were.

If the PAP had hoped that the Alliance's resounding victory at the polls would have sufficiently restored UMNO's confidence in itself, it was grievously mistaken. UMNO's fear of the PAP was not lessened. Though the immediate threat the PAP presented had been eliminated, its longer term danger to the Alliance and what it represented — Malay dominance — was not. Because the PAP espoused a pan-Malaysian and non-communal platform, and boasted a proven record of governmental capacity with a progressive social and economic programme, and represented the Singapore Chinese, it emerged in UMNO's eyes as a rival Chinese bid for power at the expense of the Malays.[17] "It can therefore be seen," observed Antony Head, the British High Commissioner, "that the prospect of … the PAP spreading into Malaya as a progressive Socialist party who would provide a better deal for the have-nots and then, judging by its performance in Singapore, attracting a considerable number of Malay supporters, seriously worried the Malay UMNO leaders."[18] Despite its defeat, the PAP had become a potential danger not only to the MCA's hold on Chinese voters but also to UMNO's sway over its Malay ground as well. "The fact that it had succeeded in getting a number of Malays in Singapore to vote for it was a political red light for the Malays," Head added.[19] The memory of the mammoth crowds attending PAP election rallies in the Malayan elections, which included many Malays, must also have haunted UMNO leaders even after the polls. Worse still, the PAP did not appear to be chastened by its defeat and, if the statements of its leaders were anything to go by, seemed as determined as ever to bring the winds of change to Malaya, a future challenge UMNO instinctively knew it had to offset.

So it was that after the heat of the elections, UMNO leaders decided to start gunning for the PAP in Singapore before it could develop further strength. Bringing the battle to the PAP's own backyard had the tactical advantage of also confining the party to Singapore, putting it on the defensive, and insulating the peninsula from its politics. With the PAP politically weakened and psychologically bruised, it was for UMNO a fortuitous moment to strike, and avenge at the same time SUMNO's

(Singapore United Malays National Organization) humiliating defeat in 1963, and recapture its Malay popular base.

Notwithstanding the fact that the PAP had triumphed in predominantly Malay constituencies in the September 1963 Singapore elections, grounds for Malay unhappiness were not altogether absent. Existing economic grievances arose from their socio-economic backwardness in relation to the other communities. After the formation of Malaysia, as Toh Chin Chye acknowledged, expectations grew among certain Malays in Singapore that with a Malay-dominated central government wielding power in Kuala Lumpur, the "special rights for the Malays as practised in Malaya will apply equally to them", even though such rights were never part of the merger agreement and would never have been acceptable to any Singapore government. It could not have escaped UMNO's calculations that no Singapore government could survive the crisis that the granting of Malay rights was bound to create. Precisely because of this, it was a potent weapon in UMNO's arsenal to bring the PAP down. Aware of this, the PAP government had made determined efforts to win over the Malays without conceding "special rights" but, as Pritchett noted, the "correction of the imbalance between the Malays and other communities in Singapore will at best be a slow process over many years". In the meantime, "the Malay feelings of resentment, suspicion and self-pity, are the stuff of communalism and racial tension" and could be "easily exploited by [those] playing upon economic jealousies and religious sentiment".[21]

Shortly after the elections, SUMNO began a campaign to prove that the PAP government was oppressing the Malays in Singapore. But it soon became clear that its intention exceeded "the resolution of legitimate grievances"; it aimed at working up Malay sentiments "against an allegedly anti-Malay and oppressive PAP government".[22] Their aim was not only to turn the Malays in Singapore against the PAP government and, thereby, discrediting the PAP's claim to being a non-communal party, but also to show Malays in Malaya that only an UMNO-led government could protect their interests. UMNO probably calculated that if it could hold the Malay votes by re-establishing its supremacy over the Malays in Singapore, and staving off any attempt by the PAP to muscle into its preserve in the Federation, it would have ensured for itself a majority over the other communities whose vote would be split by the arrangement of the constituencies.[23] The campaign was to culminate in the ugly and frightening race riots during the summer of 1964 with such devastating consequences for the state of Kuala Lumpur–Singapore relations.

Three days after the Malayan elections, the *Malayan Times* fired the opening salvo. It published a letter from Singapore accusing the PAP of insincerity and "merely bubbling with words just for the sake of winning votes from the Malays":

> ... what has it done for the Malays of Singapore? It selects a few Malays for certain high posts. These persons are active cadres of the PAP. If the PAP cares so much about the rights of Malays, why only open the doors of opportunity to only a few of them? What has Mr Lee Kuan Yew done for the thousands of jobless Malays? Does the Singapore Government realize there are more unemployed Malays than jobless Chinese though the Chinese form the majority of the population of Singapore. Regarding housing for Malays, traditionally they do not like to live in flats. Why has not Mr Lee Kuan Yew personally studied the reasons for the Malay dislike of flats?[24]

Taking up the matter the next day, its leader commented that while the PAP claimed to be multiracial in outlook, it was actually "dominated by the Chinese in numbers and in influence" with the result that "the minorities in Singapore feel their interests have been relegated into the background":

> The people who feel most keenly that they have been put on a shelf are the Malays of Singapore. ... In a society dominated by the more dynamic Chinese, the Malays emasculated by their so-called privileges have very little chance of competing for a place in the Singapore sun with the Chinese and others.[25]

On the same day, the *Berita Harian* reported the Secretary of SUMNO city division, Ahmad bin Abdul Hamid, as saying that the Alliance victory had "brought back to their senses" a small group of Singapore Malays who had previously been "deceived by certain quarters"[26] and had "chosen the wrong government"[27] in the last Singapore elections. It was the prelude to the agitation campaign SUMNO was about to foist on the PAP.

Stories of PAP persecution and discrimination of Malays soon appeared in the influential Malay press, like the *jawi*-script *Utusan Melayu*, which largely "reflected UMNO thinking". As Ali bin Haji Ahmad, UMNO's Assistant Secretary-General, admitted to Peter E. Juge, (Second Secretary, American Embassy), the impression that "the *Utusan Melayu* is UMNO's mouthpiece is substantially true" since most of the members of the Board of Directors and the editorial and reporting staff in *Utusan Melayu* were also members or officers of UMNO.[28] Sopiee noted, for instance, that the *Utusan Melayu's* attitude towards the PAP had changed perceptively after the latter's entry into the Federal fray. Whilst its leader of 28 February 1964 had praised the choice of Lee as the leader for the Truth Mission to Africa, the *Utusan Melayu* changed tack within a week, after Toh's announcement on 1 March of the PAP's token participation in the Federal polls, and launched a series of attacks on Lee and the PAP. From the beginning of March till the end of April 1964, Sopiee noted that the *Utusan Melayu* criticized the PAP on 11 occasions, "nearly as many times as it attacked all the other opposition parties put together".[29] It was the *Utusan Melayu* which took the lead in spearheading the propaganda campaign against the PAP government.

From May 1964, articles focusing on alleged PAP oppression of the Malays made their appearance in the Malay press. The PAP was accused of not allocating enough stalls in the new Geylang Serai market for Malay vendors.[30] A minor oversight by a PAP assemblyman who had sent out invitations for a meeting at the Coronation Road community centre in English and Chinese only was played up by the *Utusan Melayu* as an insult to the Malays.[31] The government's record on Malay education also came under attack. "The value of Malay education is nothing compared to the value placed on Chinese education," the editorial charged, after concluding that Malays in Singapore "are being hard pressed by the PAP Government", supposedly because of the latter's pro-Chinese bias.[32] A more suggestive treatment of the same theme by *Utusan Melayu* columnist "Bajang" appeared on 9 May:

> The reason to hold a procession [of Singapore Malay school teachers] is because they feel that they are not given fair treatment; probably not like that given to Chinese school teachers. Oh, well! When one has a step-father ...[33]

The allegation that the PAP was a "step-father" was to be repeated many times thereafter. But it was the government's ambitious scheme to resettle a large number of residents from the Kallang River basin to make way for a new housing and industrial complex that was subsequently made the focal point of agitation. On 12 May, the west coast branch of SUMNO announced that it would be passing a resolution demanding that the government withdrew eviction orders served on certain Malay residents in the West Coast area, some 500 of whom, reported the *Berita Harian* on

14 May, were affected. It said that SUMNO would protest against the government scheme to move Malays to less developed areas and urged the authorities to refrain from implementing policies that "[tend] to arouse the anxiety of the Malays".[34] Still on the same theme, on 21 May, the _Berita Harian_ carried another story about how another 600 residents living in Kampong Alexandra Terrace had been similarly served with quit notices by the Alexandra Brick Works Ltd and how the south division of SUMNO was "working hard to save these residents".[35] Some 200 of these residents were Malays.

On the same day, the _Utusan Melayu_, published a statement by SUMNO deputy chairman, Ahmad bin Haji Taff, who called on Kuala Lumpur to save the Malays in Singapore "who make up only 12 per cent of the inhabitants".[36] In another report three days later, referring to Malay residents in the Java Road, Palembang Road, Sumbawa Road and Jalan Sultan area, who were served with quit notices, the _Utusan Melayu_ ran a provocative headline: "3000 Malay Residents Threatened". It reported that an action committee had been formed to appeal to the Tunku and Syed Ja'afar Albar "to defend the residents who are now being threatened". Led by Yakob bin Mangilu and Syed Abdullah Alatas, the delegation subsequently arrived in Kuala Lumpur on 9 June, said the _Utusan Melayu_, "to explain the dark future that the Malays in Crawford are facing".[37] Replying to the Tunku's query,[38] Lee assured him that he was "very conscious of the problem some of these families face in moving into modern flats because of the rent problem" but his difficulty was "to work out a formula by which [they] can subsidize these families without creating another problem by similar demands for special treatment owing to hardship by equally poor Chinese and Indian families".[39]

The extremists' efforts to work up communal feelings against the government left Lee Kuan Yew with much misgivings about the future of Malaysia, which he expressed to the outgoing American Consul General, Sam P. Gilstrap, on 12 May, during the latter's farewell call. Unless the racial problems could be overcome in the next few years, Lee said that Malaysia only had a "50-50 chance of survival".[40] Wanting to counter the deliberate misinformation by the partisan Malay press, Lee toured the Crawford, Rochore and Kampong Glam wards on 31 May to explain the rationale behind the government's redevelopment plans, which arose, he said, out of the desire to rebuild the slums of the city so as to provide for more and better homes, healthier living conditions and office space. Only 2,500 families were affected and, of this, only 200 were Malays — not the

3,000 the *Utusan Malayu* had earlier claimed. Some 76 of the 200 Malay families, in any case, had already vacated the area by the end of May.

But the *Utusan Melayu* issued no correction. Instead, it repeated the charge with the additional allegation that the affected Malays had also become victims of the PAP's discriminatory treatment, the dark hint of victimization underscored by the new suggestion that the Chinese and Chinatown were exempted from demolition, the implication being that while "Malays were being summarily evicted ... the Chinese in the same and other areas would not be affected".[41] Thus, on 10 June, the *Utusan Melayu* ran two more stories under the following suggestive headlines: "3000 Singapore Malay PAP victims send delegation to meet Tengku. 'Save Our Future'"; "Action Committee is surprised that older houses in Chinatown are not demolished first". It quoted Yakob as asking why the Government should choose to demolish Malay houses and not older houses in Chinatown.[42] A darker rendition was given by *Utusan Melayu* columnist Bajang:

> But what about the residents in Chinatown whose houses are very old too? Oh, well! When one has a step-father ...[43]

Two days later the *Utusan Melayu* followed up with another feature headlined: "Do not treat the sons of the soil as step children".[44] Referring to an assurance given by Syed Ja'afar to the two representatives of the Crawford residents Action Committee who met him on 9 June, the Malay daily headlined another report: "Singapore UMNO directed to take steps to save PAP victims". It added that UMNO Malaya "would intervene if SUMNO was unable to resolve the matter.[45]

Subsequent reports consequently hammered home the message that it was the duty of Singapore Malays to rally behind SUMNO and that only the latter was able to take effective action "to stop the PAP Government from doing as it pleases to the Malay kampongs". To underline the point, on 17 June, the *Utusan Melayu* published a letter to the editor with another provocative caption — "PAP ordered the Malays to move out" — in which the writer suggested that Singapore Malays who had "rejected Malay parties", like SUMNO, "under the influence of the sweet words of the non-Malays" had been taught a timely lesson:

> And now what has happened to them after getting an adopted father? Why did they go to Kuala Lumpur to see the Prime Minister of Malaysia who is a Malay? When we called on the Singapore Malays to support

the party led by Malays, they rejected it. I hope this will be a lesson to all Malays in Malaysia.[46]

What that "lesson" was the *Utusan Melayu* elaborated in unambiguous terms in another inflammatory article on 18 June alleging that the reason the Malays were being summarily evicted was because the PAP wanted to disperse the Malays so as to "muffle their voice so that it will not be heard altogether". The article charged: "It is as though they [Malays] have been hunted down." The Malay leaders in the PAP could not represent Malay interests, the paper insinuated, as they were people "who have changed their skin and their mind (if not their religion) in order to serve their own ends." Declaring that it had no wish "to see the Malays being victimized and caused to suffer", the article then urged Malays to "stand solidly behind UMNO in making strong and effective protests", adding that they must "consider carefully when they cast their votes in the next general elections." When casting their votes, the Malays in Singapore "should do well to remember the benefits enjoyed by the Malays in the Federation of Malaya and in North Borneo."[47] Ali bin Haji Ahmad could not have been more explicit when he addressed the opening of the new SUMNO Tanjong Kling branch in Singapore on 28 June: "So long as there is UMNO in Singapore the PAP would not be able to sway the Malays". Chiding the PAP for imposing "colonialism on the Malays" and casting doubts on the effectiveness of Malay PAP leaders in protecting the interests of their community, Ali asserted in no uncertain terms that "If the Malays want to die out, then join the PAP; if they want good for the Malays, then they should join UMNO." He added that "only UMNO and nobody else protects the Malays ... I call upon you to join the UMNO".[48]

Concerned that the "communal agitation was but the prelude to increasingly reckless and virulent attacks", Lee Kuan Yew issued a general warning on 7 June about the "mischievous propaganda from certain quarters that the government is out to oppress the Malays".[49] And on 22 June his Minister for Social Affairs, Othman Wok, despatched letters to 144 non-political Malay organizations in Singapore inviting them to meet Lee on 19 July for informal and frank discussions on problems affecting Malays in Singapore — only to have SUMNO undercut the move by calling on 28 June a meeting of its own to meet a week earlier on 12 July to "discuss the fate and plight of Malays in Singapore under PAP rule".

A SUMNO working paper circulated for discussion prior to the meeting accused the PAP government of targeting and mistreating its Malay residents. Slamming the PAP for employing "deception and intimidation" to get Malays evicted from their settlements, and repeating the allegation that the real purpose behind the government's eviction scheme was to ensure that the Geylang Serai area would "eventually become a Chinatown and this [would] further strengthen the political position of Mr Lee Kuan Yew". The SUMNO memorandum warned that, unless Malays in other areas were watchful, the same fate would befall them, resulting in "no more Malays living in the city area". Further charging that the PAP gave the best civil service jobs to the Chinese and discriminated against Malays, the memorandum alleged that the Malays were consequently "at the mercy of others, because most departments [were] headed by Chinese and these men [gave] priority to people of their own race". Discriminatory treatment of Malays was also evident in the negligible spending on Malay education "compared with expenditure for Chinese schools", the insufficient number of Malay schools, the low standard of the teaching of Malay, and the limited bursaries and scholarships for Malay students. There was also "no sincerity in the implementation of the national language". Not only had the government refused to introduce the quota system, it had also ignored the special rights of the Malays and "failed to carry out its responsibilities towards the Malays in Singapore". Deploring "the cunning role that has often been played by the top leadership of the PAP ... to indirectly cause the Malays to fight among themselves", the memorandum urged Malays to unite to face "all sorts of pressures, suppression and threats" arising from the "policy and tactics of the PAP Government which treats the Malays as step children". It noted that "a number of Malays in Singapore who previously strongly opposed the struggle of their own race and [gave] their support to the PAP have now realized their mistake", a realization which led them to "frankly admit that they had been misled" and prompted their "return to the fold".[50]

Ignoring the fact that the Singapore government meeting had been arranged prior to the SUMNO convention, the *Utusan Melayu* came out with another misleading headline, on 2 July, accusing the former of scheming to divide the Malays by sponsoring a rival meeting: "PAP's attempt to divide Malays by inviting 56 cultural bodies. The secret of July 19 now exposed". Syed Abdullah Alatas was then quoted by the *Utusan Melayu* as saying that the government meeting was "not wise and not at the correct time" and ought to have been taken up with the Action Committee and not with the representatives of the Malay cultural organizations.[51] Condemning the *Utusan Melayu* report, on the same day, as a "deliberate lie to confuse Malays and others that the invitation to meet the Prime Minister [was] an attempt on the part of the Government to split the Malays", Othman Wok said he was saddened that the government's sincere efforts to help the Malays had been deliberately distorted by the "wilful activities of those who will consciously or unconsciously wish to bring about animosity and hatred among the races in Singapore".[52]

Two days before, in an address at the opening of the PAP Seremban branch on 30 June, Lee Kuan Yew issued another warning about the "risky line"[53] being adopted to win Malay votes by Malay extremists, such as Syed Ja'afar, who were playing on racial issues, and argued that it was futile for them to do so. This was implicit in the racial proportions of Malaysia:

> We must live together in peace. The 43% of the Malays and origins [sic] of Malaya, 40% Chinese, 10% Indians, and 7% others must live together in harmony. If they want to suppress each other then there will be dispute among them and this will lead to the destruction of Malaysia. I appeal to the people that they must be patient and understanding towards one another.[54]

On 3 July, the *Utusan Melayu* reported Lee's remarks as a stern warning instead to the Malays that "43 per cent of Malays in Malaysia could not drive away 60 per cent Chinese and other races". The next day, the *Utusan Melayu* carried Syed Ja'afar's charge against Lee not to repeat the statement about Malays not being able to drive away the Chinese: "The Malays do not intend to drive away any Chinese. But if Mr Lee attempts to colonize the Malays he will be hunted down." Lee must not "bring up the matter of 43% and 60% if he really wishes to see the various races living in harmony". Syed Ja'afar then went on to accuse Lee of opposing special rights for Malays in the Malaysia talks because he had bad intentions of suppressing the Malays in Singapore.[55] The *Utusan Melayu* asserted that "it is clear that according to Mr Lee those who are able to drive away others from Malaysia are the Chinese and other non-Malays and those who can be driven away are the Malays because their numbers are small". Turning to the situation in Singapore, the editorial went on to insinuate that Lee had similar plans to drive out the Malays from the island:

> Similarly, because the number of Chinese in Singapore is far bigger than the number of Malays, by moving the Malays from where they are residing at present and by moving Malays from predominantly Malay areas, it will cause the Malays to be split and this will make it easier for

> Lee Kuan Yew to drive away the Malays from Singapore. ... Who has the intention of driving whom out needs no clarification and who is trying to split the unity of the people in this country also needs no clarification.[56]

The allegation that Lee had opposed the special rights of the Malays brought a swift rebuttal from the Singapore government which issued a statement on 6 July to clarify the position.[57] Article 89 in the Singapore constitution,[58] it said, referred only to the "special position" of the Malays and not "special rights" as in the Malaysian constitution which reserved land, civil service jobs and licences for business for Malays, provisions which would only apply if Singapore had opted for complete merger as Penang and Malacca had done. The statement added that while the government would discharge its responsibilities to all communities fairly and justly, taking into account the "special position" of the Malays, it "cannot be coerced or intimidated by extremist groups exploiting communal sentiments". It warned that the "exploitation of the Malay issues by political parties hoping to collect Malay support can only make things more complicated and difficult for all as the Government cannot yield to intimidation by communal elements."

But there could be no let-up in the agitation. As the 12 July date drew near, the campaign intensified. On 6 July the *Utusan Melayu* carried another inflammatory article in which Mohammad Nor Awang, a committee member of the city-east branch of SUMNO, reportedly attacked the Singapore premier for brushing aside the fact that Singapore had originally been a Malay country and attempting to turn the Malays in Singapore into "tramps" by pulling down their houses. Accusing Lee for daring to "slap the faces of Malays in Singapore", he said that the Prime Minister "ha[d] been carrying out a plot against the Malays in Singapore which may lead to bloodshed between the Malays and the Chinese in Singapore". Ali Abu, SUMNO's publicity officer, in the same issue depicted Lee's speech as showing how "rough" he was towards the Malays "who ha[d] some sort of special rights in their land of birth". SUMNO, he said, "challenges Mr Lee to damage something which the Malays love and cherish, for instance, their religion and their traditions, or to oppress the Malays as he pleases".[59] Raking up the eviction issue, Talib Ahmad, secretary of SUMNO's east division, charged that government officials allegedly threatened Malay housewives in Kampong Paya Lebar, while their husbands were out at work, to put their signatures on a census survey "meant to ascertain the number of residents who will be moved out" for a road widening project in the area. "In the threats," the statement went on, "the officials said that if the owners of the houses refuse[d] to sign the forms the official would bring policemen with them and force the owners to do so, and the government would carry out its policy by demolishing the houses in two or three months' time". Talib then asked: "Why is it that the PAP Government wants to widen roads in predominantly Malay areas while roads in Chinatown like Cross Street, New Bridge Road and other roads are not affected?" The *Utusan Melayu* headlined the episode: "Another 2,000 Singapore Malays given quit notices. Now it's Paya Lebar. UMNO accuses the PAP of driving away the Malays to rural areas on purpose".[60]

With the SUMNO conference just four days away, the *Utusan Melayu* launched another salvo at the PAP government on 8 July, this time alleging that Malays who complained about the quit notices were being wrongly depicted by the government as having been "instigated by Indonesian agents" although it was the PAP that "[hunted them] down out of their places of residence." The next day, another editorial accused the PAP of attempting to "twist the facts" by claiming that Malay extremists were behind the communal politicking when they were only expressing dissatisfaction with the PAP government: "Now it is known who are trying to cause a clash between the Malays and the non-Malays, particularly the Chinese. It is known who are setting alight the fire of communalism in Singapore and attempting to do the same in Malaya and even throughout Malaysia." Ignoring again the Singapore government's earlier clarification about the special rights of the Malays, on 9 July the *Utusan Melayu* raised yet again "the bogey that the PAP was out to destroy 'Malay rights' in Singapore".[61] It published a call by the SUMNO Rochore branch urging Singapore Malays to unite to "defend the special rights laid down in the constitutions of Singapore and Malaysia", after pointing out that the PAP would not because of its emphasis on socialism: "Therefore, let us be careful and cautious so that our children and grandchildren will not accuse us of being traitors who readily accept the deceptions in the PAP's social revolution for the destruction of our race." The PAP's social revolution, it added, could "go to hell".[62]

Right up to the very day of the conference itself, there was no weakening in the intensity of the anti-PAP campaign, the *Utusan Zaman* having published on 12 July a scathing article by Wan Abdul Kadir attacking the PAP for "fishing in muddy waters" and serving notice that the Malays "cannot be easily threatened, intimidated, or frightened". Describing the convention as a time for all Malays to "roar in one clear voice at the PAP ... that the 'Malays can never be obliterated from the earth'," he warned: "When the time comes, when they are forced to, when they feel the pain of being suppressed, when pushed against the wall, the Malays who are gentle, kind-hearted and friendly, will change their attitude."[63]

The build-up of the anti-PAP agitation by the Malay extremists was deeply worrying to both the Singapore government and other political observers. As the American Consulate reported, "Spore Govt this week indicated serious concern that racial chauvinists in UMNO may incite some local Malays to violence over issue of Govt treatment of Malays". Equally nervous about the possibility of a racial flare-up, the Consulate warned:

> In community where racial animosities still lie close to surface this issue potentially explosive in hands of racial extremists. Despite risks involved, UMNO leaders exploiting issue in attempt [to] strike at PAP and regain leadership of Malay communities which party lost to PAP in Spore elections last year. Govt moving warily, offering generous compensation to resettled Malays, but obviously cannot abandon redevelopment program which in fact affects proportionately fewer Malays than Chinese. ... British urging Lee [to] exercise restraint but fear he may counterattack if UMNO continues anti-PAP campaign. Not clear what form counterattack might take. In fact British seem concerned Lee himself becoming increasingly frustrated and apparently unsure how to handle problem.[64]

Fearing the danger of a communal explosion, Lee made an urgent plea to the Tunku to call off the SUMNO campaign, when the latter was on transit in Singapore on his way to London and the United States. But the Tunku apparently "laughed off the plea with the comment that Lee was imagining things, there was really nothing to worry about".[65]

Ja'afar Albar's "Fiery Speech"

If the intention was to whip up interest in the forthcoming SUMNO-sponsored convention, it succeeded. The New Star cinema in Pasir Panjang which could accommodate up to 500 people was packed to capacity that Sunday morning on 12 July. Some 450 representatives and observers from 123 Malay and Muslim bodies, including Malay political parties like the Pan-Malayan Islamic Party (PMIP), Peninsular Malay Union (PMU), Partai Rakyat Singapura and the Singapore Malay Union, and 15 Alliance

Members of Parliament from the peninsula were in attendance.[66] Huge crowds, estimated at around 12,000 by the *Utusan Melayu*,[67] gathered outside the cinema, although both the American Embassy and the Special Branch put the number between 2,000 and 4,000.[68] Loudspeakers conveyed the proceedings to the crowds assembled outside. After the representatives had taken their seats, those who had gathered outside were invited into the hall, further fuelling the congestion inside which swelled to around 1,000 people by American Embassy estimates.[69] In the rush, one of the back doors to the cinema apparently collapsed under the weight.[70] The overwhelming turnout prompted one *Utusan Melayu* columnist to surmise if the reason behind SUMNO holding its meeting in such a small, old, dilapidated building was because it "deliberately" wanted to show "the poverty of the Malays in Singapore".[71] As thousands thronged and jostled outside, trying to get in, hundreds more huddled on congested benches and chairs inside the cinema "in an atmosphere of considerable excitement"[72] to hear the convention's three invited speakers indict the PAP government for its alleged oppressive treatment of Singapore Malays. Though intended initially as a forum for discussing the Malay situation, the convention, in the words of one *Utusan Melayu* correspondent who was there, was soon "carried away by angry shouts against Lee Kuan Yew". It resembled more and more "an UMNO meeting than a meeting of the Malays".[73] Adding to the heat was a "most fiery speech"[74] by the convention's keynote speaker, Syed Ja'afar Albar "Crowd in angry mood," reported the American Consulate, "emotions whipped up by UMNO Secretary-General".[75]

Launching "a vicious attack on Lee Kuan Yew and the PAP",[76] shortly after the convention commenced at 9.45 a.m., Syed Ja'afar, who spoke in Malay and without a prepared text, began his speech by saying, "We Malays in Singapore have for a very long time been suppressed and oppressed, either subtly or blatantly ... We Malays believed that they [the British] colonized us in order to protect and look after us, but they have betrayed our trust ...". To applause and cries of "The British are no more ... now drive the Chinese out" from the floor, Syed Ja'afar then reminded his audience of the "blatant oppression of us" by the Japanese "brand of colonialism" which followed and added that there were "different kinds of colonialism, some subtle, some blatant". Continuing, he said:

> And today, although Singapore has achieved independence through Malaysia, the fate of the Malays is even worse than it was during the

Japanese occupation. This is the reason why UMNO feels it necessary to hold this convention … I am very happy that today we Malays and Muslims in Singapore have shown unity, and are prepared to live or die together for our race and our future generation. If there is unity, no force in this world can trample us down, no force can humiliate us, no force can belittle us. Not one Lee Kuan Yew, a thousand Lee Kuan Yew … we finish them off …[77]

Breaking out in riotous applause, the crowds chanted: "Kill him! … Kill him! … Othman Wok and Lee Kuan Yew … Lee Kuan Yew … Lee Kuan Yew … Othman Wok". Accusing Lee of telling Malays, "Hey, shut up you, you minority race in this island", Syed Ja'afar asserted that the Singapore premier could never curb the Malays from expressing their anger and dissatisfaction. "Here I say to Lee Kuan Yew, 'You shut up and don't tell us to shut up'," Syed Ja'afar declared to noisy clamour and thunderous shouts of "Crush him!" from the floor. He then went on to allege that Lee's real objective was to rally the Chinese behind him in a struggle for racial hegemony:

> [T]o rally the Chinese behind him he creates a bogey and says to the Chinese "Hey you Chinese arise. Look, the Malays have arisen." … Having been defeated and having failed to get a place in Malaya, he is now trying to pit the Malays and the Chinese against each other … You know that in this country Lee Kuan Yew is trying to show the Chinese that the Malays are uniting to attack them. What is his objective in setting the two communities against each other? Lee Kuan Yew is a man who cannot survive in a peaceful atmosphere. He is like an *ikan sepat* which can live only in muddy water. [Shouts: "Arrest him"]

Expressing his misgivings also about Lee's alleged pro-communist leanings, Syed Ja'afar ranted: "It is he who is communist! It is he who is evil! It is he who is a traitor to this country." The crowd echoed in response, "Lee is a communist! Lee is a communist!" After the cries had died down, Syed Ja'afar said, "I do not want to accuse Lee Kuan Yew of being a communist … But I feel suspicious. I am doubtful of his real attitude". Although Lee was prohibited from going to Moscow, he went there, Syed Ja'afar said. The crowd then asked, "Why did Lee go to Moscow?" The UMNO Secretary-General replied, "What was whispered between Kuan Yew and officers of Soviet Russia we do not know. What made me more suspicious is that at a time when the Central Government was arresting communist youths in Singapore, Kuan Yew harboured the 'plen'." The crowd then chanted in response, "Arrest Lee! Confine Lee!" Regretting that the central government "has given way too much to Lee Kuan Yew" and had been too "soft" on him, Syed Ja'afar surmised that Kuala Lumpur did so probably in the hope that "the person to whom it is being soft may regain his senses". If he did not, Syed Ja'afar assured his audience that there were

> reasons to justify the keeping of Lee Kuan Yew inside [a prison]. …
> Whether Lee Kuan Yew will be kept inside or not, only time will tell. If
> he does not fully repent, he will one day get it.

The crowd "which could not be controlled anymore" and was "now in a stage of rage" shouted, "Arrest Lee! Confine Lee!"[78] Syed Ja'afar then told them not to worry too much because "We at the centre there have not just a pair of eyes watching Lee Kuan Yew but we have thousands of eyes watching him and his movements." What was important, he added, was that there should be unity in the Malay ranks. The purpose behind Syed Ja'afar's call for unity soon became apparent:

> I am anxious because Lee Kuan Yew is a slippery customer. I am anxious
> because on the 19th Lee Kuan Yew may throw water onto the fiery
> spirit and spirit of unity that we show today … This unity must be
> strong and must not be allowed to be shaken or undermined by any
> evil spirit. … But if there is disunity, if we are divided, on the 19th all
> the pains we have taken today, all our shouting, all the spirit that we
> have shown in the hot sun and in the rain, will be reduced to nothing
> by Lee Kuan Yew.

The crowd thundered in response, "We are united, we are ready to die!"[79] It was as clear a signal as any to the non-political Malay organizations to boycott the government-sponsored conference on 19 July. In short, what Syed Ja'afar wanted was for the Singapore government to abdicate its responsibility towards the Malays and recognize instead the 23-man Action Committee as the main vehicle for dealing with matters affecting the Malay community. That this was one of Syed Ja'afar's main motives in launching his virulent attack on the PAP government was not in doubt, as the UMNO Secretary-General himself disclosed in his speech:

> What we want is that if Lee Kuan Yew wishes to redeem his sins, if he
> wants to repent from his misdeeds, he should come and discuss things
> with us. He must not call individuals. It is the committee that we shall
> appoint today which will represent the Malays and the Muslims on this

island, and not the cultural organizations or the literary bodies that he will call on the 19th.

To the cries of "We want assistance, we want special rights for Malays …", Syed Ja'afar assured his listeners that UMNO would extend help to the Singapore Malays provided that they were fully united. "So do not feel weak and helpless," he charged them, "We must show Lee Kuan Yew that we are strong and can fight for our rights". Lee feared Malay unity, Syed Ja'afar said, "He is afraid not because we have our swords or long *parangs* at the ready, no. He is afraid because we have been united." In fact, Lee might be "scared" and "shivering" in his room that very morning, he suggested.[80] With that, the crowd burst into "thunderous applause".[81]

Although Syed Ja'afar was careful to preface and end his speech with the disclaimer that he was motivated by any desire to disrupt the "harmonious living" among the various races on the island or to "create animosity between Malays and non-Malays", the tenor of his oratory, which was designed to convince his listeners that "we are being oppressed"[82] and that the PAP was "out to oppress Malays as Malays",[83] proved otherwise. The crowd's frequent interjections and shouts, followed by Syed Ja'afar's own intervention at certain points in his address to plead for silence and calm so as to enable him to continue with his speech, showed that his listeners had, indeed, been roused and that Syed Ja'afar had no small role to play in exciting them. As an assessment prepared by the Joint Intelligence Committee (Far East) and submitted by the Commander-in-Chief (Far East), to the British Chiefs of Staff Committee put it, "The UMNO attack on the PAP reached its height on 12th July when the Secretary-General of the UMNO addressed a convention held by UMNO in Singapore *in terms which almost amounted to incitement to violence*".[84]

The two other main speeches which followed were in a similar vein: Ustaz Hassan Adli, the Vice-President of the PMIP, warned the Malays that they would be "driven into the sea" if they did not oppose the PAP and Ali bin Haji Ahmad, the Assistant Secretary-General of UMNO, accused the PAP of wanting to "turn this country into an Israel where the Muslims are pressed down and suppressed".[85] Until then the PAP had been portrayed only as being guilty of racial persecution. Ali's depiction of the PAP as anti-Muslim marked a significant escalation in the agitation campaign against the latter. As the Singapore government later commented on Ali's use of the "religious dynamite": "Clearly, the agitation against the PAP was now being carried with no inhibitions. The consequences of playing politics with religious and racial emotions as ammunition in a multiracial society should have been obvious to these persons."[86] The convention's meeting was shown over Television Malaysia the same evening.[87]

That the purpose of the convention was predominantly political was obvious to Pritchett, who reported that, although a number of memoranda concerning Malay problems were submitted to the convention, "there seem[ed] to have been little or no substantive discussion of the alleged grievances except in the context of violent denunciations of the PAP".[88] The three resolutions adopted by the convention regretted the "unjust" treatment of the Malays by the Singapore government. They promised to examine and follow up on the working papers submitted to the meeting, and called for a boycott of the government-sponsored meeting to be held the following Sunday. The conference also established a 23-man Action Committee, named *Jawatan Kuasa Bertindak Bangsa Melayu Pulau Singapura* (Singapore Malays Action Committee, or SMAC) to represent all Malays in dealings with the PAP government.[89] Apart from a handful of representatives of non-political organizations, the majority of those in the Action Committee were UMNO members[90] — its Chairman and Secretary were also Chairman and Secretary respectively of SUMNO. One member of the Singapore People's Alliance (SPA) and representatives from the other political parties, including three extremist PMIP members, and Isa Zain, the secretary of the violently chauvinistic PMU and identified by the central government as a "close Indonesian agent", were also included in the SMAC. As the American Consulate saw it, the meeting was "evidently designed [to] exploit complaints over resettlement of Malays from areas slated for redevelopment, to counter PAP inroads among Singapore Malays who hitherto had been in UMNO pocket".[91] The operation was also a "blatantly political attempt [to] undermine PAP efforts [to] gain foothold among Malays in Federation".[92] Syed Esa Almenoar himself admitted as much, in his conversation with Arthur H. Rosen and Terry T. Shima of the American Consulate on 14 July. As the minutes of the conversation recorded: "Throughout the conversation Almenoar made it clear that the UMNO campaign is designed to exploit the 'grievances' of a relative handful of Malays against the PAP and to undercut PAP efforts at developing a favourable image in the *kampongs* of Malaya."[93]

There was no let-up in the campaign against the PAP in the aftermath of the convention. Asked about SUMNO's next move, Almenoar, for example, disclosed in conversation with the American Consuls that the SMAC was preparing a report outlining their grievances which they planned to send directly to the Yang di-Pertuan Agong. When it was pointed out to him that the Agong, although leader of the Muslim religion in Malaya, had no executive power in Singapore, "Almenoar replied with a smile that this course of action is being considered simply because it would have the greatest psychological impact among Malays throughout the country". Thinking aloud, he also toyed with the idea of the SMAC sending representatives to disrupt the PAP meeting on Sunday:

> [They] would demand that the Committee be accepted as the sole negotiating representative of Singapore Malays. If the demand is accepted (and he obviously knew it would not be) the representatives would then demand immediate dissolution of the meeting on the grounds that there would be no further point in holding it. If the demand was rejected, the representatives "and others" would stage a walk-out.[94]

Pressure to boycott the government meeting on 19 July intensified, with the *Utusan Melayu* warning that those who attended the government meeting would be regarded as traitors to the Malay race. There "will be people among us who would work to destroy our unity and deviate", the *Utusan Melayu* leader asserted on 14 July, and urged Malays and Muslims to remain united in their resolve to boycott the forthcoming conference:

> If we are divided we will be destroyed. In this respect, the unity which the Malays and Muslims of Singapore have shown last Sunday will only achieve its purpose if the unity is maintained, and the people concerned uphold the resolutions which were passed. All efforts and energies will come to nothing if there is but a single person who disobeys the resolutions passed.

Since what was done at the New Star cinema constituted a challenge to the PAP, the editorial indicated that it was "sure the PAP government will take action" against those Malays it considered "extremists" who were only "expressing their dissatisfaction and who have gathered round to strengthen their spirit in opposing the oppression against them". Urging Malays to fear not, the editorial concluded by invoking a religious dictum, "Truth and sincerity will always get the blessings of the Almighty". The next day, the *Utusan Melayu* leader, warned that:

> ... if the PAP Government and the PAP leaders ... refuse to recognize the representatives that have been chosen by the convention and if the PAP persists in its efforts to split the Malays and carry out discussions with individual organizations ... [which had] expressed willingness to

> attend the meeting organized by the Singapore Government on 19th
> of July at the Victoria Theatre — _then neither the Malays, nor Dato Syed
> Ja'afar Albar, should be blamed for the consequences._[95]

Although the editorial did not elaborate on what these "consequences"
would be, the message it wanted to send was clear: if the Singapore
government proceeded with its meeting, there would be "consequences".
The ominous portent of consequences to come was to be repeated again,
this time by Syed Ja'afar himself. On 18 July, the day before the government-
sponsored conference, the _Utusan Melayu_ reported the UMNO Secretary-
General as saying that Lee Kuan Yew's efforts to "split the unity of the
Malays, Chinese and Indians (UMNO–MCA–MIC)" made him "a very
dangerous 'Father of Communalism'":

> If some undesirable incidents should happen, Dato Syed Ja'afar said,
> Lee Kuan Yew should not blame the _Utusan Melayu_ or the Malays but
> he himself should take full responsibility.[96]

As the Singapore government saw it, "Presumably by now some of the
agitators were aware that all their agitation could spark off 'undesirable
incidents' for which they disavowed responsibility in advance".[97]

Lee Meets Malay Organizations

Publicly, Lee Kuan Yew reacted to the proceedings of the SUMNO-sponsored
convention "with considerable restraint".[98] For several days, he avoided
making any direct reference to the meeting. But as pressure mounted for the
non-political Malay organizations to boycott the 19 July meeting, Lee issued
a statement on 17 July drawing attention to the political nature of the
convention and revealing that the PMU had been identified by the central
government paper _Indonesian Threat to Malaysia_ issued in April 1964 as the
body involved in recruiting agents for Indonesian terrorism. "Now they claim
that any organization which attends the meeting on Sunday is a traitor to
the Malay race," the statement said. Deploring the remarks "now daily being
made in the Malay press to confuse these non-political organizations and so
persuade them not to attend Sunday's meeting", the Prime Minister's note
disclosed that 83 of these organizations had so far accepted the government's
invitation although five subsequently withdrew after the call for boycott.
Urging them to attend the Sunday meeting, the statement gave the assurance
that Malay grievances would be carefully examined and promised to meet

Malay political parties (including the Action Committee) on a separate occasion so that their views could be aired on a "clearly party political basis". It asserted that the government had "the right and indeed the duty to solve all problems of all communities including the Malay community on its own".

Despite the SUMNO boycott, the PAP-sponsored meeting at the Victoria Theatre on 19 July "went off rather well".[99] Given extensive coverage in the press and on radio and television in Singapore, but not shown over Television Malaysia,[100] the meeting was attended by about 900 Malays,[101] said to represent 103 of the 144 organizations which had been invited, "itself an important success for Lee Kuan Yew", noted Pritchett.[102] In sharp contrast to the rabble-rousing speeches at the SUMNO convention, "the statements of PAP leaders were restrained, though firm in tone, and devoid of name calling or personal abuse."[103] In his opening address, Othman Wok regretted that the Malay press had confused the Malays with regard to their real position in Singapore and criticized the SUMNO convention as a move to split the Malays with a view to achieving its political aim.[104] Speaking after him in Malay, Lee underscored in his prepared address that the charges of unfair treatment of the Malays were basically part of an Indonesian propaganda effort to cause friction and conflict within Malaysia and subsequently exploited by SUMNO for diverse reasons. Defending the government's record in promoting the development of the Malays in the three main areas of education, employment and housing, Lee indicated that the government would take into account the Malays' "special position" and would be prepared "to go on doing everything reasonable and practicable to solve these problems". Turning to SUMNO's propaganda campaign against the government, Lee said that there "must be a limit to UMNO's political propaganda because they are in charge of the whole country, as they are the Central Government. Therefore, if they go beyond the limit the country will break up and collapse." He himself was "bewildered" that the SMAC included anti-Malaysia PMIP extremists and racists, including a "close Indonesian agent" identified by the central government, Isa Zain, the Secretary-General of the PMU. Lee insisted that the Singapore government alone held, and would not abdicate, the responsibility it had for solving the problems of all communities including the Malay community.

> For any group to say that they exclusively represent all persons of a particular community is a claim as extravagant as it is unfounded. ...
> For any group to demand the right to represent all the members of a community and so demand the exclusive right to advise what the

Government should do, is a challenge to the Constitutional rights and obligation of the Singapore Government. We do not intend to abdicate from our right to govern. It is the intention of this Government to do what is right and fair, and we will not be intimidated from doing our best in looking after the interests of the people of Singapore including the Malays who have, under our Constitution, a special position.[105]

The meeting was then given over to questions from the floor, most of which Lee fielded "deftly and sympathetically".[106]. Significantly, none of the delegates raised questions regarding the resettlement scheme which had been the spark which set off the fiery agitation campaign.[107] Lee refused to consider requests for special privileges, such as quotas for jobs, but promised every effort to train Malays to compete with non-Malays for employment. He also urged the organizations present to prepare a consolidated memorandum so that further discussions could be conducted soon.[108] As Rosen reported, citing a source who was there, Lee "encountered a certain amount of hostility at first. But before the meeting ended, Lee had won over virtually the entire audience by his explanations of PAP policies and actions on behalf of the Malay community, and his responsive handling of numerous questions from the floor."[109] "Lee clearly demonstrated he would not be pressured into making concessions which would alienate a large majority of Singapore citizens who comprise the PAP power base," the American Consulate noted, adding that thus far the Singapore government seemed to have had the "advantage in [the] public argument". But its observation was also that SUMNO officials seemed "less concerned with amelioration [of the] relatively few genuine Malay grievances than in propagandizing peninsular _kampongs_ against PAP."[110]

The American Consulate was not wrong, for the leader of the SMAC, Ahmad bin Haji Taff, immediately called the conference an "insult to the Malays" and accused the Prime Minister again of "trying to break the harmony and good relations between the Chinese and Malays, which have existed from time immemorial. Our campaign has been directed solely at Mr Lee Kuan Yew and his Government for not implementing the special rights clause in the Constitution — not campaign against the Chinese". Referring to Isa Zain, he said lamely that "He is only one of 23 people".[111] On the same day, 20 July, the _Utusan Melayu_ carried a news item on a speech by Ali bin Haji Ahmad in Pontian, on 19 July, in which the Assistant Secretary-General of UMNO reportedly warned party members about the PAP's efforts to intensify anti-Malay campaigns and divide the Malays by drawing a number of them into the PAP ranks. And then, in more inflammatory language, he alleged, "Only Malays who are ready to sacrifice the interests of their own race are willing to be supporters of the PAP." On the same issue, another news report cited Syed Esa Almenoar, the Secretary-General of SUMNO, urging the government to stop its eviction plans if it did not want the Malays "to make a noise" and demanding that it carried out its responsibilities by recognizing the special rights of the Malays. A third report quoted Kassim bin Hanafiah, the head of the Kedah West UMNO Youth Movement as saying that Lee's efforts to "cause the races in Malaysia to fight one another ... constitutes a challenge to the Malays as a whole" and this had been "proved in Singapore, where the PAP ha[d] tried in every way it can to drive away the Malays because they have succeeded in coming to power and the number of Malays is small". More suggestive were the headlines of this third news item:

> Challenge to All Malays — UMNO Youths
> Lee Kuan Yew Condemned
> Teacher forced student to smell pork — Protest[112]

As the Singapore government memorandum pointed out, the headlines "suggested that there was some connection between a teacher forcing a student to smell pork and the condemnation of Mr Lee Kuan Yew" where none in fact existed. "Only those who took the trouble to read the news story in full," the memorandum said, "would have discovered that the third of the headlines referred to a story which had nothing to do with Mr Lee and constituted the last paragraph of a lengthy news item".[113] The juxtaposition of the headlines was as mischievous as it was dangerous, for the following day, Tuesday 21 July, was a day of great religious significance to the Malays: Prophet Mohammed's birthday.

Notes

1. Mohamed Noordin Sopiee, *From Malayan Union to Singapore Separation: Political Unification in the Malaysia Region 1945–65* (Kuala Lumpur: Penerbit Universiti Malaya, 1974), p. 191.
2. *Malayan Times*, 3 May 1964.
3. Record of conversation between Lee Kuan Yew and W.B. Pritchett, 28 May 1964, A1838/280 no. 3027/2/1 Part 18.
4. *The Straits Times*, 27 April 1964.
5. Ibid., 28 April 1964.
6. W.B. Pritchett to Secretary, Department of External Affairs, 15 May 1964, A1838/280 no. 3027/2/1 Part 18.
7. *The Straits Times*, 29 April 1964.

8. W.B. Pritchett to Secretary, Department of External Affairs, 15 May 1964, A1838/280 no. 3027/2/1 Part 18.
9. Ibid.
10. Record of conversation between Lee Kuan Yew and W.B. Pritchett, 28 My 1964, A1838/280 no. 3027/2/1 Part 18.
11. Ibid.
12. W.B. Pritchett to Secretary, Department of External Affairs, 15 May 1964, A1838/280 no. 3027/2/1 Part 18.
13. Ibid.
14. Ibid.
15. _Malaysia Parliamentary Debates. Dewan Ra'ayat (House of Representatives) Official Report_, 21 May 1964, Col. 408–20.
16. Record of conversation between Lee Kuan Yew and W.B. Pritchett, 28 May 1964, A1838/280 no. 3027/2/1 Part 18.
17. Memorandum no. 1190, W.B. Pritchett to Secretary, Department of External Affairs, 12 August 1964 A1838/280 no. 3027/2/1 Part 19.
18. Head to Duncan Sandys, 15 October 1964, PREM 13/428.
19. Ibid.
20. Toh Chin Chye, "New Tasks Ahead for the PAP", in People's Action Party, _Our First Ten Years: P.A.P. 10th Anniversary Souvenir_ (Singapore: Central Executive Committee PAP, 1964), p. 126.
21. Memorandum no. 1057, W.B. Pritchett to Secretary, Department of External Affairs, 22 July 1964 A1838/280 no. 3024/2/1 Part 12.
22. "Memorandum Submitted by the Government of Singapore to the Commission of Inquiry into the Disturbances in Singapore in 1964" (March 1965), p. 12.
23. Telegram no. 514, Australian High Commission (Singapore) to Department of External Affairs, 27 July 1964, A1838/280 no. 3024/2/1 Part 12.
24. "Bubbling with Words", by Jangan Belindong Balek Teluniok, in _Malayan Times_, 28 April 1964.
25. _Malayan Times_, 29 April 1964.
26. Ibid.
27. _Berita Harian_, 29 April 1964.
28. Memorandum of conversation between Ali bin Haji Ahmad and Peter E. Juge, 18 June 1964, RG 59, Box 2454 Pol 12-8 1/1/64.
29. Sopiee, p. 192.
30. _Utusan Melayu_, 7 May 1964; _Berita Harian_, 1, 5, 6 and 11 May 1964.
31. Ibid., 28 May 1964.
32. Ibid., 5 June 1964.
33. Ibid., 6 June 1964.
34. _Berita Harian_, 14 May 1964.
35. Ibid., 21 May 1964.
36. _Utusan Melayu_, 21 May 1964.
37. Ibid., 10 June 1964.
38. Letter from the Tunku to Lee, 2 June 1964, Prime Minister's Office (PMO): Correspondence with Malaysian Prime Minister (1). The Tunku said that the residents had written to him to intercede on their behalf "as to whether the Singapore Government can see its way to allowing them to remain where they [were] until such time when they [could] be resettled somewhere outside the town, or in Malay-type _kampong_ houses". The Tunku also mentioned that the residents felt the rent which they would have to pay for the government flat was too high.

157

39. Letter from Lee to the Tunku, 9 June 1964, PMO: Correspondence with Malaysian Prime Minister (1).

40. US Naval Attaché (Singapore) to Chief Naval Operations (Washington), 19 June 1964, RG 59 Box 2450 Pol 2-1 4/3/64.

41. Airgram no. 60, American Consulate (Singapore) to Department of State, 27 August 1964, RG 59 Box 2457 Pol 23-8 1/1/64.

42. *Utusan Melayu*, 10 June 1964.

43. Ibid.

44. Ibid., 12 June 1964.

45. Ibid., 15 June 1964.

46. Ibid., 17 June 1964.

47. Ibid., 18 June 1964.

48. *Sin Chew Jit Poh*, 29 June 1964.

49. *The Straits Times*, 8 June 1964.

50. Memorandum "Working Paper of Singapore UMNO on the Position of the Singapore Malays", n.d., Appendix 3 in "Memorandum Submitted by the Government of Singapore …".

51. *Utusan Melayu*, 2 July 1964.

52. *The Straits Times*, 3 July 1964.

53. *The Malay Mail*, 1 July 1964.

54. *Sin Chew Jit Poh*, 5 July 1964.

55. *Utusan Melayu*, 4 July 1964.

56. Ibid.

57. "Statement from the Prime Minister's Office", Appendix 1.43 in "Memorandum Submitted by the Government of Singapore…".

58. Article 89 states: "(1) It shall be the responsibility of the Government constantly to care for the interests of the racial and religious minorities in the State; (2) The Government shall exercise its functions in such manner as to recognise the special position of the Malays, who are the indigenous people of the State, and accordingly it shall be the responsibility of the Government to protect, safe-guard, support, foster and promote their political, educational, religious, economic, social and cultural interests and the Malay language".

59. *Utusan Melayu*, 6 July 1964.

60. Ibid.

61. "Memorandum Submitted by the Government of Singapore …", p. 31.

62. *Utusan Melayu*, 9 July 1964.

63. *Utusan Zaman*, 12 July 1964.

64. US Naval Attaché (Singapore) to Chief Naval Operations (Washington), 10 July 1964, RG 59 Box 2451 Pol 2-1 7/1/64.

65. Airgram no. 60, American Consulate (Singapore) to Department of State, 27 August 1964, RG 59 Box 2457 Pol 23-8 1/1/64.

66. Memorandum "UMNO Convention at New Star Cinema, Pasir Panjang", 13 July 1964, ISD.

67. *Utusan Melayu*, 13 July 1964.

68. Airgram no. 60, American Consulate (Singapore) to Department of State, 27 August 1964, RG 59 Box 2457 Pol 23-8 1/1/64; Memorandum "UMNO Convention at New Star Cinema, Pasir Panjang", 13 July 1964, ISD.

69. Airgram no. 60, American Consulate (Singapore) to Department of State, 27 August 1964, RG 59 Box 2457 Pol 23-8 1/1/64.

70. Memorandum "UMNO Convention at New Star Cinema, Pasir Panjang", 13 July 1964, ISD.

71. *Utusan Melayu*, 18 July 1964.
72. Airgram no. 60, American Consulate (Singapore) to Department of State, 27 August 1964, RG 59 Box 2457 Pol 23-8 1/1/64.
73. *Utusan Melayu*, 18 July 1964.
74. Memorandum "UMNO Convention at New Star Cinema, Pasir Panjang", 13 July 1964, ISD.
75. US Naval Attaché (Singapore) to Chief Naval Operations (Washington), 17 July 1964, RG 59 Box 2451 Pol 2-1 7/1/64.
76. Memorandum no. 1057, W.B. Pritchett to Secretary, Department of External Affairs, 22 July 1964, A1838/280 no. 3024/2/1 Part 12.
77. Transcript from tape recording of speech by Syed Ja'afar Albar at the Malay convention at New Star cinema, Pasir Panjang, Singapore, on Sunday, 12 July 1964, in "Memorandum submitted by the Government of Singapore …".
78. *Utusan Melayu*, 13 July 1964.
79. Ibid.
80. Transcript from tape recording of speech by Syed Ja'afar Albar at the Malay convention at New Star cinema, Pasir Panjang, Singapore, on Sunday, 12 July 1964, in "Memorandum Submitted by the Government of Singapore …".
81. *Utusan Melayu*, 13 July 1964.
82. Transcript from tape recording of speech by Syed Ja'afar Albar at the Malay convention at New Star cinema, Pasir Panjang, Singapore, on Sunday, 12 July 1964, in "Memorandum submitted by the Government of Singapore …".
83. Ibid., p. 35.
84. COS 273/64, J.H. Lapsley to Chiefs of Staff Committee, "The Internal Security Threat to Malaya and Singapore from Indonesia", 8 October 1964, DEFE 5/154. (Emphasis mine)
85. *Utusan Melayu*, 13 July 1964.
86. "Memorandum Submitted by the Government of Singapore …", p. 38.
87. Ibid., p. 36.
88. Memorandum no. 1057, W.B. Pritchett to Secretary, Department of External Affairs, 22 July 1964, A1838/280 no. 3024/2/1 Part 12.
89. Ibid.
90. The members were as follows (source: Memorandum "UMNO Convention at New Star Cinema, Pasir Panjang", 13 July 1964, ISD:

Chairman	– Ahmad bin Haji Taff (UMNO)
Vice-Chairman	– Syed Ali Redza Alsagoff (UMNO)
Vice-Chairman	– Mohammed Kamil Suhaimi (PMIP)
Vice-Chairman	– Mahmood bin Ahmad (UMNO)
Secretary	– Syed Esa Almenoar (UMNO)
Asst. Secretary	– Ahmad bin Rahmat (UMNO)
Treasurer	– Shariff bin Ahmad (UMNO)
Auditors	– Hashim bin Abu Samah
	– Ustaz Mahmood bin Majid (Gerakan Pemuda Melayu Raya)
Committee	– Ahmad Jabri bin Mohammed Akib (UMNO)
	– Syed Ahmad bin Dahlan (PMIP)
	– M. Salleh bin Haji Mohammed Said
	– Ahmad bin Haji Yacob (SPA)
	– Isa bin Zain (PMU)
	– Yahya bin Mohammed Noor
	– Ali bin Abu (UMNO)

- Tengku Muda Mohamed (SMU)
- Syed Abdullah Alatas (UMNO)
- Esah bte Kassim (Kaum Ibu UMNO)
- Ahmad bin Abdul Rahman (UMNO)
- Mohammed Dali bin Moin (PMIP)
- Abdul Rahman bin Mohammed Zain (UMNO)
- Mohamed bin Simin (Singapore Malay Teachers" Union)
- Ustaz Ahmad Jailani Imam (Pilgrim Brokers Association)
- Mahmood bin Osman

91. Telegram no. 17, American Consulate (Singapore) to Department of State, 13 July 1964, RG 59 Box 2453 Pol 12 7/1/64.

92. US Naval Attaché (Singapore) to Chief Naval Operations (Washington), 17 July 1964, RG 59 Box 2451 Pol 2-1 7/1/64.

93. Memorandum of Conversation between Syed Esa Almenoar and Terry T. Shima and Arthur H. Rosen, 14 July 1964, RG 59 Box 2457 Pol 23-8 1/1/64.

94. Ibid.

95. *Utusan Melayu*, 15 July 1964. (Emphasis mine)

96. Ibid., 18 July 1964.

97. "Memorandum Submitted by the Government of Singapore ...", p. 41.

98. Memorandum no. 1057, W.B. Pritchett to Secretary, Department of External Affairs, 22 July 1964, A1838/280 no. 3024/2/1 Part 12.

99. Airgram no. 60, American Consulate (Singapore) to Department of State, 27 August 1964, RG 59 Box 2457 Pol 23-8 1/1/64.

100. Memorandum Submitted by the Government of Singapore ...", p. 36.

101. Memorandum "Social Gathering of Malay Cultural/Welfare/Sports Organisations at Victoria Theatre on 19th July, 1964", 28 July 1964, ISD.

102. Memorandum no. 1057, W.B. Pritchett to Secretary, Department of External Affairs, 22 July 1964, A1838/280 no. 3024/2/1 Part 12.

103. Ibid.

104. Memorandum "Social Gathering of Malay Cultural/Welfare/Sports Organisations at Victoria Theatre on 19th July, 1964", 28 July 1964, ISD.

105. "Text of Speech by the Prime Minister, Mr Lee Kuan Yew, at the meeting with Malay non-political bodies at the Victoria Theatre on Sunday, 19 July 1964, at 10.30 a.m.", in A1838/280 no. 3024/2/1 Part 12; also see *The Straits Times*, 20 July 1964.

106. Telegram no. 25, American Consulate (Singapore) to Department of State, 20 July 1964, RG 59 Box 2453 Pol 12 7/1/64.

107. "Memorandum Submitted by the Government of Singapore ...", p. 41.

108. Memorandum no. 1057, W.B. Pritchett to Secretary, Department of External Affairs, 22 July 1964, A1838/280 no. 3024/2/1 Part 12.

109. Airgram no. 60, American Consulate (Singapore) to Department of State, 27 August 1964, RG 59 Box 2457 Pol 23-8 1/1/64.

110. Telegram no. 25, American Consulate (Singapore) to Department of State, 20 July 1964, RG 59 Box 2453 Pol 12 7/1/64.

111. *The Straits Times*, 21 July 1964.

112. *Utusan Melayu*, 20 July 1964.

113. "Memorandum Submitted by the Government of Singapore ...", p. 42.

CHAPTER 6

THE SINGAPORE RIOTS

O n Tuesday 21 July, tens of thousands of Muslims, who had originally gathered at the Padang for the annual celebration of Prophet Mohammed's birthday, staged a procession through the streets of Singapore. Held just two days after the Singapore Prime Minister's meeting with Malay organizations, and three months after an intensive and sustained campaign by the Singapore United Malays National Organization (SUMNO) and the Malay press to depict Singapore Malays and Muslims as victims of a cruel racial persecution by the People's Action Party (PAP) government, the timing of the religious rally and the scale of the gathering could not have been less appropriate, or more potentially explosive. A little more than a week earlier, on 12 July, communal clashes had erupted in the town of Bukit Mertajam in Penang.[1] In brawls between Malays and Chinese, 2 persons were killed, 13 others injured and 23 arrested. A curfew was imposed for several days. This was the first serious Sino-Malay clash to occur in Malaya since the outbreak of racial violence in the immediate aftermath of the Second World War.[2] Though the Federal government played down the communal nature of the incidents, and claimed that the situation was returning to normal, it was clear that inflammable material was present and little was needed to set off another racial conflict.

The July Riots

Worried about trouble breaking out during the celebrations, Lee Kuan Yew had asked both the Commissioner of Police, John Le Cain, and Head of Special Branch, George Bogaars, for their assessment on whether anything could happen on 21 July. The police replied in the negative, while Special Branch had received unconfirmed reports that the Malays in the southern and city areas "were expecting trouble on Prophet Mohammed's birthday and that they had been told to wait for instructions".[3] But without strong evidence, it would be impossible for the Singapore government, under the circumstances, to cancel the celebrations without risking a violent backlash from within the Malay-Muslim community. It might have been feasible to request the central government to use its authority to cancel the parade. But, as the American Consul, Arthur H. Rosen, pointed out, "it is questionable whether the Central Government would under the circumstances have agreed that such action was necessary".[4] With control of the Singapore police and internal security in the hands of a Malay minister, Lee feared that the Malay extremists might be less inhibited in stirring up trouble in Singapore. On 20 July, a deeply concerned Lee warned the British Acting Deputy High Commissioner in Singapore, Frank Mills, that the Prophet's birthday the next day would be crucial.[5] It was not a good sign when inflammatory leaflets, allegedly issued by the *Kesatuan Kemajuan Islam*, were reportedly distributed in the vicinity of Geylang and Joo Chiat in the early afternoon of 21 July urging Malays to unite and crush "the dictatorial Chinese PAP Government led by the wretched Lee Kuan Yew".[6]

By 1.30 p.m., the participants for the procession had started gathering in contingents. An estimated 20,000 Malays and Muslims and members of some 73 organizations, including political parties and other Muslim associations, in Singapore had assembled for the annual celebrations.[7] But this year, something was different: amongst the thousands gathered some were out for trouble. Inflammatory leaflets, issued by a group calling itself *Pertobohan Perjuangan Kebangsaan Melayu Singapura*, had been distributed among the crowds at the Padang. These called on Malays to "destroy" the "Chinese" PAP government. "If we Malays do not oppose the PAP Government from now, within 20 years there will be no more Malays in Malaysia and there will be no more Sultans because the PAP Government does not want Malay Sultans," one charged.[8] Another warned of Chinese "planning to kill Malays" and urged Malays to unite and "wipe out the Chinese from Singapore soil because if we leave them alone they will make fools of the Malays ... Before the blood of Malays flows on Singapore soil it would be better to see the blood of Chinese flooding the country. Let us fight to the last drop of our blood!"[9] Inflammatory speeches by SUMNO leaders at the religious rally, notwithstanding a tacit understanding that speeches made by representative Muslims at the Padang would be religious and non-political in nature, did little to ease the tension.[10] Syed Ali Redza Alsagoff, SUMNO's religious officer, for instance, used his address to call upon all Malays in Singapore to unite to fight for their rights.[11] "We must show them that we can unite — the Malays must unite and arise," he said to loud shouts of "_Allahu Akhbar_" from all around the field and applause from the crowd.[12] As Othman Wok observed, "I considered that the manner in which he made this statement to the audience was one which could have stirred the feelings of all Muslims present. As a Muslim listening to his speech, I accepted that the word 'them' referred to non-Muslims."[13] SUMNO's Secretary-General, Syed Esa Almenoar, also spoke in the same vein:

> It is clear that Allah does not stop Muslims to be friendly with non-Muslims as long as they do not drive them out of their homes and disturb their religion ... but in everything that we do, there must be a limit and if it has come to that limit that such people who are non-Muslim who have disturbed our religion and who have driven us from our homes then Islam says that such people are cruel wrong-doers ... patience and understanding cannot stand the limit when people have come from within or from without, to disturb our castle, our place to live in and our religion. When it comes to such a climax, it is the duty of all Muslims to sacrifice their lives and properties for the sake of safety and for the sake of the country. The duty to the country and the duty to one's home is sacred and if any people, Muslims or non-Muslims alike, who work towards the disintegration and disruption of the country and our home such people will be treated as traitors. This is the teaching of Islam.[14]

Commenting on the address, the Singapore government asserted, "This speech cannot be called an appropriate one for the occasion in view of the communal agitation that had been going on for months. Coming as it did from the Secretary-General of Singapore UMNO, it was more like an invitation for trouble."[15] Manifestations of unruliness had in fact become starkly evident during the speech of the Yang di-Pertuan Negara, Yusof bin Ishak, who had arrived at around 3.30 p.m. to give the closing address. Towards the end of his speech, there appeared an orchestrated "booing combined with clapping from a section of the crowd slightly to the right of the stage as he faced the Padang".[16] A handful of unruly youngsters from a section of the crowd jeered and interrupted his speech with shouts of "Go home".[17] The booing, apparently, came from a section of the crowd where UMNO youths, identified by their banners, had congregated. When the jeering started, as one eye-witness noted, "a Malay youth wearing a blue shirt and a red arm-band jumped onto the steps leading to the stage and raised his left hand. He faced the group that was booing and the raising of his hand was obviously a signal for them to stop booing. In fact, the booing stopped immediately after he raised his hand".[18]

At 3.55 p.m., the Yang di-Pertuan Negara and other prominent Malay leaders led the procession. Immediately behind them were uniformed personnel from the army and police, the Workers' Brigade in their blue uniforms and contingents from the religious, welfare and cultural bodies. The political section followed with the SUMNO contingent at the head, trailed by the PAP and the Peninsular Malay Union (PMU) detachments. Directly behind the PMU group was a *bersilat* group, dressed in black, and wearing *pahlawan* caps, closely followed by the Partai Rakyat Singapura and the Pan-Malayan Islamic Party (PMIP).[19] At the junction of St Andrew's Road and Stamford Road, Yusof left the procession which then moved along Beach Road, Arab Street, Victoria Street and Kallang Road, travelling towards its dispersal point at Lorong 12 in Geylang. The procession was flanked on either side at intervals of approximately 50 yards by members of the Federal Reserve Unit (FRU) who kept in step with the marchers. A sudden shower of rain created some confusion as several marchers broke ranks to run for shelter. But otherwise the march-pass proceeded without incident, although Othman Wok, who was leading the 500-strong PAP contingent, observed that as his group turned into Victoria Street from Arab Street, "a number of Malay youths on the left side of the road on seeing our PAP flags shouted in Malay, "*Hidup China, mati Melayu*"(long live the Chinese, death to the Malays). "I cannot identify any of these Malay youths. I immediately told members of my group to keep quiet and not to reply."[20] Detective corporal Y.W. Chin, who was at a friend's house in the vicinity of Lorong 12 and Geylang Road, noticed that as the procession approached Lorong 12 from the direction of Gay World at about 5 p.m., the marchers had become "very rowdy. The participants were shouting and yelling in an emotional manner, more or less keeping in step with the tempo of the beating of the drums. ... I noticed that most of the Chinese shopkeepers along Geylang Road, quickly closed their shops."[21]

Just before 5 p.m., a Chinese FRU constable saw two Malay youths in the procession throwing unfinished packets of ice cream at a Chinese cyclist along Victoria Street, between Arab Street and Sumbawa Road, hitting him on the chest. After intervening to pacify both parties, the constable continued with the procession. Shortly after 5 p.m., near the junction of Kallang Road and Kampong Soopoo, about seven to eight Malays (including the two who had earlier been involved in the incident with the Chinese cyclist) suddenly broke away from a section of the procession which was about a third behind the PAP contingent. The constable approached them and told them in Malay to rejoin the main stream. Only one refused to return and he had to be pushed forcibly into line. "_Lu Polis boleh tolak sama orang ka?_" (You, Police, do you think you can push people around?) someone called, followed by jeering from the group. "_Pukul, pukul sama dia,_" (Strike, let's all strike him) another shouted. A group of about 20 Malays then deliberately broke away from the procession and, ignoring the constable's order to rejoin the marchers, surrounded him and shouted threateningly, "_Pukul, pukul_". By now, the size of the group had swelled to about 50. A second FRU Chinese constable who came to his rescue was also surrounded by the unruly group. Seeing the commotion, a third FRU constable, a Malay, quickly intervened and tried to pacify the crowd, which was by now becoming aggressive, but without success. He immediately ran into a coffeeshop at around 5.15 p.m. to call for more police back-up. Meanwhile, a Malay from the group of "rowdies" suddenly punched the second constable on the back. Blows then rained on the first constable, hitting him on the chest and stomach.[22] Forcing his way out, and with his attackers hot in pursuit,[23] the constable fled into a bicycle shop along Kallang Road, "his face deadly pale and panting heavily".[24] The proprietor of the bicycle shop, fifty-one-year-old Ho Kok Mong, remembered that when the policeman ran into his shop he was "bleeding from his forehead". But before Ho could close the door, the Malay chasers had rushed into his shop and assaulted him as well with their fists. Breaking free, Ho escaped through the rear entrance.[25]

Meanwhile, the commotion and shouting had also caught the attention of Othman Wok, who was marching with the PAP contingent just a few yards in front. Running to the rear to see what was happening, he witnessed "several Malay youths apparently from the PMU section crowding around, pushing and punching a uniformed policeman" whom he immediately recognized to be from the FRU by the uniform he wore. The constable was "trying to push away the Malay youths but he was outnumbered". The incident took place only a matter of yards away from the rear of the PAP contingent and beside the PMU marchers who were not wearing any distinct uniforms apart from their _songkok_.[26] At the sound of the commotion, Rahim Ishak, who was at the head of the PAP marchers, noticed "a group of about 10 Malays from the UMNO group of marchers in front of us rushing back towards Lorong Soopoo", SUMNO religious officer, Syed Ali Redza Alsagoff, among them.[27] Corroborating this account, Mohammed Ariff bin Suradi, also with the PAP marchers, said he saw "more than 10 UMNO youths breaking away from their group and rushing across the divider and passing our group".[28] "[T]hose who were rushing to the commotion spot [were] shouting '*Allahu Akhbar*'," recalled Mohammed Ghazali bin Ismail, Political Liaison Secretary at the Ministry of Culture, who was among the PAP participants. Ghazali then saw some youths from the Partai Rakyat Singapura marchers "run up to other contingents in the procession, spreading 'news' that Malays were attacked by a Chinese policeman. ... I did not see any Chinese policeman attacking any Malay from where I was."[29]

The procession had by then come to a halt, but Othman instructed his members not to break their ranks and to continue to move forward. Shortly after, as the PAP contingent approached Kallang Bridge, it encountered another incident. As Othman recalled:

> This time there was a commotion in front of us on the left side of the road, almost parallel to the UMNO section. I heard sounds of people being chased and saw a Chinese boy, about 11 to 13 years of age, being pushed against the wall on the left side of the road opposite Firestone building. Several Malay youths were pushing this boy against the wall but they did not assault him.

Rahim Ishak also witnessed "a man raise his hands and continuously beat another man who was on the ground". When the police intervened and carried him into a police car, the man's face was "spattered and streaming with blood".[30] A few seconds later, Othman "saw a cork hat hurled into the air on the left side of the road. This belonged to a male Chinese about 40 to 45 years of age, who was riding a bicycle in the direction of Geylang. I later heard that this male Chinese was set upon and assaulted." Ariff, who witnessed the "cork hat" incident noticed "about 10 to 15 Malay youths surrounding a person and beating him up with their fists and kicking him. ... Then within a few minutes, I saw this person who was bleeding from the face being carried away by two policemen who had arrived on the scene."[31] Seconds later, Othman saw an overturned scooter on the left side of the road and "several Malay youths with red arm-bands assaulting a male person a few yards ahead on the left hand side of the road. This was directly opposite the gate of the Firestone factory. I was not able to observe the race of the person being assaulted." During the same incident, Ghazali, saw "about 10 male Malays breaking off from the procession and rushed upon a Chinese bystander on the pavement", attacking him with fists and feet. Two or three of the attackers were wearing red arm-bands, he observed:

> Soon afterwards the Chinese bystander was seen to collapse to the ground but the attackers continued to kick him with their shoes. Blood was seen streaming out from the mouth and face of the victim. He staggered to lean himself against a car parked at the spot. But the attackers circled him ... and continued with their attack till their victim lay helplessly on the road.[32]

Sensing danger, Othman decided not to continue the procession and diverted the PAP contingent into the premises of the People's Association at the old Kallang Airport, locking the gates behind them. Othman immediately rang the Prime Minister.[33]

But by then it was pandemonium. Soon after the assault on the Chinese FRU constable, some 11 other Chinese pedestrians and hawkers were attacked near the vicinity of Kallang Road and Kampong Soopoo. Chinese stalls and shops were also damaged. The rioting continued for about 20 minutes until police reinforcements arrived. In the meantime, rumours were spread among the marchers that the Chinese were assaulting Malays. By 5.30 p.m., fighting had erupted in a number of _lorongs_ along Geylang Road progressing in the direction of Geylang Serai.[34] Y.W. Chin described the scene:

> [S]uddenly, a section of the procession broke through the Police cordon at the junction of Lorong 11. Trouble started. I heard broken glasses coming from that direction. I saw stones and bottles being thrown by the participants at the Chinese onlookers as well as into shophouses. A number of shop windows were broken by them. A number of Malays then attacked some Chinese. ... While this was going on at Lorong 11, the advance or forefront group then broke through the Police cordon at the junction of Lorong 12. Instead of all marching into Lorong 12, some of them charged along Geylang Road. At this stage, the whole situation was totally out of control.[35]

Running to join a police radio car at Lorong 14, Chin overheard rioters shouting "_Pukul China_" (strike the Chinese) and saw them overturning a number of cars and scooters, and smashing all the windows of cars parked along Geylang Road.[36] The group of rioters, numbering about 100 "rough looking" Malay youths, charged from the direction of Lorong 12 towards

Geylang Serai, scattering in all directions and overturning Chinese stalls as they ran.[37] As Police Commissioner, John Le Cain noted, "The majority of the victims were Chinese. It would appear that the group of persons responsible for the incidents at Kallang Road/Kampong Soopoo continued down Geylang Road beyond the dispersal point at Lorong 12 attacking [the] Chinese all the way down".[38]

Unaware that trouble had broken out, Tan Keng Cheow, a stenographer with the Public Utilities Board's gas department, was travelling along Geylang Road at about 6 p.m. on his scooter when he witnessed a mob of about 30 or 40 Malays "all in black trousers and dark coloured shirts" chasing a lone Chinese man. At Haig Road, his pursuers caught up with him and set upon him. Two other Chinese pedestrians in the vicinity were also assaulted. Eight to nine more Malay youths dressed in the same dark attire as the rest of the mob stood poise at the road divider waiting for the traffic to ease in order to join the attack. When they saw Tan, they kicked him off his scooter and started to assault him. Tan ran to the nearby Geylang Police Station where he was told that a riot had broken out and was advised to return home as quickly as possible. Walking along Guillemard Road on his way home at about 6.20 p.m., Tan saw another group of Malays on their way to Geylang Road moving towards him. One of them had a loud hailer and was shouting in Malay, "Don't be afraid. Don't be afraid. We have hundreds of our brothers to help us". Upon seeing Tan, one Malay in a gang a short distance away, pointed at him and shouted, "That is one of Lee Kuan Yew's supporters. All Chinese are Lee Kuan Yew's supporters. We must eliminate them!" As Tan recalled, "All of them at the same time rushed at me. They punched me from all directions. I defend myself as best as I could. … One of the blows hit my face and my spectacles dropped down." Another group of Malay youths soon crossed the road to join the attack, but Tan managed to escape and ran back to the Geylang Police Station. Tan observed that one of his attackers was wearing a red badge with a *keris* pointing downward.[39]

The areas most badly hit by the riots were confined along Geylang Road, Guillemard Road and Geylang Serai. But as news of the clashes became known, incidents "began to mount with each passing hour and trouble had spread to other parts of the island".[40] The Chinese who had been "purely defensive at the early stages of the trouble along Kallang Road and Geylang Road had now begun attacking Malays in the predominantly Chinese areas of the island".[41] And from 6.30 p.m., new clashes occurred on Queen Street, Rochore Road, Arab Street, Victoria

Street, Johore Road, North Bridge Road and South Canal Road.[42] By 7.30 p.m., Jalan Besar, Madras Street, Club Street and Palmer Road were added to the list of areas where riots had taken place. At about 8.15 p.m., an American Consulate car had its windscreen smashed by a hail of stones from a Chinese crowd brandishing clubs and bottles as it travelled towards the city carrying a diplomatic courier from the Paya Lebar airport, but the Malay driver was not injured.[43]

The outbreak of violence brought the entire police force into action. Reinforcements were rushed to the scenes of the clashes. Police cordons quickly sealed off the affected areas and increased mobile patrols throughout the island. The scale and spread of the violence severely taxed police resources. At 5.45 p.m., Le Cain quickly arranged for military assistance and the First and Second Singapore Infantry Regiments, the Sixth Royal Malay Regiment and the First Independent Reconnaissance Squadron were consequently put on standby. At 8.00 p.m., they were deployed to the Central, Queenstown, Joo Chiat, Orchard Road and Kandang Kerbau Police Stations. British military assistance was also sought — the Far East Command having put three of its units, including a Gurkha battalion, already on a state of high alert — but not called out.[44] A state of danger to public order was proclaimed at 8.23 p.m. and at 9.30 p.m., a curfew was imposed throughout the island. Cinemas cancelled their 9.30 p.m. shows and buses were pulled off the streets. Everyone was advised to stay indoors. Those unable to return to their homes sought refuge in police stations.[45] By midnight, 21 July, 220 incidents had been reported, 178 persons had been injured, 32 of whom were admitted to hospital, and 4 had been killed. Seven Chinese shophouses at Jalan Eunos were burnt down.[46] In Geylang Serai, 13 Chinese shophouses and 23 vehicles suffered the same fate.[47] Two policemen had been injured and a total of 113 arrests had been made.[48] Given the widespread nature of the riots, police anticipated more retaliatory action the following day.[49]

With Tunku Abdul Rahman on a visit to the United States, and Interior Security Minister Ismail bin Abdul Rahman on an inaugural Air France flight to Paris for a week, the Acting Malaysian Prime Minister, Tun Abdul Razak, was left with a "pretty thin team" to handle the crisis.[50] Reminding Malaysians in his broadcast in Malay, over Radio Malaysia, that they had lived together in peace for hundreds of years, Tun Razak urged all races in Singapore and Malaya to remain united: "You must not forget that we are facing a common enemy. ... If we fight one another, Malaysia will be destroyed and so will all of us."[51] More significantly, he underscored that the central government "would not allow any group or community to be oppressed".[52] Echoing Tun Razak's call for unity, MCA leader, Tan Siew Sin, warned in English of the "powerful enemy at our gates waiting to destroy us" and appealed to Malaysians not to "allow our minor differences to divide us … Let us remember that united we stand, divided we fall."[53] Going on the air at 10.45 p.m. and speaking in Malay, Mandarin and English, Lee asked the people to stay indoors and not to "make things worse by yourself trying to act as policemen".[54] He said the disturbances had started shortly after 5 p.m. when the procession was passing by the Kallang Gas Works. "[A] member of the Federal Reserve Unit asked a group who were straggling to rejoin the main stream. Instead of being obeyed he was set upon by them. Thereafter a series of disturbances occurred as more groups became unruly and attacked passers-by and spectators," Lee disclosed. "What or who started this situation is irrelevant at this moment," he added, "All the indications show that there has been organization and planning behind this outbreak to turn it into an ugly communal clash. All that was needed was someone to trigger it off". He promised to "sort these things out later on".[55]

The curfew brought only temporary relief. It was not strictly obeyed and "groups of Chinese and Malays armed with offensive weapons were seen in the open."[56] Twenty-four incidents were reported and a "considerable number of curfew breakers were arrested".[57] The lifting of the curfew at 6 a.m., 22 July, still left an uneasy tension in its wake, a false expectation of normalcy, soon to be crushed by the eruption of renewed violence by mid-morning, with the number of incidents totalling 35 by 10.30 a.m. Shortly before this, at 9.40 a.m., a racially mixed party of Federal ministers led by Tun Razak and included Tan Siew Sin, Mohammed Khir Johari and S. Manikavasagam, the Minister for Labour, flew into Singapore in a "display of unity"[58] to review the situation. Syed Ja'afar Albar had also intended to fly to Singapore immediately after news about the riots broke out but was apparently restrained by Tun Razak and Khir Johari. Confronted with fresh violence, Tun Razak immediately ordered a re-imposition of the curfew from 11.30 a.m. after talks with Singapore leaders and briefings by security chiefs, including the Inspector-General of Police, C.H. Fenner. But Sino-Malay clashes continued to escalate. By 2 p.m., a total of 102 new incidents had been recorded since midnight of 21 July.[59] Assaults had occurred in the Geylang, Geylang Serai, Joo Chiat and Jalan Eunos areas, and also along Victoria Street, Kallang Road, Jalan Besar and Lavender Street, with the majority of the victims being Malays. As Le Cain observed,

"It is obvious that the Chinese were the aggressors and were retaliating for the attacks made on them the previous day. … The Malays, on their part, seem to have been on the defensive".[60] Given that Chinese secret society gangsters had played a major part in the attacks on Malays, the police immediately "pursued an intensive campaign against them and made a large number of arrests".[61]

Tun Razak's party meanwhile visited casualties at the Singapore General Hospital and toured Kampong Melayu in Geylang before meeting Malay community leaders in Federation House to discuss the situation. Assured that the situation was under control, if still serious,[62] and leaving behind Khir Johari to handle matters, Tun Razak and Tan left the same evening for Kuala Lumpur. The acting Malaysian premier reportedly turned down a suggestion of a joint broadcast with Lee.[63] Both Tun Razak and Lee apparently did not get on well in Singapore. Tun Razak later claimed that Lee had wanted to talk about "all sorts of long-term problems" which the Malaysian deputy premier was loath to do in view of the immediate task of restoring order. Lee on his part felt he was "frozen off" by Tun Razak. Nor did he like Tun Razak's suggestion that he should be touring the troubled sections of the city (as Tun Razak had been) along with representatives of the other communities appealing for calm on the grounds that the SUMNO people he would be obliged to associate with were the communal agitators in the Singapore Malays Action Committee (SMAC).[64] Making his broadcast from Kuala Lumpur instead, Tun Razak reiterated his earlier plea for racial harmony in the face of the external threat. Making no mention of his talks with Lee and playing down the racial nature of the riots, Tun Razak, implicitly disagreeing with the Singapore premier's version of events, blamed the trouble instead on a bystander who had thrown an empty bottle into the procession on the Prophet's birthday. "It is clear," he said, "that the incidents were not caused by communal friction but resulted from the act of a mischievous person."[65]

The Tunku's own reaction to the disturbances, expressed as one of initial "shock", and his exhortation to his countrymen to refrain from further acts of violence, were relayed via a Voice of America hook-up and put on the air the same evening as Tun Razak's broadcast. Presenting a version different from that asserted by his deputy, the Malaysian premier put forward his suggestion that foreign agents were behind the outbreak of violence:

> I can't help but think that there must be an insidious enemy responsible for all this. The procession to celebrate the birthday of the Prophet has

been held year in and year out but never has there been anything untoward which has marred the procession. So why must it happen now? It is more than a coincidence that while we are having confrontation from Indonesia these communal clashes should have all of a sudden flared up.[66]

Lee's own statements over radio and television that night diplomatically avoided pointing a finger at who was responsible for the riots. Instead he reassured the country that there were sufficient police and troops to enforce law and order without discrimination. Lee reiterated, however, his promise that when order had been restored, "everything will be properly investigated and resolved". His public performance thus far had been good, remarked W.B. Pritchett — "calm, restrained and reasonable".[67]

Lee's outward calm, however, masked his inner dismay. He worried for the "end of Malaysia"[68] He feared, too, that Kuala Lumpur might take advantage of the situation, declare martial law, and "set about imposing a Federal solution rather than acting through the Singapore Government".[69] Only with great reluctance did he finally accede to the British Acting Deputy High Commissioner's request the day before to invite Tun Razak to Singapore in an endeavour to restore the situation.[70] As Pritchett noted, Lee took the recent events as yet further overwhelming evidence of Malayan insincerity about Malaysia and wondered if he should "throw his hand in or at least stand aside, pointing out that he was now powerless in the security field".[71] The Singapore Prime Minister was also "scathing at the failure of the Federal Government to take an explicit and resolute stand against racialism and to support his position". Kuala Lumpur appeared to him unmoved by his argument that the establishment of communalism in Malaysian politics and undermining the PAP government in Singapore were not in Malaysia's interests. He had also been "appealing strongly to the British to weigh in with the Federal Government".[72] "Lee is taking a despairing line in discussion with the British," Pritchett remarked. "His argument is that when the Chinese realize he is powerless in the security field and cannot protect them, they will turn to the Barisan Sosialis."[73] Although Pritchett commented that "Armageddon is probably further off than he thinks, or tells the British he thinks", he nevertheless conceded that the outlook from Singapore "is rather disturbing".[74] The second day of rioting had resulted in 185 incidents and 179 persons injured. Eleven more people had been killed, bringing the death toll for the first two days to 15.

Police reports for Thursday, 23 July, confirmed that the situation had not improved as the number of incidents rose sharply when the curfew was lifted from 5.30 a.m.[75] By 9.00 a.m. when the curfew was re-imposed, 19 more incidents had been added out of which six were fatal.[76] Khir Johari, accompanied by SUMNO leaders Syed Esa Almenoar and Syed Ali Redza Alsagoff, quickly toured trouble spots in Kampong Melayu and Kampong Kaki Bukit appealing for calm.[77] The forecast by Special Branch, however, remained gloomy.[78] In a departure from the sporadic nature of the previous days' pattern of attacks, unconfirmed reports received by Special Branch suggested that "large bodies of men [were now] being organized for trouble".[79] At Kampong Chai Chee, some 4,000 Chinese had apparently amassed for an attack on Kampong Melayu. More than a thousand Malays, on their part, had also assembled at a mosque in Jalan Labu where they were incited by the _Imam_ to go _jihad_ to avenge the alleged massacre of Sheikh Osman and his family by the Chinese in the area. Trouble was averted only after the Sheikh was contacted and appeared on television with Khir Johari to quell the ugly rumour.[80] A "happy note" amidst the gloom was the formation of three goodwill committees, consisting of mixed teams of Malay and Chinese community leaders who toured the _kampongs_ trying to restore calm and confidence.[81] By midnight, the total number of incidents for the day reached 105.[82]

Although the number of clashes had fallen from the previous days' highs, Tun Razak was still "clearly worried about how things would go in Singapore", reported H.M. Loveday, the Australian Acting High Commissioner in Kuala Lumpur, who dined with him earlier in the evening. The curfew was containing the situation, but Tun Razak feared that the Indonesians and communists might still exploit the fertile ground for trouble. Refusing to blame the Malay extremists entirely for the riots, the acting Malaysian deputy premier suggested that Lee's remarks about the Malays not having special privileges under the constitution, while technically correct, were nonetheless insensitive and provocative, and were more likely the cause of the present trouble than what the Malays had been doing.[83]

That same evening, in a briefing to foreign correspondents in Singapore, Lee was to give his version of the events of the past few days that put the blame squarely on UMNO's shoulders. Speaking off the record in the second part of the press conference, the Singapore premier said that the riots did not start spontaneously but were the outcome of the "machinations" of UMNO extremists, using the *Utusan Melayu* as a mouthpiece, to inflame Chinese and Malays:

> There is no real antagonism between the Malays and the Chinese. The whole thing has been cuffed up [sic]. ... At the gathering at the Padang it could be seen that something was going amiss. Some people booed the Yang and there had been some inflammatory speeches made on what should have been a religious occasion. What I want to know in the long run is whether this agitation by the Malays is all Ja'afar Albar or are they following ... UMNO. The 23-man Malay Action Committee is going right to the brink. I have agreed to Malaysia on the basis of a Malaysian nation. The tragedy is that they [the people inspiring the agitation] can never win. As long as they try to keep the Malays apart from the other people in Malaysia they make them vulnerable to Sukarno. They must be made Malaysians. We must not bend to communal bias. Malaysia has suffered a grievous blow and without real, rapid and remedial ... without a reversion of what has happened ... and taking steps to end the spread ... Malaysia is beginning to die.[84]

Critical of Kuala Lumpur's efforts to keep him in the background, the Singapore premier said he had no authority over the troops and police and had been brushed aside by Federal ministers coming to Singapore from Kuala Lumpur and criticizing him publicly. Another ploy in this humiliation campaign was for Federal ministers to make television and radio statements without consulting him or referring the script to him. He was sure Kuala Lumpur could do more to restore the situation:

> The Government in power in Kuala Lumpur should affirm that Malaysia is a Malaysian nation in which the Malays have a special position. This is in the Constitution. If I were the Tunku I would return and I would speak to the Malays who are behind all this. I would say that all this has got to stop and I do not want any more nonsense. The Tunku should say, "Let us stop all this and make Malaysia work".

The Singapore premier suggested that the British could perhaps also exert their influence towards that end: "The British have to underwrite Malaysia. They will have to pay the cheque in paying for troops and defence. If this is made clear to the British they can make a stand and spell it out to Kuala Lumpur".[85] Lee apparently made his points with "great emotion and several times almost broke down, but pulled himself together quickly". Attributing this to the Singapore premier being under "great personal strain"[86] and "frustration in a situation in which he perceives great danger, but has no authority and no confidence in or communication with those that have"[87], Pritchett warned that the political tension between Kuala Lumpur and Singapore "appears to be developing as a more dangerous threat to Malaysian stability than communalism — though Lee would argue that this is inevitable so long as Kuala Lumpur 'condones' communalism".[88] As his counterpart in the Malaysian capital subsequently commented, reports of Lee's criticism of the central government to the foreign press "are already circulating in Kuala Lumpur and will not make things any easier between Lee and Razak".[89]

By Friday, 24 July, the communal clashes had subsided considerably, with only seven incidents reported between 4.30 p.m. and 9.45 p.m., although one resulted in another death.[90] The next few days saw a further decline in the number of assaults and, on 2 August, the curfew, which had been imposed since 21 July, was lifted completely and the police and military stood down the next day.[91] Rumours of renewed clashes in Geylang, which caused a panic on 6 August and gave rise to a number of assaults on both Chinese and Malays in the evening, prompted the remobilization of the entire police force from 5 a.m. the next morning. It stood down again at 8.50 p.m. on 7 August 1964. All in all, the outbreak of racial violence had exacted its heavy toll: 23 people were dead and 454 injured. Some 3,568 persons were arrested, 715 of them charged in court and another 945 placed under preventive detention.[92] The July race riots, as Toh Chin Chye pointed out, had been "unprecedented in the history of Singapore".[93] They were not to be the last.

After the Riots, the Political Battle

Even as the racial flare-up subsided, another battle loomed. As Donald B. McCue, the American Chargé d'Affaires in Kuala Lumpur, observed, "Not all elements here are so determined to put harmony and national interest above racial and political issues"; they seemed determined instead to "continue the war on the political level".[94] Though barred from Singapore, Syed Ja'afar, for instance, did not remain silent and attempted to carry on his anti-PAP offensive at the political front through the *Utusan Melayu* and the UMNO journal, *Merdeka*, which he controlled as Secretary-General and, which by and large, served as his "mouthpiece".[95] Syed Ja'afar's intentions did not go unnoticed by the American Embassy which warned that "Albar intends [to] use UMNO house organ, *Merdeka*, which [is] directly under his control, to continue [the] campaign against Lee".[96] Efforts by more moderate UMNO leaders, like Khir Johari, to muzzle him were not entirely effective after he threatened to resign as Secretary-General. Popular among the rank and file of UMNO, Syed Ja'afar wielded influence and was not someone who could be easily controlled. The Singapore government commented: "One would have thought [that] after the outbreak of race riots in Singapore those persons conducting the campaign would have been more restrained in what they said. On the contrary, their propaganda subsequent to the riots was revealing, as it was irresponsible".[97] What the campaign subsequently revealed was not only, as the PAP had charged, the irresponsibility of its sponsors but also their more insidious political agenda — the forcible replacement of the duly elected PAP government in Singapore.

After a one-day pause in its propaganda war on 21 July, the *Utusan Melayu* returned swiftly to the fray. On 22 July, with the rioting still at a high, it carried an inflammatory report condemning Lee for "push[ing] aside the special rights of Malays in Singapore".[98] In another equally imprudent commentary on the Singapore outbreak, its leader suggested the next day that communal harmony prevailed in Malaya because non-Malays had not been treated as "step-children", the implication being that racial strife existed in Singapore because Malays had been oppressively treated. It was left to *Merdeka*, UMNO's journal, to assert more explicitly on 24 July that the incidents happened because:

> ... there is something wrong or something incorrect which has been done by the PAP Government of Singapore, which has caused a feeling of dissatisfaction or frustration amongst a section of the people about their future. This incident clearly shows the lack of integrity of the PAP Government in serving the interests of its people and of the minorities in particular who feel that they are being oppressed and victimized.[99]

The same issue also referred to a report in which Tun Razak told a *Merdeka* journalist who interviewed him on his return from Singapore that the central government "will not allow any group to oppress another group" and, henceforth, "would pay serious attention" to the Malays in Singapore.[100] Another inflammatory story appeared two days later, this time in the *Utusan Zaman* with the heading: "Lee Responsible for Singapore Riots". Based on comments by an Indonesian daily, the *Indonesian Herald*, the article implied that for "weeks and months" the

Singapore premier had been making statements that "smack of communal sentiments" and that the racial outbreak had been "ordered by an organization that is trying to do harm to ... Malays who are of the Muslim faith".[101] As the Singapore government commented, "What was the motive in printing from an Indonesian paper, while the situation was still tense, an accusation that the riots were instigated by Mr Lee and that they were tinged with 'anti-Islam' feelings?"[102] Writing in the same issue, and comparing the PAP government's record with that of the Labour Front regimes of David Marshall and Lim Yew Hock during which the people "lived in peace and harmony", *Utusan Zaman's* columnist, Pak Awang, asked: "Why now, ever since the PAP came into power under the leadership of Baba Lee Kuan Yew, there is trouble in the Island of Temasek. What is the cause?" Leaving no doubt as to where the responsibility should lie, the *Utusan Zaman* published another story on 2 August in which the Deputy Chief Minister of Sabah, Harrith bin Mohamed Saleh put the blame squarely on "communal extremists in the PAP which is the ruling party in Singapore". On the same day, Syed Ja'afar Albar, breaking his enforced silence in a speech to the Kampong Dato Keramat Hall in Kuala Lumpur, also lashed out at the "devil in Singapore who sets the Malays and the Chinese against each other". Echoing Pak Awang, the UMNO Secretary-General asked: "Why is it that under the British, Japanese, David Marshall and Lim Yew Hock governments no incidents happened in Singapore?" He attributed the unfortunate incidents to "the acts of that wretch Lee Kuan Yew".[103] The UMNO leader was to make a more serious charge in a reply to foreign correspondents in which he alleged that the Malays "were attacked by persons who were probably paid by Lee Kuan Yew to create disturbances":

> Lee Kuan Yew's object in creating disturbances in Singapore at the time when the Malays were gathered together at the Prophet's Birthday was to create the impression to the world that the Malays had been influenced by Indonesia and were causing the disturbances for the benefit of Indonesia.[104]

PAP rule was not only depicted as oppressive to the Malays and responsible for the violence, but it was portrayed as discredited and found wanting in a time of crisis. The *Merdeka* in its 24 July issue cited earlier, for instance, had asserted — erroneously as it turned out — that "Not one of the Malay leaders in the PAP went to meet the people and visited the areas involved in the disturbances" and that they were found instead "taking shelter in police stations and returned home only when the curfew order was imposed". In his speech on 2 August Syed Ja'afar made a similar charge but aimed this more personally at the Singapore premier:

> He was afraid to come out. He ran away and hid himself. While Tun Razak and the Honourable Mr Tan Siew Sin and other Ministers were in Singapore to save and pacify the people, he was shivering with fear in his steel trunk. After the police and the soldiers had come out, he also came out. ... After peace had been restored he came out, the cowardly leader.

That a sinister political purpose lurked behind the new wave of anti-PAP propaganda was not in doubt, at least to the Singapore government. Behind Syed Ja'afar's "reckless disregard for truth" and his "habit of inventing any story to work up emotions", like the "many other falsehood" in the campaign, the PAP leaders saw a political goal: it was "part of the myth the extremists were building up — that the Singapore Government and its leaders were in a state of collapse and their replacement, therefore, justified".[105] In fact, such a call for the removal of the PAP government was openly made by *Merdeka* barely three days after the riots had started:

> [W]e are of the opinion that for the good of and in the interests of peace in the island of Singapore and the State of Malaysia, the leadership of the PAP Government who are in power now should be changed and replaced ... We also have hopes that the Central Government will act firmly and realize what is happening now and pay serious attention to the fate of the Singapore Malays, so that they will not feel frustrated, because they solely depend on the Central Government now.[106]

That the bid to oust the PAP was made in the UMNO organ could not be insignificant for as UMNO Assistant Secretary-General Ali bin Haji Ahmad had intimated, the editorials in *Merdeka* reflected "some of [the] thinking in high UMNO leadership circles", including those of the Tunku and Tun Razak.[107] Extracts of its call for the replacement of the PAP leadership were reproduced in the *Utusan Melayu* the next day. "The implications of the editorial are clear," remarked the Singapore government, "The price of their stopping their campaign based on racialism was the replacement of the duly elected leaders of the PAP Government — and the Central Government, if necessary, should act firmly in this regard".[108] Harrith's remarks, reported in the *Utusan Zaman* of 2 August, carried a similar suggestion for the PAP to be proscribed:

He said the Malays have been living peacefully with Chinese for a long time, but when a multiracial party becomes the ruling party, communal extremists and those who distort facts will cause disturbances and chaos. Enche Harris then said that the evils brought by multiracial party system should be wiped out.

Another bid to remove the PAP was made by the _Menteri Besar_ of Johore, Hassan Yunos. In remarks reported by the _Utusan Zaman_ on 9 August, Hassan put the blame for the disturbances in Singapore on the PAP government and "its incompetent administration" and said that "if the PAP Government was unable to ensure peace in the island it should be replaced by another government."[109] The same issue carried a report of the resolution from the Pontian division of UMNO calling on the central government to take firm action for the sake of the Malays in Singapore.[110] As the American Chargé d'Affaires, Donald B. McCue revealed, "According to a source close to UMNO Secretary-General Ja'afar Albar, discussion of the possibility of removing Lee Kuan Yew has reached the highest circles of the Malaysian government."[111]

That the racial riots had opened up a dangerous new dimension in the threat to the PAP's political survival in Singapore was not in doubt to its leaders. Lee had originally suspected that the riots were part of a conscious UMNO plot to cause violence with the intention of letting the situation in Singapore boil to a point where the central government could declare martial law and take over.[117] But Goh Keng Swee discouraged him from this trend of thought.[113] Both Lee and Goh, however, believed that the Tunku and Tun Razak knew, and approved of, the anti-PAP campaign, even if they had not been associated with it. The attack, as the PAP leaders argued, was already in full swing long before the Tunku's departure for London and Washington, while Tun Razak later confirmed with Goh that he had full control over the extremists and the press.[114] Goh thought, however, that Tun Razak probably did not foresee the riots. But even if Tun Razak did not conspire with the extremists, the central government had displayed, in Lee's opinion, shocking irresponsibility by not reining in the extremists, such as Syed Ja'afar Albar, before the situation got out of hand.[115] Pressure by _Merdeka_ and UMNO leaders for the replacement of the PAP only added to the suspicion about Kuala Lumpur's ultimate intentions.

If the riots had been, as the PAP leadership had intimated to Pritchett, part of an UMNO plot to "damage, even wreck, the PAP in Singapore and eventually to secure the removal of Lee Kuan Yew"[116] and to "discredit

179

[the PAP] in Malaysia as a non-communal party",[117] it was very nearly successful. It was the second big blow to hit the PAP after its electoral defeat in Malaya three months earlier. As Rosen commented, "Lee's image and authority were seriously impaired in Singapore." Rosen added, "[F]or a few days, Central Government leaders virtually took over the Singapore Government ... Kuala Lumpur's muscles were flexed for all to see".[118] The racial violence and the PAP's impotence in the face of Federal power had severely affected its stature in the eyes of the Chinese community, now "gravely disquieted"[119] and angry that the government was unable to protect them and had not been forceful enough in taking action against continued Malay baiting.[120] The prevailing impression among the Chinese that the Malay security forces sent by Kuala Lumpur to quell the violence had not been entirely impartial in carrying out their duties, and had taken sides in the racial imbroglio, did not help. Special Branch, for instance, noted that the Chinese had complained that "Malays in the Police and Military have discriminated against the Chinese in their handling of incidents involving Chinese and Malays":[121]

> It is learnt that the Chinese everywhere in S'pore are talking about the unfair actions taken by the Malay soldiers and Policemen in dealing with the recent Sino-Malay clash. Somehow or other, the Chinese have been led to believe that the Malay soldiers and Policemen arrest only Chinese curfew breakers and not Malay curfew breakers. ... Rumours that the Malay soldiers and Policemen were unfair in their duties in keeping peace are everywhere, especially in coffeeshops and market places.[122]

Consequently, the view was held among the Chinese that had it not been for the Chinese secret society members who rallied to their defence, more Chinese would have been killed or injured.[123] Among the Malays, disquietude was also evident. As a Special Branch report noted, many Malays were dissatisfied with Lee's explanation of the incident that sparked off the riots in his television broadcast on 21 July and were more inclined to accept Tun Razak's version.[124] Goh himself told Pritchett that the PAP probably lost the Malay votes it won in September 1963.[125]

PAP ministers who toured their constituents in the wake of the riots were consequently "alarmed by the poor reception they [were] accorded". Both S. Rajaratnam and Toh Chin Chye were reportedly jeered. "This [convinced] PAP leaders they have at least temporarily lost their support," remarked William B. Kelly of the American Embassy. "They reportedly believe[d] that if an election were held now PAP would lose".[126] The riots had also hurt the PAP's political hopes in Malaya, discrediting its non-communal appeal and ruining its prospects with the Malay masses.[127] As Rosen ruminated, "Lee's hopes of gaining influence in the Federation have received a severe setback among *kampong* Malays, and even among some Chinese who are reluctant to have any Chinese politician 'rock the boat'."[128]

Among the PAP leaders, there was no early consensus on what constituted an appropriate response to the outrage, except that considerable pressure existed within the party to attack UMNO's communal politicking.[129] Both Rajaratnam and Toh wanted an open inquiry with UMNO admitting the bulk of the responsibility. Without this, they felt, the party would be unable to regain the support of the people who were convinced the PAP failed them by allowing the riots to occur. As Pritchett noted, "Toh says … [the] people were waiting for the next step, which has always been an inquiry previously. The people expect[ed] prompt action and … would not understand, or, eventually, tolerate any attempt to 'let things ride'."[130] After his off-the-record indictment of UMNO to the foreign correspondents on 23 July, Lee had also wanted to "come out against UMNO" more openly.[131] Favouring an inquiry, he argued that unless the PAP called for one, it would be beaten to the punch by the Barisan Sosialis (BS).[132] Goh was also "firm"[133] about an investigation. Unless the Singapore government stood up to Kuala Lumpur, he conceded, "we might not last long in power",[134] But a formal inquiry would be equally unpleasant, Goh acknowledged, and was bound to exacerbate the level of mistrust now felt by both sides. Nor did he think it would be realistic to expect UMNO to accept greater responsibility for the riots.[135] Goh reasoned that a more fruitful approach might be to emphasize the PAP's crucial role in keeping Singapore out of the hands of the communists or the other anti-Malaysia forces, and how it was in Kuala Lumpur's interests to help the PAP regain its position on the island. This meant the inclusion of PAP leaders in the national government. He had in mind Toh and Rajaratnam as possible candidates, both being influential figures in the party. Goh, who felt that "his colleagues already regarded him rather as a Kuala Lumpur man",[136] thought he should stay in Singapore to keep company with Lee. In return, Goh apparently was willing to consider withdrawal of the PAP from Malaya.[137]

Doubtful that Kuala Lumpur realized or worried about the consequences of a PAP collapse, Lee was not sanguine Tun Razak would accept the proposal. Lee felt that possibly only the threat by Britain to withhold its military support in combating *Konfrontasi* (confrontation) was likely to be more effective in bringing Kuala Lumpur to its senses,[138] using an argument he first put to the foreign correspondents on 23 July and subsequently presented to the British, Australian, New Zealand and United States governments to get them to intercede on Singapore's behalf.[139] As with merger, Lee believed that only outside pressures would get the Malay leaders to come to terms.[140] Be that as it may, Lee was prepared to give Goh's proposal a try. He felt that the threat of opening an inquiry could, in the meantime, be held in reserve while discussions proceeded with Tun Razak.[141] Should Kuala Lumpur still be unwilling to take steps to bolster the PAP — or worse, try to exploit its weakness — both Toh and Rajaratnam would favour "going down fighting". Goh and Lee, however, took a more realistic approach and were resigned to "fight another day".[142]

A more widely representative Federal government was also the solution the British High Commissioner sought. Head had in mind a national government which included two representatives from Singapore and one each from Sabah and Sarawak. He also had grave misgivings about undertaking an investigation into the disturbances. Having been forewarned by his deputy, James Bottomley, who spoke to Lee on 23 July, about the Singapore premier's wish for an inquiry into the riots,[143] Head had an hour long meeting with Tun Razak the next day. His doubts about the wisdom of an inquiry and his hope that, if one was convened, it should not be made public,[144] found a sympathetic hearing from Tun Razak who also did not want a post-mortem. The less said, the better, Tun Razak felt.[145] Head's plea for a more representative Cabinet, however, was not enthusiastically received by the Malaysian deputy premier whose antipathy towards Lee was apparent throughout the meeting.[146] Tun Razak kept blaming Lee for the riots and said he could do nothing with Lee and did not know what to do about him in the future.[147] It was up to Goh Keng Swee to talk to Tun Razak.

Goh Keng Swee had known Tun Razak since their student days in Raffles College and got on well with the Malaysian deputy premier. In March, he had accompanied Tun Razak to the tripartite ministerial conference in Bangkok and apparently did a good job at the summit of "speaking up forcefully for Malaysia".[148] In the April elections, Goh had also stayed in Singapore and did not campaign in Malaya. Credited for being a "steadying force"[149] within the Singapore Cabinet, and known for his "calm, reasoned approach",[150] Goh was the only Singapore minister Tun Razak knew well enough to discuss their mutual problems openly. So it was that when Goh suggested coming to Kuala Lumpur, Tun Razak invited him to stay at his house for several days.[151]

Goh found Tun Razak, as Head had, deeply distrusting of Lee in their discussions which began on 28 July. The Malaysian deputy premier, who "complained vigorously and at length about Lee", made Goh two offers: either a coalition government on condition that Lee resigned as Prime Minister, possibly to be given some other assignment (the United Nations was mentioned as a short-term posting), or a political truce in which both governments would operate in their respective spheres of influence to be agreed upon, on condition that the PAP dealt with the Singapore Malay community only through Khir Johari, who was also the chairman of the SUMNO Liaison Committee.[152] As a prerequisite for any settlement, there must be an end to the PAP's attempts to win the Malays.[153] Tun Razak said the politics organized along communal lines would have to continue for at least a generation.[154] When Goh asked if, as a quid pro quo for Lee's resignation, Syed Ja'afar would be removed, Tun Razak brushed this aside, saying, "We can deal with him."[155] Tun Razak's terms, as Goh later confided to Pritchett, were "those of victor to vanquished".[156]

Both alternatives were poorly received. When informed by Goh about Tun Razak's terms, Lee was prepared to resign in the interest of an enduring solution. He later told Pritchett that "if he thought he was really the barrier to cooperation he would go. But the Malays could not see that they would be bound to clash with any Chinese leader who stood up to them".[157] There were also some doubts as to whether Lee's resignation would actually resolve the more fundamental problems that confronted Malaysia. On the contrary, Lee's withdrawal could severely jeopardize his important role in containing the BS's threat in Singapore, it was argued. Nor was it likely that the PAP could accept Tun Razak's condition that it dealt with the Malays only through Khir Johari.[158]

The next morning, Tun Razak came to Goh's room before breakfast and told him that, on further reflection, he saw snags in the propositions he put forward the day before and would like to withdraw them, a reversal Head attributed to pressure from his more extreme colleagues.[159] They were hasty reflections and he needed more time before proposing a solution.[160] Tun Razak said that he could not see any satisfactory solution with Lee outside the picture and proposed meeting up with both Lee and Goh on Saturday, 2 August, when he would be passing through Singapore *en route* to Borneo. He had declined Goh's earlier suggestion that Toh and Rajaratnam met him in Kuala Lumpur on Wednesday, saying that he did not know them well enough to open his mind to them.[161]

Briefed by Goh about Tun Razak's proposals, Head opined that the terms were unworkable. R.H. Wade, the New Zealand High Commissioner, also felt that Singapore "would find it very difficult to accept" Tun Razak's proposals. Even if Lee removed himself for a period, "his successor in the event would be Toh, who though sensible is fiery and little more *persona grata* with Kuala Lumpur, rather than Goh who has become tagged as soft to Kuala Lumpur". It was also politically impossible for the PAP to deal with the Malays in Singapore only through Khir Johari and, without a quid pro quo by the Alliance to stop its anti-PAP activity, the suggestion that the PAP should suspend its politicking in Malaya was hopelessly "one-sided". When Wade pressed Tun Razak on the quid pro quo, he said "UMNO had been in Singapore a long time and was not to be repressed — as far as the MCA was concerned, however, there was no problem (I suppose because the MCA is virtually non-existent as a political force in Singapore)". Repeating what he had told Goh, Tun Razak also mentioned that "there must be no attempt to erode Malay political domination". Tun Razak's remarks suggested to Wade that the Alliance "is trying to play PAP as a communal rather than a multiracial party with an eye to the future, is ultra sensitive about its proselytizing among Malays. Government show an unfortunate tendency to try to meet present crisis by closing Malay ranks".[162] Tun Razak's back-pedalling also led to some speculation about how much authority he had for making his offers and whether the Tunku had been consulted. Goh had told Head, for instance, that Tun Razak acted like a plenipotentiary.[163] Head's own view after meeting Tun Razak was that he "would not stick his neck out for a reconciliation nor make any imaginative gesture".[164] At the very least, however, "some cards are being laid on the table" and, as H.M. Loveday, the Australian Deputy High Commissioner in Kuala Lumpur, optimistically put it, "[some] good could come of this".[165]

The meeting with Tun Razak on 2 August turned out instead to be a total failure.[166] Though Tun Razak had not renewed his demand for Lee's resignation, he had not offered any basis for cooperation either. The Malaysian deputy premier said that the only way for the PAP to cooperate with Kuala Lumpur was to join the Alliance, a prospect he would not consider for another two years, which he subsequently revised to "six months or so",[167] on condition that, in the transition, the PAP kept off the Malays in Singapore and refrained from "politicking" in the peninsula,[168] which included staying away from the Chinese.[169] He offered no quid pro quo on the part of UMNO. It was an "almost impossible demand" for Lee to fulfil, Head noted: if he accepted Tun Razak's terms, his supporters would feel that "UMNO had silenced Lee without any concession at all by UMNO" and make Lee appear to be "weak and under the thumb of UMNO".[170] To make it worse, Tun Razak had also told Lee of his intention to bring a minister from Sabah into the Cabinet, thus ensuring both Sabah and Sarawak would be represented federally, and highlighting even more starkly the exclusion of Singapore. Tun Razak's attitude left both Lee and Goh in no doubt that he was himself opposed to a coalition with the PAP and would advise the Tunku against it. Both the Singapore ministers' efforts to discuss the issues and dangers "had not gone down very well" with Tun Razak who refused to discuss them. Nor was he sympathetic to their request for an inquiry. Tun Razak's advice for them to "take things easy" and "play it on a low key" was politically impossible. As Goh ruminated to Pritchett, things could not just settle down, and the PAP could not remain quiet and would have to "make some moves" against UMNO to hold its position in Singapore. A despondent Goh saw no prospect of movement at all towards better ties with Kuala Lumpur, only a serious deterioration in relations over the next six to twelve months. Things could come to a "sticky end", he warned. In the meeting, Tun Razak had offered further talks which Lee privately professed were "pointless".[171] For Lee, the Malaysian deputy premier's attitude only confirmed what he had already suspected — that Tun Razak was uncertain of his position and would just spin out the talks until the Tunku came back.[172]

The failure of the talks left Lee with no choice but to press ahead for an inquiry. Head cabled the Commonwealth Relations Office: "Lee is quite adamant that if this is all UMNO has to offer he will reject it and will attack UMNO for part they played before riots and will demand enquiry", a process that was "likely to increase rather than diminish political bitterness" and "almost bound to lead to … more rioting".[173] Lee favoured demanding an immediate special session of the Dewan Ra'ayat (House of Representatives) to convene a commission of inquiry and publish a White Paper that would include the inflammatory articles published by the vernacular press as well as excerpts from provocative statements and speeches by UMNO leaders. If his request was turned down, the Singapore government would set up its own commission and issue its own White Paper.[174] Persuaded by Head to postpone the showdown until after the Tunku got back,[175] Lee publicly announced, on 4 August, his intention to hold a "post-mortem".[176] As the worried British High Commissioner put it, "almost everything will depend on Tunku".[177]

The Post-Mortem

Under pressure not to hush up the riots, the PAP leaders were particularly anxious to have an official inquiry which they believed would not only exonerate the Singapore government of the charge of mistreating the Malays in Singapore but would also result in an indictment of UMNO leaders in precipitating the violence. Seizing upon an inadvertent reference by Khir Johari, on 29 July, to a possible post-mortem of the incident by the central government, Toh Chin Chye said that the sooner such an inquiry was set up, the better.[178] Toh was to renew his call on 2 August: "The hands of the Singapore Government are clean. We have done nothing wrong. We want to let the people see and know the truth."[179] Kuala Lumpur, however, took the line that it was doubtful whether an inquiry would serve any useful purpose and that the major task should be the revival of good race relations. "The least said ... the better," was Ismail's terse response.[180]

If blame were to be apportioned, Khir Johari would rather see it fall on the Indonesians. "I am sure Indonesia is behind all the trouble in Singapore," he surmised.[181] But the Head of Special Branch, George Bogaars, found little evidence pointing clearly to Indonesian involvement. "Although he agreed that the riots owed something to Indonesian influence, Bogaars discounted the theory of direct Indonesian instigation of which he said there was no evidence at all," reported W.A. Luscombe (Second Secretary, Australian High Commission, Kuala Lumpur).[182] The British High Commission was also not clear about the actual part played by Indonesian agents, even though it was acknowledged that "they have been doing their best to stir up communal tension".[183] A report prepared by Headquarters Singapore Base Area, however, felt that while the Indonesians would probably "make political capital out of the disturbances" by citing them as another example of anti-Malaysia feeling in a member state, "It is not considered that Indonesia is directly involved in encouraging the disturbances."[184] This was also the conclusion of the American Consul, Arthur H. Rosen, who did not think the Indonesians played an important role in either "fomenting the riots or in exploiting them": "Although Indonesian propaganda of a racist nature had circulated in some Malay *kampongs* during recent months, this was only a contributing factor to the racial tension".[185]

Kuala Lumpur's own version certainly left little doubt that Lee and the PAP were much to blame because of "their unsympathetic handling of Singapore's Malay minority".[186] Lee, in particular, was also accused of being "the real provocateur" behind the Singapore riots.[187] As the American Ambassador, James D. Bell remarked, "Tun Razak, like other [Alliance] leaders, traced [the] beginnings of [the] Singapore riots to Lee Kuan Yew's Seremban speech of June 30."[188] Apparently, Tan Siew Sin had also "tried to put the onus of the present ruckus on Lee," Bell added. "[I]n his view the present difficulties stemmed from an exchange of polemics originating with this speech by Lee." Syed Ja'afar also took the same line, as McCue's notes of a meeting with the UMNO Secretary-General revealed: "Albar said he had been replying to Lee's Seremban speech … [which] could not be left unanswered. Statements such as the one at Seremban proved that Lee Kuan Yew would have to go, he said".[189] Alliance leaders claimed that Lee's "public and provocative reference [in his speech] to the sensitive and heretofore unmentionable fact that non-Malays outnumber the Malays in Malaysia"[190] had set the stage for the Singapore disturbances. They argued that Lee's speech "preceded inflammatory remarks by UMNO leaders which have been blamed as the cause of the July 21 race riots in Singapore … The UMNO blasts at Lee were in reaction to his goading."[191] As Peter Juge (Second Secretary, American Embassy) reported, "UMNO only took up the challenge, according to Alliance sources, and seized upon Malay discontent in Singapore, which had been growing without UMNO's prior intervention, as a way of retaliating politically against Lee in his own backyard."[192]

The Alliance's version, however, did not appear at all convincing to Rosen who remarked: "Allegations that the June 30 speech by Lee Kuan Yew … triggered hostile reactions by Malay leaders apparently ignore the fact that the campaign against Lee had already been under way for months."[193] There were also doubts as to whether Lee's remarks had been reported accurately. The American Embassy's First Secretary, Robert W. Moore, commented: "The Embassy has been unable to determine whether *Utusan Melayu* reported accurately what Lee said at Seremban. Other newspaper stories [English and Chinese language press] covered the speech in less detail. No other story known to the Embassy quoted him as being so provocative as indicated in *Utusan Melayu*."[194] As for the charge that the Singapore government had been oppressive to its Malays, Wellington's Department of External Affairs had this to say: "As far as we can gather, Lee's treatment of the Malays in Singapore has been enlightened and certainly skilful enough to attract a large slice of their votes in the last state elections".[195] And even if the government had been hasty in ordering the resettlement of Malays affected by redevelopment, "relatively few

Malays were directly affected," observed Rosen, "and channels existed to take up their complaints with the government without exciting and inflaming Malays throughout the island and in the Federation".[196]

The Singapore government's own version of the riots was that they "were not a spontaneous and unwilled manifestation of genuine animosities between the races" but had been deliberately provoked. They were "willed by irresponsible, and reckless propaganda based on falsehoods and distortions of facts"[197] in a "systematic and sustained effort to work up communal disaffection and racial and religious hatred among the Malays" in order to further the political objectives of certain communal extremists.[198] Their principal purpose was to "re-establish the political influence of UMNO among Singapore Malays". Another was to "use the Singapore Malays as pawns to consolidate Malay support for UMNO in Malaya": "By placing the blame for the riots on the Singapore Government and depicting it as oppressing and persecuting the Malays of Singapore, Malays outside Singapore could be terrified into rallying around UMNO for protection". A related objective was to intimidate the PAP into abandoning its efforts to win the Malays, and therefore, disavowing its multiracial philosophy. As the Singapore government saw it, "The communal campaign ... was in the nature of a 'Hands Off Malays' warning". Unless the PAP acquiesced to this demand, it "must be prepared to face racialist blackmail".[199]

The British did not doubt that "the riots had a political rather than a religious origin".[200] Head saw the disturbances as the outcome of the sharpening of communal tensions resulting from the propaganda campaign spearheaded by the pro-UMNO *Utusan Melayu*. Already rankled by the loss of the Malay seats in the September Singapore elections, UMNO's resentment, Head said, increased after the PAP intervened in the Federal elections, and after the party's "continuing efforts to set up a grass-roots organization in all the main Malayan towns".[201] Head had "no doubt that this extreme element of UMNO played a considerable part in stirring up the first communal riots which took place in Singapore".[202] UMNO's complicity was also not in doubt in a report prepared by the Joint Intelligence Committee (Far East) for the British Chiefs-of-Staff Committee. "The campaign against the PAP," it noted, "was carried on by UMNO branches in Singapore with the active and open support of UMNO Headquarters in Kuala Lumpur." The object of the campaign, it added, "appeared to be to prove that the PAP was essentially a Chinese communal party, and not the multiracial party it claimed to be, and to regain the support of those Singapore Malays ... who voted for the PAP in the [1963] elections".[203]

This assessment of UMNO's complicity in the racial outbreak was also shared by the American Consulate. Like Head, Rosen believed that the riots were "politically inspired"[204] and the "logical outcome" of the "long period of anti-PAP political agitation, with strong communal overtones, by UMNO leaders":

> For a long period preceding the riots UMNO leaders in Singapore, frustrated by their total defeat in the 1963 Singapore elections and abetted by UMNO national leaders in Kuala Lumpur, orchestrated a campaign to recapture Malay popular support from the Singapore Government's People's Action Party. This campaign picked up steam after the PAP made its abortive entry into the national political scene during the Federation elections last spring. ... [D]uring the past few months Malay nationalist leaders, chiefly UMNO officials, stirred up the _kampong_ Malays in Singapore (and elsewhere in the Federation) with stories of PAP mistreatment of Malays in favor of Chinese interests.[205]

In this connection, the role of Syed Ja'afar Albar in stirring up the communal disturbances remained a controversial one. Head's view was that Syed Ja'afar had made a "disgraceful and inflammatory speech whipping up Malay feelings against Chinese. As a responsible and high up member of UMNO I do not think that he should even have been allowed to do this because although object was political, namely to detach Malay votes from Lee Kuan Yew, effect was obviously bound to be divisive and destructive and likely to stir up trouble."[206] There is little doubt that the UMNO Secretary-General made an inflammatory speech, on 12 July, in his attack on Lee and the PAP. His antipathy towards Lee also ran deep. To Head's suggestion that he discussed his differences with Lee instead of attacking him, Syed Ja'afar shot back: "Talk with Lee; I'll shoot him."[207] Part of the reason why the UMNO leader attacked Lee so vehemently, surmised William Smithies (Second Secretary, Australian High Commission), was because "he hates Lee Kuan Yew so much".[208] Smithies' own view was that the Singapore riots were "largely the work of Ja'afar Albar and his Malay-extremist crowd". Although they probably did not start out to provoke the bloodshed, in their "clumsy efforts to take the leadership of the Singapore Malays away from Lee", they succeeded in "stirring up a communal hornets' nest that has not quieted down yet".[209] The more cautious Australian Acting High Commissioner, H.M. Loveday, however, felt it would be extreme to go so far and suggested that Syed Ja'afar sought to incite racial incidents in Singapore.[210] Nevertheless, there seemed to be a consensus, even from within UMNO and Alliance ranks, albeit privately, that the UMNO's Secretary-General's agitation had "worsened the atmosphere",[211] at the very least, if not "provided the spark"[212] for the July riots. In discussion with American Consulate officials, Syed Esa Almenoar, for instance, "acknowledged that Dato Ja'afar Albar ... had made an inflammatory speech against Lee Kuan Yew".[213] Jerrold M. Dion (Third Secretary, American Embassy) had also reported MCA Member of Parliament, Tan Toh Hong, as saying that "there was little question ... that Ja'afar Albar had touched off the July riots in Singapore with an inflammatory speech". And while Tan Siew Sin was not as forthcoming in blaming Syed Ja'afar, Bell noted in conversation that "Tan apparently feels that ... Ja'afar Albar has been indiscreet and unwise in his recent public statements".[214] Even Nik Daud, the Permanent Secretary at the Ministry of Internal Affairs, saw Syed Ja'afar and the Malay extremists as bearing the main responsibility for the riots. As McCue reported, "Dato Nik Daud ... has told me his Ministry [was] convinced riots [in] Singapore were caused by Malay extremists. ... He admitted July 12 Syed Ja'afar meeting and speeches [in] Singapore had further increased communal uneasiness which already existed". The significance of Nik Daud's admission was not lost to McCue who commented: "Daud, a Kelantanese, is a Malay Malay. If there were any doubt regarding Malay extremists being responsible for Singapore riots Daud would give them the benefit of doubt. Fact Daud's Ministry convinced Malays responsible for riots may eliminate or at least keep out of public eye any ... investigation of disturbances [in] Singapore".[215]

Having an important bearing on the issue of whether the riots were "spontaneous or deliberately provoked"[216] is also the question of who set off the actual fighting. Controversy still surrounds the matter. According to Tun Razak's version, the outbreak of violence was presumably spontaneous in origin, caused by someone, possibly a mischief-maker (by implication Chinese), throwing a bottle into the procession celebrating the Prophet's birthday. Lee's version said that the trouble began when a group (by implication Malay) broke off and resisted instructions from a policeman to return to the procession. As the *Merdeka* of 24 July put it, "Who is right, Lee or Tun?"[217]

Tun Razak's "bottle throwing" explanation was probably based on an account concerning one Syed Alwi bin Syed Mohamed, a part-time actor, who was allegedly hit on the head by a bottle, while following the procession near Kampong Soopoo, and sustained an injury which bled profusely. Just prior to this, Syed Alwi had confronted and scolded a male Chinese youth for throwing some joss-papers through the window of the first floor of a coffeeshop called Yew Seng Restaurant. The youth, in turn, threw a bottle at him, wounding Syed Alwi on the left side of his head and causing blood to gush all over his face. While he was being led away by two Malays, Syed Alwi apparently told members of the procession that a bottle thrown by some Chinese hit him. Angered by the provocation, some Malays from the procession ran into the coffeeshop and assaulted the Chinese there. A Chinese FRU constable tried to intervene but he too was set upon. Some of the Malays then ran towards Geylang Road, overturning stalls and roadside dustbins along the way.[218] However, there were a number of versions to the Syed Alwi incident. Special Branch, for instance, noted that the "exact location and time of this incident [were] very dubious and [were] in no way corroborated by any other independent witness." One of the two witnesses, Mohamed bin Saaban, subsequently denied having seen the incident and confirmed only that he saw Syed Alwi along Kallang Road with blood on his face. The occupants of the first floor of the coffeeshop also denied throwing joss-paper or any other object during the evening of 21 July. [219]

Lee's explanation that the riots began with the assault on the FRU officer, on the other hand, appeared to be borne out much better by eyewitness accounts. A subsequent Special Branch report on the riots noted that "Numerous witnesses residing along Kallang Road have been interviewed and have confirmed that the incidents in which the crowd beat the FRU PC sparked off the disturbances which occurred along Kallang Road and which subsequently spread throughout the State of Singapore".[220] What was more significant, at least from the Singapore government's perspective of the origins of the riots, was its corollary charge that the disturbances did not occur spontaneously, as Tun Razak had presumed, but represented the machinations of conspiratorial agitators. "The troublemakers were organized," Othman Wok had maintained, "They purposely assaulted the policeman near us, with the intention of blaming us later on. When the youths from the PMU group stopped assaulting the policeman, the UMNO groups started assaulting other Chinese. We were sandwiched. Obviously they wanted it to appear that we were responsible for the disturbances."[221] Corroborating Othman's account, Luscombe noticed that most of the troublemakers "appeared to have been in the PMU section of the procession and this [was] where the initial outbreak occurred. Once the fighting had started, members of this group left the procession and concentrated on keeping the heat on."[222] UMNO marchers were also not free from blame. The New Zealand High Commission noted for instance that "the Malays in the UMNO party did not look like fervent supporters of the Prophet and many were obviously thugs who had no religious interest. During the procession the UMNO party began to straggle and a Chinese policeman attempted to get them back into line whereupon he was attacked by some 20 to 30 Malays." The High Commission maintained that there were doubts that the whole incident happened entirely by accident.[223] Special Branch also dismissed the possibility of the riots being spontaneous in origin. There were "organizers ... [who] created the incidents at the Prophet Mohamed's birthday procession on 21st July, 1964".[224]

Even if it could not be ascertained with exactitude which incident came first, what was clear, commented Luscombe, was that the "troublemakers were bent on starting a fight and if neither incident had occurred they would have found something else".[225] In the final analysis, if blame was to be allocated, Pritchett remarked that "there can be no doubt that the responsibility for the riots rests squarely with UMNO whose members ran the communalist campaign or condoned it".[226] This was also the view of the New Zealand Department of External Affairs: "[T]he fact remains that UMNO (and ultimately UMNO's leaders) must bear the main burden of responsibility for the recent outbreak by virtue of their recourse to the excitation of Malay racial sentiment. It appears to us that Razak and other UMNO leaders did not act soon enough to curb the excesses of extremists like Ja'afar Albar and we [were] left in even more disturbing doubt by the reaction of the Federal Government to the riots".[227] Head also had "little doubt that this press campaign has been inspired for political reasons by UMNO. For Federal Government to condone it is in my view indefensible and irresponsible".[228] It is perhaps not surprising why Alliance leaders had no wish to want to have an official inquiry into the riots. As Head pointed out, "I also think it quite likely that UMNO would not come [out] well [in] an enquiry".[229]

The Tunku Returns

Everyone waited expectantly for the Tunku to return and put his reconciling magic to work. Since the outbreak of the clashes, Head had been looking to Whitehall to "have a serious talk"[230] with the Tunku who was due to return to London for medical treatment.[231] A day after the riots had broken out, the British High Commissioner had cabled the Commonwealth Relations Secretary, Duncan Sandys, about his dismay at the mismanagement of Malaysian affairs by the central government which, he felt, was "placing party political advantage way ahead of any aims toward maintaining or creating Federal unity", Tan Siew Sin's intention "to do all he can in economic field to favour Malaya at expense of Singapore" being one striking example. Noting that the representation of the rest of Federation in the Malaysian Cabinet was "still restricted to one nice old semi-educated man from Sarawak",[232] Head said that "It [was] becoming increasingly apparent that Federal Government's policy is one of empirical self-advantage for UMNO with marked disregard for interests or feelings of Singapore, Sarawak and Sabah".[233] Arguing that "we can no longer sit by" and "do nothing", Head suggested that the Prime Minister or Sandys himself should try to press the Tunku for a more inclusive national government. "We have in our military, financial and other forms of aid fairly strong reason and sanction for bringing pressure to bear on [the] Malaysian Government if we think things are going wrong," Head said.[234]

Head was not alone in asking for pressure to be put on the Tunku. Sir Robert Menzies, the Australian premier, had urged his British counterpart, Sir Alec Douglas-Home, to do the same.[235] So did the Commonwealth Relations Office and the Foreign Office, both worried about how the troubles "behind the frontier"[236] might embarrass the British government not only domestically but also internationally[237] and adversely affect the campaign to thwart Indonesian *Konfrontasi*. Fears were also expressed about the possibility of further riots eroding the PAP's ability to act as an "essential bulwark" against communism in Singapore.[238] "Lee's fear that many Chinese supporters would desert to Barisan may well be justified," noted the British High Commission in Singapore. "We do not believe that Malaysians could effectively counter this threat by force in long term."[239] As it turned out, the meeting between the two Prime Ministers on 6 August went rather well, with Douglas-Home recalling that the Tunku was quite easy to talk to and very well aware of this problem and anxious to do what he could but found that "the politics of the matter were not easy" and he had been unable to bring Lee into his Cabinet owing to opposition from his colleagues. But he hoped in other ways, like through the National Defence Council, to bring in representatives from Singapore.[240]

The Tunku returned to Kuala Lumpur on 14 August to an emotional welcome — and broke down before the estimated 10,000 strong crowd gathered to greet him. His response was a masterpiece, recalled Musa Hitam to Jerrold M. Dion of the American Embassy: "With total sincerity and in the Malay words a father would use to admonish quarrelling children, the Tunku had struck chords of deep emotion here".[241] Between sobs, the Tunku said, "I have always reminded leaders to be careful when they speak and to be cautious in wording their speech so that disturbances would not occur among the people of the country".[242] The Malaysian premier's performance during his visit to Singapore, at Lee's invitation, four days later, to "undo the harm the disturbances had done"[243] was no less skilful. It brought about the "beginning of a thaw", according to Lee, who pledged to "go to the end of the world" to help him resolve the problem. "If there is one man who can resolve it, it is he," Lee said.[244] The Tunku's "flair" had also impressed Goh, reported Pritchett: "Everybody was pleased with him, he said, except the Malays. They had expected the Father to come down to Singapore and give Lee Kuan Yew the stick. In fact, the Tunku had spoken quite sharply to them ... he had called them 'hysterical'."[245] "This goes at least some way towards recognizing publicly UMNO's share of responsibility for the disastrous rioting," remarked the New Zealand High Commission.[246] Nothing much, however, issued from the visit on the political front,[247] as the Tunku had not made any concrete proposals, apart from persuading the Singapore government to agree to the introduction of the Federation's rural development schemes into the island. Lee had sought the Tunku's opinion on Syed Ja'afar Albar and was satisfied with his reply that he did not side with him. Lee's expressions of loyalty and trust in the Tunku had apparently also made "an excellent impression and strengthened the Tunku's resolve to deal firmly with Syed Ja'afar Albar and his associates".[248] Lee got the impression that the Tunku had been shaken and angered by the riots which had marred his American visit and was critical of Tun Razak's handling of the situation.[249] The Tunku, in turn, had told Lee that it would split his party to take the PAP into the Federal Cabinet at the moment and indicated that the PAP should withdraw from Malaya and confine itself to Singapore.[250] But while the Tunku's good intentions were beyond doubt, it remained to be seen whether he could persuade his associates,[251] or deal firmly with the extremists.[252]

The Tunku had a major task cut out for him. The day after he returned to Kuala Lumpur, *Merdeka* renewed its anti-Lee campaign with a provocative leader: "Lee Kuan Yew's antics arouse anger of Malays". Repeating its charges of PAP cowardice during the riots, the editorial alleged that Lee "had always hurt the Malays because they refused to support the PAP" and that he had inspired the unfavourable reporting of the Singapore disturbances by foreign journalists[253] to "remove the bloodstains from his hands". Drawing attention to the differing explanations of the causes of the riots offered by both Tun Razak and Lee, the editorial asserted that it trusted Tun Razak's version more because it was based on police statements, and quoted the Malaysian deputy premier as having said that "Lee Kuan Yew wanted to see bloodshed between the two friendly communities for his own political ends."[254] The *Utusan Melayu* followed the next day with a report asserting that the majority of UMNO's 98 divisions had proposed that the forthcoming UMNO General Assembly on 5 September "should take action against the PAP government and Lee Kuan Yew".[255] As American Ambassador, James D. Bell, had earlier noted, plans were already afoot to "stop" Lee: "Activist UMNO elements who seek [to] persuade Tunku to deal firmly with Lee may try [to] influence him by seeking mass support for their views at national UMNO conference … Ahmad bin Taff plans a 'hot' speech at conference on Lee's alleged perfidy".[256] Bell surmised that although the Tunku might be more amenable to a *modus vivendi* with Lee, "it seems fairly certain Tun Razak [was] under pressure from chauvinist Malay leaders insisting on hard line", and was probably "genuinely concerned over possibilities of split in UMNO ranks with ultra-nationalists breaking with government leaders if any compromise made on racial issues". Tun Razak also seemed to believe "that Malay political control depends on Malay unity and keeping Lee Kuan Yew out of the political picture in Malay states … [He] views conflict as in large part personal battle with Lee Kuan Yew."[257]

Three days before the UMNO General Assembly convened, race riots broke out in Singapore — a second time.

The September Riots and a New Rift

On 2 September, at about 8.50 p.m., a Chinese on a scooter was hit by a stone catapulted by two Malays. The incident took place at East Coast Road in front of Kampong Amber. Ten minutes later, another Chinese at Paya Lebar Road was suddenly fisted by two Malays while all three were alighting from a bus.[258] The incidents culminated in the mysterious killing of a Malay trishaw-rider opposite the Changi market at Geylang Serai by a group who were alleged to be Chinese, "with the motive of inciting racial feeling of Malays against the Chinese", some one and a half hours later.[259] The unprovoked murder of the 57-year-old Malay trishaw-rider sparked off immediate retaliatory action by the Malays in the area, resulting in isolated cases of attempted arson, assaults and stabbing.[260]

By daybreak the next morning, nine other persons were injured, two seriously. All were Chinese. Geylang Serai, the scene of the clashes, remained "very tense". Most shops were shut, the streets deserted. Investigations by Special Branch revealed that a clandestine organization with Indonesian backing had been responsible for fanning and exploiting Malay feelings prior to the outbreak of the disturbances. An unconfirmed report it received suggested that about four or five suspected Indonesian agents had moved into the Jalan Ubi area, having arrived on the morning of 3 September. Six others had been arrested at 11.00 a.m., in a boat without cargoes, near Kusu Island. It was strongly suspected that roving bands of Malays were possibly acting under the direction of these Indonesian agents to "create incidents".[261] Both Kuala Lumpur and Singapore immediately came out with statements blaming Indonesia for the latest outbreak of racial violence, which appeared to coincide with the infiltration of Indonesian commandos into Labis in Johore.[262] The American Ambassador, however, saw "little evidence of any direct link between Indonesian agents and the Singapore riots" although he conceded that the "tense atmosphere" in the aftermath of the July riots unquestionably "presented every opportunity to external agitators". Accusations of Indonesian complicity, Bell added, would detract little from the fact, which the politicians had chosen publicly to ignore, that "racial unrest here is never far below the surface and little is needed to touch it off".[263] On the same day, the Malaysian Cabinet finally consented to an inquiry into the racial disturbances in Singapore.[264]

Although the Chinese had not retaliated so far, the police feared that they might be "provoked into retaliating if Malays continue[d] to attack them".[265] The fear was not unfounded, for, the following day, 4 September, "large crowds of Chinese and Malays were seen gathered in front of markets and roadsides" and had to be dispersed by the police. The racial tension that had been building then exploded. Between 11.00 a.m. and 2.00 p.m., 25 incidents were reported in the Geylang Serai area. They were also of a more serious nature, claiming seven deaths, and were more widespread. The rioters also appeared to be better organized and not entirely communal. They stoned police cars and, on one occasion, a gang of 15 threatened a military radio transmitting station but fled when the lone guard opened fire.[266] With the military recalled into action and an island-wide curfew imposed from 2.00 p.m., only three incidents took place. In his evening radio broadcast, Toh Chin Chye, deputizing for Lee, who had left for Brussels on 31 August to attend the centenary celebrations of the Socialist

International, urged the people not to fall prey to the "invidious whispers and rumours" of the Indonesian agents and their sympathizers.[267] But during the period when the curfew was lifted — between 5.30 a.m. and 9.00 a.m. on 5 September, 21 incidents occurred in the Geylang Serai area, claiming two more lives. At 5 p.m., the police launched Operation Walnut leading to the arrest of 14 suspected members of a clandestine group and 15 more subsequently.[268] On 8 September, Tun Razak visited Singapore, and, accompanied by Toh and Lim Kim San, toured the riot-hit areas of Geylang Serai, Changi Road, Jalan Eunos, Kaki Bukit and Kampong Chai Chee, calling on the *kampong* folks to ignore Indonesian efforts to stir up racial hatred.[269] The situation returned to almost normal by 9 September. But three more persons had died over the last three days. The curfew was finally lifted at 4 p.m. on 11 September 1964. The military stood down the following day, and the police, on 14 September.

Efforts were also made to contain the racial flare-up politically. At the opening of the UMNO General Assembly on 5 September, the Tunku warned delegates to keep the "still smouldering" Singapore situation out of their discussions. Hinting that "unwise politicians" were being restrained, he urged all UMNO members to refrain from "wild talk" that could unwittingly play into the hands of Sukarno. But that did not stop Ahmad Haji Taff from accusing the central government of frequently being hesitant to act firmly against the Singapore government. A request that the central government "take over the administration of Singapore" was also made.[270]

By the time Lee returned on 13 September, the riots were over. Thirteen lives were lost in this latest wave of racial violence that left another 106 injured. Some 1,439 persons were arrested, of whom 268 were placed under preventive detention orders, and 154 charged in court.[271] But another political controversy was about to unfold. On the same day, the *Sunday Telegraph* in London published a scathing editorial attack on the Tunku's "complacent attitude about the pace of Chinese advancement to parity" and compared him to Sir Roy Welensky, the former premier of the Federation of South Rhodesia and Nyasaland. Arguing that British military aid be made conditional on Kuala Lumpur's willingness to "build a non-racial united community really worth saving", the leader urged the British premier to "bring the strongest possible pressure on the Tunku to give the Chinese a fair deal".[272] Since Lee was in London after Brussels from 7 September, meeting with the government and Labour Party members and the press, and speaking to Malaysian students, the belief that he was the inspiration behind "this sudden burst of criticism" was rife among

Alliance leaders. Pointing out that the editorial appeared soon after Lee's visit to Britain, the Publicity Secretary of the Alliance, Yap Chin Kwee, said in a statement: "We do not know whether this editorial is inspired by some of Mr Lee's more candid remarks there or the outcome of his chats with the leader-writer".[273] Privately, the Tunku was hopping mad. Bitterly critical of Lee's "meddling" in his affairs, he resolved never to give him an appointment overseas and determined to keep him at home "where he could be watched".[274]

The Tunku's reply — an "angry, anti-PAP speech"[275] — was delivered during an address at a reception in Singapore, given by the Singapore Alliance (SA), on 20 September. Touching on the probable causes of the riots in July and September, the Malaysian premier suggested that while the former "might have been" because Singapore Malays felt neglected and were being "driven out of their homes", and the latter "manufactured by Sukarno", "some politicians in Singapore" were not free from blame either. Referring to the "mischievous" *Sunday Telegraph* report, the Tunku retorted that there was "an undercurrent to contest my leadership of the Malaysian people by trying to make out that I am a leader of Malays only". He reminded the PAP bluntly that it had no right to interfere in Malaysian affairs and should stay in Singapore where "so much" remained to be done. The Tunku maintained that "the first signs" of PAP interference appeared when it participated in the April elections, something "quite contrary to what we agreed". As if to confirm his intention not to allow the PAP a national role, the Malaysian premier then called on the UMNO, MCA and MIC (Malayan Indian Congress) in Singapore to strengthen their organizations because the people of Singapore were "fed up with all these petty and stupid politics" and "want them to lead them along the path to unity with the rest of Malaysia". The Tunku also announced plans to scrap the "goodwill committees" in favour of new "peace committees", after charging that the former "could not function properly because they composed of members of one party".[276] As the American Consul, Richard H. Donald, commented, "Replacing these committees, which at least represent PAP grassroots leadership, with peace committees under the control of the police (and ultimately the central government) doubtless offers political advantages to the Alliance".[277] Speculating on the Tunku's motives for his hard hitting speech, Donald suggested that "what may have angered the Tunku was probably not so much Lee's statements to the press and public as his lobbying with the leaders of the Labour Party ... in the hope that a Labour government would be more inclined to bring pressure to bear on the Tunku". The Malaysian High Commissioner's report on Lee's activities in London[278] could also have contributed to the Tunku's "highly partisan" outburst which had all but "shattered" the fragile political truce.[279] As Pritchett remarked, the Tunku was "carrying the fight to Lee".[280]

PAP leaders were surprised and saddened by the Tunku's outburst, not least of all Lee himself, who had publicly praised the Tunku as a "tolerant and benign leader" on the same day. Rajaratnam felt a PAP retort to set the record straight was unavoidable, for in both riots, it was UMNO that was "supplying fuel" and "setting [the] stage for the extremists to light the match".[281] But pressed by the British to exercise restraint, Lee, accompanied by Goh Keng Swee, Toh Chin Chye and Lim Kim San, accepted the Tunku's invitation for peace talks on 25 September at the Cameron Highlands. Toh subsequently announced that a two-year "truce" had been agreed upon. The supposed "truce", however, was actually only a general agreement to avoid for three months — not two years — provocative remarks likely to exacerbate communal relations. The Tunku apparently referred particularly to references regarding the numerical proportions of the various communities in Malaysia. In return, the Tunku would control the Malay extremists and put an end to their anti-PAP campaign,[282] including keeping Syed Ja'afar Albar out of Singapore.[283] No explicit restrictions were placed on the political operations of the Alliance in Singapore or PAP political activity on the mainland.[284] But while the PAP need not withdraw from Malaya, it was not to expand its organization any further.[285] The Tunku apparently warned Lee that Singapore "could be expelled from Malaysia if trouble continued".[286] E.W. Barker, the Singapore Assembly Speaker, predicted that the truce was unlikely to last "two months".[287] He was right.

Notes

1. *Straits Echo*, 13 July 1964.
2. For an excellent study of the Sino-Malay clashes in the immediate aftermath of the Second World War, see Cheah Boon Kheng, *Red Star Over Malaya: Resistance and Social Conflict During and After the Japanese Occupation, 1941–1946* (Singapore: Singapore University Press, 1983).
3. Memorandum "Malay/Chinese Racial Riots, 21st July, 1964", n.d., ISD.
4. Airgram no. 60, American Consulate (Singapore) to Department of State, 27 August 1964, RG 59 Box 2457 Pol 23-8 1/1/64.
5. Telegram no. 98, American Consulate (Singapore) to Department of State, 26 July 1964, RG 59 Box 2457 Pol 23-8 1/1/64.
6. Memorandum "The Racial Riots in Singapore in July–August 1964", 7 October 1964, ISD.
7. Memorandum "Prophet Mohamed Birthday Celebration", 29 July 1964, ISD.

8. See Appendix 12 in "Memorandum Submitted by the Government of Singapore to the Commission of Inquiry into the Disturbances in Singapore in 1964", March 1965.
9. See Appendix 11 in Ibid.
10. Ibid., p. 43.
11. Memorandum "Prophet Mohamed Birthday Celebration", 29 July 1964, ISD.
12. Singapore Police Force, Statement by Othman Wok to J.C. Cooke, 4 August 1964, ISD.
13. Ibid.
14. See Appendix 10, "Speech by Dato Syed Esa Almenoar, The Singapore UMNO Secretary-General, on the Padang, on 21st July, 1964" in "Memorandum Submitted by the Government of Singapore …".
15. Ibid., p. 44.
16. Singapore Police Force, Statement by Othman Wok to J.C. Cooke, 4 August 1964, ISD.
17. Memorandum, "Prophet Mohamed Birthday Celebration", 29 July 1964, ISD.
18. Singapore Police Force, Statement by Othman Wok to J.C. Cooke, 4 August 1964, ISD.
19. Ibid.
20. Ibid.
21. Report by Y.W. Chin, 21 July 1964, ISD.
22. Memorandum "The Racial Riots in Singapore in July–August 1964", 7 October 1964, ISD.
23. Singapore Police Force, Statement by Yusof bin Ali to L.L. Woo, 4 August 1964, in Appendix 15, "Memorandum Submitted by the Government of Singapore …".
24. Ibid.
25. Singapore Police Force, Statement by Ho Kok Mong to Yong Ser Hiong, 4 August 1964, Appendix 16, Ibid.
26. Singapore Police Force, Statement by Othman Wok to J.C. Cooke, 4 August 1964, ISD.
27. Signed Affidavit by A. Rahim Ishak, 28 July 1964, Appendix 17 in "Memorandum Submitted by the Government of Singapore …".
28. Singapore Police Force, Statement by Mohammed Ariff bin Suradi to Lim Cheng Pah, 3 August 1964, Appendix 18 in Ibid.
29. Singapore Police Force, Statement by Mohammed Ghazali bin Ismail, 3 August 1964, Appendix 20 in Ibid.
30. Signed Affidavit by A. Rahim Ishak, 28 July 1964, Appendix 17 in Ibid.
31. Singapore Police Force, Statement by Mohammed Ariff bin Suradi to Lim Cheng Pah, 3 August 1964, Appendix 18 in Ibid.
32. Singapore Police Force, Statement by Mohammed Ghazali bin Ismail, 3 August 1964, Appendix 20 in Ibid.
33. Singapore Police Force, Statement by Othman Wok to J.C. Cooke, 4 August 1964, ISD.
34. Memorandum "Racial Disturbances in Singapore in July–September, 1964", 8 October 1964, ISD.
35. Report by Y.W. Chin, 21 July 1964, ISD.
36. Ibid.
37. Diary of Ag. DSP J.C. Cooke, 21 July 1964, ISD.
38. Memorandum "Racial Disturbances in Singapore in July–September, 1964", 8 October 1964, ISD.
39. Singapore Police Force, Statement by Tan Keng Cheow to O.H. Lim, 11 August 1964, Appendix 21 in "Memorandum Submitted by the Government of Singapore …".
40. Memorandum "Malay/Chinese Racial Riots 21st July, 1964", n.d., ISD.
41. Ibid.
42. Memorandum "Racial Disturbances in Singapore in July–September, 1964", 8 October 1964, ISD.

43. Telegram no. 30, American Consulate (Singapore) to Department of State, 22 July 1964, RG 59 Box 2457 Pol 23-8 1/1/64.
44. Telegram no. 237, New Zealand High Commission (Singapore) to Department of External Affairs (Wellington), 22 July 1964, in A1838/280 no. 3024/2/1 Part 12.
45. *The Straits Times*, 22 July 1964.
46. Memorandum "Malay/Chinese Racial Riots 21st July, 1964", n.d., ISD.
47. Memorandum "Racial Disturbances in Singapore in July–September, 1964", 8 October 1964, ISD.
48. Memorandum "Malay/Chinese Racial Riots 21st July, 1964", n.d., ISD.
49. Telegram no. 237, New Zealand High Commission (Singapore) to Department of External Affairs (Wellington), 22 July 1964, A1838/280 no. 3024/2/1 Part 12.
50. Telegram no. 811, Australian High Commission (Kuala Lumpur) to Department of External Affairs, 23 July 1964, A1838/280 no. 3024/2/1 Part 12.
51. *The Straits Times*, 22 July 1964.
52. Telegram no. 28, American Consulate (Singapore) to Department of State, 22 July 1964, RG 59 Box 2457 Pol 23-8 1/1/64.
53. *The Straits Times*, 22 July 1964.
54. Ibid.
55. Ibid.
56. Memorandum "Racial Disturbances in Singapore in July–September, 1964", 8 October 1964, ISD.
57. Memorandum "Malay/Chinese Racial Riots 21st July, 1964", n.d., ISD.
58. Telegram no. 814, Australian High Commission (Kuala Lumpur) to Department of External Affairs, 24 July 1964, A1838/280 no. 3024/2/1 Part 12.
59. Memorandum "Malay/Chinese Racial Riots 21st July, 1964", n.d., ISD.
60. Memorandum "Racial Disturbances in Singapore in July–September, 1964", 8 October 1964, ISD.
61. Ibid.
62. *The Straits Times*, 23 July 1964.
63. Telegram no. 34, American Consulate (Singapore) to Department of State, 22 July 1964, RG 59 Box 2457 Pol 23-8 1/1/64.
64. Telegram no. 814, Australian High Commission (Kuala Lumpur) to Department of External Affairs, 24 July 1964.
65. *Merdeka*, 24 July 1964.
66. Telegram no. 80, Department of State to American Embassy (Kuala Lumpur), 22 July 1964, RG 59 Box 2457 Pol 23-8 1/1/64.
67. Telegram no. 505, Australian High Commission (Singapore) to Department of External Affairs, 23 July 1964, A1838/280 no. 3024/2/1 Part 12.
68. Telegram no. 237, New Zealand High Commission (Singapore) to Department of External Affairs (Wellington), 22 July 1962, A1838/280 no. 3024/2/1 Part 12.
69. Ibid.
70. Ibid.
71. Telegram no. 505, Australian High Commission (Singapore) to Department of External Affairs, 23 July 1964, A1838/280 no. 3024/2/1 Part 12.
72. Ibid.
73. Telegram no. 507, Australian High Commission (Singapore) to Department of External Affairs, 23 July 1964, A1838/280 no. 3024/2/1 Part 12.
74. Ibid.
75. Ibid.

76. The murders took place in Geylang Serai, Paya Lebar, Arab Street and Sembawang Road. Four Chinese and two Malays were killed. Memorandum "The Racial Riots in Singapore in July–August 1964", 7 October 1964, ISD.
77. *The Straits Times*, 24 July 1964.
78. Telegram no. 507, Australian High Commission (Singapore) to Department of External Affairs, 23 July 1964, A1838/280 no. 3024/2/1 Part 12.
79. Memorandum "Malay/Chinese Racial Riots 21st July, 1964", n.d., ISD.
80. Ibid.
81. Ibid.
82. Ibid.
83. Telegram no. 814, Australian High Commission (Kuala Lumpur) to Department of External Affairs, 24 July 1964, A1838/280 no. 3024/2/1 Part 12.
84. "Note prepared by Mr Brokenshire", A1838/280 no. 3024/2/1 Part 12.
85. Ibid.
86. Memorandum no. 1070, W.B. Pritchett to Secretary, Department of External Affairs, 25 July 1964, A1838/280 no. 3024/2/1 Part 12.
87. Telegram no. 509, Australian High Commission (Singapore) to Department of External Affairs, 24 July 1964, A1838/280 no. 3024/2/1 Part 12.
88. Ibid.
89. Telegram no. 820, Australian High Commission (Kuala Lumpur) to Department of External Affairs, 25 July 1964, A1838/280 no. 3024/2/1 Part 12.
90. The victim, a Malay, was murdered at Lorong 1, Geylang Road. Memorandum "The Racial Riots in Singapore in July–August 1964", 7 October 1964, ISD.
91. Memorandum "The Racial Riots in Singapore in July–August 1964", 7 October 1964, ISD.
92. Appendix A in Memorandum "Racial Disturbances in Singapore in July–September, 1964", 8 October 1964, ISD.
93. *The Straits Times*, 30 July 1964.
94. Airgram no. 71, American Embassy (Kuala Lumpur) to Department of State, 31 July 1964, RG 59 Box 2451 Pol 2-1 7/1/64.
95. Ibid.
96. Telegram no. 114, American Embassy (Kuala Lumpur) to Department of State, 31 July 1964, RG 59 Box 2453 Pol 12 7/1/64.
97. "Memorandum Submitted by the Government of Singapore ...", p. 47.
98. *Utusan Melayu*, 22 July 1964.
99. *Merdeka*, 24 July 1964.
100. Ibid.
101. *Utusan Zaman*, 26 July 1964.
102. "Memorandum Submitted by the Government of Singapore ...", p. 51.
103. Text of speech by Syed Ja'afar Albar at the Kampong Dato Keramat Hall on 2 August 1964, Apendix 22 in "Memorandum Submitted by the Government of Singapore ...".
104. Syed Ja'afar Albar, "A Letter to Dennis Bloodworth", n.d., in A1838/280 no. 3024/2/1 Part 13.
105. Text of speech by Syed Ja'afar Albar at the Kampong Dato Keramat Hall on 2 August 1964, Apendix 22 in "Memorandum Submitted by the Government of Singapore ..."; also p. 52.
106. *Merdeka*, 24 July 1964.
107. Telegram no. 114, American Embassy (Kuala Lumpur) to Department of State, 29 July 1964, RG 59 Box 2453 Pol 12 7/1/64.
108. "Memorandum Submitted by the Government of Singapore ...", p. 49.

109. *Utusan Zaman*, 9 August 1964.
110. Ibid.
111. Airgram no. 88, American Embassy (Kuala Lumpur) to Department of State, 7 August 1964, RG 59 Box 2456 Pol 18 8/7/64.
112. Telegram no. 514, Australian High Commission (Singapore) to Department of External Affairs, 27 July 1964, A1838/280 no. 3024/2/1 Part 12; Telegram no. 51, American Consulate (Singapore) to Department of State, 27 July 1964, RG 59 Box 2456 Pol 18 1/1/64.
113. Telegram no. 514, Australian High Commission (Singapore) to Department of External Affairs, 27 July 1964, A1838/280 no. 3024/2/1 Part 12.
114. Memorandum no. 1190, W.B. Pritchett to Secretary, Department of External Affairs, 12 August 1964, A1838/280 no. 3027/2/1 Part 19.
115. Telegram no. 51, American Consulate (Singapore) to Department of State, 27 July 1964, RG 59 Box 2456 Pol 18 1/1/64.
116. Memorandum no. 1190, W.B. Pritchett to Secretary, Department of External Affairs, 12 August 1964, A1838/280 no. 3027/2/1 Part 19.
117. Telegram no. 514, Australian High Commission (Singapore) to Department of External Affairs, 27 July 1964, A1838/280 no. 3024/2/1 Part 12.
118. Airgram no. 60, American Consulate (Singapore) to Department of State, 27 August 1964, RG 59 Box 2457 Pol 23-8 1/1/64.
119. Telegram no. 514, Australian High Commission (Singapore) to Department of External Affairs, 27 July 1964, A1838/280 no. 3024/2/1 Part 12.
120. Telegram no. 48, American Consulate (Singapore) to Department of State, 27 July 1964, RG 59 Box 2456 Pol 18 1/1/64.
121. Memorandum "Malay/Chinese Racial Riots: Events of 26th July 1964", n.d., ISD.
122. Special Branch report, "Alleged partiality of the Malay soldiers & policemen in dealing with the Sino-Malay clash", 29 July 1964, ISD.
123. Special Branch report, "Chinese reaction towards recent racial riots", 4 August 1964, ISD.
124. Special Branch report, "General Report touching Malay reaction on recent disturbances in Singapore", 31 July 1964, ISD.
125. Memorandum no. 1082, W.B. Pritchett to Secretary, Department of External Affairs, 29 July 1964, A1838/280 no. 3024/2/1 Part 13.
126. Telegram no. 51, American Consulate (Singapore) to Department of State, 27 July 1964, RG 59 Box 2456 Pol 18 1/1/64.
127. Memorandum no. 1190, W.B. Pritchett to Secretary, Department of External Affairs, 12 August 1964, A1838/280 no. 3027/2/1 Part 19.
128. Airgram no. 60, American Consulate (Singapore) to Department of State, 27 August 1964, RG 59 Box 2457 Pol 23-8 1/1/64.
129. Telegram no. 51 American Consulate (Singapore) to Department of State, 27 July 1964, RG 59 Box 2457 Pol 23-8 1/1/64.
130. Memorandum no. 1128, W.B. Pritchett to Secretary, Department of External Affairs, 5 August 1964, A1838/280 no. 3027/2/1 Part 19.
131. Telegram no. 514, Australian High Commission (Singapore) to Department of External Affairs, 27 July 1964, A1838/280 no. 3024/2/1 Part 12.
132. Telegram no. 98, American Embassy (Kuala Lumpur) to Department of State, 26 July 1964, RG 59 Box 2457 Pol 23-8 1/1/64.
133. Telegram no. 514, Australian High Commission (Singapore) to Department of External Affairs, 27 July 1964, A1838/280 no. 3024/2/1 Part 12.
134. Telegram no. 48, American Consulate (Singapore) to Department of State, 27 July 1964, RG 59 Box 2456 Pol 18 1/1/64.

135. Ibid.
136. Telegram no. 1082, W.B. Pritchett to Secretary, Department of External Affairs, 29 July 1964, A1838/280 no. 3024/2/1 Part 13.
137. Telegram no. 51, American Consulate (Singapore) to Department of State, 27 July 1964, RG 59 Box 2456 Pol 18 1/1/64.
138. Telegram no. 56, American Consulate (Singapore) to Department of State, 30 July 1964, RG 59 Box 2456 Pol 18 1/1/64.
139. Telegram no. 514, Australian High Commission (Singapore) to Department of External Affairs, 27 July 1964, and Telegram no. 837, Australian High Commission (Singapore) to Department of External Affairs, 29 July 1964, A1838/280 no. 3024/2/1 Part 12.
140. Telegram no. 530, Australian High Commission (Singapore) to Department of External Affairs, 31 July 1964, A1838/280 no. 3024/2/1 Part 12.
141. Telegram no. 250, New Zealand High Commission (Singapore) to Department of External Affairs (Wellington), 31 July 1964, A1838/280 no. 3024/2/1 Part 12.
142. Telegram no. 51 American Consulate (Singapore) to Department of State, 27 July 1964, RG 59 Box 2456 Pol 18 1/1/64.
143. Telegram no. 819, Australian High Commission (Kuala Lumpur) to Department of External Affairs, 24 July 1964, A1838/280 no. 3024/2/1 Part 12; also reported in Telegram no. 98, American Embassy (Kuala Lumpur) to Department of State, 26 July 1964, RG 59 Box 2457 Pol 23-8 1/1/64.
144. Telegram no. 97, American Embassy (Kuala Lumpur) to Department of State, 26 July 1964, RG 59 Box 2457 Pol 23-8 1/1/64.
145. Telegram no. 837, Australian High Commission (Kuala Lumpur) to Department of External Affairs, 29 July 1964, A1838/280 no. 3024/2/1 Part 12.
146. Telegram no. 97, American Embassy (Kuala Lumpur) to Department of State, 26 July 1964, RG 59 Box 2457 Pol 23-8 1/1/64.
147. Telegram no. 819, Australian High Commission (Kuala Lumpur) to Department of External Affairs, 24 July 1964, A1838/280 no. 3024/2/1 Part 12.
148. Telegram no. 113, American Embassy (Kuala Lumpur) to Department of State, 29 July 1964, RG 59 Box 2456 Pol 18 1/1/64.
149. Telegram no. 51, American Consulate (Singapore) to Department of State, 27 July 1964, RG 59 Box 2457 Pol 23-8 1/1/64.
150. Telegram no. 113, American Embassy (Kuala Lumpur) to Department of State, 29 July 1964, RG 59 Box 2456 Pol 18 1/1/64.
151. Telegram no. 837, Australian High Commission (Kuala Lumpur) to Department of External Affairs, 29 July 1964, A1838/280 no. 3024/2/1 Part 12.
152. Telegram no. 520, Australian High Commission (Kuala Lumpur) to Department of External Affairs, 29 July 1964, A1838/280 no. 3024/2/1 Part 12.
153. Telegram no. 523, Australian High Commission (Kuala Lumpur) to Department of External Affairs, 30 July 1964, A1838/280 no. 3024/2/1 Part 12.
154. Ibid.
155. Telegram no. 1339, British High Commissioner (Kuala Lumpur) to Commonwealth Relations Office, 28 July 1964, DEFE 24/63.
156. Telegram no. 520, Australian High Commission (Singapore) to Department of External Affairs, 29 July 1964, A1838/280 no. 3024/2/1 Part 12
157. Telegram no. 530, Australian High Commission (Singapore) to Department of External Affairs, 31 July 1964, A1838/280 no. 3024/2/1 Part 12.
158. Telegram no. 520, Australian High Commission (Singapore) to Department of External Affairs, 29 July 1964, A1838/280 no. 3024/2/1 Part 12.

159. Telegram no. 1362, British High Commission (Kuala Lumpur) to Commonwealth Relations Office, 3 August 1964, PREM 11/4909.
160. Telegram no. 848, Australian High Commission (Kuala Lumpur) to Department of External Affairs, 30 July 1964, A1838/280 no. 3024/2/1 Part 12.
161. Ibid.
162. Telegram no. 250, New Zealand High Commission (Singapore) to Department of External Affairs (Wellington), A1838/280 no. 3027/2/1 Part 19.
163. Telegram no. 848, Australian High Commission (Kuala Lumpur) to Department of External Affairs, 30 July 1964, A1838/280 no. 3024/2/1 Part 12.
164. Telegram no. 250, New Zealand High Commission (Singapore) to Department of External Affairs, 31 July 1964, A1838/280 no. 3027/2/1 Part 19.
165. Telegram no. 848, Australian High Commission (Kuala Lumpur) to Department of External Affairs, 30 July 1964, A1838/280 no. 3024/2/1 Part 12.
166. Telegram no. 531, Australian High Commission (Singapore) to Department of External Affairs, 2 August 1964, A1838/280 no. 3024/2/1 Part 12.
167. Telegram no. 536, Australian High Commission (Singapore) to Department of External Affairs, 3 August 1964, A1838 no. 3024/2/1 Part 12.
168. Telegram no. 850, Australian High Commission (Kuala Lumpur) to Department of External Affairs, 3 August 1964, A1838/280 no. 3024/2/1 Part 12.
169. Telegram no. 1362, British High Commission (Kuala Lumpur) to Commonwealth Relations Office, 3 August 1964, PREM 11/4909.
170. Ibid.
171. Telegram no. 850, Australian High Commission (Kuala Lumpur) to Department of External Affairs, 3 August 1964, A1838/280 no. 3024/2/1 Part 12.
172. Telegram no. 530, Australian High Commission (Kuala Lumpur) to Department of External Affairs, 31 July 1964, A1838/280 no. 3027/2/1 Part 19.
173. Telegram no. 1362, British High Commission (Kuala Lumpur) to Commonwealth Relations Office, 3 August 1964, PREM 11/4909
174. Telegram no. 152, American Embassy (Kuala Lumpur) to Department of State, 11 August 1964, RG 59 Box 2457 Pol 23-8 1/1/64.
175. Ibid.
176. *The Straits Times*, 5 August 1964.
177. Telegram no. 1362, British High Commission (Kuala Lumpur) to Commonwealth Relations Office, 3 August 1964, PREM 11/4909.
178. *The Straits Times*, 30 July 1964.
179. Ibid., 3 August 1964.
180. Ibid., 3 August 1964.
181. Ibid., 30 July 1964.
182. Memorandum no. 1114, W.A. Luscombe to Secretary, Department of External Affairs, 18 August 1964, A1838/280 no. 3027/2/1 Part 19.
183. Telegram no. 102, Head to Commonwealth Relations Office, 1 August 1964, "Malaysia Fortnightly Summary, Part I, 15th–29th July, 1964", Foreign and Commonwealth Office source.
184. Memorandum no. 1095, W.B. Pritchett to Secretary, Department of External Affairs, 29 July 1964, A1838/280 no. 3024/2/1 Part 12.
185. Airgram no. 60, American Consulate (Singapore) to Department of State, 27 August 1964, RG 59 Box 2457 Pol 23-8 1/1/64.
186. Telegram no. 169, American Embassy (Kuala Lumpur) to Department of State, 13 August 1964, RG 59 Box 2450 Pol 2 1/1/64.

187. Airgram no. 118, American Embassy (Kuala Lumpur) to Department of State, 18 August 1964, RG 59 Box 2450 Pol 2 1/1/64.

188. Telegram no. 180, American Embassy (Kuala Lumpur) to Department of State, 17 August 1964, RG 59 Box 2457 Pol 23-8 1/1/64.

189. Memorandum of Conversation among Tran Kim Phuong (Chargé d'Affaires, Embassy of the Republic of Vietnam), Syed Ja'afar Albar, Lord Head, Syed Nasir (Director, Institute of Language and Literature), Donald B. McCue (Chargé d'Affaires, American Embassy), 30 July 1964, RG 59 Box 2450 Pol 2 1/1/64.

190. Memorandum by Peter E. Juge, "Background to Malay/UMNO Political Behavior in Dispute with Lee Kuan Yew and the PAP", n.d., (August 1964), RG 59 Box 2450 Pol 2 1/1/64.

191. Airgram no. 118, American Embassy (Kuala Lumpur) to Department of State, 18 August 1964, RG 59 Box 2450 Pol 2 1/1/64.

192. Memorandum by Peter E. Juge, "Background to Malay/UMNO Political Behavior in Dispute with Lee Kuan Yew and the PAP", n.d., (August 1964), RG 59 Box 2450 Pol 2 1/1/64.

193. Airgram no. 60, American Consulate (Singapore) to Department of State, 27 August 1964, RG 59 Box 2457 Pol 23-8 1/1/64.

194. Airgram no. 118, American Embassy (Kuala Lumpur) to Department of State, 18 August 1964, RG 59 Box 2450 Pol 2 1/1/64.

195. Telegram no. 398, Department of External Affairs (Wellington) to New Zealand High Commission (Kuala Lumpur), 21 August 1964, A1838/280 no. 3027/21/1 Part 19.

196. Airgram no. 60, American Consulate (Singapore) to Department of State, 27 August 1964, RG 59 Box 2457 Pol 23-8 1/1/64.

197. "Memorandum Submitted by the Government of Singapore ...", p. 60.

198. Ibid., p. 58.

199. Ibid., pp. 59–60.

200. Telegram no. 102, Head to Commonwealth Relations Office, "Malaysia Fortnightly Summary, Part I: 15th–29th July, 1964", 1 August 1964, Foreign and Commonwealth Office source.

201. Ibid.

202. Head to Duncan Sandys, 15 October 1964, PREM 13/428.

203. COS 273/64, J.H. Lapsley to Chiefs of Staff Committee, "The Internal Security Threat to Malaya and Singapore from Indonesia", 8 October 1964, DEFE 5/154.

204. Airgram no. 60, American Consulate (Singapore) to Department of State, 27 August 1964, RG 59 Box 2457 Pol 23-8 1/1/64.

205. Ibid.

206. Telegram no. 1301, Head to Duncan Sandys, 22 July 1964, PREM 11/4909.

207. Memorandum of Conversation among Tran Kim Phuong (Chargé d'Affaires, Embassy of the Repulic of Vietnam), Syed Ja'afar Albar, Lord Head, Syed Nasir (Director, Institute of Language and Literature), Donald B. McCue (Chargé d'Affairs), 30 July 1964, RG 59 Box 2450 Pol 2 1/1/64.

208. Memorandum of Conversation between William Smithies and Jerrold Dion, 30 July 1964, RG 59 Box 2450 Pol 2 1/1/64.

209. Ibid.

210. Telegram no. 831, Australian High Commission (Kuala Lumpur) to Department of External Affairs, 28 July 1964, A1838/280 no. 3024/2/1 Part 12.

211. Memorandum "Malaysia: Communal Troubles in Singapore", n.d., A1838/280 no. 3024/2/1 Part 12.

212. Memorandum of Conversation between Tan Toh Hong and Jerrold M. Dion, 26 October 1964, RG 59 2450 Pol 2 1/1/64.

213. Memorandum of Conversation between Syed Esa Almenoar, Terry T. Shima and Arthur H. Rosen, 14 July 1964, RG 59 Box 2457 Pol 23-8 1/1/64.

214. Memorandum of Conversation between Tan Siew Sin and James Bell, 12 August 1964, RG 59 Box 2450 Pol 2 1/1/64.

215. Telegram no. 99, American Embassy (Kuala Lumpur) to Department of State, 27 July 1964, RG 59 Box 2457 Pol 23-8 1/1/64.

216. Memorandum no. 1190, W.B. Pritchett to Secretary, Department of External Affairs, 12 August 1964, A1838/280 no. 3027/2/1 Part 19.

217. *Merdeka*, 24 July 1964.

218. Special Branch report, "Sino-Malay clashes: re: Incident at Kg. Soopoo", 28 July 1964, ISD.

219. Memorandum, "The Racial Riots in Singapore in July–August 1964", 7 October 1964, ISD.

220. Ibid.

221. "Report by the Minister for Social Affairs on Maulud Procession on July 21, 1964", in "Memorandum Submitted by the Government of Singapore ...", Appendix 13. In an interview in 1997, Othman Wok explained how he concluded that the riots were "planned by a few people". He said: "One week after the riots, I was in Kuala Lumpur. A senior *Utusan Melayu* reporter met me, obviously to find out about the situation in Singapore. He told me that at 2 p.m. on July 21, 1964, he already knew that the riots were going to happen. I said, 'How did you know beforehand when the riots took place?' He replied: 'Oh yes, we knew beforehand. We have our sources, you know.' That clicked. *Utusan Melayu* must have been informed by those responsible for the impending riots because it was going to be big news". See *The Straits Times*, 25 January 1997, 23 July 1997.

222. Memorandum no. 1114, W.A. Luscombe to Secretary, Department of External Affairs, 18 August 1964, A1838/280 no. 3027/2/1 Part 19.

223. Telegram no. 237, New Zealand High Commission (Singapore) to Department of External Affairs (Wellington), 22 July 1964, A1838/280 no. 3024/2/1 Part 12.

224. Memorandum "The Racial Riots in Singapore in July–August 1964", 7 October 1964, ISD.

225. Memorandum no. 114, W.A. Luscombe to Secretary, Department of External Affairs, 18 August 1964, A1838/280 no. 3027/2/1 Part 19.

226. Telegram no. 514, Australian High Commission (Singapore) to Department of External Affairs, 27 July 1964, A1838/280 no. 3024/2/1 Part 12.

227. Telegram no. 398, Department of External Affairs (Wellington) to New Zealand High Commission (Kuala Lumpur), 21 August 1964, A1838/280 no. 3027/2/1 Part 19.

228. Telegram no. 1301, Head to Duncan Sandys, 22 July 1964, PREM 11/4909.

229. Telegram no. 1362, British High Commission (Kuala Lumpur) to Commonwealth Relations Office, 3 August 1964, PREM 11/4909.

230. Minutes, J.O. Wright to Sir Alec Douglas-Home, 24 July 1964, PREM 11/4909.

231. Telegram no. 141, American Consulate (Singapore) to Department of State, 23 September 1964, RG 59 Box 2457 Pol 23-8 1/1/64.

232. This was the Temenggong Jugah, the Minister for Sarawak Affairs.

233. Telegram no. 1301, Head to Duncan Sandys, 22 July 1964, PREM 11/4909.

234. Ibid.

235. Allen Brown to Sir Alec Douglas-Home, 31 July 1964, PREM 11/4909.

236. CRO Memorandum, "Brief for the Prime Minister's Talk with the Tunku on Thursday, 6th August 1964", PREM 11/4909.

237. R. Butler to Alec Douglas-Home, 5 August 1964, PREM 11/4909.

238. CRO Memorandum, "Brief for the Prime Minister's Talk with the Tunku on Thursday, 6th August, 1964", PREM 11/4909.
239. Telegram no. 1373, British High Commission (Kuala Lumpur) to Commonwealth Relations Office, 3 August 1964, PREM 11/4909.
240. "Note by the Prime Minister of his private conversation with Tunku Abdul Rahman at No. 10 Downing Street on Thursday, August 6, 1964", n.d., PREM 11/4909.
241. Memorandum of Conversation between Musa bin Hitam (Political Secretary, Ministry of Transport) and Jerrold M. Dion (Political Officer, American Embassy), 17 August 1964, RG 59 Box 2453 Pol 12 7/1/64.
242. *Utusan Melayu*, 15 August 1964, in A1838/280 no. 3024/2/1 Part 13.
243. Ibid., 20 August 1964.
244. *The Straits Times*, 21 August 1964.
245. Memorandum no. 1246, W.B. Pritchett to Secretary, Department of External Affairs, 28 August 1964, A1838/280 no. 3024/2/1 Part 13.
246. Telegram no. 273, New Zealand High Commission (Singapore) to Department of External Affairs (Wellington), 24 August 1964, in A1838/280 no. 3027/2/1 Part 19.
247. During his visit, the Tunku held discussions on 18 August also with SUMNO members and met with a delegation from the BS and UPP (the United People's Party), including Ong Eng Guan, during which he persuaded them to withdraw their parties' resolutions demanding a commission of inquiry into the riots. Special Branch report "Tengku Abdul Rahman, Malaysian Prime Minister: His visit to Singapore in connection with the recent disturbances", 19 August 1964, ISD.
248. Memorandum no. 1234, W.B. Pritchett to Secretary, Department of External Affairs, 25 August 1964, A1838/280 no. 3027/2/1 Part 19.
249. Ibid.
250. Ibid.
251. Memorandum no. 1246, W.B. Pritchett to Secretary, Department of External Affairs, 28 August 1964, A1838/280 no. 3024/2/1 Part 13.
252. Memorandum no. 1234, W.B. Pritchett to Secretary, Department of External Affairs, 25 August 1964, A1838/280 no. 3027/2/1 Part 19.
253. The Malaysian leaders were incensed over the poor light in which UMNO and the Malays were portrayed by much of the international press reporting on the Singapore disturbances. A *Time* article with the heading "Amok But Not Asunder" (31 July 1964) particularly incensed Kuala Lumpur. Another by Dennis Bloodworth, entitled "Malaysia Premier's Party Extremists Inflame Killing", in *The Observer* (26 July 1964), stirred especially the ire of Syed Ja'afar Albar who responded with a lengthy reply in *Merdeka*. Alliance leaders felt that the Western press had been influenced by Lee into believing that the PAP were the "good guys" and UMNO and Syed Ja'afar the "bad guys". See also telegram no. 169, American Embassy (Kuala Lumpur) to Department of State, RG 59 Box 2450 Pol 2 1/1/64.
254. *Merdeka*, 21 August 1964, in A1838/280 no. 3024/2/1 Part 13.
255. *Utusan Melayu*, 22 August 1964.
256. Telegram no. 169, American Embassy (Kuala Lumpur) to Department of State, RG 59 Box 2450 Pol 2 1/1/64.
257. Telegram no. 180, American Embassy (Kuala Lumpur) to Department of State, RG 59 Box 2457 Pol 23-8 1/1/64.
258. Memorandum "Racial Disturbances in Singapore in July–September, 1964", 8 October 1964, ISD.
259. *Royal Malaysia Police (Singapore) Intelligence Journal*, no. 9, 30 September 1964, p. 103.
260. Ibid.

261. Singapore Police Force, "General Situation Report — 4th September, 1964", ISD.
262. *The Straits Times*, 4 September 1964. On 2 September 1964,at least two groups of infiltrators were airdropped into the Labis area of northeast Johore. The first group, consisting of 34 Indonesian regulars and 16 Malaysian Chinese (who had undergone training in Indonesia), was detected by security forces and engaged within a few hours. The existence of the second group of 36 Indonesian regulars and 12 Malaysian Chinese, was only discovered on 9 September 1964. See COS 273/64, J.H. Lapsley to Chiefs of Staff Committee, "The Internal Security Threat to Malaya and Singapore from Indonesia", 8 October 1964, DEFE 5/154.
263. Airgram no. 186, American Embassy (Kuala Lumpur) to Department of State, 11 September 1964, RG 59 Box 2451 Pol 2-1 7/1/64.
264. Airgram no. 165, American Embassy (Kuala Lumpur) to Department of State, 4 September 1964, RG 59 Box 2451 Pol 2-1 7/1/64. On 10 October 1964, a five-man commission to inquire into the causes of the Singapore riots was established. The Singapore government submitted a memorandum to the commission in March 1965.
265. Singapore Police Force, "General Situation Report — 4th September, 1964", ISD.
266. Telegram no. 110, American Consulate (Singapore) to Department of State, 6 September 1964, RG 59 Box 2457 Pol 23-8, 1/1/64.
267. *The Straits Times*, 5 September 1964.
268. *Royal Malaysia Police (Singapore) Intelligence Journal*, no. 9, 30 September 1964, p. 103.
269. *The Straits Times*, 9 September 1964.
270. *Utusan Melayu*, 8 September 1964.
271. Memorandum "Racial Disturbances in Singapore in July–September, 1964", 8 October 1964, ISD.
272. *Sunday Telegraph*, 13 September 1964.
273. "Press statement by the Publicity Secretary of the Alliance Party, Inche Yap Chin Kwee in reply to Sunday Telegraph editorial", 15 September 1964, in A1838/280 no. 3024/2/ 1 Part 13.
274. Telegram no. 1029, Australian High Commission (Kuala Lumpur) to Department of External Affairs, 25 September 1964, A1838/280 no. 3027/2/1 Part 19.
275. Airgram no. 95, American Consulate (Singapore) to Department of State, 4 October 1964, RG 59 Box 2453 Pol 12 7/1/64.
276. Telegram no. 137, American Consulate (Singapore) to Department of State, 21 September 1964, RG 59 Box 2457 Pol 23-8 1/1/64; Telegram no. 642, Australian High Commission (Singapore) to Department of External Affairs, 21 September 1964, A1838/280 no. 3024/ 2/1 Part 13.
277. Airgram no. 95, American Consulate (Singapore) to Department of State, 4 October 1964, RG 59 Box 2453 Pol 12 7/1/64.
278. Ibid.
279. Telegram no. 137, American Consulate (Singapore) to Department of State, 21 September 1964, RG 59 Box 2457 Pol 23-8 1/1/64.
280. Telegram no. 645, Australian High Commission (Singapore) to Department of External Affairs, 21 September 1964, A1838/280 no. 3024/2/1 Part 13.
281. Telegram No. 138, American Consulate (Singapore) to Department of State, 22 September 1964, RG 59 Box 2457 Pol 23-8 1/1/64.
282. Memorandum 1415, W.B. Pritchett to Secretary, Department of External Affairs, 2 October 1964, A1838/280 no. 3027/2/1 Part 19.
283. Memorandum of Conversation between Tan Toh Hong (MCA MP) and Jerrold M. Dion (Third Secretary, American Embassy, Kuala Lumpur), 26 October 1964, RG 59 Box 2450 Pol 2 1/1/64.

284. Airgram no. 246, American Embassy (Kuala Lumpur) to Department of State, 2 October 1964, RG 59 Box 2451 Pol 2-1 7/1/64.

285. M.W.B. Smithies to Secretary, Department of External Affairs, 1 October 1964, A1838/280 no. 3024/2/1 Part 13; Memorandum 1415, W.B. Pritchett to Secretary, Department of External Affairs, 2 October 1964, A1838/280 no. 3027/2/1 Part 19.

286. Telegram no. 1039, Australian High Commission (Kuala Lumpur), 26 September 1964, A1838/280 no. 3024/2/1 Part 13.

287. US Naval Attaché (Singapore) to Chief Naval Operations (Washington), 4 October 1964, RG 59 Box 2451 Pol 2-1 7/1/64.

CHAPTER 7

"WE ARE ON COLLISION COURSE"

N otwithstanding the truce, Alliance leaders had not abandoned their strategy to take the fight to Singapore. The first phase of the Alliance campaign, according to the Singapore United Malays National Organization's (SUMNO) Secretary-General Syed Esa Almenoar, was to discredit the People's Action Party (PAP) among the Malays and win them back into UMNO's (United Malays National Organization) fold.[1] If successful, the Alliance would have dealt a serious blow to the PAP's efforts to spread its influence beyond Singapore. Forced back on its Chinese base, the PAP would have little choice but to take on a more communal role and champion Chinese interests in Malaysia, in which case, according to Alliance leaders, the Chinese in Malaya would reject it in favour of the concept of a communal Malayan Chinese Association (MCA) within the Alliance. The PAP, in their view, was a potential threat to the Alliance only so long as it remained a non-communal force. The next phase in the Alliance scheme was to defeat the PAP in the 1968 elections in Singapore, and for this the strengthening of the Alliance organization on the Island was imperative, as was the need for some image-building. The Alliance was convinced, as was the PAP, that if the latter was contained in Singapore, its political demise was certain. To survive, the PAP, on its part, could not afford to be confined to Singapore nor to succumb to the temptation of becoming a Chinese party. It needed, in the first instance, to expand and seek not just national influence but also national power. It also had to emphasize more aggressively rather than play down its ideological differences with the Alliance. As Goh Keng Swee was later to remark to W.B. Pritchett, the Australian Deputy High Commissioner, the forecast was indeed bleak: "We are on collision course".[2]

Barred by the terms of the truce from raising communal issues, the Alliance turned instead to build support from among the Chinese in Singapore. It opened a "second front" aimed at discrediting the PAP among the Chinese in Singapore.[3] On 17 October, in an address before the Hokkien *huay kuan* in Singapore, Tan Siew Sin fired the first shot and called upon the wealthy Chinese to take a more active interest in politics and urged them not to be deterred by the false proposition that "the great mass of people in Singapore will only be attracted to a political philosophy distinctly socialistic or savouring of socialism".[4] Acting on the principle that "the enemy of my enemy is my friend", the Alliance also consorted publicly with disaffected elements like the Barisan Sosialis (BS) and Tan Lark Sye in order to woo the Chinese ground. Syed Esa Almenoar, for instance, told American Consulate officials that he had met with BS leaders who indicated that they would prefer the Alliance to the PAP government in Singapore. Alliance–BS cooperation, he rationalized, would not only strengthen the anti-PAP campaign but would prevent these two left-wing factions (the BS and the PAP) from reuniting to oppose the Alliance.[5] When Tunku Abdul Rahman visited Singapore in August 1964, he had also met with BS leaders and urged them to join the goodwill committees which were later replaced by "peace committees". Tan Siew Sin, on his part, also openly consorted with Tan Lark Sye, the former chairman of the Nanyang University Council who had supported BS candidates in the 1963 Singapore elections, possibly in the hope of capitalizing on the latter's considerable influence in the Hokkien community. Syed Ja'afar Albar's appointment as a member of the board of directors in Tan Lark Sye's cement factory in Perak[6] marked a further consolidation in this alliance of unlikely parties.

It was not long before UMNO decided to work its Malay ground again. On 25 October, Mohammed Khir Johari came to Singapore to open five new UMNO branches and announced plans to overhaul the Singapore Alliance (SA) organization "so that in the next general elections in Singapore in 1967, the Singapore Alliance will win enough votes to form the next Government".[7] Given banner headlines in *The Straits Times*, Khir Johari's challenge to the PAP on its home ground was impossible to ignore. Seen from Singapore, it was, in Pritchett's words, a "provocative breach" of the understanding its leaders thought they had with Kuala Lumpur to refrain from sharpening political differences for the sake of national unity.[8] It was also, in the Australian High Commission's reckoning, "an unnecessary and tactless statement".[9] Crying foul almost immediately, on

26 October, Toh Chin Chye charged that Khir Johari's "ostentatious call" for the "ouster" of the PAP government "ill accords" with the terms of the truce which the PAP interpreted as a two-year halt to UMNO–PAP politicking. "We cannot accept a pause which is only applicable to the PAP," he said.[10] On the same day, another Singapore minister, Jek Yeun Thong, described the recent statements by some Alliance ministers as unethical and contrary to their agreement: "We are not afraid of the Alliance, but any competition must be on fair terms."[11] Lee Kuan Yew immediately rang the Tunku who told him that he had not seen the papers but he reassured Lee: "if they make a speech then you can make a speech".[12]

On his return to Kuala Lumpur, Khir Johari "tried to make the best of a bad job"[13] by issuing a statement on 27 October disclaiming knowledge of any existing truce. Clarifying that the reorganization of the SA was necessary to "strengthen democracy, freedom and fair-play in Singapore", he then added more provocatively that Kuala Lumpur had no intention of abandoning its "loyal party members or our silent supporters" and leaving them to be "exploited by people with evil intentions".[14] Referring to the new controversy as "a storm in a teacup" when he addressed the National Press Club of Malaya in Kuala Lumpur that same evening, the Tunku explained that the Alliance had operated in Singapore for many years and it would continue to do so, as it was a reminder of the presence of the central government.[15] The next day, however, after meeting SA leaders in Kuala Lumpur to discuss plans for the reorganization of the Alliance machinery in Singapore, the Tunku said that the truce applied only to communal issues and did not bar the revitalization of the SA. As T.K. Critchley commented, "The Alliance argues, of course, that it has long been established in Singapore (pre-dating the PAP) and its continued political activities there do not change the existing pattern of party politics in the State. The PAP, on the other hand, entered Malayan politics only after the formation of Malaysia gave it the opportunity to do so and its activities in Malaya have upset the Malayan politico-communal status quo."[16]

In a carefully worded response on 28 October, Toh disputed the Tunku's interpretation of their agreement. Asking whether Khir Johari's provocative comments were "in the spirit of the pause or conducive to national unity", Toh said that his "declared innocence" of any knowledge of a pause "comes strangely" after a lapse of more than a month after it was disclosed to the press. The PAP, however, "welcomes this invitation" to present alternative programmes to the people.[17] On 1 November, in what appeared to the

Australian High Commission's Second Secretary, M.W.B. Smithies, as "direct retaliation"[18] for Khir Johari's remarks, Toh declared that the PAP was also to be "reoriented and reorganized so that we can get at Malaya". He added, "We have members scattered all over Malaya. When the time is ready, we will organize them into branches."[19] Coming after the exchange had apparently run its course, Smithies thought Toh's remarks "badly timed", even if only a brief mention was made on an inside page of *The Straits Times*, and even less publicity in the other newspapers.[20] Fortunately, Toh's remarks did not provoke much of a rise from Kuala Lumpur, apparently anxious to dampen further political controversy.

The Budget Debate

But controversy could not be avoided when, at the budget debate in the Dewan Ra'ayat (House of Representatives) on 25 November, the Malaysian Finance Minister, Tan Siew Sin, unveiled his "shock" tax plans, ostensibly for the purpose of raising an extra $147 million to help redress a huge Federal deficit of $543 million incurred largely from *Konfrontasi*-related expenditure.[21] "'Incompetent, iniquitous and politically inept' is how the Federal Budget ... is being described in Singapore," reported Pritchett.[22] The reactions from the business circles and the press were hostile, and justifiably so, for Singapore taxpayers, in Goh Keng Swee's calculations, would contribute an "incongruous" 39.8 per cent towards the yield of the new taxes, even though the Island's population was only 17 per cent of the total population of Malaysia.[23]

Tan's controversial proposals for a turnover tax and a payroll tax, in particular, attracted heated criticisms, especially from Singapore. Large turnovers, it was pointed out, were no index of large profits. Coming after the brunt of Indonesia's economic confrontation, the riots in July and September, and the loss of the barter trade, the imposition of the turnover tax at half a per cent per annum would fall especially hard on a merchant community like Singapore where so many operated to extremely fine margins and relied on a high turnover for their profit. Describing the turnover tax as both "repressive and regressive",[24] Lee warned that it "may work freak and inequitable results on businesses with large turnovers but small profit margins".[25] The proposed two-per-cent payroll tax also came under heavy fire, on the grounds that it would discourage employment of labour, lead to retrenchments, and adversely affect labour intensive industries like rubber. It was also an anti-labour tax in that it would hinder

214

efforts by unions to press their claims.²⁶ New taxes on diesel oil and sugar
— introduced in Singapore for the first time — were attacked as yet another
attempt to squeeze the poor,²⁷ while the plans to reduce the rate of taxation
for the highest income earners from 55 per cent to 50 per cent were criticized
by Jek Yeun Thong as favouring the rich by giving them an *ang pow*
equivalent to 5 per cent of their total income.²⁸ The Malaysian Finance
Minister, Lee said, had been unable to resist "the desire to help one's own
kind. In the end temptation was stronger than conscience."²⁹ The new
taxes favoured the "haves" rather than the "have-nots," Lee charged, and
added that Singapore had not been consulted in advance on his proposals.³⁰

However much the PAP might have wanted, as Lee said, to "make
future relations easier", it was clearly impossible after the budget
announcements for the PAP "to hold back our views",³¹ especially when
the proposed tax changes so adversely affected Singapore's interests. Still,
Lee decided to call on the Tunku at the Residency on the morning of 30
November before the Dewan Ra'ayat budget debate, to forewarn him of
the PAP's concern over the proposed taxes, and to urge him to review
them. Knowing from his experience in the merger discussions, however,
that the Malaysian Finance Minister was "allergic to arguments from
me", Lee declined the Tunku's offer of a meeting with Tan Siew Sin
but agreed to record his views on a tape-recorder so that Tan could
later be acquainted with them. He could then send Goh Keng Swee to
sort matters out with Tan.³²

But despite Lee's best efforts to "put over our case in Parliament on a
low key",³³ the PAP's blast (considered "moderate" by Pritchett) still "clearly
stung Tan Siew Sin and one has the impression in Singapore that the
Alliance has been rattled by the PAP's criticism."³⁴ John A. Lacey, the
American Consul General, reporting the remarks of Philip Moore, the
British Deputy High Commissioner, commented in the same vein: "Lee is
a masterful debater with a stinging tongue and indeed his performance …
was less stinging than usual. But even though he may have attempted to
have mooted his criticism, Moore observed that his remarks were still quite
biting, and could not help but engender Alliance hostility."³⁵ The Malaysian
Finance Minister reacted sharply to the PAP's charges. Observing that the
PAP had always spoken of the necessity for the "haves" to share their
wealth with the "have-nots", Tan retaliated by threatening to raise "in the
near future" prosperous Singapore's contribution to the central government
from 40 per cent to 60 per cent of its revenue.³⁶ He added that the Singapore
government "need have no fear it would ever be consulted" unless the

Malaysia agreements so provided.[37] Tan's "somewhat intemperate comment" appeared to Pritchett "politically inept ... smacking of a domineering Federal attitude to a State, and [showed an] unwillingness to answer criticism".[38] It did not help that Tan repeated his threat the following day and cast more doubt on Singapore's sincerity in wanting to become a fully participating member of Malaysia. "[I]n their first test," he said, "[they] have failed lamentably. Their proposal in effect is 'Don't tax us, tax the Malayan tin miners!'"[39]

The Finance Minister's remarks drew an angry response from Lee that same night about dealing with "irrational people" who replied to criticisms by asking for 60 per cent of Singapore's revenue: "No argument, nothing. ... When they cannot answer you, they get their back-benches to shout at you and threaten you. Why waste time threatening us? ... [W]e will never be intimidated."[40] To prove its retaliatory capability, the PAP campaigned hard against the taxes, not only in Singapore but also by widening its attacks through PAP branches in Malaya. "With support throughout Malaysia," Lee declared, "a new climate of public opinion may be built whereby the Finance Minister may find he has got to adjust policies to face realities."[41] In Singapore, the pro-PAP National Trades Union Congress (NTUC) consequently planned a mass rally of workers at the National Theatre to protest against the anti-labour provisions of the budget. When the police, apparently "on orders from Kuala Lumpur",[42] refused permission for the rally, the NTUC, after seeking legal advice and ignoring police warning that the meeting was illegal, went ahead to hold an indoor "delegates conference" instead at the Victoria Memorial Hall on 14 December.[43] Defying the ban, Jek Yeun Thong, the Minister for Labour, spoke against the budget at the meeting. So did Lee Kuan Yew who attended at the last minute "so that if the police prosecuted they would have to prosecute him".[44] Lee's presence, however, was kept out of the newspapers.

The Kuala Lumpur–Singapore rift worsened considerably as the month-long debate on the budget tarried. Like Pritchett, Antony Head the British High Commissioner, also attributed the deterioration in ties largely to Tan Siew Sin, whom he said had "done more than most ... to keep Singapore/Centre relations uneasily simmering".[45] In a withering blast against the Singapore government during the introduction of his bill in the Dewan Negara (Senate) on 30 December, Tan, for instance, accused the PAP leaders of not only working hand in hand with the communists to undermine the central government but also inflaming "mob passions"

His voice filled with emotion, Lee Kuan Yew declares from the steps of City Hall on 16 September 1963 that Singapore "shall forever be a part of the sovereign democratic and independent State of Malaysia". Looking on are the Yang di-Pertuan Negara, Yusof bin Ishak, Malaysian Internal Security Minister, Ismail bin Abdul Rahman, representing the Malaysian government, and Duncan Sandys, British Commonwealth Relations Secretary.

(The Straits Times)

Huge poster of detained Barisan Sosialis Secretary-General, Lim Chin Siong, at a Barisan rally during the September 1963 hustings.

PAP election victory rally at City Hall on 26 September 1963.

The Singapore Alliance campaigning in Katong, next to the Hollywood cinema, on 14 September 1963.

Heated anti-PAP speeches were made at the rally, including one by UMNO Secretary-General, Syed Ja'afar bin Hasan Albar.

(The Straits Times)

SUMNO reacts bitterly to the defeat of its candidates after the Singapore elections. At its Kampong Ubi branch on the night of 27 September 1963, angry crowds subsequently burn an effigy of Lee Kuan Yew.

(The Straits Times)

The banner reads: 'We oppose the policy of the PAP'.

(The Straits Times)

The Tunku, who also spoke at the rally, hits out at Malay "traitors" and vows to personally direct the affairs of SUMNO.

S. Rajaratnam discussing election strategies with PAP Malayan candidates on 23 March 1964.

Billboard announcing the PAP presence in Malaya.

PAP chairman Toh Chin Chye.

Lee Kuan Yew
campaigning on
the streets.

(Courtesy of the National
Archives of Singapore)

Huge crowds at a
PAP election rally
on 11 April 1964.

(Courtesy of the National
Archives of Singapore)

Lee Kuan Yew reaching out to the crowds.

Large crowds gather outside the New Star Cinema on 12 July 1964.

Inside the packed cinema, representatives from some 123 Malay and Muslim bodies, including political parties assemble to hear the invited speakers indict the PAP for its alleged oppressive treatment of Singapore Malays.

The government holds its own meeting with Malay bodies. Lee Kuan Yew and Othman Wok entering Victoria Theatre on 19 July as supporters stand by.

Syed Ja'afar Albar delivers his controversial keynote address.

Malay procession during Prophet Mohammed's birthday on 21 July 1964.

Police cordon beside the Kallang Gas Works after the outbreak of riots.

Fearsome violence:
overturned and burnt cars.

(Courtesy of the National
Archives of Singapore)

A victim of the riots.

(Courtesy of the Internal
Security Department)

Another victim
along Telok
Kurau Road.

(Courtesy of the Internal
Security Department)

Tun Razak (third from the left) and SUMNO deputy chairman, Ahmad Haji Taff (fourth from the left), visiting a riot affected area on 22 July 1964.

Lee Kuan Yew visits a Housing and Development Board estate to reassure residents on 26 July 1964.

Delegates at the rally.
(Courtesy of the National Archives of Singapore)

Lee Kuan Yew giving his keynote address at the first Malaysian Solidarity Convention (MSC) rally at the Singapore National Theatre on 6 June 1965.
(Courtesy of the National Archives of Singapore)

Delegates rallying to the MSC's call for a Malaysian Malaysia.
(Courtesy of the National Archives of Singapore)

S. Rajaratnam bids farewell to Alex Josey, Lee's press secretary, who had been served an expulsion order by the Malaysian government.

(Courtesy of the National Archives of Singapore)

Lee's press conference on 9 August 1965 after announcing Singapore's separation from Malaysia.

(Courtesy of the National Archives of Singapore)

The Tunku returns on 5 August 1965.

An emotional moment for the Prime Minister.

against the turnover and payroll taxes and inciting the populace "to action, perhaps even violent action, in order to bring the Central Government to its knees".[46] His announcement on the same day that Kuala Lumpur had decided to close down, in due course, the Bank of China in Singapore also drew S. Rajaratnam's ire and provoked his retort that the Singapore government would not agree to its closure simply "because of the personal likes or dislikes of the Malaysian Finance Minister". The bank's position, Rajaratnam added, had been "thrashed out" in the Malaysia negotiations and he had not heard any convincing arguments for a reconsideration of its useful role.[47]

The political fallout from the budget debate was more serious. For Kuala Lumpur, ever fearful of the political organizing power of the PAP, and mindful of the next elections, the writing was on the wall. The open demonstration of PAP power within and without the House was deeply worrying. It showed that the PAP could not be intimidated and was capable of hitting back hard. It was also an ominous warning to Kuala Lumpur of the PAP's strength in eventually being able to mobilize opinion throughout Malaysia, using Parliament and its branches in Malaya, to bring influence to bear on the policies of the central government. As Siow Loong Hin, the Alliance member for Seremban Barat, saw it, the PAP's intention was to "launch an extensive and massive pan-Malayan campaign"[48] utilizing all their cadres and supporters to "escalate the discontent of the people".[49] Something should be done, he said, "to separate the people from the PAP".[50]

The Tunku was thinking of doing just that.

Secret Negotiations for "Disengagement"

By early December, the Tunku was already having second thoughts about keeping Singapore within Malaysia. "If they [the PAP] want to get out they are welcome to," the Tunku told Critchley on 6 December.[51] On 9 December, in a speech at King Edward VII Hall, University of Singapore, the Tunku complained of the adverse political activity which was disrupting peace in the State. "[U]nnecessary excitement" and the sometimes unhealthy aspects of Singapore politics were the reasons why the Tunku was "once not very anxious to bring Singapore into the Federation". He had taken risks in the interest of Malaysia but if Singapore chose "to make politics the main springboard", Malaysia would suffer. Referring to the "many types of politicians in Singapore", including the "lightning flash ones" (a pointed reference to the PAP emblem), the

217

Tunku said that if Singapore politicians disagreed with him the only solution was a "breakaway" which would be a calamity for Singapore and Malaysia though it would be welcomed by Indonesia and the communists.[52] Although Critchley did not take the Tunku's breakaway remarks too seriously,[53] Head suspected that both the Tunku and Tun Abdul Razak were hatching some sort of scheme to deal with Singapore: "They clearly wish to prevent Singapore from playing any significant part in the politics of Malaya."[54]

Head was not wrong. On 27 December, the suggestion of a new constitutional "rearrangement" was apparently made by Tun Razak to Goh Keng Swee.[55] Lee first heard of Kuala Lumpur's intention from political contacts in the Malaysian capital and from journalists with whom Tun Razak had been speaking off the record.[56] Antony Head, the British High Commissioner, had also obtained confirmation of the secret talks from a "most delicate and confidential" Kuala Lumpur source. The Tunku's offer, which was put to Goh on 22 January 1965, Head found out, envisaged Singapore giving up its seats in the Federal Parliament in exchange for complete autonomy, except for foreign affairs and defence. Apart from the latter two subjects, Singapore would regain control over all the subjects it held before Malaysia Day, including internal security. In short, the effect of the Tunku's scheme would make Singapore and the rest of Malaysia virtually independent of each other, except for foreign affairs and defence. "[P]resumably with no seats in Parliament," Head commented, "the Malays would think that they could eliminate any likelihood of Lee Kuan Yew scoring political success in Malaya".[57]

Further confirmation came on 25 January when Lee informed Philip Moore, the British Deputy High Commissioner, that he was going to make the following offer to the Federal government: All "Federal" subjects would revert to Singapore, except foreign policy and defence; Singapore was to retain its seats in Parliament and the right to criticize the Federal government's foreign and defence policies but a Defence Council would be established for these questions to be normally thrashed out in private; the PAP, however, would close its branches in Malaya in return for the Alliance doing the same in Singapore; and a detailed agreement was to be drawn up to settle the introduction of the Common Market.[58] As Head noted, apart from the "very great exception of Parliamentary representation", Lee's scheme was "a close parallel" to the Tunku's offer.[59]

The proposals filled Head with alarm. "It is as far as I know unprecedented for one member of a Federation to be excluded politically from the Federal Government," the High Commissioner informed Sir Saville Garner, the Permanent Under-Secretary of State, at the Commonwealth Relations Office. "[W]orld opinion ... may consider that this is the first sign of a crack in the new Federation of Malaysia," Head warned, "and that maybe the Indonesians are right after all and this is only an artificial and ephemeral construction, not deserving of strong support." He had no doubt that "such a move would be much played up by the Indonesians". Head particularly had deep misgivings about giving internal security back to Singapore and knew from his Kuala Lumpur source that Ismail bin Abdul Rahman, now the Malaysian Minister of Home Affairs and Minister of Justice, had also disapproved of this. "[I]t would be highly dangerous," he said, "for Singapore to have to rely on its own somewhat meagre resources for internal security and to be in a position whereby Federal reinforcement might be uncertain or late and in a situation for which the Federal Government had no direct responsibility." What was disturbing was also that both the Tunku and Tun Razak were "deliberately keeping us in the dark, no doubt because they have a guilty conscience and want to face us with a *fait accompli* which — they calculate — we should decide to make the best of."[60] For the moment, Head was loath to confront the Tunku so as not to compromise his source: "[U]ntil we learn of it more properly we must keep very quiet about our knowledge of the Malaysian ideas — otherwise our source will be immediately suspect, which we cannot afford". He hoped, however, to be able soon "to use what Lee told Moore as a lever to get Razak to talk, but first Moore must get Lee's concurrence".[61]

In the meantime, Lee had apparently forced the pace by meeting the Tunku to discuss disengagement. On 1 February, Head learnt from his confidential source that Lee had visited Kuala Lumpur secretly and "had stated he would accept loss of seats [in] Federal Parliament".[62] Fearing that the scheme now seemed "virtually agreed", Head found himself in a dilemma. To intervene and block a possible solution, he argued, could result in the British being blamed for all future Tunku–Lee rows. Not to do so would adversely affect British interests. His instinct was to play it slow and merely get the Tunku's assurance that nothing would be settled irrevocably without consulting the British. If British objectives could be achieved only "through an almighty row" it was better to let it go, he counselled, "On the other hand, if there are signs of weakness or wobble when full implications of such a policy on British and world confidence in Malaysia are pointed out then we could weigh in hard".[63]

Head saw the Tunku on his birthday, 8 February. The Tunku finally confirmed the existence of the plan but spoke reassuringly to the High Commissioner that the talks had not gotten far and he foresaw long and detailed negotiations leading to a formal amendment of the constitution, a process likely to take at least a year and possibly more, at the end of which the British government would be free to express its views. Meanwhile, he aimed to set up a working committee, possibly assisted by a British constitutional adviser, to produce a concrete plan, which might then be discussed with the British government at the time of the next Commonwealth Prime Ministers' meeting. Brushing aside Head's remarks about the bad effect on world opinion, the Tunku said that the continuance of the row between the two governments would create an even worse international image. He also discounted the possibility of the changes leading to similar demands from Borneo. But would not the plan be likely to leak, with disastrous consequences for all, Head asked? Again, the Tunku assured the High Commissioner that it would not leak. Only five persons knew of its existence, the Tunku revealed. "On this I have serious doubts," Head opined.

The High Commissioner left the meeting reassured at least that the Tunku would consult the British.[64] But he remained concerned that the Tunku, driven as he was by his overriding determination to get Singapore out, was still "blind and unimaginative" to the serious effect his plan would have on world confidence in Malaysia. "He professes to regard this as simply a matter of presentation," Head complained to Garner. Knowing this, Head felt it was imperative that the British government, instead of waiting to be consulted in 12 months' time, should make known immediately its strong objections to the scheme, otherwise the Tunku might assume "we had no general dislike of his ideas in principle". Head thought the "best peg" on which to hang British disapproval might be to tell the Tunku that his new plan would alter the essential basis of the United Kingdom–Malaysia defence arrangements in the Malaysia agreement,[65] which was that internal security in Singapore must be under direct control of the Federal government so as to ensure the security of the British bases.[66] The timely visit to Malaysia by the British Chief of the Defence Staff, Admiral Lord Louis Mountbatten, on 10 February, in the course of a world tour, afforded just such an occasion to put across that point to him.[67]

Head and Mountbatten consequently discussed the situation in turn with Tun Razak and the Tunku when he called on them the following day, on 11 February. Tun Razak appeared "receptive to Mountbatten's arguments" and "undertook to reconsider the matter in the light of them" but Head thought this might be no more than a desire not to give offence. As the High Commissioner saw it, "very often Razak is apt to be receptive and pliant at the time of an interview, but his subsequent actions often show that this is a mixture of good manners and desire not to give offence". The Tunku, however, stood pat on his plan. As Head reported, "His theme was: there is plenty of time, I will consult you, there is nothing to worry about". What did emerge, according to Head, was that Tunku was strongly in favour of "getting his scheme through, and did not relish the idea of Mountbatten and myself talking to Lee Kuan Yew. Only reluctantly, did the Tunku finally give his consent for Head to approach Lee.[68]

The next day, Head explained quite frankly to Lee the very serious consequences which might stem from the Tunku's plan. Lee then proposed an alternative solution which Head saw as almost "identical to that which Mountbatten and I, discussing the matter previously, had thought might be the best compromise". In essence, Lee's plan was similar to the Tunku's, the main difference being that Singapore would retain its Federal seats, but would abstain from using them for any controversial purposes or for attacking the central government. Should this undertaking be broken, the new self-governing powers to be given to Singapore could be freely withdrawn by the Federal government. Unlike the Tunku's plan, which required the constitution to be amended, a process taking a year or more, Lee's proposal would be achieved by purely internal administrative action, without the need for a formal amendment to the Federal constitution, and could be worked out and agreed on in about three weeks.[69] All PAP branches in Malaya would also be closed down in return for the closure of UMNO and MCA branches in Singapore. So long as *Konfrontasi* (confrontation) was still in force, Lee personally undertook not to rock the boat by agreeing to a forfeiture of the Federal seats but said he would be prepared to reconsider the matter afresh upon the ending of the troubles with Indonesia.

Compared to the Tunku's original proposals, Lee's compromise scheme was "certainly an improvement",[70] the main advantage being that it would make Singapore's separation *de facto* rather than *de jure*, and somewhat less apparent. But, still, there were drawbacks. Lee's insistence on controlling internal security, for instance, "leaves gravely open to doubt the issue of ultimate responsibility for internal security in Singapore".[71] And although the Singapore premier might be prepared to assure the Tunku concerning the good behaviour and restraint of Singapore members in the Federal Parliament, and was even ready to "write out a guarantee in the strongest terms and sign it", and agree to the withdrawal of the extra powers, if such a political truce were broken, Head surmised that the Tunku might still want a firm agreement about the forfeiture of seats after *Konfrontasi*, which Lee was not yet ready to give.[72] Nor was it at all clear that the Tunku would agree to the closure of UMNO branches in Singapore. Getting the Tunku's acceptance of the compromise plan might also present a problem since he was, at the moment, "so naïve about the effect of forfeiture of seats that it will need a lot of talking and convincing to get him out of it".[73]

Given the urgency of resolving the existing tensions, Head recommended, with Mountbatten's backing, that support be given to Lee's proposals. Despite its drawbacks, Lee's compromise plan was still less objectionable than the Tunku's earlier proposals.[74] Head believed that if he were to lobby Tun Razak and Ismail there was a good chance the Tunku could be deflected from insisting on his original plans. He suggested that the New Zealanders, who were not yet aware of Lee's thinking, and also the Australians, particularly Critchley or Menzies who "stands high in Tunku's estimation and has not got disadvantage of being the ex boss", could be taken into Whitehall's confidence and asked to forward the solution to the Tunku on their own initiative. Head would then add his own representation in support of Lee's plan. "Lee Kuan Yew stated, in my view accurately," Head reported, "that for him to propose such a scheme [to the Tunku] would give it a very bad chance".[75]

London reacted to the High Commissioner's intimation of secret negotiations between the Tunku and Lee with grave foreboding. Any major change less than 18 months after the formation of Malaysia, the Commonwealth Relations Office opined, would be "a pretty dramatic development, and we do not see how it could be wrapped up so as to avoid causing most serious consequences internationally". Commenting on the Tunku's proposals, Sir Saville Garner maintained that the exclusion of Singapore from parliamentary representation, would not only make Malaysia a "farce", but would also "alarm and dishearten Malaysia's friends" and swing sympathy within Britain against underwriting Malaysia. To make it worse, Singapore's disengagement would have an "extremely disturbing effect in Sarawak and Sabah", leading possibly to "seriously disruptive moves inside those States".[76] On internal security, Garner was also emphatic that the Federation must retain some responsibilities and the right to intervene, fearing an otherwise "nasty problem" if Singapore's own limited security forces failed to deal with a situation.[77]

The concern was also shared by the British Defence Secretary, Denis Healey, who found the ramifications alarming. With British troops "holding the ring militarily for Malaysia", Healey feared that, with a loosening of the bonds between Malaya and Singapore, the Borneo territories "will be on the cards [again]" and "thrust back into our lap, in practice if not by constitution". He warned, however, that any development that made "less of a reality of the Malaysian Federation will inevitably increase the extent to which we appear to be 'neo-Colonialist' in respect of Borneo". Nor was he happy about finding "ourselves landed again with massive internal security responsibilities in Singapore", a role British forces certainly could not take on.[78]

The Foreign Office was just as worried. "[T]he world in general would begin to think that Malaysia was breaking up," it warned, "This would be a godsend for Indonesian propaganda and would encourage other countries, notably the USA, to work for peace at all costs." With internal security invested in Singapore, "it remains a fact that we should probably have to abandon the Singapore base ... if pressed to do so by a strongly left-wing government in Singapore". The effect on Sabah and Sarawak would also be very "unsettling, even if they did not lose faith in Malaysia entirely". It agreed with Head's assessment, however, that if the principals were determined to proceed, it would be counter-productive to attempt to block a settlement.[79]

Forewarned about the secret talks, the British premier, Harold Wilson, also expressed his misgivings. "I know Lee Kuan Yew very well and he might listen to me," he minuted, "Is there a case for getting him over on some pretext and twisting his arm?"[80] A week later, Wilson was still toying with the idea of getting Lee to London. When he was told that the Tunku's plan might not come into fruition until a year later, Wilson penned, "If it is a year, that gives us time to get LKY over on, e.g., Soc. Int. business".[81]

Instructed by Wilson to have the merits of the proposals examined, an interdepartmental committee was set up on 11 February.[82] A draft memorandum was subsequently prepared and submitted on 16 February for consideration three days later by a Cabinet committee chaired by the Prime Minister himself. The view of the departments in Whitehall was that both schemes had "very grave disadvantages for us"[83] and were, therefore, unacceptable "basically because they would make it impossible for the United Kingdom to help defend Malaysia".[84]

The memorandum concurred that Tunku's plan would have "a most damaging effect on the Malaysian image abroad", and weaken international resolve behind Britain's efforts to defend Malaysia. Although Lee's proposals might have less immediate public impact, "its international effects would be the same in the end, while internally it would cause confusion in government".[85] The committee thought it highly unlikely that Lee's scheme could be kept confidential, as he suggested, "and it might well lead to even greater confusion and acrimony in the long run than the more drastic solution proposed by the Tunku", since it would rest on no clear-cut public division of responsibilities and be open to constant misunderstanding, both unintentional and otherwise. If responsibility for internal security was no longer in the hands of the Federal government, and the Singapore government was unable to control the situation, the security of the Singapore base might be imperiled, and "we might find ourselves saddled in practice with the ultimate responsibility and previous experience suggests that it would not be tolerable where we have no formal status."[86]

The effect of either plan on the Borneo territories could be such as to "produce a break up, in fact if not in name, of the Federation".[87] Political disintegration from within would also make it more difficult for Britain to defend Malaysia against threats from without, including the long-term danger from China. If the division between Singapore and Malaya led to the break-up of Malaysia, the "whole weight of defence against Indonesia would have to be carried by Britain to an even greater extent than at present." In the Borneo territories, Britain would find itself saddled, not only with defence, but also, in effect, with civil administration, if the territories were not to be abandoned to Indonesia — a prospect which would lead to "a virtual reimposition of colonial rule, but without the formal position and powers that enabled us to carry it out previously."[88]

The committee, therefore, recommended that both schemes be opposed, and that the support of the Australian and New Zealand governments be enlisted to lend weight to British efforts to dissuade both the Tunku and Lee from pursuing their proposals for the time being. British ministers, who considered the committee's report on 19 February, agreed that both plans were fraught with danger for British interests and decided that in private discussion with the Tunku and Lee, Head should resist any radical amendment of the Federal constitution or any administrative arrangements designed to secure the same ends.[89]

Meanwhile, a new round of talks between the Tunku and Lee in Singapore on 15 February resulted in another set of proposals which had "gone far to reach agreement"[90] between them. The Tunku, who was in Singapore to open the new UMNO headquarters the day before, had apparently changed his tune and was agreeable to having Singapore representatives remain in the Federal Parliament, a breakthrough Lee attributed to the influence of Mountbatten and Head. External affairs and defence, as before, would remain Federal responsibilities, although the latter would continue to be deliberated in the National Defence Council in which Singapore, Sabah and Sarawak were already represented. On the thorny internal security issue, the Tunku showed some readiness to let Singapore have day-to-day control of its own police and Special Branch in return for a joint Internal Security Council (ISC), chaired by Ismail, having the power to overrule Singapore on internal security questions. Any request for British assistance in internal security operations would have to be discussed by the ISC and channelled through the central government to Britain. Probably to avoid future state-centre fiscal quarrels, the Tunku was prepared to restore all financial powers to Singapore in return for an agreed financial contribution towards the cost of defence and external affairs. Singapore was also to pay for its own police and Special Branch.[91] Both parties would cease their attacks on each other.[92] Although they had not discussed political activities in each other's territory, Lee's own assessment was that the Tunku could not close UMNO branches in Singapore and that probably the best compromise might be for their respective ministers to undertake not to speak at party political occasions in each other's territory, thus rendering their respective branches less effective and controversial.[93]

But the ideas soon ran into several snags and, by 18 February, James Bottomley, Head's deputy, was reporting that "things are now to some extent back in the melting pot".[94] First, SUMNO, which got wind of the talks, resented being abandoned by Kuala Lumpur and "were creating serious difficulties" for the Tunku. Next, Tan Siew Sin "was threatening to resign if Singapore was given degree of fiscal autonomy" envisaged in the Tunku's plans, and "Tan's threat will at least hold up this side of the plan". Ismail had also "temporarily convinced Tunku that Federal Government must retain full responsibility for internal security in Singapore".[95] Despite the setbacks, the Tunku was apparently still "busily looking for ways out of these difficulties and could not be counted on to remain on Ismail's side over internal security, particularly if [the] British showed any sign of being prepared to accept some compromise on this aspect".[96]

The British, however, discounted such a prospect. The new proposals still suffered from the same "very serious objections" that led to the rejection of the previous two schemes.[97] British concerns over internal security were still not allayed. The compromise of an Internal Security Council, Bottomley thought, would probably be adequate in normally quiet times but might prove unworkable in a crisis, like a repeat of the communal disturbances. "If it came to a showdown," Bottomley argued, "it seems almost certain that either there would be serious delays caused by arguments between Ismail representing Federal government, with their Malay sensitivities, and Singapore authorities; or else that Ismail would use his overriding powers and Singapore authorities publicly disclaim responsibility leaving the police (paid and promoted by them) in [the] most unenviable position in carrying out Ismail's orders."[98] The consequences could be serious. Weakening Federal control over internal security, would prospectively imperil the functioning of the Singapore base. "Our ability to fulfill our SEATO obligations could be prejudiced," the Commonwealth Relations Office warned.[99]

On 23 February, Head went to work. First, he spoke to both his Australian and New Zealand counterparts. Critchley apparently had known generally of what was afoot for some time.[100] The New Zealand High Commissioner, R.H. Wade, was also aware after Lee disclosed to his deputy, Brian Lendrum, on 16 February the main points of his discussion with the Tunku the day before.[101] Both high commissioners, however, were "sound on the two major points, Singapore seats and internal security", and Head felt "reasonably confident that they will be prepared to help if and when major crunch develops".[102] Later in the morning, Head saw the Tunku alone and, after putting across to him the British government's strong apprehensions about the surrender of the Singapore seats, he secured the Malaysian leader's personal assurance that the seats would remain. Head confirmed that while the Tunku was still determined to negotiate a deal with Lee, he had encountered strong resistance from Ismail and Tan Siew Sin. "Tunku hopes to reach some compromise but from what I have found out it is not going to be easy," Head reported. After lunch, Head had about an hour with Lee who was in Kuala Lumpur for talks with Ismail and the Tunku. Lee told Head he had run into difficulties over internal security but he was nevertheless convinced that some compromise had to be found to take the heat out of the tensions between Kuala Lumpur and Singapore. Head opined that he foresaw a protracted period of negotiations and suggested that Lee could perhaps persuade the Tunku to agree to a joint interim statement to the effect that negotiations were going on but no radical changes were contemplated in order to forestall damaging press leakages, "kill current rumours of more radical changes" and afford both sides a better opportunity to observe a political truce. Lee said he would put the point to the Tunku. On the whole, Head was pleased and surmised that the "views held by Tan Siew Sin, Ismail and Lee Kuan Yew could well stop anything from happening".[103]

He was right. British pressure on the Tunku, augmented by those of their local allies "fighting our battle for us",[104] had the desired effect. The Tunku backed away from pursuing a settlement. Nor did he wish to issue any statement. By 4 March, Head was able to report that British objectives had been achieved, though probably at a cost:

> As far as your original apprehensions are concerned, I think you can be entirely certain that there will be no giving up of seats in Federal Parliament and reasonably certain Lee will not be given complete autonomy for internal security. On [the] other hand, prospect of improved relations between Singapore and Kuala Lumpur are not, in my view, at all good.[105]

Securing Allies: The Malaysian Solidarity Convention

It was not British pressure alone that dissuaded the Tunku from pursuing a settlement with Lee. A secret report, which had reached the Tunku's ears, of a meeting in Singapore between Lee and certain dissident politicians[106] from Malaya, Sabah and Sarawak on 12 February 1965, with the object of establishing a united front of non-communal opposition political parties,[107] had upset the Tunku extremely and closed his mind to any further meeting with Lee or to try to reach any agreement. As Head reported, the Malaysian premier had formed the impression that Lee was "deliberately sticking pins" into him to get him to negotiate and reach some agreement and that "the more Lee did the less inclined the Tunku was to negotiate".[108] Both Ismail and Tun Razak also grew firm in their resolve not to give control of internal security to Singapore. On seeing the report, "Razak thought they could not hand over internal security to a man who was operating in this kind of way while in the middle of negotiations with the Tunku."[109] Speculating on Lee's motive for calling the meeting, the Commonwealth Relations Office (CRO) surmised that "Lee pretty certainly must have known that all this would leak to the Federal authorities before long; it is possible that his object is to frighten them into agreeing to his other proposals by means of this threat of a really big row if they reject his terms." Whatever might have been Lee's intentions, the CRO thought that while it was "a perfectly legitimate political manoeuvre" for Lee, "in [the] local circumstances, it is a highly inflammable tactic".[110]

Discussion within the PAP concerning the advisability of forming a united opposition front began in the fall of 1964 leading to a decision by its Central Executive Committee in November 1964 to seek common ground with like-minded political groups in Sabah, Sarawak and Malaya. But the inspiration for such a grouping went much further back. Prior to the formation of Malaysia, the PAP was already in touch with political parties in Sarawak and Sabah, like the Sarawak United People's Party (SUPP) and the United National Kadazan Organization (UNKO), though relations with the former cooled after the extremist wing within the party opposed the formation of Malaysia. The value of a Singapore–Sarawak–Sabah united front as a negotiating lever was not lost on Lee during the final stages of the Malaysia discussions. Frustrated by the bitter negotiations with Kuala Lumpur, Lee had made an eleventh-hour trip to the two Borneo states and proposed that if the Malayan government would not give in, then Sabah, Sarawak and Singapore would "go it alone" as the "United States of Malaysia".[111] Whether Lee's intentions were "real or only for bluff",[112] the birth of Malaysia on 16 September 1963, in any case, made the possibility of a tie-up academic. For a time after that, the PAP deliberately avoided being too closely associated with the other opposition parties, anxious as it was to portray itself as a loyal and moderate party, in line with its tactical objective of working with UMNO. Its participation in the Federal elections in April 1964 brought it into contact this time with Malayan-based parties like the People's Progressive Party (PPP) and United Democratic Party (UDP). Although there were reports — subsequently denied by the PAP — of "a three-cornered agreement between the PAP, PPP and UDP",[113] tactical expediency again prevented any close liaison being forged. Still hoping to strike a tune with the Alliance after its ill-judged foray into Federal politics, Lee had refused the Tunku's offer to lead the anti-Alliance opposition bloc, and in one of his first speeches in the new Dewan Ra'ayat in May 1964, the Singapore premier spoke deliberately of the "unbridgeable" chasms between the pro-Malaysia PAP and the communist-penetrated anti-Malaysia SUPP, Socialist Front (SF) and the Barisan Sosialis on the other.[114] Lee said that the PAP had also "yet to find [their] water-level" with the PPP and the UDP.[115] In reply, the SUPP chairman, Ong Kee Hui, wryly remarked that in the near future the PAP might find the chasms not so unbridgeable after all.[116]

Indeed, by the latter half of 1964, the PAP came under pressure to reassess its policy of cooperation with Kuala Lumpur. A PAP–Alliance tie-up had failed, and appeared unlikely to materialize. The crisis in the post-election ties between Singapore and Kuala Lumpur had also worsened, and reached a crescendo in the aftermath of the race riots in July and September. As PAP–Alliance recriminations heated up, the frost between the PAP and the other opposition parties began to thaw at the top. Ong Kee Hui revealed, for instance, that while attending the Dewan Ra'ayat sessions in July 1964, he "had been in close liaison with both Lee and Dr Lim Chong Eu over the possibility of forming a cohesive parliamentary opposition".[117] The American Consul in Kuching, William A. Brown, reported, "In fact, Ong and Lee had agreed to hold a preliminary 'summit' meeting, but Lee backed off during the end of the parliamentary session on the grounds that he foresaw an outbreak of communal tension in Singapore and would be fully occupied with the problem."[118] A tie-up with the PAP was not without its attractions to the SUPP, as Robert W. Moore commented: "Ong may well have come to the conclusion that he and the other SUPP moderates cannot lead the party out of the wilderness on their own. Therefore, some sort of cooperation with and assistance from the experienced PAP leadership might be welcome under certain conditions."[119] The crisis in the Sabah Alliance,[120] the result of an internal power struggle between the United Pasok-Momogun Kadazan Organization (UPKO) — a link-up of Donald Stephens' UNKO and the Pasok Momogun — and the Kuala Lumpur-backed United Sabah National Organization (USNO)–Sabah National Party (SANAP), representing the Malay-Muslim and Chinese respectively, had also driven Donald Stephens, in danger of being ousted as Chief Minister, to turn to Lee for help. Despite the mediation efforts by the Tunku, no acceptable solution was found, and Stephens subsequently lost his post in a scheme brokered by the Tunku, in return for his appointment as Minister for Sabah Affairs in the Federal Cabinet. Apparently "discouraged and embittered by what he considers Federal betrayal", Stephens had "stated flatly that in the event of a break-up he would ally with the Singapore People's Action Party".[121] When he was informed by Brown that the PAP might be hesitant to jump into Borneo politics, Stephens declared, "Well, I have had long talks with Lee Kuan Yew and I think they might be interested."[122]

Lee was tempted to help but did not think it was the right time to do so. Queried by Pritchett on 3 July about the PAP's intentions in Sarawak, Lee again said that he thought this was the wrong time for the PAP to move to Borneo. It would only cause misunderstanding and friction and was also likely to be regarded as a hostile act by Kuala Lumpur: "Lee said that if the Borneo States and Singapore all joined together and looked like increasing their power they would all be put in gaol".[123] As for Sabah, it seemed to Lee that the Tunku really wanted to "get rid of Donald Stephens" and he toyed with the idea of helping Stephens. As Pritchett reported, "He said Donald Stephens would need the Chinese vote to hang on and he (Lee Kuan Yew) was probably the one to fix this for him. What if Toh Chin Chye were to take his holidays in Sabah?"[124] E.W. Barker, now Minister for Law, who had visited Sabah in November, had told Lee of his assessment that the "PAP could win support [of] SANAP rank and file and join with Stephens to demand and then win direct elections".[125] Such an intervention by the PAP, however, would risk a serious rupture with Kuala Lumpur, as Lee told Pritchett: "Lee Kuan Yew ... said that of course the PAP were the only ones who could deal with it. But they could never go in: the Tunku would explode". Lee related how the Tunku "hit the roof" after learning that Barker whom he met by accident at Jesselton airport was a PAP man from Singapore.[126]

But in the aftermath of the race riots, there also emerged tremendous pressures within the PAP to attack UMNO's communal politicking, though such tendencies were held temporarily in check by the truce negotiated between Lee and the Tunku in September. PAP leaders were still hopeful that the transition could be used to restore Alliance confidence in the PAP. But to no avail. In October 1964, when the Tunku defined the truce as barring only the exploitation of sensitive issues but not Alliance efforts to unseat the PAP, party leaders began to wonder if the time had not come to seriously formulate a new policy. Whether the PAP liked it or not, it was being forced increasingly into opposition, a position Lee did not relish, as he confided to Pritchett on 27 October, two days after Khir Johari's "defeat PAP" speech in Singapore:

> Lee Kuan Yew spoke of being forced into opposition and spoke two or three times of calling a conference of socialist, non-communal parties in Malaysia, including [Donald] Stephens' UPKO and Ong Kee Hui's SUPP. He spoke of such a conference calling for autonomy for the Borneo States and a revision of the status of Singapore and Penang. (He seemed to be thinking of securing constitutional safeguards against Malay domination.) Such a conference would come out in full campaign against the Federal Government and really give it the works. Of course, it would be the end of Malaysia.[127]

As the price to pay was probably too high, Pritchett surmised that Lee was very likely only "talking well ahead of his intentions" and that he "has no plan at all for arranging any such thing".[128]

What seems clear is that by November 1964, the PAP had all but abandoned any hope of working with the UMNO-led Alliance, even if for tactical reasons it had not yet chosen to openly confront the latter. Convinced by now that the Alliance was not interested in having the PAP in a coalition and that Kuala Lumpur did not have the will nor capacity to "make a go" of Malaysia,[129] the PAP in a major strategy shift at its 10th anniversary party congress on 22 November, declared that it would seek not just national influence but national power on a platform of non-communalism and socialism. The PAP emphasized that the phase of allying with the right wing was over and the party now planned to become an opposition party advocating non-communal, class-based politics and socialism as against the communal politics and capitalism of the Alliance. Instead of playing down the ideological differences between the PAP and the Alliance, the party would now call attention to these differences and seek to unite all like-minded political groups in Malaysia, including the non-communist elements within the Socialist Front and the SUPP.[130] "To be silent about our non-communal beliefs now is not only to betray Malaysia but make inevitable its doom," Rajaratnam was to warn later.[131]

It had become abundantly clear by November that Kuala Lumpur was determined to reorganize the SA to unseat the PAP in Singapore. By January 1965, Khir Johari had spoken again of how the SA was being reorganized in readiness "to fight such a solid party as the PAP" in the next elections.[132] "We must move as fast as the PAP," he said, "to compete effectively with them".[133] Tun Razak had apparently also threateningly warned PAP leaders on 31 January that Kuala Lumpur would "use force to implement policies which we believe will benefit the people".[134] Addressing the opening of the new MCA Sembawang branch on 14 February 1965, Tan Siew Sin had also called for the establishment of an opposition party "which could be an alternative" to the PAP regime, which he compared to Hitler's Nazi government. Tan also spoke of the "price" Singapore must pay for entry to the elusive common market — "acceptance of the full range of import duties at present borne by the States of Malaya ... They cannot have it both ways." Tan also threatened manufacturers who opened factories in Singapore with dire consequences for their folly in investing in Singapore.[135] As Lee saw it, "knuckle dusters were put on and authority crudely flaunted in the people's faces".[136]

After deciding to embark on a course of engagement, political mobilization was inevitable. First, in view of the heightening tension between Kuala Lumpur and Singapore, and threats to undermine the party in Singapore, the PAP needed to move quickly to end its political isolation. Toh Chin Chye, who initiated the idea of the political grouping, recalled: "We were more and more isolated. The PAP needed friends to talk to in Malaysia."[137] More than that, the PAP needed political allies in Malaya, Sabah and Sarawak, not only to break free from containment by Kuala Lumpur, but also to spread its ideals and put pressure, in turn, on the Alliance by demonstrating, in a concrete way, that its call for political equality and non-communalism would strike a responsive chord throughout Malaysia. The PAP realized that an aggressive attempt to form PAP branches outside Singapore would take too long and might serve to alarm the Malays. As Toh put it, "The PAP has too long been isolated from the mainstream of politics outside Singapore and it will take a considerable time to organize on a pan-Malaysian basis. We must, therefore, learn how to work in cooperation with other political groups."[138] Presumably, the presence of allies would make any attempt to suppress the PAP more difficult since the central government would also be obliged to move against its partners. The need to move swiftly to secure political allies was made all the more urgent by new developments at the political front in the early months of the new year. Since December 1964, talks between Singapore and Kuala Lumpur on "disengagement" had started, and the PAP's ability to mobilize political allies would invariably strengthen its hand in the negotiations.

So it was that early in 1965, the search for political allies was stepped up. On 12 February, PAP leaders met representatives of the UPKO, SUPP,[139] UDP, and PPP in Singapore to consider a draft statement for convening a Malaysian Solidarity Convention (MSC) of non-communal opposition political parties to fight for a Malaysian Malaysia. Apart from Toh Chin Chye, S. Rajaratnam, Jek Yeun Thong, E.W. Barker and Lee Kuan Yew, the others present at the first meeting were Peter Mojuntin and Amadeus Leong, both from the UPKO, Ong Kee Hui, Lim Chong Eu and S.P. Seenivasagam. Noticeably absent was Donald Stephens who, though invited, opted out at the last minute. Stephens, apparently, feared that his participation in a line-up against Kuala Lumpur might compromise his position as a minister in the central government. All were keen on the convention, though concerns were expressed that it should proceed slowly and not appear as a gang-up against the Malays.[140] At the next meeting in Kuala Lumpur, held at Temasek House on 1 March, the PAP team of Lee, Toh, Rajaratnam and Devan Nair entered into further discussions with Lim, Seenivasagam and Ong, now joined by another colleague, Stephen

Yong. Not bothering to conceal his visit this time was Donald Stephens who, accompanied by Ganie Gilong, another UPKO leader, "came in his official car with flags unfurled". Rajaratnam was heartened that "there was less suspicion that the Convention was primarily a gimmick for the convenience of the PAP." It was agreed at the meeting to launch the MSC some time in April or May 1965.[141]

With the backing of political allies assured, the PAP opened a "frontal assault"[142] on the Alliance government by escalating the "war of words".[143] As Pritchett noted, Lee had started to attack the Alliance "with a directness that until now he has avoided".[144] On 24 February, the Singapore premier openly challenged the Alliance to "competition" to see who could "do as much, if not more for the Malays".[145] Taking his challenge further, in Seremban, on 2 March, Lee dismissed the practicality of the Alliance formula of "communally segregated" political parties "either in Singapore, Sabah or Sarawak. And in the long run it will not work in Malaysia as a whole."[146] In Malacca the next day for the opening of a new PAP branch, Lee took the opportunity to hit out at the "ultras" and *Utusan Melayu* for attempting to foster Malay dominance over Malaysia and hinted that "Malaysia will soon see a re-alignment of political forces" between those who wanted a "Malaysian nation" and those who preferred a "communally segregated nation dominated by one of the constituent parts":

> Ranged on behalf of a multiracial nation will be the PAP, groups preaching multiracialism in Sabah, in Sarawak and in Malaya which will include all those who whilst they were not enthusiastic over the formation of Malaysia, are determined now Malaysia is formed that this shall be a Malaysian nation.[147]

The Australian Deputy High Commissioner commented that "the speeches are a well-calculated tactical move".[148] Speculating on Lee's motives, Pritchett surmised that the "significance of all this seems to lie primarily in relation to Lee's advocacy of a disengagement".[149] He "wants to underline the conflict with Kuala Lumpur and increase the pressure for 'some adjustments'."[150]

> Lee's purpose is to bring on a situation in which the Alliance comes to feel that a major disengagement is the best course, both because of the manifest incompatibility of the PAP's and the Alliance's platform and the need to disengage for a time to avoid clashes disastrous to Malaysia ... and because of the Alliance's realization that there is no prospect of imposing a settlement, which is the purpose of many of Lee's actions

and statements, such as his repeated references to the percentage strengths of the various communities and avowals ... that the PAP was not afraid to use knuckle-dusters if necessary. He said to me he deliberately planned to get this back to the Alliance so as to discourage them from any thought of force. From this aspect, Lee appears to be seeking to establish a position of strength from which to conduct his negotiations with the Alliance for a disengagement.[151]

Lee's secondary objective, Pritchett added, might be related to preparing public attitudes in Singapore for the changes which must be made:

He has eschewed until now the normal levers of domestic politics. Nevertheless, the basic public attitudes have been created: suspicion and apprehension of the Malays; irritation with the Alliance; resentment of the Tunku; scepticism about whether Malaysia will work. If the conflict were sharpened and the issues taken to the people, which is the direction the PAP seems to have been moving in recently, confidence in the Malaysian arrangement could dwindle rapidly.[152]

Prior to his departure on 5 March for a month long tour of New Zealand and Australia, Lee was to hint again that it was inevitable for "all those who believe that Malaysia should become a Malaysian nation should come together ... if we want this thing to survive". This time, however, he was to link the still undisclosed plans for the MSC to his advocacy of "disengagement", mentioned publicly for the first time: "It might be quite some time before we get certain groups, influential groups in Malaya to accept this position, and I think for the time being it might not be unprofitable for us to find a *modus vivendi*, [a] means of disengagement to take the heat out of intensity of feeling on this matter."[153]

Holding the Ring: New Zealand and Australia

Not all of Lee Kuan Yew's colleagues in the PAP, however, saw the MSC as a mere tactical device to urge disengagement on the Tunku. While Lee had persuaded his ministers to agree to disengagement, apparently not all had supported it wholeheartedly. Some had advocated a full-scale incursion into Malayan politics as an opposition party. They had argued, Lee said, that once disengagement had become a reality, there could be no hope of coming together again. Two days before leaving for his tour, Lee had confided in Head of his fears that, unless the Tunku showed a clear indication that he was committed to restart the negotiations for disengagement, he "would not be able to stop his supporters from attacking UMNO and Tunku".[154] Pritchett thought that "Rajaratnam would certainly be one of these and, I think, Toh Chin Chye".[155] He felt that Lee did not have complete control over them and was under pressure by Rajaratnam and Toh to be more aggressive. Toh, indeed, had given the impression to the Australian High Commission's First Secretary, W.A. Vawdrey, on 2 March, of being strongly critical of Kuala Lumpur's attempt to foist Malay dominance. "[T]he tone of his remarks suggested that the PAP was more likely to plunge into a fight for its views than 'disengage'," Vawdrey minuted, recalling that Toh had spoken "as a man who had made up his mind and for whom further discussion was not really worthwhile".[156] Should disengagement fail, it was unlikely that Lee would be able to rein in his more interventionist lieutenants "eager for political battle",[157] and for whom the MSC was being prepared as their political vehicle. It could not have escaped PAP calculations that the course of "serious collision", as Head put it, "might well bring reciprocal attacks"[158] — including the possibility of threatening police action against Lee and his colleagues. Always alive to the danger, the PAP needed influential friends to hold the ring for the forthcoming contest. New Zealand and Australia were strategic in this respect.

Lee's visit to New Zealand from 6 to 15 March, therefore, had the objective of creating a broad understanding of the issues involved in the survival of Malaysia. By speaking publicly in fairly broad and general terms, and avoiding direct attacks upon the Tunku and Alliance leaders, Lee apparently left an "excellent impression", observed a confidential New Zealand Ministry of Defence report on his visit. It added: "The personal impression Lee created and the persuasiveness, balance and reasonableness of his arguments for (and about) Malaysia should have strengthened public opinion in New Zealand in Malaysia's favour." Press editorials were "both complimentary to him and staunch in their support of Malaysia". The visit was also "a considerable personal success for Lee" who came across as a leader "whose loyalty was firmly attached to Malaysia".[159] He was praised by the New Zealand premier, Keith Holyoake, after their talks on 10 March, as one who had worked "unremittingly" for Malaysia.[160] But there was another side to Lee's mission. His policy of "conscious restraint" in public, however, was complemented in private by his more "obvious attempt ... to persuade the Government to bring pressure to bear on the Malaysian Government to act in what he would regard as a reasonable and far-sighted way".[161]

The Singapore premier's mission in Australia from 15 March to 2 April was no less motivated by his "strong sense of political purpose". As a confidential Australian Ministry of External Affairs report noted, Lee "had a specific interest in getting Australia a little more on his side; if not the Government then as much of the press and the people as he could manage".[162] In private discussions with top Australian officials a day after arriving in the country, Lee spoke of his difficulties with Kuala Lumpur, as his talks with Paul Hasluck, the Australian Minister for External Affairs, on 16 March revealed:

> Mr Lee spoke of the impasse that had now been reached. The Malays and their associates in the Alliance sought to cut back the PAP and confine it to Singapore and even there reduce its position. Its presence made the situation too unstable for them in Malaya. The PAP refused to be extinguished. But its only weapon was to make clear that if attacked, though it could not win, the conflict would wreck Malaysia.[163]

Invited to address the Australian Cabinet on the same day, Lee spoke, as the minutes indicated, of the racial, as distinct from multiracial, quality of Malaysian internal policies, designed to consolidate the Malays and to insulate the non-Malays as constituting the "gravest" threat in Malaysia since its formation. The strong Malay accent of the policies of the Malaysian government, he added, was causing anxiety and some reaction on the part of the non-Malays, especially in Singapore, Sabah and Sarawak, as a result of which both Sabah and Sarawak "are having great doubts at present about adherence to Malaysia and a new determination, whether by plebiscite or by a process of consultation with the political leaders, would not necessarily confirm the original adherence". In Lee's view, the policy of Malay domination could not continue to be endured indefinitely. Either there must be a struggle within Malaysia with one racial group conquering the others, or there must be separation, or there must be an accommodation of policies to the requirements of a multiracial nation. But because of the way things developed, it had been necessary for him and the Tunku to discuss political disengagement, notwithstanding the internal and external risks.[164]

The Australian government was not unsympathetic to Lee's arguments, as a Department of External Affairs memorandum put it: "We do not want to see the 'Malay' Malaysia Lee warns against. Nor do we want to see the Chinese giving up the inevitably long-term effort to build a multiracial society."[165] But while Canberra conceded that "Lee's charges are not to be dismissed lightly", it was not convinced that the overall situation had deteriorated to such an extent that accommodation was no longer possible. Australian policy was, therefore, to discourage him from over-reacting to his immediate difficulties, either by "forcing a political crisis and asserting his demand for 'disengagement' through pressure tactics" or by "yielding to the view in his Party that the PAP should turn itself into a Malaysia-wide party and fight the Alliance." Either course would only "sharpen communal difficulties very considerably and will dangerously threaten Malaysia."[166] Hasluck consequently informed Lee during their meeting on 16 March that Australia "had taken a stand on the need to preserve the 'integrity of Malaysia'. If the basis of this stand were to change we should need to re-think our position. Mr Lee said he understood this."[167]

Lee's efforts to win support outside Australian government circles appeared more successful. As the Ministry of External Affairs report noted, the Prime Minister "made a quite remarkable impression wherever he went on the people he met and on the people who saw him or heard him on TV and radio". The reasons why Malaysia was worthwhile defending, and why it deserved Australian support, were argued "most effectively" by Lee who succeeded in "producing among his audiences everywhere quite [an] astounding level of support and even enthusiasm". Lee's efforts to enlist what Australian support he could in his struggle with the Federal government were also put across pretty discreetly, at least in public, though the Singapore premier "seemed to accept that, however cautious he might be, any reference to the subject of whatever kind would be taken amiss in Kuala Lumpur". He was consequently "careful to ensure that all his public addresses were taped, and full texts flown to Singapore as early as possible".[168]

But controversy could not be avoided altogether. The day after his discussion with Australian ministers, the Sydney *Mirror*, in a report likely to anger the central government, disclosed that Lee was "privately urging Australian leaders that they give support to Malaysia as a country, not to the regime in Kuala Lumpur". The article further alleged that Lee told Australian leaders that the Tunku "was suffering from diabetes and failing eyesight and was losing control of day-to-day government".[169] An exclusive interview with the *Sunday Telegraph* on 28 March also quoted the Singapore premier as having made slighting remarks about the Tunku,[170] which Lee subsequently denied.[171] Adding to the controversy were also Lee's off-the-record remarks to Malaysian students in Australia, which invariably found their way home. In an address to the students in Sydney on 20 March, for instance, Lee spoke on essentially familiar themes "but he said it with much more fire and impatience than on any other occasion, and he put a lot of stress on the idea of not flinching from the struggle (with the diehard Malay supremacists)."[172] Though Lee spoke "very moderately and reasonably" at his next Malaysian students' meeting in Adelaide on 29 March, he reportedly made a "highly political" speech when he addressed Malaysian students at the University of Western Australia in Perth on the eve of his departure for home:

> He spoke at length of the intense political pressure on Singapore from Kuala Lumpur and said that he had made it clear to the Central Government that whilst his Government recognized that Kuala Lumpur had all the sanctions at its disposal (he referred to guns) he and his supporters would never concede the principles for which they stood: namely equal opportunity for all in a Malaysian Malaysia. ... There should and could be no flinching from the struggle he said. If need be, we must be and are ready to stand up and be counted and to die if necessary, for the cause of a Malaysian Malaysia. If ten men in this hall on return to Singapore, he declared, were prepared to stand up on a platform on these terms there was no doubt in his mind that their cause must succeed.[173]

By the time Lee returned on 2 April, the barrage of criticism at home had already done much to cast suspicions about his ultimate intentions in Australia — from "trying to brainwash Malaysian students in Australia"[174] to using "foreign powers to stab the Central Government in the back and raise up the PAP" and painting the central government as "a bunch of the worst fellows in the world".[175] The Tunku himself warned, on 29 March, that Singapore might become a Cuba instead of a New York unless its leaders were careful.[176] He criticized Singapore leaders for wanting the "limelight" so that "people know ... there is such a thing as Mr Lee Kuan Yew".[177] Communal tensions had also increased. On 29 March and 1 April, minor communal clashes broke out again in the Geylang district of Singapore, where race riots in July 1964 had started.[178]

Lee's subsequent make-up session with the Tunku in Kuala Lumpur on 15 April "had been rather difficult",[179] as Lee later admitted to Critchley. Nor was the Tunku fully satisfied with Lee's explanations, as his remarks two days later revealed: "I personally feel that there must be some truth in it as otherwise the statements would not have been published."[180] In the circumstances, it came as no surprise that the Tunku's interest in disengagement waned. Suspicious of Lee, the Tunku was in no mood to negotiate. As Critchley had earlier predicted, "I doubt whether the Tunku in his present mood will give Lee much of a hearing let alone encouragement."[181] Nor were the Tunku's hands entirely free, especially when Ismail was dead set against transferring internal security to Singapore — which Lee had put down as one of the two essentials for negotiating disengagement, the other being the common market — and had even hinted he would resign if the Tunku saw it differently, a prospect Lee too hoped to avoid "as Ismail was the only Minister in the Cabinet he could talk to".[182] Lee's own reading, as told by Pritchett, was that "the British had got at the Tunku and twisted his arm. He was in a paralysis of indecision; he did not dare now to go for disengagement, but in his heart he yearned for it."[183]

Open Conflict

If Lee had been, as Critchley suspected, "deliberately playing up a sense of crisis" so as to achieve disengagement on terms especially favourable to the PAP,[184] Alliance leaders on their part balked at such pressure tactics, and refused to give in to him. An irate Tunku declared at an Alliance convention two days after his meeting with Lee that "[w]e must not be pushed around by a State Government if this Federation is to have a meaning".[185] A prevailing deep resentment of PAP tactics was also what the Commonwealth Secretary, Arthur Bottomley, discerned when he visited the Malaysian capital from 23 to 25 April on his way to Australia and New Zealand.[186] By the end of April, Kuala Lumpur had abandoned disengagement[187] and now "prefers collision with the PAP".[188] In Singapore, the SA had been reorganized and renamed the Alliance Party Singapura, its members now directly recruited to boost its multiracial image, in readiness for battle with the PAP.[189] As Critchley observed, "In Razak's opinion, it seemed the only course was to fight Lee politically."[190]

Lee had also reluctantly accepted that, without the support of either Kuala Lumpur or Britain, disengagement was not on the cards. He consequently assured Bottomley in Singapore, on 25 April, that while he disagreed with London's view, he would not press for disengagement[191] though reserving, at the same time, the option of returning to it should new circumstances permit.[192] In his mind, Lee saw no credible alternative to disengagement. The Malaysian polity could not otherwise stand the strain of an open competition for power. "Malaysia would blow up in our faces," Lee warned.[193] Since the PAP could not remain politically inert during the transition, Lee said that it would have to keep on expanding to maintain its tactical position so that "when the Tunku finally sought negotiations, he would find that the PAP had become even more strongly entrenched."[194] He also kept up the pressure on the "ultras". On 26 April, he filed two writs suing Syed Ja'afar Albar for libel.[195]

If Lee hoped that by varying the pressure on the central government, Kuala Lumpur could eventually be "forced into cooperation",[196] he found the Tunku a stubborn opponent. Shrewd politician that he was, the Tunku had no wish to be outflanked by the PAP. Instead, to force an early realignment of the new political forces at play, he publicly disclosed on 24 April that he knew of plans by Lee and the PAP to forge the pro-Malaysia opposition parties into a "Grand Opposition", whose "main grouse", he said, seemed to be Malay rights. Defending the need for Malay rights to be protected, he urged people "to make a study of this man before they give their heart and soul to such a move".[197] The Tunku's tactical disclosure had its intended effect. After the Tunku's public goading, the PAP could hardly remain silent, even if it might have wanted to keep its plans for the MSC hushed up until more definite commitments had been received from the other parties, and a tactically opportune date decided upon, probably after the UMNO 18th General Assembly scheduled for 15 and 16 May.[198] So on 27 April, three days after the Tunku's disclosure, Toh confirmed publicly that a grand convention of pro-Malaysia opposition parties, which he declined to name but excluded the SF and Pan-Malayan Islamic Party (PMIP), would be held in the future. The next day, in a show of solidarity, both Lee and Lim Chong Eu spoke in support of the new opposition front, followed by Seenivasagam the day after. In Kuching, leaders of the SUPP and Party Machinda disclosed that they had also been in touch with the PAP to discuss the formation of the front.[199]

In another effort to regain some initiative, leading office holders[200] of the PAP, UDP, PPP, SUPP and Machinda, met in Singapore on 9 May and, after a two-hour closed-door session, issued a declaration that formally launched the MSC with its aim of establishing a Malaysian Malaysia. Emphasizing that it was the transgression of the spirit and intent of the basic principles of a "Democratic Malaysian Malaysia" embodied in the Malaysia Agreement that posed the greater threat to the country than the Indonesian confrontation and pro-communist subversion, the declaration called for the establishment of a Malaysia "that is not identified with the supremacy, well-being and the interests of any one particular community or race":

> A Malaysian Malaysia is the antithesis of a Malay Malaysia, a Chinese
> Malaysia, a Dayak Malaysia, an Indian Malaysia or Kadazan Malaysia
> … The people of Malaysia did not vote for a non-democratic Malaysia.
> They did not vote for a Malaysia assuring hegemony to one community.
> Still less would they be prepared to fight for the preservation of so
> meaningless a Malaysia.[201]

Absent at the launch, to the PAP's disappointment, was the UPKO, which
had decided to stay in the Sabah Alliance for the time being,[202] still
undecided where its advantage lay.[203]

Lee Kuan Yew was also away — in Bombay with Ong Kee Hui and
Peter Mojuntin, attending a two-day conference organized by the
International Union of Socialist Youths, before embarking on his tour of
Asian countries; his itinerary included New Delhi, Calcutta, Rangoon,
Bangkok, Vientiane and Phnom Penh. Given the constant danger of Kuala
Lumpur succumbing to extremist pressure to act unconstitutionally and
remove the PAP or its partners in the MSC, Lee needed to insure against
this threat by adopting a higher international profile and projecting the
PAP as a "democratic socialist party with worldwide connections to
international socialist and labour organizations". As he put it, "They
know that if they crush us by undemocratic means there will be uproar
in Britain, Australia, New Zealand and elsewhere who are sending
troops to guard our borders".[204]

But before his departure for Bombay, Lee was to make a controversial
speech to party cadres on 4 May, which had the effect of heating up the
political atmosphere considerably during his absence. Offering his view
that none of the three major races in Malaysia could claim to be more
native than the others, since all their ancestors came to Malaysia not more
than 1,000 years ago, Lee pointed out that of the 39 per cent of Malays,
about one-third were "comparatively new immigrants", like the UMNO
Secretary-General Syed Ja'afar Albar who arrived in Malaya from Indonesia
just before the war.[205] Lee's remarks were deliberately provocative, and,
according to the American Consul, Richard Donald, probably calculated
to "bait" the Malay "ultras" into making more and more extreme statements
— a tactic the PAP had used in 1961 to precipitate the split with its own
extremist wing — and force the moderates to choose between abandoning
their principles or supporting the extremists. This would force a split in
UMNO at the forthcoming UMNO General Assembly in slightly over a
week's time. "By mentioning Ja'afar Albar by name … as one of the

'comparatively new immigrants'," Donald said, "Lee could count on a reply from Albar and knowing Albar, he could be reasonably certain the reply would be irresponsible enough to embarrass the moderates at the May 15 UMNO Convention in Kuala Lumpur".[206] Presumably, Lee had decided that the time had come to isolate the extremists who had been conducting a relentless and virulent propaganda campaign, using what Lee called "their own VHF, their private circuit"[207] — the Malay press, particularly the *jawi*-script *Utusan Melayu* — to attack the PAP and Lee in person. If he did not, as he later confided in Pritchett, he doubted the moderates would control the extremists "who were fighting their battle".[208]

What Lee said, as Sopiee put it, "incensed the Malays to a man".[209] The next day, Syed Ja'afar hit back at Lee. Calling Lee's remarks "wicked and mischievous", he said what Lee implied was that the Malays "should not have special privileges because they are recent immigrants". He added that the statements were a "slap in the face of the Malays who are insisting that this country is theirs, hence they are given special rights".[210] As Donald commented, "In one sentence, Ja'afar Albar stated two propositions which Lee would oppose and which he hopes the UMNO moderates would also oppose: (1) Malaysia belongs to the Malays and the non-Malays live on sufferance; and (2) Malay special rights are given to Malays as their due, because this is their country, and not simply because they are a depressed community which needs special and temporary help".[211] Predictably, Syed Ja'afar reverted to threatening Lee with arrest again. "If the Government allows such provocation to continue," he declared, "I am certain the Malays will lose their patience."[212] It was no secret in Alliance circles "that Ja'afar Albar and some of his friends would dearly like to put Lee out of the way for a while",[213] observed the Australian High Commission, a point Syed Ja'afar himself admitted in his conversation with Australian officials on 11 May. Denouncing Lee as the man who would "destroy Malaysia", Syed Ja'afar said he did not know why the Government, with the Internal Security Act behind it, did not "lock him up".[214] Lee retorted that he understood from the constitution that, while Malays were given special rights "which we agreed to and will abide by", he had "an equal right as a Malaysian citizen to decide the destiny of this country".[215]

Lee's remarks forced Government leaders, who could hardly be expected to remain silent, to declare their stand. Charging Lee of having reckless ambitions to be the Prime Minister of Malaysia, the Minister of Information and Broadcasting, Senu bin Abdul Rahman, accused Lee of "humiliating the Malays" and wanting to take away their privileges and rights.[216] Tun Razak also lashed out at Lee for making "mischievous and dangerous" remarks that had upset not only the Malays but also their rulers. "If the people of Singapore wish to maintain this relationship with us," he declared, "they must find another leader who is sincere".[217]

It was in this highly politically charged atmosphere that UMNO Youth tabled a resolution at the two-day UMNO 18th General Assembly, held at the Dewan Bahasa in Kuala Lumpur, calling for "serious action against PAP leaders". Speaker after speaker demanded Lee's arrest. Only the concerted efforts of both the Tunku and Ismail helped to calm them down. Urging delegates to "play down" the exchanges between PAP and Alliance leaders, the Tunku shrewdly chided Lee for saying that the Malays were not Malaysia's natives — the hereditary position of the rulers "alone is sufficient proof that the Malays were natives of this country". Ismail, on his part, assured everyone that "If Mr Lee uses force, I'll put him in detention. I have been given this power and will have to use it very carefully." But while he had the power to detain subversives, Ismail said, "We must act constitutionally." Ismail argued that Lee had confined his attacks to speeches and they should reply in like manner: "To use force in these circumstances is wrong and undemocratic." The resolution was unanimously passed, after Senu, who was also the head of UMNO Youth, spoke on its behalf but with the qualification that the Government be "urged to take action, not now, but when the time comes".[218]

If the PAP strategy was to press the moderates to disassociate themselves openly from the actions and tactics of the extremists, they were only partially successful. Though the moderate speeches of the Tunku and Ismail were "probably precisely the reaction Lee hoped to get",[219] there was no convincing evidence that the moderate leaders were really in control, or that they were in a strong enough position to disown the extremists, who, in the opinion of Singapore Minister of Labour, Jek Yeun Thong, appeared to be "winning more and more grassroot support".[220] Donald observed, for instance, that an "extremely worried" Jek had asked him three times during their conversation, "you don't really think they will arrest Lee Kuan Yew, do you?"[221] Asked for his comments by reporters on his arrival in Vientiane on 16 May, Lee shrugged it off, saying, "The thought has, from time to time, entered my head that some people might feel that my arrest would provide a simple solution to what is a complicated and delicate problem." At dinner with the Australian Ambassador that evening, Lee, however, expressed his confidence that Ismail would act constitutionally and he "had no worry about Ismail who knew and understood him well".[222]

243

So long as Ismail remained as Minister of Home Affairs, Lee probably felt more assured that Kuala Lumpur would "act constitutionally". But pressures to act extra-constitutionally had also been strong, as the debate in the UMNO General Assembly meeting had shown. On this occasion, it took the combined stature of both the Tunku and Ismail to dissuade delegates calling for Lee to be detained. There was no guarantee they could forestall them again under different circumstances. Because of their opposition to Lee's detention, both Malay leaders were criticized for being too "soft" on the PAP.[223] The PAP's survival as a pan-Malaysian political party in pursuit of its objective of a Malaysian Malaysia necessitated that the constitutional arena be kept open. If this was not to be, Lee would prefer, in the last resort, a "separation between Singapore, Malacca, Penang and other States on the one hand and Malaya on the other",[224] a point the Singapore premier had made privately to the Australian Ambassador in Vientiane.

Lee was not prepared to let the matter rest and, upon his return on 21 May, he pressed the point again — this time publicly. Would Kuala Lumpur succumb to pressures to use its police powers to scrub out a constitutional challenge by the PAP? Lee wanted to know. By bringing matters to a head, he would at least know where he stood and whether he should begin his campaign for alternative arrangements. In a rousing speech to a large crowd upon his arrival at the airport, Lee demanded to know who the Malaysians were and how the term was to be defined. He declared that the PAP "will not retreat" from building a Malaysian Malaysia, "the only kind of Malaysia we will agree to. No other." He added, "I say to those who believe that Malaysia was supposed to be a communal Malaysia that they better say so now that it is a ghastly mistake." Rebutting charges that he was attacking Malay rights and privileges, Lee said, "we don't want to deny anybody their special rights, no point ... distorting what I have said about special rights. I have never denied it and never will." Commenting on calls for his arrest, Lee said that "nothing will intimidate us":

> Is it so simple? If they issued a telegram, I will come back to be arrested. Do they think that will solve the problem of Malaysia. Is that going to solve it? You think when we went into Malaysia that we did not consider all these things ... We calculated the odds very carefully ... being arrested is the least of our problems ... After all, the British failed to make us heroes, perhaps somebody else will make us heroes. ... What do you think we fought the British for? To change masters? You think we were prepared to fight the British and fought the communists in the process — that we would just stay back quietly?

He warned that he was quite sure that the British, Australians and New Zealanders "who can calculate", and whose navy kept the lines open between Malaya, Singapore, Sabah and Sarawak, would not support a communal Malaysia. At the close of his speech, Lee then declared:

> If we must have trouble, I say let us have it now. Why wait 5, 10 years? If really Malaysia can't work, let us know now, because now we can make alternative arrangements. Later, [it is] more complicated.[225]

Lee gave his speech in "a notably excitable and rousing manner", observed the Australian Commission, "This has been interpreted by officers of the British High Commission as an indication that he has returned to Malaysia determined to launch into a political battle".[226] Not wanting his point to be missed, Lee repeated his charge, but on a lower key,[227] at a press conference the next day.[228]

Lee's speeches elicited considerable response from the MCA and UMNO spokesmen. Tan Siew Sin warned of the "futility" of secession as Singapore could not exist by itself and urged the 1.5 million Chinese to be realistic about their minority position, being surrounded by 100 million Malays.[229] Syed Ja'afar challenged Lee to say whether Singapore wanted to secede and asked if Lee regretted what he had already done to bring about Malaysia. As the *Utusan Melayu* reported:

> Why only now has he regretted? "Why?" asked Albar in a high-pitched tone, and his audience replied, "Crush Lee, crush Lee". "Lee," continued Albar in a lower tone, "was really like an *ikan sepat* which cannot live save in muddy water". "Several voices shouted, 'Arrest Lee and preserve him like entrails in pickle'." Dato Albar smiled for a moment and then he replied, "Shout louder! — Shout louder so that Dr Ismail can hear the people's anger."[230]

Syed Ja'afar then repeated his call for the government to act against Lee. "I reiterate that Mr Lee is a danger to the peace of Malaysia and I urge immediate action before it is too late."[231]

Replying on 23 May, Lee emphatically denied that Singapore wanted to secede. "The question of secession is out," Lee said. Any change must be a step forward and not backward.[232] In a belligerent mood, Lee retorted the next day, "Let us be quite frank, why should we go back to old Singapore and once again reduce the non-Malays in Malaya into a minority?" His "alternative arrangements" did not mean secession, Lee amplified, but referred to "a complete rearrangement either of Malaysia itself within

Malaysia — or Malaysia into different component parts." The PAP's position was now clear: it had no intention of seceding but if a Malay Malaysia was contemplated, it would like the moderate UMNO leaders to say so, or else refute it, publicly and unequivocally, so that all who disagreed with it would know where they stood and could decide on "alternative arrangements".

The next day, Toh Chin Chye, announced that the MSC would be holding a rally in Singapore on 6 June to explain its objectives. He emphasized that the PAP expected the MSC to grow into a "movement".[233] Speaking on the same subject in a television interview the same day, Lee asserted that if it was "necessary to have a Malaysian Malaysia through such a group of parties making an effort to win the majority of seats in Malaysia to form the Government, well so be it. It has to be done."[234] Lee's implicit message — and threat — was also clear: the PAP was ready to launch a constitutional challenge to bring about a Malaysian Malaysia, if all else should fail. It was a threat Kuala Lumpur took seriously.

British observers, however, perceived a deeper purpose behind Lee's "play at brinkmanship". They saw it as part of an elaborate tactical manoeuvre to "force Kuala Lumpur to seek a disengagement", which would enable Lee to stand by his own undertaking to Bottomley not to pursue the earlier disengagement proposal and put him in a stronger bargaining position, "confident that the personal success of his recent visit to Australia and Asia would prevent the central government from detaining him".[235]

Showdown at the Dewan Ra'ayat

The confrontation took a more dramatic turn in the Dewan Ra'ayat. In his speech at the opening of Parliament on 25 May, the Yang di-Pertuan Agong made general references to "threats from within the country", adding that "If those concerned achieve their objective, it will mean chaos for us and an end to democracy." At the very start of the debate, it was clear that UMNO was determined to carry the fight to the PAP. Moving the motion of thanks the next day and setting the tone for the debate, a prominent UMNO backbencher, the member from Kota Star Selatan, Mahathir bin Mohamed, in what Lee later called "very fierce words to tell us, face to face, in Parliament",[236] criticized the Singapore premier as a good example of a Chinese from a wholly Chinese environment who "have never known Malay rule and could not bear the idea that the people that they have so long kept under their heels should now be in a position to rule them"[237] —

"the implication being we ought to be", Lee later said.[238] "They are not words uttered in haste," Lee observed, "they were scripted, prepared and beautifully read out; and if we are to draw the implications from that, the answer is quite simple: that Malaysia will not be a Malaysian nation."[239] "Had we melted, I say it would have been lost,"[240] Lee subsequently recalled. "When we joined Malaysia, we never agreed to Malay rule; we agreed to Malaysian rule. ... Somebody has made a grave error of judgment if they believe that we agreed to Malay rule."[241]

The next day, speaking in Parliament, Lee requested that the government be specific about the "threats from within". Reading excerpts from the *Utusan Melayu*[242] and *Merdeka*, Lee said he could only assume that the threats referred to the PAP. "No useful purpose is served for us to pretend that we do not know what was intended," he said. Criticizing Syed Ja'afar for calling upon Malays to unite by saying "Wherever I am, I am a Malay", Lee asked why he did not say instead "Wherever I am, I am a Malaysian".[243] Accusing the extremists of seeking, and even threatening the use of force, to ensure a Malaysia in which the Malays would rule, and of preferring union with Indonesia rather than submerge their interests in a Malaysian Malaysia, Lee said that if that was really the intention, it should be made clear. If that was not the intention, Lee suggested that the government disown Syed Ja'afar and his associates and come out clearly and unequivocally with a statement disclaiming the intention to work towards a Malay-dominated Malaysia in favour of a Malaysian Malaysia. Lee reiterated that the threat to use force was not credible: "You want to hold little Malaya, may be, to hold Malaysia on that basis — no" because "you haven't got enough guns".[244] The PAP and the MSC, on their part, would act constitutionally — "never offside" — and "play in accordance with the rules to wait 5 years, 10 years, 15 years" for a Malaysian Malaysia as it believed "the ideas we represent must come true".[245]

In demanding a Malaysian Malaysia, Lee emphasized that he was not asking for the abrogation of the constitutional provisions for Malay to be the national language and for the Malay community to have certain special rights. "[W]e uphold that, we accept it," he declared.[246] But these provisions, in Lee's view, were inadequate to uplift the Malays generally, favouring only a special few, and that his own party had a more effective programme. Delivering a section of his speech in fluent Malay, Lee then posed the Alliance a challenge — one which he later said was "so radical" because it "broke all the taboos ... that you should not make an appeal to the Malays":[247]

> If the UMNO leaders really cared for the common people — and not
> merely seeking to preserve their own social status, but really cared for
> the ordinary man in the street — then let us compete by showing who
> has a programme or policy that could better the Malays' standard of
> living and those of the other *bumiputera* like our friends from Sarawak
> and Sabah. Let us compete on these grounds.[248]

"I had made a very simple point," Lee later recalled, "I am speaking to you
in Malay. In 20 years, all the non-Malays would be able to speak in Malay
to you."[249] Restating his point in English, Lee repeated his challenge — to
compete with the PAP in modernizing the Malay way of life, and uplifting
the lot of the poor, Malays and non-Malays, which was the crux of the
matter, not Malay rights or language.

Lee ended by proposing a motion — backed by the MSC
parliamentarians — expressing regret that the Yang di-Pertuan Agong's
speech "did not reassure the nation that Malaysia will continue to progress
in accordance with its democratic constitution toward a Malaysian
Malaysia" but had instead "added to the doubts over the intentions of the
present Alliance Government and to the measures it will adopt when faced
with a loss of majority popular support".[250] It was the first time since
independence in 1957 that an opposition party had moved to censure the
Yang di-Pertuan Agong's speech.[251]

On Sunday, 30 May, in a speech to the Delta Community Centre,
while Parliament adjourned for the weekend, Lee dropped another
bombshell when he elaborated on the alternative arrangements he had
in mind:

> And the alternative arrangements? Well, we don't want to talk too
> much about it. But if really it is necessary, then I say, "Look, all those
> States that want a Malaysian Malaysia can come together". I can think
> of three straightaway: Sabah, Sarawak, Singapore. I can think of a few
> others like Penang and Malacca. I can even believe that Johore — the
> Sultan of Johore may not like to go and join Indonesia as has been
> suggested by UMNO Merdeka. Why should he?[252]

Though Lee had not used the word,[253] "partition" was suspected.[254] "This
is rash and heady stuff," commented Head, "especially in the middle of
confrontation, and many people have taken it as reference to a form of
partition."[255]

If Lee had wanted to force a showdown, he was, as Willard Hanna put
it, "exactly 100% successful".[256] Lee's remarks, both inside and outside

Parliament, immediately triggered another political storm. Federal ministers and backbenchers met the PAP challenge head-on. To a man, they heaped abuse on Lee and assailed him. Shouts of "Traitor", "Sit down", "Get out", and "Shame" rang out in the House when Lee interrupted the debate to clarify remarks made by Alliance ministers. He was also denied the right of reply under standing orders. Accusing Lee of misquoting him, Syed Ja'afar angrily shot back, "Even if I did call on Malays to unite, what's wrong with that?" He asked what was the use of "thumping your chest and shouting that you are not racialist, communalist or chauvinist, when there are riots in your State?"[257] Ismail, who was shrewdly chosen to give the government's opening reply, placed himself clearly with those who wanted to take a hard line of confrontation with Lee, and compared the PAP with Dr Jekyll and Mr Hyde, "a party which shouts, 'Fire! Fire!' while committing arson".[258] For the first time, Ismail essayed to place the onus of the political ruckus on Lee. V.T. Sambanthan, the Minister of Works, Posts and Telecommunications, charged that Lee's speech was the talk of a megalomaniac, who would "calmly and quietly propose the cutting up of our country" — just as it had happened in Pakistan and India where millions died during the partition.[259] Calling Lee and the PAP "the greatest disruptive force in the entire history of Malaya and Malaysia", Tan Siew Sin said that, so long as Lee was Prime Minister of Singapore, "it will be far easier for the camel to go through the proverbial needle's eye than for the Central Government to cooperate with the Government of Singapore".[260] Senu charged that Lee wanted to destroy the nation and build a new one and suggested that his statement about partition would be received "with jubilation in Indonesia".[261] Tun Razak, who wound up the debate on 3 June, delivered a 40-minute broadside against Lee. He explained that the "threat from within" referred to the communists, not the PAP. By "whipping this anti-Malay feeling", Lee was "playing a dangerous game … this mad seeking for power," Tun Razak warned. He threatened that "if, as a result of his adventure, troubles should break out in this country, we must hold him fully responsible".[262] The gulf dividing the Alliance and the PAP was "now wide and clear", the Deputy Prime Minister said. The Malaysia Alliance Party stood for "Malaysia, Abundance, Progress"; the PAP, he said, stood for "Partition and Perish".[263] The Tunku did not say a word during the bitter debate. It was only with difficulty, he later revealed, that he forced himself not to rise and attack Lee during the debate as he wanted to play the role of an elder statesman and help resolve issues.[264] Privately, however, he told Critchley that he did not want to give Lee an importance he did not deserve.[265] By then, the Tunku was completely disillusioned.

While the overwhelming defeat of Lee's motion was expected,[266] what mattered from the PAP's ideological viewpoint was that the debate had finally elicited from top Federal leaders a public admission that the Alliance, no less the PAP, subscribed to the concept of a "Malaysian Malaysia". "[T]he concept of 'Malaysian Malaysia'," as Ismail conceded, "was accepted even before Malaysia was launched ... both the Alliance and the PAP subscribe to the concept of a 'Malaysian Malaysia', but they differ in their approach to make it a living entity".[267] Tan Siew Sin argued that "there would have been no Alliance at all if we had not believed in a Malaysian Malaysia".[268] Of significance, too, was Tun Razak's clarification that neither Lee nor the PAP was "the enemy from within":

> *Lee Kuan Yew*: ... am I safe to assume that the Deputy Prime Minister is speaking with the full approval of the Prime Minister and that he disagrees profoundly with the view made by the Secretary-General of UMNO and the Assistant Secretary-General of UMNO that I am the enemy?

> *Tun Razak*: I am speaking on behalf of the Government with the full authority of the Prime Minister. I am stating the view of the Government.[269]

No less comforting was the Deputy Prime Minister's public assurance that the Alliance would fight Lee and the PAP "democratically and constitutionally".[270] In its fight against the UMNO "ultras", the PAP had scored an important gain, as Lee was to say later:

> [W]hat is important is that the top leadership has for the first time conceded publicly in Parliament, "Yes, we will follow the Constitution. Yes, this is a Malaysian concept, ... Yes, we will be democratic. Yes, the PAP is not subversive." ... Now that we have had this clear official admission that we are not subversives, therefore, it is our right to continue democratically and constitutionally in a peaceful way. ... In other words, ... if we continue to be Malaysians and not to be traitors to Malaysia, they cannot, and therefore will not, act undemocratically and unconstitutionally.[271]

But the price paid to extract the public admissions was high, indeed, perhaps too high. "One result of Lee's tactics," observed the Australian Department of External Affairs, "is that he has quite alienated the Alliance leadership ... now, UMNO leaders, particularly the Tunku who is the crucial figure, are thoroughly fed up with him and say they cannot possibly work with him. This is a very serious situation; Malaysia was largely the creation of the Tunku and Lee."[272] By the end of the debate, PAP–Alliance relationship had reached such a new low that Head felt "a serious crisis" was at hand. Hard words had been exchanged in the heated and bitter debate, "such as had never been heard aloud there before".[273] In Critchley's view, the gulf between the two had necessarily widened and "there seems no early prospect of bridging it".[274] The Tunku, as Head found out, was determined "never again to try and treat with Lee Kuan Yew, whom he did not trust a yard and about whom he was completely disillusioned". Blaming Lee for the crisis, the Tunku told Head, on 1 June, that he had a duty to preserve the Federation and if Lee was destroying it, "I know my duty and I shall not hesitate to do it". Taking the Tunku's intimations as a strong hint that he was contemplating having Lee "put inside", Head immediately warned the Tunku that Lee's detention, without due cause, might warrant a serious reappraisal of Britain's attitude to Malaysia. In "obstinate mood" the Tunku icily retorted, "very well then, I should have to make peace with Indonesia".[275] For Lee, the time for patience and delay had also passed. As Head reported of his interview with him on 1 June, right after his talk with the Tunku: "Lee said that the time had now come to fight for a Malaysia that would not be dominated by Malays. This, in his view, was why he had created [a] new opposition grouping and if Federal Government decided to put him inside he would welcome it because it would strengthen his position." Head predicted serious trouble if the present trend continued for another five or six months.[276]

The British High Commissioner's alarming intimations about the possible arrest of Lee were received in London with grave concern. The Commonwealth Relations Office immediately warned that not only would world opinion turn against Malaysia, there was also the danger of serious retaliatory trouble breaking out in Singapore should Lee be arrested, and this could spill over into the Borneo territories. Told about the danger, the British premier, Harold Wilson, suggested that Lee should perhaps go abroad for a week or two, "We do not want him put inside before PMs Conference".[277] To forestall such an action, Head was instructed to tell the Tunku that Wilson was very anxious to discuss the situation with him during his forthcoming visit to the Prime Ministers' meeting in London and "assume[d] that the Tunku will not in the meantime commit himself to any irrevocable step".[278] Wilson's message to the Tunku was clear, as he later wrote: "I felt it necessary to go so far as to let the Tunku know that if he were to take action of this kind, it would be unwise for him to show his face at the Commonwealth conference, since a large number of his colleagues — including myself — would feel that such action was totally opposed to all we believed in as a Commonwealth."[279]

On 4 June, Head made another attempt to break the impasse. Little headway was made at his talks with Lee. The Singapore premier was still perfectly prepared to go for disengagement but Head did not think the Tunku or his ministers were in any mood for it. Lee said that if he could have common market, he would soft-pedal his political line provided UMNO laid off its politicking in Singapore. But since the PAP could not agree to a quid pro quo with regard to its activities in Malaya because of its involvement in the MSC, Head said the PAP proposal was a non-starter. Lee, in turn, had no faith in Head's suggestion of an unconditional truce, saying that the Alliance would not honour it. Complaining bitterly of the provocative propaganda in the Malay vernacular press campaign against him, Lee said that he had to fight now because to adopt a mild line would be misinterpreted as tacit acceptance of a Malay-dominated Malaysia.[280]

Head's interview with the Tunku afterwards was no better. As Head had suspected, the Tunku confirmed that things had gone much too far for either disengagement or political détente. "We have to deal with the situation as it is," he told Head. He was determined to remain resolute in the hope that Lee would lose Chinese sympathy and find himself in difficulties. The possibility of replacing Lee with an alternative prominent PAP leader was also considered. The Tunku made it clear that if Lee retained support and continued with his agitation and caused unrest, he "would have no alternative but detain him". To Head's caution about the bad effect this would have, the Tunku reiterated that he "[would] not fear to do" his duty but assured Head that "I will not detain Lee without good reason which can be fully justified". The Tunku added, "This is an internal situation which I have got to settle. You must not get involved in our internal affairs. Americans did in Viet Nam and look what a mess they made of it." He gave Head an undertaking that Lee would not be arrested before the Commonwealth Prime Ministers' Conference. As Head saw it, "We were thus back to square one." Viewing the situation pessimistically, Head opined that both Singapore and the Federation were "embarked on a collision course which will end in serious communal rioting and possibly suppression of Lee". The only uncertain factor, according to Head, was "whether Tunku has ace up his sleeve, such as some plan for dealing with [the] situation which he is not prepared to tell me".[281]

The Fateful Decision: Separation

If the Tunku was making plans, so was the MSC. Plans for a series of public rallies, beginning in Singapore but spreading to the other Malaysian states, were already set in motion. As Critchley intimated to Lee on 4 June, these rallies were hardly calculated to ease the tension.[282] But with dim prospect of a constitutional disengagement, Lee could no longer urge restrain on his lieutenants — Toh Chin Chye and S. Rajaratnam in particular — who were "as happy as larks about the new situation" and anxious to join the political battle. Lee himself was under no illusion about the risks of an open political conflict and greatly regretted that disengagement had not been possible.[283] According to Philip Moore, the British Deputy High Commissioner, Lee was supposed to remain aloof from the MSC so as to keep himself free in the event developments proved adverse.[284] But as he could hardly refuse to address the MSC at its first public rally in Singapore on Sunday, 6 June, without giving the impression that he was disassociating himself from the convention, Lee agreed subsequently to deliver the closing address. By identifying himself so openly with the MSC in launching its "crusade" for a Malaysian Malaysia throughout the country,[285] Lee had, in Moore's words, "crossed the Rubicon".[286] He was now committed publicly to pan-Malaysian politics to which he could no longer withdraw.[287] Cognizant of its implication, Lee had twice mentioned to Pritchett in their conversation on 11 June, that "constitutional disengagement was now out".[288] It seemed to Lee by then that only the prospect of a political battle so favoured by Toh and Rajaratnam was the only way ahead. The other alternative — separation — would negate all that he fought for to bring about merger between the two territories. "Whatever PAP's original purpose may have been in backing creation of MSC," observed the American Consul General, John A. Lacey, "this movement appears to be developing dynamic of its own".[289]

Malaysian ministers, on their part, worried at the prospect of a series of MSC rallies spreading to other Malaysian states.[290] Alliance leaders read the launch of the PAP-backed MSC's campaign correctly as the start of a new phase in the open war[291] between the two antagonists and reacted vigorously — despite Lee's deliberate efforts[292] not to unduly alarm the Malays in his rally speech on 6 June by saying that "it will take some time … five, ten, fifteen, twenty years"[293] for the MSC to achieve its objectives. In the Senate debate on the Yang di-Pertuan Agong's speech on 7 June, Alliance senators spearheaded the attack. Warning that Lee and the MSC were leading the country to "the holocaust of inter-racial strife", the Alliance whip, T.H. Tan, called on the government to stop Lee and "his partners in this perfidy ... before perdition sets in" and urged the authorities to either put Lee away "to sober him up" or to exclude Singapore from Malaysia.[294] Speaking to UMNO Youth in Negri Sembilan on 10 June, the Minister of Information and Broadcasting, Senu bin Abdul Rahman, also hinted that "there is a limit to our patience", after accusing the PAP of wanting to "get rid of our Rulers", and warned the PAP that they "will be responsible for the consequences" if it pushed UMNO too far.[295] The next day, in his first public comment on the Sunday rally, the Tunku accused the MSC of "trying to create issues which are likely to generate ill-feeling, suspicion and hatred among the people".[296] On the same day, Sarawak Chief Minister, Stephen Ningkan, said that the MSC could not hold rallies in Sarawak — where the next meetings had been scheduled — because of the general ban on political rallies under the emergency regulations.[297]

The Tunku hoped to contain the situation, fearing for the worst. To take some heat off the dispute during his absence from Malaysia to attend the Commonwealth Prime Ministers' Conference, the Tunku made known in a pre-departure press interview on 11 June, his readiness to sit down at the table and listen to what Lee had to say "about what is giving him all these worries and anxieties". His disappointment was obvious, as he added ruefully that he wished he "had not listened to all the persuasive talk before. Then Malaya would still be a very happy Malaya — no confrontation, nothing".[298] Also hoping for a talk with the Tunku,[299] Lee was "cheered" by the Tunku's "soft, polite and reasonable line" and publicly accepted the offer to "talk things over". He indicated that he was prepared to go to Kuala Lumpur earlier to talk to Tun Razak if necessary. But he insisted that while he welcomed the Tunku's offer to talk, the issues could not be resolved by concluding another vague truce but by discussing fundamental objectives — if the Alliance sincerely accepted the principle of a democratic, non-communal Malaysia why did it allow the *Utusan Melayu* to continue "pouring poison" into the Malay *kampong* in the Malay-language media?

Lee's talk with Tun Razak on 29 June, however "amounted to nothing".[300] Lee had wanted all future agreements to be in writing and made known to all, including secondary leaders, and the "shriek of hate" in the *Utusan Melayu* and *Merdeka* to stop, without which any political accommodation was meaningless. He had also insisted that the extremists be cast off.[301] Though Tun Razak could well stop them if he wanted to, he had refused to do so, and pointed out instead that Lee "should have confidence" in the Malay leaders to deal with them if he really wanted to cooperate with UMNO.[302] Tun Razak, on his part, had wanted an assurance that the MSC would stop its "provocative remarks against the Malays" and stop interfering in UMNO's domestic affairs,[303] an undertaking Lee was equally unwilling to give. Having committed himself to the MSC, it was hard for him to keep quiet and he probably felt that, unless he spoke out against a Malay Malaysia, his case would go by default. As Head reported, "Talks were conducted on rather ginger basis of concealed hostility".[304] There was no meeting of minds.

Pressure continued to be exerted by both sides. On 6 July, Lee Kuan Yew's press assistant, Alex Josey, who was also a freelance correspondent in Kuala Lumpur, was served an expulsion order to leave Malaysia within 14 days.[305] Tun Razak said he was being expelled because he had interfered in Malaysia's internal politics while not being a citizen of the country.[306] "The mail fist was shown at us, not against Alex Josey," was Lee's reading of the expulsion.[307] On 8 July, Toh Chin Chye declared that Josey's expulsion was only the first step in a plan of suppression and disclosed that the PAP knew that soon after the last meeting of Parliament and the first public rally of the MSC on 6 June, "instructions were given to make a case for Mr Lee's arrest".[308] He warned the central government against seeking further to placate its extremist elements by arresting Lee. Though Tun Razak responded to Toh's remarks by calling them "wild and mischievous", he did not deny the specific charge that a case was being prepared to justify Lee's detention. Neither did the Tunku, when he issued a statement in London, on 13 July, saying only that he knew of "no evidence" against Lee to warrant his arrest.[309] Commenting on the episode, the American Consul, Robert W. Sullivan, remarked that there was "reliable information that a dossier [was] in fact being compiled on Lee", possibly for use in political attacks against him and not necessarily for his arrest, "although, of course, the two possibilities are not mutually exclusive".[310] Critchley also confirmed that "Some time ago, Special Branch looked into the case that could be made for arresting Lee Kuan Yew" but found nothing substantial. Tun Razak had admitted to him that there was no case and it would be a mistake to arrest Lee in the present circumstances.[311]

If the PAP's victory in the Hong Lim by-election[312] in Singapore on 10 July[313] made repressive measures less likely, it also helped the party not only to consolidate its position in Singapore but also to strengthen its hand in its dispute with the central government. What it revealed was that the PAP could count on almost solid political support in Singapore, for if it could win in a strong opposition ward like Hong Lim, it was certain to win in almost any electoral district in Singapore. The results confirmed that there was no possibility of UMNO or the Alliance dislodging the PAP from its Singapore base. Tacitly admitting that it had no chance, the Alliance fielded no candidate but indirectly sought to undermine the PAP by supporting the BS candidate. In what Lee called the beginning of the "big fix", the *Utusan Melayu* editorially urged the 30-odd Malay voters in Hong Lim to vote for the BS candidate, the irony of the right-wing communalists working in tandem with the left-wing communists to crush the middle socialists.[314] By fighting and winning the by-elections on a Malaysian Malaysia platform, the PAP's triumph was, therefore, also a vote against the central government and had, as Lee put it, "strengthened my voice to speak for a Malaysian Malaysia when the Tunku returns from London".[315] During the electioneering, Lee had kept up the pressure for a Malaysian Malaysia. Referring to the Malayan Union episode in a speech on 2 July, Lee warned that the non-Malays should not allow another opportunity to insist on the acceptance of a multiracial nation to slip by and urged them to take a stand against Malaysia becoming a Malay country.[316] This provoked the *Malayan Times* which accused Lee of endorsing the "infamous MacMichael Treaty" and that his Malaysian Malaysia campaign and other arrangements for Penang, Malacca, Singapore, Sabah and Sarawak meant a return to a "Colonial Malaya".[317]

The MSC was also gearing itself to launch a series of rallies in Penang, Ipoh, Kuala Lumpur, Seremban and other Malayan urban centres from 1 August, a decision reached at a conference in Singapore from 17 to 18 July. An official statement said that the MSC was convinced "that its cause for a Malaysian Malaysia will get more support once people are allowed fully to listen to our case just as at the moment they are only free to listen to the case against the convention". The formation of an MSC parliamentary group was also confirmed. It would try "to reach a consensus on as many specific issues as possible" that come before Parliament without abandoning the fundamental party standpoint of its individual members.[318] It was possible that in the longer period, the MSC campaign might threaten Malay political hegemony itself. "Over time, our ideas would prevail," Lee later reflected, "I think, within two to three years, there would have been a very solid bloc".[319] There was no constitutional or other way to check the Malaysian Malaysia campaign apart from repressive actions against Singapore. The only other alternative was separation.

The first hint that Kuala Lumpur was thinking about separation was given by Tun Razak to his old college friend, Singapore's Law Minister, E.W. Barker, on 28 June. Barker did not at that time take him seriously, thinking that some looser form of federation was meant,[320] and Tun Razak did not pursue the matter.[321] Separation was also the solution the Tunku was considering. Recuperating from shingles — "a nerve disease of racking, unbearable pain"[322] — in a London clinic, the Tunku came to his "painful" decision that a parting of ways was the only course. Forced to lie on his back for a considerable time while in hospital, the Tunku spent much time reflecting on events.[323] He recalled:

> I had never been in a hospital bed in my life and I never knew before
> what it felt like to be stretched out on a bed without being able to
> move one's legs or to turn to one side or the other for days on end.
> Every movement caused grinding pain, but my mind was alive and
> active; so as I lay there, I was thinking of Mr Lee Kuan Yew. ...
> Whichever way my restless mind turned, I could not help but come
> to one conclusion — and that was to cut Singapore adrift from the
> rest of Malaysia.[324]

He had, as he said later, "weighed the pros and cons" of evicting Singapore on a balance sheet running into several foolscap pages and concluded that "it was best that the two territories should part". He had reached his decision on 29 June, the same day that Lee and Tun Razak were holding their inconclusive talks in Kuala Lumpur. Both Tun Razak and Ismail apparently claimed they had also independently reached the same conclusion at about the same time.[325] Having so decided, the Tunku told Lim Kim San, the Singapore Minister for National Development and a member of his delegation, who was returning to Singapore that day, exactly how he felt about Singapore.[326] "Thus a Singapore minister knew before Malaysian ministers," commented Critchley.[327]

Still in hospital, the Tunku wrote on 1 July to instruct his deputy, Tun Razak, to sound out other senior Malaysian ministers as well as lay the necessary groundwork. He said that he had spoken to Ismail on the line of action to take to confront Lee and feared that "ultimately ... we will have no choice but to cut out Singapore from Malaysia in order to save the rest of the body from gangrene".[328] On 6 July, after leaving the hospital, the Tunku hinted that, upon his return to Kuala Lumpur, he intended to meet Lee "to smooth things over once and for all" and "bring about a quick settlement of this unnecessary trouble".[329] On 13 July, Goh Keng Swee came to Kuala Lumpur, ostensibly to see Lim Swee Aun, the Minister of Commerce and Industry, but asked instead to see Tun Razak, "the first hint the Malaysians had of a new Singapore initiative". Goh suggested disengagement, emphasizing Singapore's desire for financial autonomy, but appeared to have "fallen in quite readily with Malaysian views that disengagement could only be based on complete separation".[330] According to Tun Razak, "Keng Swee strongly believe[d] that the only way to stop a headlong collision between us and Singapore is to separate Singapore from the Central Government":[331]

> I told him that if this was his view we would be ready to discuss this, and that I would consult my senior colleagues, i.e. Datuk Dr Ismail, Siew Sin and Sambanthan, and that he should first go back and consult Kuan Yew and his colleagues. I did not at this stage commit ourselves one way or the other.[332]

Goh had never been enthusiastic about the PAP's intervention in Malaya and, given his difficulties on economic matters with Kuala Lumpur, probably saw Malaysia as offering Singapore nothing more than an economic prospect, and even that was fast dimming. Goh subsequently told Pritchett that Singapore might just as well be out of Malaysia if Kuala Lumpur was not going to cooperate economically.[333] That Kuala Lumpur was "deliberately not cooperating on economic matters so as to bring political pressure against Singapore" was not in doubt, as Tun Razak himself had admitted,[334] and, confronted with UMNO's determination to fight, it was likely that Goh pressed Lee to accept. "We should have been butchered," he later told Pritchett.[335]

On 20 July, Goh met Tun Razak and Ismail and reached agreement on how the separation should be achieved.[336] In Tun Razak's reportage, Goh said he had consulted Lee, Lim Kim San and E.W. Barker who all agreed that "this would be the best way to avoid collision and trouble".[337] Goh persuaded Tun Razak that "the only way out was for Singapore to secede, completely".[338] Tun Razak said he would have to consult the Tunku first.[339] Goh added that the break "should be done quickly, and before we get more involved in the Solidarity Convention". And it should also be done "quietly". Goh stressed the imperative of absolute secrecy since Toh and Rajaratnam were too deeply involved in the MSC and they were likely to oppose the scheme should word leak out.[340] Toh later confirmed that he was "ignorant" of the top secret negotiations. "It must have been a hush-hush operation," he said.[341] Goh also insisted that the British, who "would have never agreed to Singapore leaving Malaysia", must not be told, and stressed the imperative of the plan being presented to them as a *fait accompli*.[342] Barker was asked by Lee, in the meantime, to go ahead with the legal drafting. To prevent any leak, Barker had to do all the drafting himself, and he told no one, not even his wife. "When you work on a matter like this, you don't tell anybody," he recalled.[343]

On 22 July, while convalescing in France, the Tunku received Tun Razak's reply that the senior Malaysian Cabinet members had agreed to separation. Tun Razak wrote that his talk with Lee "did not get very far":

> We went round and round, and he definitely said he had to take a position against what he calls the "ultras" in UMNO ... I told him that if he wanted to fight our "ultras" in UMNO there would be trouble. He must leave it to us to handle members of our parties. He said quite clearly he had no confidence in the leadership of UMNO, other than yourself, to handle the "ultras". It is clear, as we believe, that he will continue with his campaign against us, or as what he calls a crusade against a feudal Malay-dominated Alliance Party.[344]

Three days later, on 25 July, the Tunku wrote back, giving his input and instructed Tun Razak to proceed in his negotiations with Goh and Barker on the terms of the separation agreement. Replying by cable, Tun Razak said he would be convening Parliament on 9 August to go through the readings of a bill to amend the constitution on a certificate of urgency.[345] Goh apparently had further talks with Tun Razak on 26 July and 3 August.[346] On 3 August, Lee took a week's leave in the Cameron Highlands until 9 August when Parliament would convene in Kuala Lumpur.[347] By the time the Tunku returned on Thursday, 5 August, the agreement was to all intents and purposes complete. He was greeted at the Singapore airport by Lim Kim San and Alliance supporters carrying posters inscribed with slogans like "Crush Lee Kuan Yew".[348]

The next day, the Tunku met his senior ministers in Kuala Lumpur and agreed on the inevitability of separation. Barker and Goh had also arrived for their scheduled meeting. Barker had flown to the Malaysian capital that morning, while Goh had taken the night train from Singapore on 5 August evening. They met Tun Razak, Ismail and Attorney-General, Kadir Yusof, in the late afternoon before adjourning to Sri Taman, Tun Razak's Lake Gardens home, where the draft agreement, which Barker brought, was read carefully by Tun Razak and his colleagues. Feeling hungry, Goh had wanted to return to Sri Temasek, the official Singapore residence in the heart of the capital. Don't bother, Tun Razak told him, "I'll give you dinner." And then, in jest, he added, "I've told the policemen outside not to let you and Eddie go until I give permission." Tan Siew Sin and V.T. Sambanthan joined them after dinner. The six ministers — Goh and Barker for Singapore and Tun Razak, Ismail, Tan and Sambanthan for Malaysia — signed the agreement just after midnight. Barker recalled that when it came to signing, the Malaysians were very swift about it. When it came to Barker's turn, he wanted to read the document again but "Razak turned to me and said: 'Eddie, it's your draft, it's your chap who typed the final document, so what are you reading it for?' So I signed."[349]

Lee Kuan Yew then telephoned Toh and Rajaratnam separately and asked them to get to Kuala Lumpur urgently. The purpose, as Toh later surmised, was apparently to keep them from travelling together "so as to prevent us from exchanging notes" about what the emergency meeting was all about.[350] On his phone call, Toh later disclosed that "It was pointed out to me by Mr Lee that an ultimatum had been given to us — either Singapore withdrew from Malaysia or else the situation might not be under control."[351] He was surprised that Lee had called from Kuala Lumpur. "I thought he was in Cameron Highlands for a rest".[352] By the time Toh, his driver and bodyguard crossed the Causeway, it was already past midnight. They drove all night and "nearly ended up in a ditch because the car did not have any yellow fog light." They arrived at Singapore House quite early in the morning. Toh was met by Lee when he stepped into the bungalow — and was told the news. Shocked, Toh tried to gather his many thoughts as he sat in the living room: foremost in his mind was that a Singapore out of Malaysia would mean letting down all those who had supported the PAP's cause.

Rajaratnam's recollection was that all Lee said to him was that they needed to discuss something very important face to face. He telephoned Othman Wok, telling him, without elaborating, that they needed to be in Kuala Lumpur, which got Othman worrying whether something had happened to Lee. "I became very apprehensive. I kept wondering: What's happening? What's happening? I asked Raja: 'We go by train or what?' Raja said, 'You drive.' So early in the morning, I drove up to his house and we set off, him, me and his bodyguard".[353] When they arrived at Singapore House, it was already past eight in the morning on Saturday, 7 August. Rajaratnam found Toh scribbling away and was told the news. Neither agreed to sign the agreement, and both were quite prepared to take the risk of resisting separation. Lee remembered that fateful day very well:

One picture stays etched in my mind: Toh Chin Chye sitting at the desk near the staircase of the drawing room; he pondered the awesome decision. Rajaratnam sat out in the patio facing the golf course, smoking furiously, equally adamant to see the battle through to the end. Walking up and down the stairs, I watched Toh Chin Chye at the desk. He had a piece of paper with a line drawn down the middle — one side "for", the other "against".

Methodically, he jotted down points "for" and points "against". It seemed ages, about two and a half hours. Finally, I suggested he see the Tunku himself. But the Tunku refused to see him.[354]

At half past noon, Lee and Goh drove to the Tunku's Residency where the Malaysian premier and some of his senior ministers had been waiting. Lee spoke to the Tunku privately, thinking that he could "still convince the Tunku that there were a number of other ways to reduce communal tensions, such as a looser federation" but "realized there was no other way … I knew from what he said — and he has an intuition about these matters — that we would all be in for big communal trouble if Singapore, or if I and my colleagues, insisted on going on with Malaysia as it is."[355] Lee later related to Harold Wilson and A. Bottomley how the Tunku presented him with two choices: either leave Malaysia while remaining under the umbrella of the Anglo-Malaysian Defence Treaty, or face the consequence of "communal trouble and 'bloodshed', leaving unspoken the inevitable consequence which is either Fascist method with temporary success in holding the situation or chaos resulting in eventual communist victory".[356] The Tunku later told Critchley that, while Lee raised no objection personally to the separation, he said that both Toh and Rajaratnam had resisted signing on the dotted line and suggested that the Malaysian premier might write a brief letter of explanation to Toh, which he did on the spot, in his own handwriting. Lee said that with this letter, Toh and Rajaratnam would sign.[357] The Tunku underscored in his letter that there was absolutely no solution. "If I were strong enough and able to exercise complete control of the situation," he wrote, "I might perhaps have delayed action, but I am not, and so while I am able to counsel tolerance and patience, I think the amicable settlement of our differences in this way is the only possible way out."[358] Before leaving the Residency with the Tunku's note, Lee said to Tan Siew Sin: "Today is the day of your victory, the day of my defeat; but five or ten years later, you certainly will feel sad about it."[359]

Reluctantly, both Toh and Rajaratnam agreed to put their signatures to the separation document. The Tunku's strong hint of trouble leading to bloodshed, was a "very compelling argument," recalled Rajaratnam, "we realized we could be responsible for loss of lives and worse".[360] Replying to the Tunku in writing the next day, Toh referred to the decision as "sad" and "a blow" to him and his colleagues who had "rejoiced at the reunification of Singapore with Malaya in September 1963". But he accepted that if expulsion was the price of peace, "then we must accept it, however agonizing our inner feelings may be".[361] Rajaratnam, who hailed from Seremban, spoke of his agony in an interview published in 1996:

> Separation to me, was the crushing of my dreams. I believed in one nation, regardless of race and religion. My dreams were shattered. ... To me, it was also my family. They were from Malaysia. My brother, my father, were all in Malaysia. So to me it was a separation from kith and kin.[362]

Two other Singapore ministers also signed the document. Ong Pang Boon, the Singapore Minister of Education, was "struck speechless" for quite a while when a grim Toh broke the news to him in Singapore House that afternoon. Ong had just been in Kuala Lumpur that week helping to set up PAP branches. He too asked, "Is this the only way?" Toh replied that the alternative was bloodshed. Ong recalled that it took him some time to accept that separation was a better alternative. "The rational part of me accepted it," he said, "but the emotional part took some time."[363] Othman Wok, also a signatory, was relieved that the bickering was going to stop but worried at the same time about the communists in Singapore. "Don't worry. That's my problem, I'll handle it," Lee assured him.[364]

The next day, 8 August, as Toh, Rajaratnam and Ong fanned out to the various states in Malaya to inform PAP branch leaders and supporters, Lee made another abortive bid to persuade the Tunku to consider a looser federation instead of separation. Returning to Singapore, he got the three remaining ministers — Lim Kim San, Jek Yeun Thong and Yong Nyuk Lin to put their signatures on the agreement.[365]

So strong, in fact, had been the opposition among some of his ministers that it threatened a split in the Cabinet. As Lee acknowledged, "a number of my colleagues felt very strongly against this ... a good number of my colleagues were born, bred in Malaya. And they feel passionately about what they consider to be their homeland."[366] Given Goh Keng Swee's role in negotiating the separation, some of his other colleagues had been "explicitly prepared to see Goh resign until worked on by Lee himself".[367] Lee apparently was able to get them to sign only because support from Lim

Kim San, E.W. Barker, Jek Yeun Thong, Goh Keng Swee and Othman Wok had been sufficient to carry the day.[368]

Meanwhile, in Kuala Lumpur, the Tunku informed his ministers and *Mentris Besar* that the Separation bill would be introduced the following morning. All parliamentarians were told of a special announcement the next day and instructed to be present in Parliament at 9.30 a.m.[369] During the day, a special RMAF aircraft was sent to Singapore to collect the separation agreement bearing the signatures of the entire Singapore Cabinet and bring it back to Kuala Lumpur.[370]

That evening, at 7.30 p.m., a Federal Cabinet minister came to see the British High Commissioner and asked him what he thought of the latest decision, and that if Head did not know, then he must not tell him. Head "got it out of him". Convinced he was telling the truth and stunned by this "startling development", Head went immediately to the Tunku's house. Not finding him there, he searched for him and finally found him at a party in a penthouse with Tun Razak, Tan Siew Sin, and Ismail. Head said he thought it was "extraordinary that we had neither been told nor even consulted about this drastic step" and pleaded with them to postpone it for 24 hours. "They would not do so and were obstinate in the way of conscious sinners," Head reported afterwards.[371]

First thing in the morning at 9 a.m. on 9 August, Head saw the Tunku with a message from the British premier expressing his hope that the announcement would not be made: "I am astonished that you should be taking this step ... Have you really thought out the implications of what you propose to do, or considered the difficulties which this will create for us who have done so much in so many ways to uphold the integrity of Malaysia?"[372] But to no avail. The Tunku told Head it was too late to reverse the process now and "it was no good arguing about the step which, in his view, was inevitable. He could see no other course to take." At Head's concern that Singapore might pursue a foreign policy that would be prejudicial to both British and Kuala Lumpur's interests, the Tunku said he was not to worry. If Singapore's foreign policy ran counter to Malaysia's interests, "they could always bring pressure to bear on them by threatening to turn off the water in Johore" — "a startling proposal of how to coordinate foreign policy," commented Head.[373] Two days later, still on foreign policy, the Tunku intimated to Critchley that if Lee "tried any funny business" with China or Indonesia, "he would not hesitate to take direct action. Force was the only thing Lee understood."[374]

At 9.30 a.m. on 9 August, Alliance Members of Parliament gathered at Committee Room 1 of Parliament House. They were told the news and asked to vote for the bill.[375] Half an hour later, as the Dewan Ra'ayat was called to order, the Tunku informed the House of the decision he had been forced to take to separate Singapore from Malaysia. He spoke of the many differences with Singapore, since the formation of Malaysia, that brought relations to "this breaking point" and that separation to give Singapore complete independence and sovereignty, though a "shock", seemed the preferred course to take, since the alternative — repression — was "repulsive to our concept of a parliamentary democracy".[376] Supporting the Tunku's motion, Tan Siew Sin said that "it was clear to those of us who were in full possession of the facts that things had gone too far" and that there was a grave likelihood of a large-scale Sino-Malay clash erupting. Those who had to make the "fateful decision", he said, had "searched [themselves] deeply and in anguish" but found no other alternative.[377] Speaking in his capacity as the lone PAP voice in the House — all the other 12 PAP members, as agreed, had absented themselves — Devan Nair alleged that the agreement had not been freely reached but forced on Singapore by threats of repression and violence. Singapore had been "ejected", he said, "for no other reason" than because it refused to submit to a communal Malaysia. It was no accident that Kuala Lumpur's ultimatum came two months after the formation of the MSC and one month after its by-election victory in Hong Lim in which the Alliance joined forces with the anti-Malaysia BS to attack the PAP and its Malaysian Malaysia programme.[378] To Lim Chong Eu, the day "will be remembered as the death of the principle of constitutional procedure in this country".[379] Ong Kee Hui complained about the lack of consultation with the Borneo states, but to no avail.[380] The bill was given its first, second and third readings immediately and passed with 126 votes in favour, none against and one abstention.[381] Seventeen others, including UMNO Secretary-General, Syed Ja'afar Albar, did not turn up. The Dewan Negara approved the bill unanimously a few hours later.

In Singapore, the Prime Minister briefed representatives of the British, Australian, New Zealand and Indian High Commissions at 10 a.m. in City Hall and explained that his decision to pull Singapore out had been difficult. It was not the threat of internment or assassination which had persuaded him to give in. Six of his ministers were prepared to fight it out at the risk of their lives, and three had threatened to resign.[382] He agreed only because the alternative offered was rioting, communal violence all over Malaysia, and an eventual communist victory. Lee regretted that he had not been able to let them know in advance because he knew they would have done everything possible to stop it. In this, he recognized that he had not been able to keep his side of the bargain with Bottomley but felt he had no choice.[383] He then left for Caldecott Hill to prepare for his televised press conference. To a packed press conference at noon, a visibly distraught Lee recounted the sequence of events that led to the final break. In a voice choked with emotion, he added, "Every time we look back on this moment when we signed this agreement which severed Singapore from Malaysia, it will be a moment of anguish. For me it is a moment of anguish because all my life … the whole of my adult life … I have believed in merger and the unity of these two territories … It broke everything we stood for."[384]

And then the Prime Minister wept.

Notes

1. Airgram no. 147, American Consulate (Singapore) to Department of State, 23 November 1964, RG 59 Box 2453 Pol 12 7/1/64.
2. Memorandum no. 266, W.B. Pritchett to Secretary, Department of External Affairs, 6 March 1965, A1838/280 no. 3027/2/1 Part 21.
3. US Naval Attaché (Singapore) to Chief Naval Operations (Washington), 25 October 1964, RG 59 Box 2451 Pol 2-1 10/9/64.
4. *The Sunday Times*, 18 October 1964.
5. Airgram no. 147, American Consulate (Singapore) to Department of State, 23 November 1964, RG 59 Box 2453 Pol 12 7/1/64.
6. Ibid.
7. *The Straits Times*, 26 October 1964.
8. Telegram no. 736, Australian High Commission (Singapore) to Department of External Affairs, 28 October 1964, A1838/280 no. 3027/2/1 Part 20.
9. Telegram no. 39, Australian High Commission (Kuala Lumpur) to Department of External Affairs, 5 November 1964, A1838/280 no. 3027/2/1 Part 20.
10. *The Straits Times*, 27 October 1964.
11. Memorandum no. 1548, Peter J. Curtis to Secretary, Department of External Affairs, 27 October 1964, A1838/280 no. 3027/2/1 Part 20.
12. *The Straits Times*, 27 October 1964; Telegram no. 736, Australian High Commission (Singapore) to Department of External Affairs, 28 October 1964, A1838/280 no. 3027/2/1 Part 20.
13. Telegram no. 39, Australian High Commission (Kuala Lumpur) to Department of External Affairs, 5 November 1964, A1838/280 no. 3027/2/1 Part 20.
14. Press statement by Khir Johari, 27 October 1964, in A1838/280 no. 3027/2/1 Part 20.
15. "Prime Minister addresses National Press Club of Malaya", 27 October 1964, *Siaran Akhbar*, in A1838/280 no. 3027/2/1 Part 20.
16. Telegram no. 1175, Australian High Commission (Kuala Lumpur) to Department of External Affairs, 29 October 1964, A1838/280 no. 3027/2/1 Part 20.
17. *The Straits Times*, 29 October 1964.
18. Memorandum no. 1615, M.W.B. Smithies to Secretary, Department of External Affairs, A1838/280 no. 3027/2/1 Part 20.
19. *The Straits Times*, 2 November 1964.

20. Memorandum no. 1615, M.W.B. Smithies to Secretary, Department of External Affairs, A1838/280 no. 3027/2/1 Part 20.

21. *The Straits Times*, 26 November 1964.

22. Memorandum no. 1815, W.B. Pritchett to Secretary, Department of External Affairs, A1838/280 no. 3027/2/1 Part 20.

23. *Malaysia Parliamentary Debates. Dewan Ra'ayat (House of Representatives) Official Report*, 16 December 1964, Col. 4807.

24. Ibid., 30 November 1964, Col. 3069.

25. Ibid., 30 November 1964, Col. 3073.

26. Ibid., 30 November 1964, Col. 3074.

27. Ibid., 1 December 1964, Col. 3216.

28. Ibid., 1 December 1964, Col. 3214.

29. Ibid., 30 November 1964, Col. 3062.

30. Ibid., 30 November 1964, Col. 3061.

31. Letter from Lee Kuan Yew, *The Straits Times*, 22 December 1964.

32. Ibid.

33. Ibid.

34. Memorandum no. 1815, W.B. Pritchett to Secretary, Department of External Affairs, 16 December 1964, A1838/280 no. 3027/2/1 Part 20.

35. Memorandum of conversation between Philip Moore and John A. Lacey, 29 December 1964, RG 59 Box 2456 Pol 18 1/1/64.

36. *The Straits Times*, 3 December 1964.

37. Ibid.

38. Memorandum no. 1815, W.B. Pritchett to Secretary, Department of External Affairs, 16 December 1964, A1838/280 no. 3027/2/1 Part 20.

39. *Malaysia Parliamentary Debates. Dewan Ra'ayat (House of Representatives) Official Report*, 3 December 1964, Col. 3539.

40. *The Straits Times*, 5 December 1964.

41. Ibid., 14 December 1964.

42. Telegram no. 168, British High Commission (Singapore) to British High Commission (Kuala Lumpur), 29 December 1964, "Singapore Summary No. 26, 15th–28th December, 1964", Foreign and Commonwealth Office source.

43. Telegram no. 1, Australian High Commission (Singapore) to Department of External Affairs, 5 January 1965, A1838/280 no. 3027/2/1 Part 20. Ismail later clarified that the police was only following previous practice requiring permits to be issued for meetings held in the Victoria Memorial Hall. The police consequently warned the organizers that the meeting was illegal, not knowing that the latter had already sought legal advice earlier and were told that a permit was unnecessary. See *Malaysia Parliamentary Debates. Dewan Ra'ayat (House of Representatives) Official Report*, 18 December 1964, Col. 5036.

44. Telegram no. 168, British High Commission (Singapore) to British High Commission (Kuala Lumpur), 29 December 1964, "Singapore Summary No. 26, 15th–28th December, 1964", Foreign and Commonwealth Office source.

45. Telegram no. 9, British High Commission (Kuala Lumpur) to Secretary of State for Commonwealth Relations, 18 January 1965, "Malaysian Fortnightly Summary No. 1, 31st December, 1964–13th January, 1965", Foreign and Commonwealth Office source.

46. *Malaysia Parliamentary Debates. Dewan Negara (Senate) Official Report*, 30 December 1964, Col. 925–26.

47. *The Straits Times*, 31 December 1964.

48. *Malaysia Parliamentary Debates. Dewan Ra'ayat (House of Representatives) Official Report*, 15 December 1964, Col. 4622.

49. Ibid., 15 December 1964, Col. 4623.
50. Ibid., 15 December 1964, Col. 4625.
51. Telegram no. 44, Australian High Commission (Kuala Lumpur) to Department of External Affairs, 7 December 1964, A1838/280 no. 3027/2/2 Part 20.
52. *Siaran Akhbar*, PEN.12/64/142 (PM), in A1838/280 no. 3027/2/1 Part 20.
53. Telegram no. 44, Australian High Commission (Kuala Lumpur) to Department of External Affairs, 7 December 1964, A1838/280 no. 3027/2/2 Part 20.
54. Head to Sir Saville Garner, n.d. (January 1965), PREM 13/429.
55. This was revealed by Lee on 4 June 1965. See *The Straits Times*, 5 June 1965.
56. "Summary Record of Conversation of Mr Hasluck with Mr Lee Kuan Yew, Prime Minister of Singapore, 16th March, 1965", in A1838/280 no.3027/2/1 Part 21.
57. Head to Sir Saville Garner, n.d. (January 1964), PREM 13/429.
58. Ibid.
59. Ibid.
60. Ibid.
61. Ibid.
62. Telegram no. 164, Head to Garner, 1 February 1965, PREM 13/429.
63. Ibid.
64. Telegram no. 176, Head to Garner, 8 February 1965, PREM 13/429.
65. These were incorporated under Article VI and Annex F of the 1963 Malaysia Agreement.
66. Telegram no. 185, Head to Garner, 9 February 1965, PREM 13/429.
67. Mountbatten, accompanied by Lady Brabourne and Sir Solly Zucherman, arrived in Malaysia on 10 February 1965. From 14 to 17 February 1965, he visited British units in the forward areas in Borneo.
68. Telegram no. 47, Head to Garner, 12 February 1965, PREM 13/430.
69. Ibid.
70. Telegram no. 488, Garner to Head, 15 February 1965, PREM 13/430.
71. Ibid.
72. Telegram no. 17, Head to Garner, 12 February 1965, PREM 13/430.
73. Ibid.
74. Ibid.
75. Ibid.
76. Telegram no. 340, Garner to Head, 30 January 1965, PREM 13/429.
77. Telegram no. 365, Garner to Head, 3 February 1965, PREM 13/429.
78. Denis Healey to A. Bottomley, 3 February 1965, PREM 13/429.
79. Minutes by Joint Malaysia/Indonesia Department, 3 February 1965, FO 371/181454.
80. Minutes by Wilson, 2 February 1965, PREM 13/429.
81. See Burke Trend to Wilson, 9 December 1965, and Wilson's comments, n.d., PREM 13/429.
82. Minutes of Misc. 36/1st meeting, 11 February 1965, CAB 130/225. The departments involved were the Treasury, Foreign Office, Commonwealth Relations Office, Department of Economic Affairs, Ministry of Defence, and Board of Trade.
83. Memorandum "Malaysia", in MISC 36/2nd meeting, 16 February 1965, CAB 130/225.
84. Minutes of Misc. 36/2nd meeting, 16 February 1965, CAB/130/225.
85. Ibid.
86. Memorandum "Malaysia", in Misc. 36/2nd meeting, 16 February 1965, CAB 130/225.
87. Ibid.
88. Ibid.
89. Minutes of Misc. 39/1st meeting, 19 February 1965, CAB 130/225. Chaired by Wilson, the ministers present included George Brown, First Secretary of State and Secretary of

State for Economic Affairs, Michael Stewart, Secretary of State for Foreign Affairs, Arthur Bottomley, Secretary of State for Commonwealth Relations, James Callaghan, Chancellor of the Exchequer, Denis Healey, Secretary of State for Defence, Douglas Jay, President of the Board of Trade.

90. Telegram no. 253, Bottomley to Garner, 18 February 1965, PREM 13/430.
91. Telegram no. 255, Bottomley to Garner, 18 February 1965, PREM 13/430.
92. Telegram no. 151, Australian High Commission (Singapore) to Department of External Affairs, 17 February 1965, A1838/280 no. 3027/2/1 Part 20.
93. Telegram no. 255, Bottomley to Garner, 18 February 1965, PREM 13/430.
94. Telegram no. 253, Bottomley to Garner, 18 February 1965, PREM 13/430.
95. Telegram no. 254, Bottomley to Garner, 18 February 1965, PREM 13/430.
96. Ibid.
97. Telegram no. 450, Commonwealth Relations Office to British High Commission (Canberra), 20 February 1965, PREM 13/430.
98. Telegram no. 253, Bottomley to Garner, 18 February 1965, PREM 13/430.
99. Telegram no. 450, Commonwealth Relations Office to British High Commission (Canberra), 20 February 1965, PREM 13/430.
100. Telegram no. 253, Bottomley to Garner, 18 February 1965, PREM 13/430.
101. Telegram no. 151, Australian High Commission (Singapore) to Department of External Affairs, 17 February 1965, A1838/280 no. 3027/2/1 Part 20.
102. Telegram no. 292, Head to Commonwealth Relations Office, 23 February 1965, PREM 13/430.
103. Ibid.
104. Telegram no. 610, Commonwealth Relations Office to British High Commission (Kuala Lumpur), 24 February 1965, PREM 13/430.
105. Telegram no. 360, Head to Commonwealth Relations Office, 4 March 1965, PREM 13/430.
106. Those present at the meeting included Peter Mojuntin and Amadeus Leong (both from UPKO); Ong Kee Hui (SUPP); Lim Chong Eu (UDP); S.P. Seenivasagam (PPP); and Lee Kuan Yew, Toh Chin Chye, S. Rajaratnam, Jek Yeun Thong, E.W. Barker (all from PAP). See S. Rajaratnam, "Notes by Rajaratnam of Meeting Between PAP Representatives and those from Sabah, Sarawak and Malaya held at Sri Temasek on February 12, 1965", 16 February 1965, PMO: MSC.
107. Commonwealth Relations Office Memorandum, "Relations Between Kuala Lumpur and Singapore", 5 March 1965, PREM 13/430.
108. Telegram no. 360, Head to Commonwealth Relations Office, 4 March 1965, PREM 13/430.
109. Commonwealth Relations Office Memorandum, "Relations Between Kuala Lumpur and Singapore", 5 March 1965, PREM 13/430.
110. Ibid.
111. Airgram no. 704, American Embassy (Kuala Lumpur) to Department of State, 19 March 1965, RG 59 Box 2453 Pol 12 1/1/65.
112. Ibid.
113. M.W.B. Smithies to Secretary, Department of External Affairs, 14 May 1964, A1838/318 no. 3024/2/2/1 Part 1.
114. *Malaysia Parliamentary Debates. Dewan Ra'ayat (House of Representatives) Official Report*, 21 May 1964, Col. 410.
115. Ibid.
116. Ibid., 22 May 1964, Col. 483.

117. Record of Conversation between Ong Kee Hui and William A. Brown, 28 July 1964, RG 59 Box 2450 Pol 2 1/1/64.
118. Ibid.
119. Airgram no. 103, American Embassy (Kuala Lumpur) to Department of State, 14 August 1964, RG 59 Box 2450 Pol 2 1/1/64.
120. For a discussion of the internal politics of the Borneo territories, see Chapter 20 in Gordon P. Means, *Malaysian Politics* (London: Hodder and Stoughton, 1976).
121. Record of Conversation between Donald Stephens and William A. Brown, January 1965, RG 59 Box 2456 Pol 18 1/1/65.
122. Ibid.
123. Record of Conversation between Lee Kuan Yew and W.B. Pritchett, 3 July 1964, A1838/280 no. 3024/2/1 Part 12.
124. Record of Conversation between Lee Kuan Yew and W.B. Pritchett, 27 October 1964, A1838/280 no. 3024/2/1 Part 14.
125. Telegram no. 223, American Consulate (Singapore) to Department of State, 12 December 1964, RG 59 Box 2456 Pol 18 8/7/64.
126. Record of Conversation between Lee Kuan Yew and W.B. Pritchett, 19 November 1964, A1838/280 no. 3024/2/1 Part 14.
127. Ibid.
128. Memorandum no. 1707, W.B. Pritchett to Secretary, Department of External Affairs, 23 November 1964, A1838/280 no. 3024/2/1 Part 14.
129. Memorandum no. 266, W.B. Pritchett to Secretary, Department of External Affairs, 6 March 1965, A1838/280 no. 3027/2/1 Part 21.
130. See People's Action Party, *Our First Ten Years: PAP 10th Anniversary Souvenir* (Singapore: PAP, 1964), p. 112; also *The Straits Times*, 23 November 1964.
131. *Malayan Times*, 15 February 1965.
132. Telegram no. 5, Australian High Commission (Kuala Lumpur) to Department of External Affairs, 8 February 1965, A1838/280 no. 3027/2/1 Part 20.
133. *The Straits Times*, 29 January 1964.
134. *Utusan Melayu*, 1 February 1965.
135. *The Straits Times*, 15 February 1964; Text of speech by Tan Siew Sin at the opening of the MCA Sembawang ward branch, 14 February 1965, in A1838/280 no. 3027/2/1 Part 20.
136. Speech by Lee Kuan Yew in Kuala Lumpur, 24 February 1965, in A1838/280 no. 3027/2/1 Part 21.
137. Interview with Toh Chin Chye, in Melanie Chew, *Leaders of Singapore* (Singapore: Resource Press, 1996), p. 95.
138. *The Straits Times*, 23 November 1965.
139. The PAP recognized that there was a risk in associating with a party like the SUPP that had taken an anti-Malaysia position and which had been infiltrated by the communists but decided that the risk was worth taking because it needed a base in Sarawak and the moderate leadership of the SUPP were now willing to accept Malaysia as a political reality. By bringing the SUPP into the MSC (over the objections of the left-wing), the PAP presumably also hoped to provide the moderate leaders in the SUPP with an issue to precipitate a split, with the moderates emerging victorious by defeating the left-wing faction just as the PAP had done in weeding out its own left-wing by using the merger issue.
140. "Notes by Rajaratnam of meeting between PAP Representatives and those from Sabah, Sarawak and Malaya held at Sri Temasek on February 12, 1965", 16 February 1965, PMO: MSC.

141. Ibid.
142. Memorandum no. 266, W.B. Pritchett to Secretary, Department of External Affairs, 6 March 1965, A1838/280 no. 3027/2/1 Part 21.
143. Mohamed Noordin Sopiee, *From Malayan Union to Singapore Separation: Political Unification in the Malaysia Region 1945-65* (Kuala Lumpur: Penerbit Universiti Malaya, 1974), p. 199.
144. Memorandum no. 266, W.B. Pritchett to Secretary, Department of External Affairs, 6 March 1965, A1838/280 no. 3027/2/1 Part 21.
145. *Malayan Times*, 25 February 1965.
146. Speech by Lee Kuan Yew at Seremban, 2 March 1965, in A1838/280 no. 3027/2/1 Part 21.
147. Speech by Lee Kuan Yew at Malacca, 3 March 1965, in A1838/280 no. 3027/2/1 Part 21.
148. Telegram no. 194, Australian High Commission (Singapore) to Department of External Affairs, 1 March 1965, A1838/280 no. 3027/2/1 Part 21.
149. Memorandum no. 266, W.B. Pritchett to Secretary, Department of External Affairs, 6 March 1965, A1838/280 no. 3027/2/1 Part 21.
150. Telegram no. 194, Australian High Commission (Singapore) to Department of External Affairs, 1 March 1965, A1838/280 no. 3027/2/1 Part 21.
151. Memorandum no. 266, W.B. Pritchett to Secretary, Department of External Affairs, 6 March 1965, A1838/280 no. 3027/2/1 Part 21.
152. Ibid.
153. "Transcript of a press conference by Prime Minister, Mr Lee Kuan Yew at TV Singapura studios on 5th March 1965 at 10.30 a.m.", in A1838/280 no. 3027/2/1 Part 21.
154. Telegram no. 360, Head to Commonwealth Relations Office, 4 March 1965, PREM 13/430.
155. Memorandum no. 266, W.B. Pritchett to Secretary, Department of External Affairs, 6 March 1965, A1838/280 no. 3027/2/1 Part 21.
156. Record of Conversation between Toh Chin Chye and Brian Lendrum (New Zealand Deputy High Commissioner, Singapore), P. Cotton (First Secretary, New Zealand High Commssion, Kuala Lumpur), and W.A. Vawdrey, (First Secretary, Australian High Commission, Kuala Lumpur), 2 March 1965, A9735/6 no. 205/10 Part 1.
157. Memorandum no. 266, W.B. Pritchett to Secretary, Department of External Affairs, 6 March 1965, A1838/280 no. 3027/2/1 Part 21.
158. Telegram no. 360, Head to Commonwealth Relations Office, 4 March 1965, PREM 13/430.
159. G.N. Parkinson to McIntosh, "Visit to New Zealand of Mr Lee Kuan Yew 6 to 16 March 1965", 29 March 1965, in A9735/6 no. 205/10 Part 1.
160. *The Malay Mail*, 10 March 1965.
161. G.N. Parkinson to McIntosh, "Visit to New Zealand of Mr Lee Kuan Yew 6 to 16 March 1965", 29 March 1965, in A9735/6 no. 205/10 Part 1.
162. "Report by Escort Officers on Visit to Australia of Mr Lee Kuan Yew, Prime Minister of Singapore, 15th March–2nd April, 1965", n.d., A9735/6 no. 205/10 Part 1.
163. Paul Hasluck, "Summary Record of Conversation of Mr Hasluck with Mr Lee Kuan Yew, Prime Minister of Singapore, 16th March, 1965", n.d., A1838/280 no. 3027/2/1 Part 21.
164. Cabinet minutes, Decision no. 786, 16 March 1965, A4940/1 no. C4142.
165. Department of External Affairs, "Mr Lee Kuan Yew's Interview with the Prime Minister", 18 March 1965, A4940/1 no. C4142.
166. Department of External Affairs, "Briefing Notes on the Visit of Mr Lee Kuan Yew", 15 March 1965, A4940/1 no. C4142.

167. Paul Hasluck, "Summary Record of Conversation of Mr Hasluck with Mr Lee Kuan Yew, Prime Minister of Singapore, 16 March, 1965", n.d., A1838/280 no. 3027/2/1 Part 21.
168. "Report by Escort Officers on Visit to Australia of Mr Lee Kuan Yew, Prime Minister of Singapore, 15th March–2nd April, 1965", n.d., in A9735/6 no. 205/10 Part 1.
169. *Mirror*, 17 March 1965, in Telegram no. 465, Department of External Affairs to Australian High Commission (Kuala Lumpur), 18 March 1965, A1838/280 no. 3027/2/1 Part 21.
170. *Sunday Telegraph*, 28 March 1965, in A9735/6 no. 205/10 Part 1.
171. Telegram no. 515, Department of External Affairs to Australian High Commission (Kuala Lumpur), 29 March 1965, A1838/280 no. 3027/2/1 Part 21.
172. "Report by Escort Officers on Visit to Australia of Mr Lee Kuan Yew, Prime Minister of Singapore, 15th March–2nd April, 1965", n.d., in A9735/6 no. 205/10 Part 1.
173. Ibid.
174. *Malayan Times*, 24 March 1965.
175. *The Straits Times*, 19 April 1965.
176. Telegram no. 31, Head to A. Bottomley, "Malaysian Fortnightly Summary No. 7, 25 March 1965–7 April 1965", 10 April 1965, Foreign and Commonwealth Office source.
177. *The Straits Times*, 6 April 1965.
178. Telegram no. 31, Head to A. Bottomley, "Malaysian Fortnightly Summary No. 7, 25 March 1965–7 April 1965", 10 April 1965, Foreign and Commonwealth Office source.
179. Telegram no. 17, Australian High Commission (Kuala Lumpur) to Department of External Affairs, 16 April 1965, A1838/280 no. 3027/2/1 Part 21.
180. Speech by Tunku at the Malaysian Alliance Convention on 17 April 1965, in A1838/280 no. 3027/2/1 Part 21.
181. Telegram no. 953, Australian High Commission (Kuala Lumpur) to Department of External Affairs, 15 April 1965, A1838/280 no. 3027/2/1 Part 21.
182. Ibid.
183. Telegram no. 86, Australian High Commission (Singapore) to Australian High Commission (Kuala Lumpur), 21 April 1965, A9735/6 no. 205/10 Part 1.
184. Telegram no. 16, Australian High Commission (Kuala Lumpur) to Department of External Affairs, 14 April 1965, A1838/280 no. 3027/2/1 Part 21.
185. Speech by Tunku at the Malaysian Alliance Convention on 17 April 1965, in A1838/280 no. 3027/2/1 Part 21.
186. Telegram no. 1006, Australian High Commission (Kuala Lumpur) to Department of External Affairs, 26 April 1965, A1838/280 no. 3027/2/1 Part 21; Telegram no. 3613, Australian High Commission (London) to Department of External Affairs, 7 May 1965, A1838/280 no. 3027/2/1 Part 21.
187. Telegram no. 711, Head to Commonwealth Relations Office, 22 April 1965, PREM 13/430.
188. Memorandum no. 266, W.B. Pritchett to Secretary, Department of External Affairs, 6 March 1965, A1838/280 no. 3027/2/1 Part 21.
189. *The Straits Times*, 2 April 1965.
190. Telegram no. 1006, Australian High Commission (Kuala Lumpur) to Department of External Affairs, 26 April 1965, A1838/280 no. 3027/2/1 Part 21.
191. Telegram no. 3613, Australian High Commission (London) to Department of External Affairs, 7 May 1965, A1838/280 no. 3027/2/1 Part 21.
192. Philip Moore to Commonwealth Relations Office, 30 April 1965, in A1838/280 no. 3027/2/1 Part 22.
193. Telegram no. 16, Australian High Commission (Kuala Lumpur) to Department of External Affairs, 14 April 1965, A1838/280 no. 3027/2/1 Part 21.

194. Telegram no. 356, Australian High Commission (Singapore) to Department of External Affairs, 21 April 1965, A1838/280 no. 3027/2/1 Part 21.

195. The first writ referred to an open and undated letter from Syed Ja'afar to Denis Bloodworth on or about 7 August 1964, and the second to statements in two articles appearing in *Utusan Melayu* on 25 March and 27 March 1964 headed respectively "Lee is accused of being an enemy of Malaysia and an agent of Indonesia" and "Albar accuses Kuan Yew of being an agent of the Communists". *Utusan Melayu* and its editor, Melan bin Abdullah, were also being sued in connection with the second issue. Before the writs were filed, Syed Ja'afar was given seven days in which to apologize. The notice expired on 23 April 1965. On 22 September 1967, the newspapers printed the news that the libel suit was discontinued after all the defendants admitted that "there is no foundation for any of the disgraceful allegations" they made against Lee and agreed to apologize to him and indemnify him for the whole cost of the proceedings. R.C. Hoffman, acting for Syed Ja'afar, acknowledged that the allegations made by the latter "are unfounded and he unreservedly withdraws them ... and he apologizes to him for the distress and embarrassment caused to him by such publication." See Memorandum no. 729, C. Tadgell (Third Secretary) to Secretary, Department of External Affairs, n.d., A1838/280 no. 3027/2/1 Part 21; *The Sunday Times*, 25 April 1965; *The Straits Times*, 23 September 1967.

196. Telegram no. 413, Australian High Commission (Singapore) to Department of External Affairs, 7 May 1965, A1838/280 no. 3027/2/1 Part 21.

197. *The Sunday Times*, 25 April 1965.

198. Telegram no. 17, US Naval Attaché (Singapore) to Chief Naval Operations, 29 April 1965, RG 59 Box 2451 Pol 2-1 4/9/65.

199. Memorandum no. 205/10, C. Tadgell to Secretary, Department of External Affairs, 30 April 1965, A1838/280 no. 3027/2/1 Part 21.

200. The convenors were: Lim Chong Eu and Abdul Wahab bin Mohd Yassin (UDP); D.R. Seenivasagam and T. Selvarassan (PPP); Stephen Yong and Marican Salleh (SUPP); M. Buma and Leong Ho Yuen (Machinda); Toh Chin Chye and Othman Wok (PAP).

201. "Declaration by the Convenors of the Malaysian Solidarity Convention", in A1838/280 no. 3027/2/1 Part 22.

202. Telegram no. 108, Australian High Commission (Singapore) to Australian High Commission (Kuala Lumpur), 10 May 1965, A9735/6 no. 205/10 Part 1.

203. Telegram no. 413, Australian High Commission (Singapore) to Department of External Affairs, 7 May 1965, A1838/280 no. 3027/2/1 Part 21.

204. *The Sunday Times*, 1 August 1965.

205. Memorandum no. 571, C.E. McDonald to Secretary, Department of External Affairs, 8 May 1965, A9735/6 no. 205/10 Part 1.

206. Airgram no. 258, American Consulate (Singapore) to Department of State, 24 May 1965, RG 59 Box 2454, Pol 12 5/1/65.

207. Transcript of a press conference given in the Federal Parliament by Lee Kuan Yew and other leaders of the Malaysian Solidarity Convention, 3 June 1965, in A1838/277 no. 3027/2/2/15.

208. Memorandum by W.B. Pritchett, 12 June 1965, A1838/280 no. 3027/2/1 Part 23.

209. Sopiee, p. 201.

210. *Berita Harian*, 6 May 1965; cited in Airgram no. 258, American Consulate (Singapore) to Department of State, 24 May 1965, RG 59 Box 2454 Pol 12 5/1/65.

211. Airgram no. 258, American Consulate (Singapore) to Department of State, 24 May 1965, RG 59 Box 2454, Pol 12 5/1/65.

212. *Malayan Times*, 6 May 1965; *The Straits Times*, 6 May 1965.
213. Telegram no. 11-09, Australian High Commission (Kuala Lumpur) to Department of External Affairs, 7 May 1965, A1838/280 no. 3027/2/1 Part 21.
214. Record of Conversation among Syed Ja'afar Albar, Ali bin Haji Ahmad, C. Tadgell and G. Bentley, 11 May 1965, A1838/280 no. 3027/2/1 Part 22.
215. Cited in Memorandum no. EA.796, C. Tadgell to Secretary, Department of External Affairs, 11 May 1965, A1838/280 no. 3027/2/1 Part 22.
216. *Malayan Times*, 9 May 1965.
217. *The Straits Times*, 10 May 1965.
218. *The Sunday Times*, 16 May 1965.
219. Airgram no. 258, American Consulate to Department of State, 24 May 1965, RG 59 Box 2454, Pol 12 5/1/65.
220. Memorandum of Conversation between Jek Yeun Thong and Richard H. Donald, 17 May 1965, RG 59 Box 2454 Pol 12 5/1/65.
221. Ibid.
222. Telegram no. 94, Australian Embassy (Vientiane) to Department of External Affairs, 19 May 1965, A1838/280 no. 3027/2/1 Part 22.
223. *The Straits Times*, 17 May 1965.
224. Telegram no. 94, Australian Embassy (Vientiane) to Department of External Affairs, 19 May 1965, A1838/280 no. 3027/2/1 Part 22.
225. Text of speech by Lee Kuan Yew at the airport on his return from a tour of Asian countries, 21 May 1965, in A1838/280 no. 3027/2/1 Part 22.
226. Memorandum no. 658, C.E. McDonald (Second Secretary, Australian High Commission, Singapore) to Secretary, Department of External Affairs, 26 May 1965, A1838/280 no. 3027/2/1 Part 22.
227. *The Australian*, 24 May 1965, in A1838/280 no. 3027/2/1 Part 22.
228. Transcript of a press conference by Lee Kuan Yew at the studios of Television Singapura, 22 May 1965, in A1838/280 no. 3027/2/1 Part 22.
229. *The Sunday Times*, 23 May 1965.
230. *Utusan Melayu*, 24 May 1965; See also *Malaysia Parliamentary Debates. Dewan Ra'ayat (House of Representatives) Official Report*, 27 May 1965, Col. 543–44.
231. *The Straits Times*, 24 May 1965.
232. Ibid.
233. Ibid., 25 May 1965.
234. Ibid.
235. The British views were reported in Telegram no. 469, Australian High Commission (Singapore) to Department of External Affairs, 26 May 1965, A1838/280 no. 3027/2/1 Part 22.
236. Cited in Han Fook Kwang, Warren Fernandez, and Sumiko Tan, *Lee Kuan Yew: The Man and His Ideas* (Singapore: Times Editions, 1998), p. 77.
237. *Malaysia Parliamentary Debates. Dewan Ra'ayat (House of Representatives) Official Report*, 26 May 1965, Col. 84.
238. Ibid., 27 May 1965, Col. 545.
239. Ibid., 27 May 1965, Col. 546.
240. Han *et al.*, p. 78.
241. Transcript of a speech by Lee Kuan Yew at the Delta Community Centre on the occasion of its 4th anniversary celebrations, 4 May 1965, in A1838/280 no. 3027/2/1 Part 22.
242. The *Utusan Melayu* of 25 May, for instance, headlined a report "Lee is an enemy of the people of Malaysia" and quoted the Mentri Besar of Selangor, Harun bin Haji Idris,

describing Lee as "an enemy of the people of Malaysia and was endangering the peace of the country".

243. *Malaysia Parliamentary Debates. Dewan Ra'ayat (House of Representatives) Official Report*, 27 May 1963, Col. 543.
244. Ibid., 27 May 1965, Col. 562–63.
245. Ibid., 27 May 1965, Col. 566–67.
246. Ibid., 27 May 1965, Col. 541.
247. Han *et al.*, p. 78.
248. *Malaysia Parliamentary Debates. Dewan Ra'ayat (House of Representatives) Official Report*, 27 May 1965, Col. 555.
249. Han *et al.*, p. 78.
250. Ibid., 27 May 1965, Col. 568.
251. Airgram no. 936, American Embassy (Kuala Lumpur) to Department of State, 28 May 1965, RG 59 Box 2451 Pol 2-1 4/9/65.
252. Transcript of a speech by Lee Kuan Yew at the Delta Community Centre on the occasion of its 4th anniversary celebrations, 30 May 1965, in A1838/280 no. 3027/2/1 Part 22.
253. Lee said, "I never used the word 'partition', never suggested it and never will. ... I said those states that want a Malaysian Malaysia if there is going to be an alternative arrangement they are bound to get together, isn't it? ... I will not ever be the person who would be even remotely accused of having started partition". See Transcript of a press conference given in the Federal Parliament by Lee Kuan Yew and other leaders of the Malaysian Solidarity Convention, 3 June 1965, in A1838/277 no. 3027/2/2/15.
254. *The Straits Times*, 1 June 1965.
255. Telegram no. 960, Head to Commonwealth Relations Office, 1 June 1965, PREM 13/430.
256. Willard A. Hanna, *The Separation of Singapore from Malaysia*, (New York: American University Field Staff, 1965), p. 20.
257. *Malaysia Parliamentary Debates. Dewan Ra'ayat (House of Representatives) Official Report*, 27 May 1965, Col. 616–17.
258. Ibid., 31 May 1965, Col. 714.
259. Ibid., 1 June 1965, Col. 875, 884.
260. Ibid., 1 June 1965, Col. 838–39.
261. Ibid, 1 June 1965, Col. 952, 957.
262. Ibid., 3 June 1965, Col. 1005.
263. Ibid, 3 June 1965, Col. 1011.
264. *The Straits Times*, 12 June 1965.
265. Telegram no. 1301, Australian High Commission (Kuala Lumpur) to Department of External Affairs, 5 June 1965, A9735/6 no. 205/10 Part 2.
266. Fourteen voted for the PAP motion; 108 against. There were 9 abstentions. *Malaysia Parliamentary Debates. Dewan Ra'ayat (House of Representatives) Official Report*, 3 June 1965, Col. 1011.
267. *Malaysia Parliamentary Debates. Dewan Ra'ayat (House of Representatives) Official Report*, 31 May 1965, Col. 703–4.
268. Ibid., 1 June 1965, Col. 839.
269. Ibid., 3 June 1965, Col. 995–96.
270. Ibid., 3 June 1965, Col. 1000.
271. Text of speech by Lee Kuan Yew at the Malaysian Solidarity Convention at the National Theatre , 6 June 1965, in A1838/277 no. 3027/2/2/15.

272. Memorandum "Malaysia — Internal", n.d., A1838/280 no. 3027/2/1 Part 23.

273. Airgram no. 936, American Embassy (Kuala Lumpur) to Department of State, 28 May 1965, RG 59 Box 2451 Pol 2-1 4/9/65.

274. Telegram no. 1296, Australian High Commission (Kuala Lumpur) to Department of External Affairs, 4 June 1965, A9735/6 no. 205/10 Part 2.

275. Telegram no. 960, Head to Commonwealth Relations Office, 1 June 1965, PREM 13/430.

276. Ibid.

277. Minutes by Harold Wilson, 5 June 1965, PREM 13/430.

278. Telegram no. 1594, Commonwealth Relations Office to British High Commission (Kuala Lumpur), 3 June 1965, PREM 13/430.

279. Harold Wilson, *The Labour Government 1964–1970: A Personal Record* (London: Weidenfeld and Nicolson, 1971), p. 131.

280. Telegram no. 980, Head to Commonwealth Relations Office, 4 June 1965, PREM 13/430.

281. Ibid.

282. Telegram no. 1301, Australian High Commission (Kuala Lumpur) to Department of External Affairs, 5 June 1965, A9735/6 no. 205/10 Part 2.

283. Memorandum by W.B. Pritchett to Paul Hasluck, 12 June 1965, A1838/280 no. 3027/2/1 Part 23.

284. Memorandum of Conversation between Philip Moore and John A. Lacey (Consul General), 28 June 1965, RG 59 Box 2450 Pol 2 1/1/65.

285. *The Straits Times*, 7 June 1965.

286. Memorandum of Conversation between Philip Moore and John A. Lacey (Consul General), 28 June 1965, RG 59 Box 2450 Pol 2 1/1/65.

287. Memorandum by W.B. Pritchett to Paul Hasluck, 12 June 1965, A1838/280 no. 3027/2/1 Part 23.

288. Ibid.

289. Telegram no. 435, American Consulate (Singapore) to Department of State, 8 June 1965, RG 59 Box 2454 Pol 12 5/1/65.

290. Telegram no. 1352, Australian High Commission (Kuala Lumpur) to Department of External Affairs, 10 June 1965, A1838/280 no. 3027/2/1 Part 23.

291. *Malaysia Parliamentary Debates Dewan Negara (Senate) Official Report*, 7 June 1965, Col. 409.

292. After Critchley expressed his concerns about the MSC heating up the political temperature in his interview with the Singapore premier on 4 June 1965, Lee said he would use the Sunday rally to try to direct thinking away from the present by emphasizing that the objectives of the Convention could not be achieved quickly but would have to be worked for quietly and patiently over a long period of time. See Telegram no. 1301, Australian High Commission (Kuala Lumpur) to Department of External Affairs, 5 June 1965, A9735/6 no. 205/10 Part 2.

293. Text of speech by Lee Kuan Yew at the Malaysian Solidarity Convention at the National Theatre, 6 June 1965, in A1838/277 no. 3027/2/2/15.

294. Ibid.

295. *Malayan Times*, 11 June 1965.

296. *The Straits Times*, 12 June 1965.

297. Airgram no. 276, American Consulate (Singapore) to Department of State, 21 June 1965, RG 59 Box 2451 Pol 2-1 4/9/65.

298. *The Straits Times*, 12 June 1965.

299. Lee had asked Critchley on 4 June 1965 whether he ought to see the Tunku. Critchley thought that "now was not the time", to which Lee said it was up to the Tunku to restore confidence in Malaysia by "making appropriate public statements". See Telegram no. 1301, Australian High Commission (Kuala Lumpur) to Department of External Affairs, 5 June 1965, A9735/6 no. 205/10 Part 2.

300. Telegram no. 1143, Head to Bottomley, 30 June 1965, in A1838/280 no. 3027/2/1 Part 23.

301. *The Straits Times*, 29 July 1966.

302. Ibid., 28 July 1966.

303. Ibid.

304. Telegram no. 1143, Head to Bottomley, 30 June 1965, in A1838/280 no. 3027/2/1 Part 23.

305. *The Straits Times*, 7 July 1965.

306. Ibid., 8 July 1965.

307. Ibid., 9 July 1965.

308. Ibid., 9 July 1965.

309. Ibid., 14 July 1965.

310. Airgram no. 13, American Consulate (Singapore) to Department of State, July 1965, RG 59 Box 2451 4/9/65.

311. Telegram no. 1568, Australian High Commission (Singapore) to Department of External Affairs, 13 July 1965, A6364/4 KL565/6.

312. The by-election was necessitated by the resignation on 16 June of Ong Eng Guan, the leader and sole representative of the UPP. Ong had charged, in his letter of resignation, that the PAP had suppressed all effective opposition in Singapore and that "no useful purpose" would be served by his continuing as an assemblyman. *The Straits Times*, 17 June 1965.

313. The by-election was fought between the PAP and the BS, the other parties having opted out. The PAP's candidate was Lee Khoon Choy, who had been Lee Kuan Yew's political secretary. Standing against him was the BS's Ong Chang Sam, who fought on a "Crush Malaysia" platform. See John Drysdale, *Singapore: Struggle for Success* (Singapore: Times Books International, 1984), p. 389.

314. *The Sunday Times*, 1 August 1965.

315. Airgram no. 20, American Consulate (Singapore) to Department of State, 26 July 1965, RG 59 Box 2454 Pol 12 5/1/65.

316. Memorandum no. 933, C.E. MacDonald (Second Secretary) to Secretary, Department of External Affairs, 21 July 1965, A9735/6 no. 205/10 Part 2.

317. *Malayan Times*, 13 July 1965.

318. Telegram no. 37, Australian High Commission (Kuala Lumpur) to Department of External Affairs, 6 August 1965.

319. Han et al., p. 79.

320. Telegram no. 332, New Zealand High Commission (Singapore) to Department of External Affairs (Wellington), 10 August 1965, A1838/333 no. 3006/10/4 Part 4.

321. Telegram no. 678, Australian High Commission (Singapore) to Department of External Affairs, 10 August 1965, A1838/333 no. 3006/10/4 Part 4.

322. Tunku Abdul Rahman, *Looking Back: Monday Musings and Memories* (Kuala Lumpur: Pustaka Antara, 1977), p. 122.

323. Memorandum no. 1378, Critchley to Secretary, Department of External Affairs, A1838/333 no. 3006/10/4 Part 6.

324. Tunku Abdul Rahman, *Looking Back*, p. 122.

325. Memorandum no. 1378, Critchley to Secretary, Department of External Affairs, A1838/333 no. 3006/10/4 Part 6.
326. *The Sunday Times*, 15 August 1965.
327. Telegram no. 1795, Australian High Commission (Kuala Lumpur) to Department of External Affairs, 16 August 1965, A6364/4 no. KL65/6.
328. Tunku Abdul Rahman, *Looking Back*, p. 123.
329. *The Straits Times*, 7 July 1965.
330. Telegram no. 1795, Australian High Commission (Kuala Lumpur) to Department of External Affairs, 16 August 1965, A6364/4 no. KL65/6.
331. Tunku Abdul Rahman, *Looking Back*, p. 123.
332. Ibid.
333. Telegram no. 678, Australian High Commission (Singapore) to Department of External Affairs, 10 August 1965, A1838/333 no. 3006/10/4 Part 4.
334. Telegram no. 669, Australian High Commission (Kuala Lumpur) to Department of External Affairs, 10 August 1965, A1838/333 no. 3006/10/4 Part 4.
335. Ibid.
336. Telegram no. 1795, Australian High Commission (Kuala Lumpur) to Department of External Affairs, 16 August 1965, A6364/4 no. KL65/6.
337. Tunku Abdul Rahman, *Looking Back*, p. 123.
338. Interview with Goh Keng Swee, cited in Chew, p. 147.
339. Tunku Abdul Rahman, *Looking Back*, p. 123.
340. Interview with Goh Keng Swee, cited in Chew, p. 147.
341. Interview with Toh Chin Chye, cited in Chew, p. 97.
342. Ibid.
343. Cited in Leslie Fong, "The week before separation", *A Straits Times Special*, 9 August 1990.
344. Tunku Abdul Rahman, *Looking Back*, p. 123.
345. *The Sunday Times*, 15 August 1965.
346. Interview with Goh Keng Swee, cited in Chew, p. 147.
347. *The Straits Times*, 4 August 1965.
348. Drysdale, p. 391.
349. Fong, p. 9.
350. Interview with Toh Chin Chye, cited in Chew, p. 97.
351. *The Sunday Times*, 15 August 1965.
352. Interview with Toh Chin Chye, in Chew, p. 97.
353. Cited in Fong, p. 10.
354. Speech by Lee Kuan Yew at a valedictory dinner on 22 August 1981 at the Istana, printed in *Petir*, (March 1982), pp. 7–8.
355. Ibid.
356. "Message from Lee Kuan Yew to Prime Minister and Mr Bottomley, Secretary of State for Commonwealth Relations", n.d., PREM 13/589.
357. Telegram no. 1795, Australian High Commission (Kuala Lumpur) to Department of External Affairs, 16 August 1965, A6364/4 KL65/6.
358. Drysdale, p. 391.
359. Sopiee, p. 210.
360. Cited in Fong, p. 10.
361. Ibid.
362. Interview with Rajaratnam, cited in Chew, p. 155.
363. Cited in Fong, p. 10.

364. Ibid., p. 12.
365. Ibid.
366. Transcript of a press conference given by Lee Kuan Yew at Broadcasting House, Singapore, at 1200 hours, 9 August 1965, A1838/333 no. 3006/10/4 Part 6.
367. Telegram no. 239, British High Commission (Singapore) to Commonwealth Relations Office, 10 August 1965, PREM 13/589.
368. Ibid.
369. *The Sunday Times*, 15 August 1965, cited in Sopiee, p. 211.
370. Drysdale, p. 393.
371. Telegram no. 1340, Head to Commonwealth Relations Office, 8 August 1965, PREM 13/589.
372. Telegram no. 2021, Commonwealth Relations Office to British High Commission (Kuala Lumpur), 8 August 1965, PREM 13/589.
373. Telegram no. 1344, Head to Commonwealth Relations Office, 9 August 1965, PREM 13/589.
374. Telegram no. 1745, Australian High Commission (Kuala Lumpur) to Department of External Affairs, 11 August 1965, A1838/333 no. 3006/10/4 Part 6.
375. Sopiee, p. 211.
376. *Malaysia Parliamentary Debates. Dewan Ra'ayat (House of Representatives) Official Report*, 9 August 1965, Col. 1459–66.
377. Ibid., Col. 1472.
378. Ibid., Col. 1473-75.
379. Ibid., Col. 1503–4.
380. Ibid., Col. 1509.
381. Ibid., Col. 1518.
382. Telegram no. 660, Australian High Commission (Singapore) to Department of External Affairs, 9 August 1965, A1838/333 no. 3006/10/4 Part 4.
383. Telegram no. 228, British High Commission (Singapore) to Commonwealth Relations Office, 9 August 1965, PREM 13/589.
384. Transcript of a press conference given by Lee Kuan Yew at Broadcasting House, Singapore, at 1200 hours, 9 August 1965, in A1838/333 no.3006/10/4 Part 6.

CHAPTER 8

"SINGAPORE IS OUT"

T he headlines in *The Straits Times* of 10 August said it all.[1] Calling
the news a "cruel shock", its page-one leader commented that it
was "a thousand pities that the clock had been thus set back". The
destinies of the two countries, it insisted, remained interwoven.[2] The
political aftershocks followed immediately.

On 11 August, Syed Ja'afar Albar resigned from his post as the
Secretary-General of the United Malays National Organization (UMNO).[3]
Tunku Abdul Rahman subsequently told T.K. Critchley, the Australian
High Commissioner, that Syed Ja'afar had actually been "sacked" because
he had been "so excitable that he had played into Lee's hands".[4] Lee Kuan
Yew's own view, as told to Frank Mills, the British Acting Deputy High
Commissioner, was that the Tunku "would have to get rid not merely of
Albar but also five others".[5] If Syed Ja'afar had been asked to resign or was
sacked soon after the riots started in Singapore, Lee surmised that separation
would not have taken place. But it was too late now.[6]

On his part, Lee was having some initial trouble keeping order
within his own ranks. While the Cabinet gave an outward impression
of unity, there were simmering tensions within. Both Toh Chin Chye and
S. Rajaratnam were apparently still angry at Goh Keng Swee and Lee for
advocating separation and had not accepted that the People's Action Party
(PAP) could no longer participate in the Malaysian Solidarity Convention
(MSC). They professed to see nothing wrong in helping PAP branches in
Malaysia to organize and expand their activities. Lee's efforts to "moderate
their enthusiasm", observed Mills, had "met such hostile reception that
he had had to withdraw quickly".[7] By 12 August, however, cooler heads
had prevailed and things had simmered down somewhat after the PAP

leaders had, in Lee's words, crossed the "last hurdle" in saying their final farewell to the PAP cadres from Malaya who met Toh and Rajaratnam to discuss the future of the party in Malaysia. Toh said that henceforth, PAP Malaysia would act independently of its Singapore counterpart.[8] Though Lee was no longer as worried about his Cabinet colleagues, some residue tension remained. A number of his ministers were still suspicious that "Goh Keng Swee had engineered the whole affair and would never quite trust Goh again". The reshuffling of Goh from the Finance ministry to head the newly created Defence and Security portfolio helped as "they would not have to have so much work to do with him".[9] As the New Zealand High Commission in Singapore commented, "It is a moment of anguish for them all".[10]

The possibility of another re-merger was immediately held out by leaders from both sides. "All of us must hope that the separation will not be permanent," Tan Siew Sin said.[11] The Malacca Chief Minister, Abdul Ghafar bin Baba remarked that a reunion might be possible once communal tensions had cooled down.[12] Lee Kuan Yew was also sure that "they will open the door for us again".[13] Reunification, however, would be on very different terms from those in 1963, Lee said, and would only be accepted if Singapore's interests were firmly safeguarded.[14] But unlike in 1946, the separation document in 1965 gave no assurance about the possibility of re-merger or the inevitability of re-integration.[15] Twice bitten, both sides shy away from considering merger again.

Why was merger unsuccessful? Even before its formation it was already evident that the integration of Singapore into the Federation would pose one of Malaysia's most difficult tasks. The basic problem lay in the historical consciousness of the Malays that Malaya was primarily a Malay country and that the non-Malays, who had settled there under British rule, were in Malaya on sufferance and were not entitled to citizenship rights except on Malay terms. For this reason the Malays had opposed the Malayan Union scheme and agitated for its replacement by the Federation of Malaya. Singapore had always posed a special problem because of its large Chinese population, and was left out from the Malayan Union precisely for this reason. Yet, it could not be ignored, for a hostile, and especially a communist Singapore, would pose a security threat to the Federation. The creation of Malaysia in 1963 brought to the fore the difficult problems of political accommodation between these two power centres which represent two major racial groupings. By then the differences between the two territories had also become so marked as to make any political reconciliation even more difficult. That Kuala Lumpur never evinced much interest in wanting Singapore to return to the Malayan fold did not help. The Tunku only became more inclined to Malaysia after he reached the conclusion that Singapore must be absorbed before it could threaten Malaya while Singapore agreed to the scheme as the only possible way to become independent. In order that the racial balance of the existing Federation should not be disturbed, and racial harmony with it, the Borneo territories were added. The fact that the majority of the people in Sarawak and North Borneo were not Malays was tolerable: at least they were not Chinese. While this might have had psychological value in attracting Malay support for Malaysia, in concrete terms, it did not really address the fundamental challenge that the inclusion of a largely Chinese-dominated state posed to the communally organized and racially weighted political system in the Federation. Left unresolved also was the question raised by Milne: "[T]o what extent, if at all, were politics in Malaya to be insulated from politics in Singapore?"[16] Whilst the merger negotiations represented some attempts to arrive at such a political framework, no real understanding was ever reached between the PAP and the Alliance. As Antony Head, the British High Commissioner, put it, Malaysia "was something of a shotgun wedding"[17] and the basic question of how the two centres of power would get along after merger was not thoroughly examined. "With the advantage of hindsight," observed Sopiee, "it is clear that most of the major factors which were to lie at the base of PAP-Alliance dissension after the formation of Malaysia had reared their heads even before it".[18]

In the Tunku's mind, Malaysia was very much an extension of the "Old Malaya", with political parties organized on a communal basis, under the hegemony of UMNO. Indeed, he had sought to duplicate the Alliance system in the rest of Malaysia, including Singapore. Kuala Lumpur would make no major accommodation to suit the PAP.[19] What Kuala Lumpur desired was for the left-wing, socialist and non-communal PAP to adjust itself to a Malaysia run along conservative and communal lines by the Alliance. "Singapore came into the Federation with their eyes wide open and they came in on their own accord", said the Tunku. Kuala Lumpur was not obliged to "make any further openings" to allow the PAP to do "something more than just to run Singapore as a State and as an important business centre of Malaysia".[20] Given the PAP's political and ideological incompatibilities with the Alliance, the Tunku's view was basically that the PAP should keep out of Malaya and confine its mission instead to making Singapore the commercial heart of Malaysia. "We dreamt of Singapore in connection with Malaya as what New York is to America," the Tunku had said.[21] But because Kuala Lumpur never completely trusted the PAP, and had considered the party instead as a potential political challenger, it had sought not only to confine the PAP to Singapore but also to circumscribe its influence there. To the Malayan Chinese Association (MCA) in particular, the PAP was its natural enemy, competing as it was for the same Chinese votes. Consequently, even before merger became an accomplished fact, MCA leaders already started to interfere in the Island's political arena in order to undermine the PAP's support among the Chinese there.[22] PAP leaders, on their part, had no wish to see the party's role reduced to that of "running a Town Council in Singapore".[23] Nor did they envision Malaysia as simply an expanded version of the Old Malaya underpinned by Malay hegemony when Malays no longer formed the majority race. They saw Malaysia instead as a new entity requiring a more dynamic form of political organization in which they could play a more prominent part. Efforts by the Alliance to confine the PAP to, and undermine its influence in, Singapore only confirmed their suspicions about Kuala Lumpur's sincerity in wanting Malaysia,[24] and not just Malaya "writ large",[25] with Singapore, Sabah, and Sarawak as "mere appendages".[26]

"The PAP understandably, and surely legitimately, has ambition to participate in the central affairs of the nation it has helped to found," commented W.B. Pritchett, the Australian Deputy High Commissioner, "It cannot be expected to confine itself to Singapore; expansion to Malaya, and eventually to Borneo, must take place".[27] The PAP had always been a multiracial party, non-communal in outlook and pan-Malayan in its ambitions. Short of recanting its political objectives and philosophy, the PAP would sooner or later have extended its political activities outside Singapore. Given such considerations, in the view of the Australian Department of External Affairs, it was even more unrealistic of Kuala Lumpur to expect that it could simply "establish Federal authority and control over Singapore without giving Singapore the right to participate in shaping central policy — Singapore cannot be made a 'colony' of Kuala Lumpur".[28] The New Zealand Department of External Affairs concurred, emphasizing that Alliance leaders should recognize that "Malaysia is a federation, not an empire".[29] Whilst there is evidence to suggest that Kuala Lumpur was fully cognizant of the desirability of involving the PAP more fully in national affairs, there was at the same time little political will to do so. G.A. Jockel's (First Assistant Secretary, Australian Department of

External Affairs) notes of meeting with Federal ministers between 19 and 21 May 1965 revealed, for instance, that:

> In the discussions, Malaysian Ministers offered no clear answer to the current problem whereby the 1.7 million Malaysians in Singapore had no official participation in the processes of decision-making in the Central Government. This was recognized as a weakness by Dr Ismail. He said that one had to go back to the original bargain ... concerning the terms and conditions of Singapore's entry into Malaysia. That had been a quickly contrived arrangement but there was no hope in present circumstances of altering it. It was necessary to make the best of it and to live with it.[30]

In retrospect, given their deep-seated and contrary conceptions of what Malaysia represented, the conflict between the PAP and the Alliance was perhaps inevitable. But it would probably be erroneous to surmise that the Malaysia enterprise was doomed to fail from the start. Much of the friction and difficulties, as Head observed, could have been avoided had Kuala Lumpur adopted a more "tactful" and "less partisan" approach in its dealings with Singapore.[31] "Since Malaysia was established," Pritchett argued, "the old Malayan regime has continued in power. It has also made little effort to develop cooperation with the Singapore and other State Governments and to bring them into regular consultation on matters of general national concern".[32] If blame was to be apportioned, the New Zealand Department of External Affairs was clear that it should not be apportioned equally: "It is inescapable, however, that the Federal Government has the prime responsibility for making the Federation work".[33]

In the chain of events and circumstances that contributed to separation, the PAP's overwhelming victory in the September 1963 elections in Singapore, five days after Malaysia Day, probably gave UMNO its first serious apprehensions about the political and ideological threat the PAP posed to the Federation. Scholars who have written on the subject are in agreement that the September 1963 election constituted an important landmark in the saga of Singapore's separation. Bellows wrote, for instance, that it laid the "basis for renewed confrontation between UMNO and the PAP".[34] For Ostrom, this began the "first round in the PAP–UMNO political competition within Malaysia".[35] Tae Yul Nam similarly saw its importance in sowing "the seeds of power politics between the two territories".[36] The significance of the PAP's overwhelming victory was not only that it consolidated the PAP position in Singapore and afforded it a strong base for expansion into Federation politics, the fact that it had succeeded in getting a number of Malays to vote for it was a major "political red light" for UMNO as well. As Head put it:

> Why? Because ... in order to retain political and administrative control of their own country, the Malays rely on a purely communal vote. "Vote Malay to keep the Malays in power" is UMNO's main attraction and appeal to their supporters. It can, therefore, be seen that the prospect of Lee Kuan Yew's party, the PAP, spreading into Malaya as a progressive socialist party who would provide a better deal for the have-nots and then, judging by its performance in Singapore, attracting a considerable number of Malay supporters, seriously worried the Malay UMNO leaders. The possibility of having their solid communal UMNO vote eroded by the PAP is the basic cause of Malaya's major problem today, mutual fear and tension between Malay and Chinese.[37]

Prior to the 1963 Singapore elections, UMNO probably never thought the PAP would ever have much appeal to the Malays. Head's assessment was not far from Lee Kuan Yew's own interpretation of the significance of the 1963 elections:

> [T]he irony of this is that because in Singapore we were so successful, too successful, without special rights and privileges written into the Constitution, nevertheless making that adjustment consciously, that we won all the three predominantly Malay constituencies the last time. That, in turn, triggered off a reaction on the other side that we should never be allowed to do that in Malaya. ... [I]f we had lost the three Malay constituencies, the problem would not have arisen. We won, and they were determined that we will not win in Malaya.[38]

After the total political defeat of the Singapore United Malays National Organization (SUMNO), there remained, as Abdullah Ahmad put it, only "slender hope indeed of any prospect of Lee Kuan Yew, who was known to be wanting to work closely with UMNO in the Central Government, achieving his objective". Citing his interview with Tun Abdul Razak, Abdullah surmised that had Lee saved the Tunku's "face" by arranging for SUMNO candidates to win at least in Malay-majority constituencies, he "might well have achieved his desire to work with UMNO at the Centre in future ... [and] the course of the history of Malaysia would have been different".[39] Whilst it is true that the PAP was not confident of victory in the Malay wards, it is doubtful whether it would have been politically possible for the PAP to quietly abdicate its responsibility over its own Malay community to SUMNO for the sake of political peace with UMNO. To do so would also be to countenance communal politicking, something contrary to the PAP's own ideological beliefs. The PAP, in any case, expected a close fight with the Barisan Sosialis (BS) and needed every vote it could get. But the extent of SUMNO's humiliation also made it politically inopportune for the Tunku to immediately adopt a more enlightened policy of involving the PAP in the central government. Instead, SUMNO's defeat added another "root cause of future Alliance–PAP dissension … to the already long list".[40]

Significant though it was, the outcome of the 1963 election did not close the door completely to PAP–Alliance cooperation. After the initial uproar over SUMNO's defeat had subsided, there were encouraging signs that the moderate UMNO leaders had begun thinking about getting the PAP more closely involved in the central government, including the possibility of bringing a PAP minister or two into the Federal Cabinet. The Tunku apparently was thinking of taking two ministers from the PAP into the Federal government and Head "believe he would have done it".[41] Tun Razak himself saw advantages in such an arrangement and had declared to Critchley that the Alliance would have "no difficulty" in getting along with most of the PAP ministers.[42] But because of opposition from the MCA and the more extremist elements in UMNO, and the prospects of Federal elections in early 1964, not much headway was made by way of involving the PAP more intimately with the national government, apart from despatching Lee on an ad hoc assignment to rally support for Malaysia from amongst the African states from 20 January to 26 February 1964. In retrospect, this was an opportunity lost because the PAP had wanted to develop a cooperative relationship with Kuala Lumpur, and was likely to accept a position in the Federal Cabinet if offered.[43] R.A. Woolcott argued that if UMNO was afraid of the PAP, "I would have thought that it might be preferable to have [Lee] or another Singapore State Minister within the Federal Cabinet and under Cabinet control and discipline rather than outside of the Cabinet where there would be a tendency to attempt to rally opposition to the Central Government".[44]

However, whatever prospect there was for such accommodation evaporated after the PAP's participation in the 1964 Federal elections. To Head, this was the "first really critical event" that soured relations and contributed to the bitterness between the PAP and the Alliance.[45] Scholars who had commented on the reasons for Singapore's eventual separation from Malaysia were also in agreement. Ostrom, for instance, saw the PAP's decision to participate in the Federal election as constituting an important "watershed" in PAP–Alliance ties, "comparable to Caesar's crossing of the Rubicon", for in so doing, the PAP came into direct political combat with the Alliance for the first time.[46] It was perhaps this decision, "more than any other," according to Catley, "which set in motion the events leading to Singapore's secession".[47]

To the Tunku, the PAP's foray into Federal politics was not only "quite contrary"[48] to an understanding which Lee Kuan Yew was supposed to have made with him, but it was also an attempt to circumvent the constitutional terms by which Singapore was accepted into the Federation, which limited Singapore's representation in the Dewan Ra'ayat (House of Representatives) to 15 seats. Exactly what the two leaders agreed has not been documented. All that is clear is that the Tunku was convinced that such an agreement existed and that the PAP had broken it. "Lee said to me before that 15 seats were enough for him in the Federal Parliament," the Tunku had charged.[49] As he put it:

> With the return of the PAP to power we considered that the State of Singapore was safe from the communists ... little did we realize that the leader of the PAP had in his mind a share in the running of Malaysia. This we considered as unacceptable since the Alliance is strong enough to run the country on its own.[50]

What the available evidence showed, however, is that while Lee had assured Kuala Lumpur publicly on numerous occasions, both before and after merger, that the PAP would keep out of the 1964 Federal elections, there appeared to be no blanket assurance that the PAP would not contest subsequent Federal elections. This would seem to support Fletcher's suggestion that there did not seem to be much "concrete evidence of any firm commitment by the leadership of the PAP permanently to refrain from extending their party organization into Malaya or from campaigning in Malaya to elect PAP candidates who were not Singapore citizens".[51] Lee, on his part, had assumed that a quid pro quo existed, for he had stated publicly that the Tunku had also "given an assurance that he will not come down to Singapore to participate in the elections. So there will be no collision in Singapore and elsewhere".[52] It would appear that the understanding between the two premiers was probably only, as Lee put it, a "gentleman's understanding" to "stay out of each other's backyard".[53] After the Tunku and other Federation leaders campaigned on behalf of the SA in the 1963 Singapore elections, the PAP probably did not feel bound anymore by Lee's assurance to the Tunku that it would not contest the elections in the Federation. As Lee put it, "the CEC [Central Executive Committee] considered all bets off".[54]

Lee's role in the decision to contest the Federal polls has been the subject of some controversy. While Leifer believed that the decision "was taken only in the few weeks preceding the announcement"[55] when Lee was in Africa, Sopiee felt that this was "most convenient" in view of his "solemn undertaking to the Tunku made before the formation of Malaysia that the PAP would not participate in the 1964 Malayan elections".[56] Although Lee said subsequently that he did not take part in the decision and that Toh Chin Chye and Rajaratnam "led the CEC in taking them", Barr insisted that "it was Lee himself, not Rajaratnam and Toh Chin Chye, who took the decision to enter the 1964 Federal elections, which proved to be the event which began the decline in UMNO–PAP relations". Barr came to his conclusion not from any documentary evidence but from an inference he made from an interview with Goh Keng Swee some three decades after the event.[57] What seemed clear is that, although the matter of the PAP's participation in Federal politics had been considered for some time, no firm decision was taken before Lee's departure for Africa. Just before he left on 20 January 1964, Lee had, in fact, asked the Publicity and Propaganda Coordinating Committee not to make any decision in his absence.[58] When he returned on 26 February, Lee found that the decision had already been taken by the CEC, led by Toh and Rajaratnam, and that he had been presented with a *fait accompli*. He was not enthusiastic but abided by the decision.[59] Pang Cheng Lian's interviews with senior PAP leaders showed that not all the CEC members were in agreement that the PAP should stay out of Malaya. Rajaratnam, for one, had "denied that the Party had ever claimed that it would not take part in the Malayan elections". Another CEC member added that "the PAP had all along meant to participate in the Malayan elections" and that while Lee "had come to some sort of an understanding" with the Tunku, "the rest of the CEC were against this".[60] Chan Heng Chee's interview with a PAP minister also led her to conclude that it "appears that Lee Kuan Yew during the merger talks did give some form of promise to Alliance leaders that the PAP would not participate in the 1964 elections, but this was without prior discussions with other PAP leaders who therefore did not feel bound by Lee's words".[61] From what is known, it would appear that the PAP's CEC took the fateful decision to participate in the Federal elections, not Lee, during the latter's absence in Africa. The popular perception "that the PAP was Lee Kuan

Yew" — a proposition that Lee said was "simply not true" — probably contributed to some of the ambiguity about Lee's role.[62]

The PAP's motives for contesting the 1964 Federal elections could be viewed within the context of the party's unsuccessful bid to become an acceptable partner in the Alliance and its assessment that, without such a show of power, Kuala Lumpur was unlikely to agree to a share of power with the PAP so as to allow the party to play a wider national role and fulfil its ideological mission. So long as the PAP remained confined to Singapore, its long-term political survival could not be guaranteed, for the Alliance would be able to bring the full weight of Federal power to bear on the Island and erode the influence of the PAP there over time. Kuala Lumpur's decision to hold the Malayan state and Federal elections simultaneously, on the other hand, added an urgency to PAP calculations, for it denied the party an intermediate opportunity to test Malayan opinion until the next elections in 1969. It, therefore, probably saw the 1964 elections as, in Lee's words, "the preliminary of the elections in 1969" and that if it were possible to get the "winds of change" to blow gently in 1964, "so much less of an upset it will be all around in 1969".[63] Underlying the PAP's rationale for intervention was the assumption that it could work with the moderate Malay leaders in UMNO and that, should the PAP be successful against the MCA, the Tunku would have to come to terms with the PAP much earlier and bring it as a partner into the national government. The PAP acknowledged that intervention carried risks but the alternative of the PAP remaining in the opposition was also fraught with dangers for it must mean that UMNO would, sooner or later, have to fight the PAP, and face all the consequences that would entail for the stability of Malaysia.

Whatever the PAP's intentions, its decision "immediately resulted in a serious deterioration in PAP–Alliance relations as a whole".[64] The MCA was convinced that the PAP had designs to supplant it, while UMNO read the intervention as an attempt to divide the Alliance and closed ranks with the former to defeat the PAP. Federation leaders all saw the PAP as a worrying political and ideological threat to the Alliance system. The very aggressiveness of the PAP campaign, its ability to draw unprecedented crowds, and its socialist appeal to the have-nots — all struck fear in the hearts of conservative Alliance leaders, alarmed at the prospect of a PAP expanding actively outside Singapore. Until the appearance of the PAP in Federal politics, UMNO's hegemony over the Malays had no real contender, except for the Pan-Malayan Islamic Party (PMIP). Now, a

Singapore party, on a non-communal, socialist programme, had eroded UMNO support in the Malay-dominated constituencies on the Island. It had also completely defeated the Alliance candidates in the non-Malay urban constituencies in the Singapore elections. Both these developments worried UMNO and its partner, for in the urban areas in the 1964 Federal elections, the PAP attracted huge crowds, including Malays. Though the PAP was decisively defeated, winning only one seat and presented no threat to the Alliance, UMNO saw the PAP participation as a rehearsal for an ultimate Chinese challenge to a political arrangement that would end Chinese political passivity as represented by the MCA. The PAP's defeat, as Parmer put it, was "probably the key to the events which followed and which culminated in Singapore's separation".[65]

Henceforth, Alliance policy deliberately sought to confine the PAP to Singapore. UMNO saw the opportunity presented by the PAP's defeat to weaken or possibly destroy the PAP in its own backyard, and exploited it to the fullest. Immediately after the elections, UMNO activists began a campaign to undermine the multiracial basis of the PAP's support by wooing back Malay voters. Through Malay newspapers like the *Utusan Melayu* and *Utusan Zaman*, and the UMNO organ, *Merdeka*, and speeches, the PAP was accused of being anti-Malay. Seen from Singapore, the strategy appeared to be to inflame the Malays, possibly to riot, with the objectives of intimidating the PAP government into submission, and causing the Singapore Malays to fear the PAP and withdraw their support for the party, thus discrediting the PAP's multiracial platform. Another goal was probably to use the supposed plight of the Singapore Malays as a means to rally and consolidate Malay support for UMNO throughout Malaysia. The tense racial situation created by the communal politicking in Singapore by the UMNO-led campaign and extremists played no small part in contributing to the two race riots in Singapore in July and September 1964.

The race riots had a profound effect on the prospects of future PAP–UMNO cooperation. Before the riots, the PAP had assumed that it could work with UMNO. After the riots, the PAP knew it could not. The extremists in UMNO did not want it, and the moderates were apparently not sufficiently strong to control them. Seen from Singapore, the Malay leadership appeared determined to preserve Malay hegemony even at the expense of alienating Chinese support, not only in Singapore but also in the rest of Malaysia, by condoning the extremists' campaign to use the communal weapon against the PAP. UMNO probably calculated that the risks were worth taking. As Pritchett commented:

Alliance leaders have not only not moved towards multiracialism, but have insisted on the need to maintain the communal organization of politics for at least a generation. They have failed to control their more extreme followers and permitted them to wage a vigorous and openly communal campaign against the PAP, even to the extent of carrying agitation to a point where conspirators were able to provoke mass riots for several days in July and, less successfully, in September.[66]

The riots demonstrated how the PAP was vulnerable in Singapore without a measure of control over its own internal security. With a Malay Federal minister in charge of Singapore's police and internal security, the Malay extremists were less likely to exercise restraint in their anti-PAP activities in Singapore. Even though Internal Security minister, Ismail, and the Tunku were considered moderates, neither of them apparently put a stop to the anti-PAP agitation campaign which was in full swing for some three months prior to the outbreak of the riots. When the July riots erupted, both Malay leaders were overseas, leaving no moderate check on the extremists. After the riots, PAP leaders realized that unless the party expanded across the Causeway into Malaya and possibly into Sabah and Sarawak, it would be finished off by the "ultras" if it remained isolated and vulnerable in Singapore. Influence was not sufficient. Formal power was now necessary.[67] The riots had probably also convinced the PAP that it "had to aggressively agitate for the suppression of these extremists"[68] since the moderate English-educated leaders in UMNO seemed either reluctant or unable to take action to inhibit the activities of the extremists within their ranks. The survival of Malaysia, in the PAP's reckoning, depended on whether the extremists could be kept out of the leadership of both the Malay and Chinese communities, for Malay extremism would invariably produce a counter-reaction from the Chinese and afford the Barisan Sosialis an opportunity to outbid the government in its efforts to secure the allegiance of the Chinese.[69] The PAP had done its share by neutralizing the Chinese extremists in Singapore and expected UMNO to do the same and restrain its own extremists in Malaysia. When UMNO did not, the PAP took upon itself the task of actively campaigning against the Malay ultras and pushing more resolutely for a multiracial Malaysia. Convinced by now that an Alliance–PAP coalition was a non-starter, the PAP, in a major strategy shift in November 1964, announced its decision to assume the role of an opposition party and to intensify efforts to expand into the Federation and to form what eventually crystallized as the united front of like-minded opposition parties in support of a Malaysian Malaysia. In the budget debates from November to December 1964, PAP parliamentary and organizational muscles were flexed for the Alliance to see.

It was within this context that the Tunku made his offer of what became known subsequently as "disengagement" in late December 1964. Essentially, Singapore would gain much greater autonomy in economic and fiscal matters, including internal security, without interference from Kuala Lumpur whose powers were confined to external affairs and defence. Apart from averting immediate conflict, disengagement would also afford the PAP a breathing space in the expectation of a future re-integration under better conditions. But the price was the abandonment of the PAP's capacity to influence the ground directly in Malaya, Sabah and Sarawak and compete for power at the centre. The PAP was to surrender its seats in the Federal Parliament and abstain from politicking in Malaya or Borneo. In stark communal terms, UMNO was prepared to give up its control over 1.7 million people in Singapore, including its sway over a quarter million Malays there, to the PAP in order to preserve its influence over some 4.7 million non-Malays in Malaysia. In any case, the disengagement proposals lapsed, partly because the British opposed the scheme, fearing that it might prove to be the start of a drift towards increasing separatism, and also because a number of the Tunku's key ministers, Tan Siew Sin and Ismail in particular, were bitterly against giving up any of the levers of control the Federal government had acquired over Singapore. Reports that the PAP had, in the meantime, been organizing a united front of opposition parties also closed the Tunku's mind to any further attempt to achieve disengagement.

Having failed to confine the PAP to Singapore, Alliance leaders embarked on a course of "collision" instead — to fight the PAP politically. The PAP reacted in kind. Realizing that its strength lay in its capacity to gather the support of the non-communal groups in Malaysia, including nearly all the non-Malays, and bring pressure to bear on the Alliance government, the PAP proceeded with the tactical expansion of its branches in Malaya; investigated the possibility of starting operations in the Borneo states; formed the Malaysian Solidarity Convention to spearhead its Malaysian Malaysia campaign; and used the "open argument"[70] both within and outside Parliament to champion its cause. The latter two developments, in particular, contributed in no small measure to warming up the political battle and strengthening the hand of the Malay extremists. Lee probably calculated that the result of all these activities would be the creation of such a degree of tension that Kuala Lumpur would be drawn back to the negotiating table to discuss disengagement or perhaps even "partition". But confronted with PAP tactics, Alliance attitudes hardened instead. To the Malays, their fears about the addition of the large Chinese population of Singapore seemed on the verge of being realized. What was even more fearsome was the possibility that the indigenous peoples of Sabah and Sarawak, instead of providing a balance against the Chinese, might side with the latter against the Malays. Such a development, though not imminent, would be a threat to Malay political hegemony, and there was no constitutional way to check the Malaysian Malaysia campaign short of repressive actions against Singapore, which would have national and international repercussions.

Though Lee was confident that the PAP could keep its campaign against the Alliance within constitutional limits, the threat of repression nevertheless loomed large because of Kuala Lumpur's monopoly of coercive powers. Ever since the PAP had decided to test the possibilities of an eventual bid for power at the centre, Malay extremists had made persistent and vehement calls for Lee's arrest and the forcible takeover of the Singapore government. While the moderate UMNO leaders had successfully resisted taking repressive action against PAP leaders, there was little doubt that they could always do so if necessary. Their initial reluctance was probably on account of the fact that the British, Australians and New Zealanders, who were actively defending Malaysia, could never acquiesce to such drastic measures, not only because their electorates would not support repression against the PAP, but also because they knew that this would mean the disintegration of Malaysia through communal conflict. Seen from this perspective, Lee's strategically timed overseas tours were probably motivated as much by the need to cultivate influential friends to insure against possible proscription by Kuala Lumpur as by the desire to fulfil wider political objectives in Afro-Asia and in the Commonwealth countries he visited. Nevertheless, in the end, according to the Tunku, matters came to such a head that repressive measures against the Singapore government "for the behaviour of some of their leaders"[71] were, indeed, seriously contemplated but dropped in favour of its alternative — separation.

There could be little doubt, as Head argued, that the personal antagonisms which grew between the Tunku and Lee had possibly compounded the situation, and made it more serious than it should.[72] According to Critchley, Lee apparently had been bothered by the "extent to which his problems with Kuala Lumpur were created by a clash of personalities. Should he step back and put forward people more acceptable to Kuala Lumpur such as Goh Keng Swee?"[73] But it was unlikely that a change in the PAP leadership, as was occasionally hinted at, would have resolved the basic conflict, which was that any arrangement that confined the PAP to Singapore without giving it a large measure of control over its own affairs, especially internal security, was a non-starter as far as the party was concerned, while any alternative that could not keep Singapore out of Malaysia was equally unacceptable to UMNO and its partners. Neither the PAP nor UMNO, in the months before separation, could find a mutually acceptable constitutional re-arrangement within Malaysia. Though Lee had suggested, in his meeting with the Tunku on 7 August, a looser form of federation, the Tunku by then was no longer interested. "There would have been all this acrimony still if there had been a little string tying Singapore to Malaysia," the Tunku said later, "The best thing was to cut Singapore off completely".[74] In the circumstances, separation was the only realistic option. After less than 23 months in Malaysia, Singapore separated on 9 August 1965 to become a sovereign independent nation.

If Singapore had not agreed to merger in 1963, it would have neglected what appeared, at one point, to be the most obvious and logical solution to the political future of Singapore. To have merged and separated was to have discovered that the considerations that led to its initial separation in 1946 had, indeed, been deep-seated ones. Not to have consented to separation, in the circumstances of August 1965, would have precipitated possible communal clashes and chaos and denied the people of Singapore their sovereign right to determine their own future and chart their own destiny as a truly non-communal, multiracial nation. Separation for Singapore, on the other hand, reopened the whole series of problems that the formation of Malaysia sought to resolve. Almost overnight, Singapore's future was put to question.[75] Would Singapore survive? Lee's answer to Harold Wilson was illuminating. "Do not worry about Singapore," Lee wrote to the British premier a fortnight after separation, "My colleagues and I are sane, rational people even in our moments of anguish. We weigh all possible consequences before we make any move on the political chessboard". He added, "Our people have the will to fight and the stuff that makes for survival".[76]

Notes

1. *The Straits Times*, 10 August 1965.
2. Ibid.
3. *The Straits Times*, 12 August 1965. Musa bin Hitam was appointed to replace him as acting Secretary-General of UMNO.
4. Telegram no. 1745, Australian High Commission (Kuala Lumpur) to Department of External Affairs, 11 August 1965, A1838/333 no. 3006/10/4 Part 6.
5. Telegram no. 270, British High Commission (Singapore) to Commonwealth Relations Office, 13 August 1965, PREM 13/589.
6. Summary of a press interview with Lee Kuan Yew in Chinese, recorded at the TV studios, 13 August 1965, A1838/333 no. 3006/10/4 Part 6.
7. Telegram no. 239, British High Commission (Singapore) to Commonwealth Relations Office, 10 August 1965, PREM 13/589.
8. Transcript of the proceedings of meeting between Singapore and Malaysian PAP leaders, 12 August 1965, A1838/333 no. 3006/10/4 Part 6.
9. Telegram no. 270, British High Commission (Singapore) to Commonwealth Relations Office, 13 August 1965, PREM 13/589.
10. Telegram no. 332, New Zealand High Commission (Singapore) to Department of External Affairs (Wellington), 10 August 1965, A1838/333 no. 3006/10/4 Part 4.
11. *Malaysia Parliamentary Debates. Dewan Ra'ayat (House of Representatives) Official Report*, 9 August 1965, Col. 1471.
12. *The Straits Times*, 11 August 1965.
13. Ibid., 13 August 1965.
14. Summary of a press interview with Lee Kuan Yew in Chinese recorded at the TV studios, 13 August 1965, A1838/333 no. 3006/10/4 Part 6.
15. The only common bond that linked both territories was the joint effort for defence and security. The Independence of Singapore Agreement called for the establishment of a treaty on external defence and mutual assistance which provided for a joint defence council; Malaysian defence assistance for Singapore; and the latter, in turn, allowing Malaysia to continue to utilize those facilities being used by its military forces in Singapore as Malaysia "may consider necessary" for its external defence. Both states also agreed not to enter into any treaty or agreement with a foreign state that might be detrimental to the independence and defence of the other. Singapore would continue to allow the United Kingdom access to its bases for the defence of Singapore and Malaysia, Commonwealth defence, and the "preservation of peace in South-East Asia". On economic matters, the agreement merely stated that the two states would cooperate "for their mutual benefit and interest". To make it worse, the common provision in Annex J of the 1963 Malaysia Agreement was rescinded. However, the Malaysian parliamentary act that amended the Malaysian constitution and the 1963 Malaysia Act specifically provided that Johore would abide by the terms of the 1961 and 1962 water agreements with Singapore which was dependent upon this source for most of its fresh water. See Charles Richard Ostrom, "A Core Interest Analysis of the Formation of Malaysia and the Separation of Singapore" (Unpublished PhD dissertation submitted to the Faculty of Claremont Graduate School, 1970), pp. 270–72; *The Straits Times*, 10 August 1965.
16. R.S. Milne, "Singapore's Exit from Malaysia: The Consequences of Ambiguity", *Asian Survey* 6, 3 (March 1966), p. 177.
17. "Note for Mr Thorneycroft by the British High Commissioner on the political situation", 11 January 1964, DEFE 7/1557.

18. Mohamed Noordin Sopiee, _From Malayan Union and Singapore Separation: Political Unification in the Malaysia Region 1945–65_ (Kuala Lumpur: Pernebit Universiti Malaya, 1976), p. 183.

19. Abdullah Ahmad, _Tengku Abdul Rahman and Malaysia's Foreign Policy 1963–1970_ (Kuala Lumpur: Berita Publishing, 1985), p. 86.

20. Speech by the Tunku at the Malaysian Alliance Convention, 17 April 1965, A1838/280 no. 3027/2/1 Part 21.

21. Ibid.

22. John Drysdale, _Singapore: Struggle for Success_ (Singapore: Times Books International, 1984), pp. 328–39.

23. Telegram no. 530, Australian High Commission (Singapore) to Department of External Affairs, 31 July 1964, A1838/280 no. 3027/2/1 Part 19.

24. Telegram no. 35, Australian High Commission (Singapore) to Department of External Affairs, 31 July 1964, A1838/280 no. 3027/2/1 Part 19.

25. Nancy McHenry Fletcher, _The Separation of Singapore from Malaysia_ (Ithaca: Southeast Asia Program, Department of Asian Studies, Cornell University, Data Paper no. 73, 1969), p. 78.

26. Memorandum of Conversation between Toh Chin Chye and William P. Bundy (Assistant Secretary of State for Far Eastern Affairs), Robert W. Barnett (Deputy Assistant Secretary of State for Far Eastern Affairs), and Albert D. Moscotti (Officer in Charge of Malaysian Affairs), 16 December 1964, RG 59 Box 2450 Pol 2 1/1/64.

27. Memorandum no. 266, W.B. Pritchett to Secretary, Department of External Affairs, 6 March 1965, A1838/280 no. 3027/2/1 Part 21.

28. Memorandum "Constitutional Discussions between the Tunku and Lee: The Problem of Singapore", n.d. (1965), in A1838/280 no. 3027/2/1 Part 23.

29. Telegram no. 398, New Zealand Department of External Affairs to High Commission (Kuala Lumpur), 21 August 1964, A1838/280 no. 3027/2/1 Part 19.

30. Memorandum by G.A. Jockel, "Notes on Visit to Kuala Lumpur and Singapore", n.d., A9735/6 no. 205/10 Part 2.

31. Telegram no. 1301, British High Commission (Kuala Lumpur) to Commonwealth Relations Office, 22 July 1964, PREM 11/4909.

32. Memorandum no. 1190, W.B. Pritchett to Secretary, Department of External Affairs, 12 August 1964, A1838/280 no. 3027/2/1 Part 19.

33. Telegram no. 398, New Zealand Department of External Affairs to High Commission (Kuala Lumpur), 21 August 1964, A1838/280 no. 3027/2/1 Part 19.

34. Thomas J. Bellows, _The People's Action Party of Singapore: Emergence of a Dominant Party System_ (New Haven: Southeast Asian Studies, Yale University, Monograph Series No. 14, 1970), p. 57.

35. Ostrom, p. 182.

36. Tae Y. Nam, _Racism, Nationalism, and Nation-Building in Malaysia and Singapore: A Functional Analysis of Political Integration_ (India: Sadhna Prakashan, 1973), p. 62.

37. Letter from Head to Secretary of State for Commonwealth Affairs, 15 October 1964, PREM 13/428.

38. Speech by Lee Kuan Yew to Malaysian students at Malaysia Hall in London, 10 September 1964, A1838/280 no. 3024/2/1 Part 13.

39. Abdullah, p. 89.

40. Sopiee, p. 189.

41. Memorandum no. 9, British High Commissioner (Kuala Lumpur) to Secretary of State for Commonwealth Relations, 21 July 1965, PREM 13/430.

42. Memorandum no. 1126, T.K. Critchley to Secretary, Department of External Affairs, 6 November 1963, A1838/333 no. 3006/10/4 Part 3.

43. Woolcott said that Goh Keng Swee had hinted to him that the PAP would accept a Cabinet position, if it was offered one. Toh Chin Chye, however, had reservations about the advantages of the PAP being represented in the Federal Cabinet because it would then be obliged to share collective responsibility for Federal policies some of which could be prejudicial to the standing of the PAP in Singapore. Letter from R.A. Woolcott to T.K. Critchley, 23 October, 1963, A1838/333 no. 3006/10/4 Part 3; Telegram no. 55, Australian High Commission (Singapore) to Department of External Affairs, 30 November 1963, A1838/333 no. 3006/10/4 Part 3.

44. Letter from R.A. Woolcott to T.K. Critchley, 23 October 1963, A1838/333 no. 3006/10/4 Part 3.

45. Memorandum no. 9, British High Commissioner (Kuala Lumpur) to Secretary of State for Commonwealth Relations, 21 July 1965, PREM 13/430.

46. Ostrom, p. 184.

47. R. Catley, "Malaysia: The Lost Battle for Merger", The Australian Outlook, 21, 1 (1967), p. 55.

48. The Straits Times, 21 September 1964.

49. Transcript of an interview between Garry Barker (Melbourne Herald) and Tunku Abdul Rahman, 11 a.m., 16 August 1965, A1838/333 no. 3006/10/4 Part 6.

50. Speech by Tunku Abdul Rahman at the Malaysian Alliance Convention, 17 April 1965, A1838/280 no. 3027/2/1 Part 21.

51. Fletcher, p. 30.

52. The Straits Times, 18 May 1963; cited in Drysdale, p. 329.

53. Speech by Lee Kuan Yew at a valedictory dinner on 22 August 1981 at the Istana, printed in Petir, (March 1982), p. 7.

54. Ibid.

55. Michael Leifer, "Singapore in Malaysia: The Politics of Federation", Journal of Southeast Asian History, 6, 2 (September 1965), p. 60.

56. Sopiee, p. 189.

57. Michael D. Barr, "Lee Kuan Yew in Malaysia: A Reappraisal of Lee Kuan Yew's Role in the Separation of Singapore from Malaysia", Asian Studies Review, 21, 1 (July 1997), p. 2.

58. See Chapter 4.

59. Ibid.

60. Pang Cheng Lian, Singapore's People's Action Party: Its History, Organization and Leadership (Singapore: Oxford University Press, 1971), p. 34.

61. Chan Heng Chee, "Singapore Out of Malaysia: The Politics of Survival" (Unpublished MA dissertation submitted to Cornell University, 1967), p. 24.

62. Speech by Lee Kuan Yew at a valedictory dinner on 22 August 1981 at the Istana, printed in Petir (March 1982), p. 9.

63. The Straits Times, 23 March 1964.

64. Sopiee, p. 190.

65. J. Norman Parmer, "Malaysia 1965: Challenging the Terms of 1957", Asian Survey, 6, 2 (February 1966), p. 114.

66 Memorandum no. 266, W.B. Pritchett to Secretary, Department of External Affairs, 6 March 1965, A1838/280 no. 3027/2/1 Part 21.

67. On 31 July 1964, Lee Kuan Yew, for instance, had told Pritchett that the PAP did not seek to contest Malay dominance and was ready to undertake not to work among the Malays in Malaya or Singapore. But the Malays must permit genuine cooperation in

making Malaysia work, including bringing the PAP into a national government. Pritchett reported that "Lee spoke of two or three seats and mentioned housing". When Pritchett reminded Lee that he had told him earlier that formal power was not important, only influence, Lee said that this was before the riots. Telegram no. 530, Australian High Commission (Singapore) to Department of External Affairs, 31 July 1964, A1838/280 no. 3027/2/1 Part 19.

68. Sopiee, p. 194.

69. Telegram no. 250, New Zealand High Commission (Singapore) to Department of External Affairs, 31 July 1964, in A1838/280 no. 3027/2/1 Part 19.

70. See speech by Lee Kuan Yew at a Hari Raya and Chinese New Year dinner at Joo Chiat Community Centre, 5 February 1965, in A1838/280 no. 3027/2/1 Part 20. Lee said, "[W]e are accustomed to the open society, the open debate, the open argument."

71. *Malaysia Parliamentary Debates. Dewan Ra'ayat (House of Representatives) Official Report*, 9 August 1965, Col. 1460.

72. Head to Duncan Sandys, 15 October 1964, PREM 13/428.

73. Telegram no. 35, Australian High Commission (Kuala Lumpur) to Department of External Affairs, 13 October 1964, A1838/280 no. 3027/2/1 Part 19.

74. Transcript of an interview between Gary Barker (*Melbourne Herald*) and Tunku Abdul Rahman, 11 a.m., 16 August 1965, A1838/333 no. 3006/10/4 Part 6.

75. Chan Heng Chee, *Singapore: The Politics of Survival 1965–1967* (Singapore: Oxford University Press, 1971), p. 1.

76. Lee Kuan Yew to Harold Wilson, 23 August 1965, PREM 13/589.

GLOSSARY

"Allahu Akhbar"	"God is Great"
ang pow	traditional Chinese red packet containing a gift of money
bersilat	an adverb of *silat* (n) which is the Malay art of self-defence
bumiputera	native, indigenous people
dato	respectful title for a man of rank
Dewan Negara	Senate
Dewan Ra'ayat	House of Representatives
huay kuan	clan association
ikan sepat	a type of small freshwater fish, sea-perch; a degoratory term
Imam	Muslim spiritual leader
jawi	Malay-Arabic characters
jihad	holy war
kampong	village
keris	a Malay dagger with a straight or wavy blade
lorong	narrow street
Konfrontasi	confrontation
Menteri Besar	Chief Minister
pahlawan	warrior
parang	a type of cleaver
songkok	a type of Malay headdress usually made of velvet
Yang di-Pertuan Agong	King
Yang di-Pertuan Negara	Head of State

BIBLIOGRAPHY

Unpublished Sources

United Kingdom (Public Record Office, London)

DO 169 — Commonwealth Relations Office. Far East and Pacific Department: Registered Files, 1960–1964.

DEFE 5 — Ministry of Defence. Chiefs of Staff Committee. Memoranda, 1947–1964.

DEFE 7 — Ministry of Defence. Registered Files: General Series, 1942–1979.

DEFE 24 — Ministry of Defence. Defence Secretariat: Registered Files, 1958–1973.

CAB 130 — Cabinet Office. Ad Hoc Committees: General and Miscellaneous Series.

FO 371 — Foreign Office. General Correspondence: Political Departments.

PREM 11 — Prime Minister Office. Correspondence and Papers, 1951–1964.

PREM 13 — Prime Minister Office. Correspondence and Papers, 1964–1970.

Australia (Australian Archives)

A1838 — Department of Foreign Affairs and Trade: Correspondence files, 1948–1989.

A4940 — Cabinet Office: Menzies and Holt Ministries — Cabinet files "C", 1958–1967.

A6364 — Department of Foreign Affairs and Trade: Printed copies of inward cables, secret and below, 1942–1979.

A9735 — Department of Foreign Affairs and Trade/Australian International Development Assistance Bureau Central Office: Correspondence files (Kuala Lumpur).

Singapore

National Archives of Singapore

Prime Minister's Office (PMO)

Correspondence with Malaysian Prime Minister (1)

Malaysia Solidarity Convention File (MSC)

Memorandum Submitted by the Government of Singapore to the Commission of Inquiry into the Disturbances in Singapore in 1964 (March 1965)

Publicity and Propaganda Coordinating Committee File

Internal Security Department (ISD)

Royal Malaysia Police (Singapore) Intelligence Journal (1963–1965)

Files from the Internal Security Department, Ministry of Home Affairs.

United States

RG 59   General Records of the Department of State.

Published Official Sources

Singapore

Lee Kuan Yew. *The Battle for Merger*. Singapore: Government Printing Office, 1961.

———. *Malaysia Will Succeed*. Singapore: Government Printing Office, 1964.

———. *Some Problems in Malaysia*. Singapore: Ministry of Culture, 1964.

———. *Are There Enough Malaysians to Save Malaysia?* Singapore: Ministry of Culture, 1965.

———. *The Battle for a Malaysian Malaysia*. Singapore: Ministry of Culture, 1965.

Malaysia – Age of Revolution. Singapore: Ministry of Culture, 1965.

———. *Malaysia Comes of Age*. Singapore: Ministry of Culture, 1965.

Malaysia: Agreement Concluded between the United Kingdom of Great Britain and Northern Ireland, the Federation of Malaya, North Borneo, Sarawak and Singapore. Cmd. 22 of 1963.

Memorandum Setting Out Heads of Agreement for a Merger between the Federation of Malaya and Singapore, Cmd. 33 of 1961 (15 November 1961).

Mirror of Opinion. Singapore: Ministry of Culture, 1965.

Republic of Singapore. *Lee Kuan Yew. Prime Minister's Speeches, Press Conferences, Interviews, Statements, etc.* Singapore: Prime Minister's Office, 1962–63.

Singapore Government Press Statements. Singapore: Publicity Division, Ministry of Culture, 1963–65.

Singapore Legislative Assembly Elections (Amendment) Ordinance, 1960, Ordinance No. 23 of 1960.

Singapore Legislative Assembly Debates (1961–65).

Federation of Malaysia

Malaysia Parliamentary Debates. Dewan Negara (Senate) Official Report. (1961–65).

Malaysia Parliamentary Debates. Dewan Ra'ayat (House of Representatives) Official Report. (1961–65).

Great Britain

Malayan Union and Singapore. *Statement of Policy on Future Constitution*. Cmd. 6723. London: HMSO, 1946.

Newspapers and Periodicals

Berita Harian
Far Eastern Economic Review
The Malay Mail
Malayan Times
Nanyang Siang Pau

The Observer
Sin Chew Jit Poh
Straits Echo
The Straits Times
Sunday Telegraph
Time Magazine
The Times
Utusan Melayu
Utusan Zaman

Party Publications

Plebian (Barisan Sosialis)
Petir (People's Action Party)
Our First Ten Years: PAP 10th Anniversary Souvenir (Singapore: PAP, 1964)
Lee Kuan Yew. *The Winds of Change* (Singapore: PAP Political Bureau, 1964)
Petir 25th anniversary issue. People's Action Party, 1954–1979 (Singapore: PAP, 1979)
Fong Sip Chee. *The PAP Story — The Pioneering Years* (Singapore: PAP, 1979)
The People (Singapore People's Alliance)
Merdeka (United Malays National Organization)
Unity (United People's Party)

Books

Abdul Rahman, Tunku. *Looking Back*. Kuala Lumpur: Pustaka Antara. 1977.
———. *As a Matter of Interest*. Kuala Lumpur: Heinemann Educational Books. 1981.
———. *Lest We Forget: Further Candid Reminiscences*. Singapore: Eastern Universities Press. 1983.
———. *Political Awakening*. Malaysia: Pelanduk. 1986.
———. *Viewpoints*. Kuala Lumpur: Heinemann. 1979.
Abdullah Ahmad. *Tengku Abdul Rahman and Malaysia's Foreign Policy 1963–1970*. Kuala Lumpur: Berita Publishing. 1985.
Allen, J. de.V. *The Malayan Union*. New Haven: Yale University, Southeast Asia Studies. 1967.
Allen, Richard. *Malaysia: Prospect and Retrospect*. London: Oxford University Press. 1968.
Ang, Hwee Suan. *Dialogues with S. Rajaratnam: Former Senior Minister in the Prime Minister's Office*. Singapore: Shin Min Daily News. 1991.
Bedlington, Stanley Sanders. *Malaysia and Singapore: The Building of New States*. Ithaca: Cornell University Press. 1978.
———. *The Singapore Malay Community: The Politics of State Integration*. Ithaca: Cornell University, Southeast Asia Program. 1974.
Bellows, Thomas J. *The People's Action Party of Singapore*. New Haven: Yale University, Southeast Asia Studies Mimeograph Series, No. 14. 1970.
Bloodworth, Dennis. *The Tiger and the Trojan Horse*. Singapore: Times Books International. 1986.

Chan Heng Chee. *Singapore: Politics of Survival 1986–67*. Singapore: Oxford University Press. 1984.

Cheah Boon Kheng. *The Masked Comrades: A Study of the Communist United Front in Malaya, 1945–1948*. Singapore: Times Books International. 1979.

———. *Red Star Over Malaya: Resistance and Social Conflict During and After the Japanese Occupation, 1941–1946*. Singapore: Singapore University Press. 1983.

Chew, Ernest C.T. and Edwin Lee (eds.). *A History of Singapore*. Singapore: Oxford University Press. 1991.

Chew, Melanie. *Leaders of Singapore*. Singapore: Resources Press. 1996.

Chin, Aloysius. *The Communist Party of Malaya: The Inside Story*. Kuala Lumpur: Vinpress. 1994.

Chin Kin Wah. *The Defence of Malaysia and Singapore: The Transformation of a Security System 1957–1971*. Cambridge: Cambridge University Press. 1983.

Clutterbuck, Richard. *Conflict and Violence in Singapore and Malaysia, 1945–1983*. Singapore: Graham Brash. 1984.

Drysdale, John. *Singapore, Struggle for Success*. Singapore: Times Books International, 1984.

Falk, Stanley L. *Seventy Days to Singapore: The Malayan Campaign, 1941–1942*. London: Robert Hale. 1975.

Fletcher, Nancy McHenry. *The Separation of Singapore from Malaysia*. Ithaca: Cornell University, Southeast Asia Program Data Paper No. 73, 1969.

Gill, Ranjit. *Of Political Bondage: An authorised biography of Tunku Abdul Rahman, Malaysia's first Prime Minister and his continuing participation in contemporary politics*. Singapore: Sterling Corporate Services. 1990.

Gullick, J.M. *Malaysia*. London: Ernest Benn. 1969.

———. *Malaysia and its Neighbours*. London: Routledge & Kegan Paul. 1967.

Han Fook Kwang, Warren Fernandez and Sumiko Tan. *Lee Kuan Yew: The Man and His Ideas*. Singapore: Times Editions. 1997.

Hanna, Willard A. *The Formation of Malaysia: New Factor in World Politics*. New York: American Universities Field Staff. 1964.

———. *The Separation of Singapore from Malaysia*. New York: American University Field Staff. 1965.

Heng Pek Koon. *Chinese Politics in Malaysia: A History of the Malaysian Chinese Association*. Singapore: Oxford University Press. 1988.

Ho Ah Chon (comp.). *The Formation of Malaysia*. Kuching: A.C. Ho. 1991.

Josey, Alex. *Lee Kuan Yew Vol. 1*. Singapore: Times Books International. 1968.

Lau, Albert. *The Malayan Union Controversy 1942–1948*. Singapore: Oxford University Press. 1991.

Lee Khoon Choy. *On the Beat to the Hustings: An Autobiography*. Singapore: Times Books International. 1988.

Lee Ting Hui. *The Open United Front: The Communist Struggle in Singapore 1954–1966*. Singapore: South Seas Society. 1996.

Mackie, J.A.C. *Konfrontasi: The Indonesia–Malaysia Dispute 1963–1966*. Kuala Lumpur: Oxford University Press. 1974.

Macmillan, Harold. *Winds of Change*. London: Macmillan. 1966.

Means, Gordon P. *Malaysian Politics*. London: Hodder and Stoughton. 1976.

Milne, R.S. *Government and Politics in Malaysia*. Boston: Houghton Mifflin. 1967.

Milne, R.S. and Diane K. Mauzy. *Politics and Government in Malaysia*. Singapore: Times Books International. 1978.

———. *Singapore: The Legacy of Lee Kuan Yew*. Boulder, Colorado: Westview Press. 1990.

Montgomery, B. *Shenton of Singapore, Governor and Prisoner of War*. Singapore: Leo Cooper. 1984.

Morais, J. Victor. *Tun Tan: Portrait of a Statesman*. Singapore: Quins. 1981.

Nam, Tae Yul. *Racism, Nationalism and Nation-Building in Malaysia and Singapore: A Functional Analysis of Political Integration*. India: Sadhna Prakashan. 1973.

Ong Chit Chung. *Operation Matador: Britain's War Plans against the Japanese 1918– 1941*. Singapore: Times Academic Press. 1997.

Ongkili, James P. *Modernization in East Malaysia 1960–1970*. Kuala Lumpur, Oxford University Press. 1972.

———. *Nation-Builiding in Malaysia 1946–74*. Singapore: Oxford University Press. 1985.

Osborne, Milton E. *Singapore and Malaysia*. Ithaca: Cornell University, Southeast Asia Program Data Paper No. 531. 1964.

Pang Cheng Lian. *Singapore People's Action Party*. Singapore: Oxford University Press. 1971.

Purcell, Victor. *The Chinese in Malaya*. Kuala Lumpur: Oxford University Press. 1967.

Ratnam, K.J. and R.S. Milne. *The Malayan Parliamentary Election of 1964*. Singapore: University of Malaya Press. 1967.

Ratnam, K.J. *Communalism and the Political Process in Malaya*. Kuala Lumpur: University of Malaya Press. 1965.

Ross-Larson, Bruce. *The Politics of Federation: Syed Kechik in East Malaysia*. Singapore: Bruce Ross-Larson. 1976.

Shafruddin, B.H. *The Federal Factor in the Government and Politics of Peninsular Malaysia*. Singapore: Oxford University Press. 1987.

Shaw, William. *Tun Razak. His Life and Times*. Kuala Lumpur: Longman. 1976.

Sheppard, Mubin. *Tunku: His Life and Times*. Malaysia: Pelanduk Publications. 1995.

Short, Anthony. *The Communist Insurrection in Malaya 1948–60*. London: Frederick Muller. 1975.

Smith, Simon C. *British Relations with the Malay Rulers from Decentralization to Malayan Independence 1930–1957*. Kuala Lumpur: Oxford University Press. 1995.

Sopiee, Mohamed Noordin. *From Malayan Union to Singapore Separation: Political Unification in the Malaysia Region 1945–65*. Kuala Lumpur: Penerbit Universiti Malaya. 1974.

Stockwell, A.J. *British Policy and Malay Politics during the Malayan Union Experiment, 1942–1948*. Kuala Lumpur: Malaysian Branch of the Royal Asiatic Society. Monograph No. 8. 1979.

Stockwell, A.J. (ed.). *British Documents on the End of the Empire, Series B Volume 3: Malaya, Part I: The Malayan Union Experiment 1942–48*. London: HMSO. 1995.

———. *British Documents on the End of the Empire, Series B, Volume 3: Malaya, Part II: The Communist Insurrection 1948–1953*. London: HMSO. 1995.

———. *British Documents on the End of the Empire, Series B, Volume 3: Malaya, Part III: The Alliance Route to Independence*. London: HMSO. 1995.

Stubbs, Richard. *Hearts and Minds in Guerrilla Warfare: The Malayan Emergency 1948– 1960*. Singapore: Oxford University Press. 1989.

Tilman, Robert O. (ed.). *Man, State, and Society in Contemporary Southeast Asia*. New York: Praeger. 1969.
Turnbull, C.M. *A History of Singapore 1819–1975*. Singapore: Oxford University Press. 1977.
Vasil, R.K. *Ethnic Politics in Malaysia*. New Delhi: Radiant Publishers. 1980.
Warner, Dennis. *Reporting Southeast Asia*. Sydney: Angus and Robertson. 1966.
Wilson, Harold. *The Labour Government 1964–1970: A Personal Record*. London: Wiedenfeld and Nicolson. 1971.
Yeo Kim Wah. *Political Development in Singapore, 1945–1955*. Singapore: Singapore University Press. 1973.
Yong, C.F. *The Origins of Malayan Communism*. Singapore: South Seas Society. 1997.

Articles
Barker, Elisabeth. "Malaysia and Singapore", *The Indian Review*, 64, 9 (September 1965), pp. 461–62.
Barr, Michael "Lee Kuan Yew in Malaysia: A Reappraisal of Lee Kuan Yew's Role in the Separation of Singapore from Malaysia", *Asian Studies Review*, 21, 1 (July 1997), pp. 1–17
Bass, Jerome R. "Singapore's Relations with Malay(si)a: Merger and After", *Solidarity*, 4, 10 (October 1969), pp. 16–24.
Bellows, Thomas J. "The Singapore Party System", *Journal of Southeast Asian History*, 8, N1 (March 1967), pp. 122–38.
Boyce, Peter. "Singapore as a Sovereign State", *The Australian Outlook*, 19, 3 (1965), pp. 259–71.
———. "Policy Without Authority: Singapore's Foreign Affairs Power", *Journal of Southeast Asian History*, 6, 2 (September 1965), pp. 87–104.
Bradley, Paul C. "Rupture in Malaysia", *Current History*, 50, 294 (February 1966), pp. 98–105.
———. "The Formation of Malaysia", *Current History*, 46, 270 (February 1964), pp. 89–94.
Catley, R. "Malaysia: The Lost Battle for Merger", *The Australian Outlook*, 21, 1 (1967), pp. 44–60.
Esslemont, Don. "Malaysia: Politics Before the Split", *Venture*, 17, 8 (September 1965), pp. 18–20.
Gamer, Robert E. "Urgent Singapore, Patient Malaysia", *International Journal*, 21, 1 (1965–66), pp. 42–56.
Grossholtz, Jean. "An Exploration of Malaysian Meanings", *Asian Survey*, 6, 4 (April 1966), pp. 227–40.
Han, Suyin. "Singapore Separation", *Far Eastern Economic Review* (19 August 1965).
Hatta, Mohammad. "One Indonesian View of the Malaysian Issue", *Asian Survey*, 5, 3 (March 1965), pp. 139–43.
Josey, Alex. "Why Malaysia Failed", *New Statesman* (13 August 1965), pp. 207–8.
Leifer, Michael. "Communal Violence in Singapore", *Asian Survey*, 4, 10 (October 1964), pp. 1115–21.

————. "Singapore in Malaysia: The Politics of Federation", _Journal of Southeast Asian History_, 6, 2 (September 1965), pp. 54–70.

————. "Singapore Leaves Malaysia", _The World Today_, 21, 9 (September 1965), pp. 361–64.

————. "Astride the Straits of Johore: The British Presence and Commonwealth Rivalry in Southeast Asia", _Modern Asian Studies_, 1, 3 (1967), pp. 283–96.

————. "Singapore Leaves Malaysia", _The World Today_, 21, 9 (September, 1965), pp. 361–64.

Milne, R.S. "Malaysia: A New Federation in the Making", _Asian Survey_, 3, 2 (February 1963), pp. 507–18.

————. "Malaysia", _Asian Survey_, 4, 2 (February 1964), pp. 695–701.

————. "Singapore's Exit from Malaysia: The Consequences of Ambiguity", _Asian Survey_, 6, 3 (March 1966), pp. 175–84.

Ong, Noel. "A Bridge-Builder: Dr Thio Chan Bee (1904–1978)", _Journal of the Malaysian Branch of the Royal Asiatic Society_, Vol. LXX, Part I (1997).

Pang Cheng Lian. "The People's Action Party 1954–63", _Journal of Southeast Asian History_, 10, 1 (March 1969), pp. 142–54.

Parmer, J. Norman. "Malaysia 1965: Challenging the Terms of 1957", _Asian Survey_, 6, 2 (February 1966), pp. 111–18.

Roff, Margaret. "The Malayan Chinese Association, 1948–1965", _Journal of Southeast Asian History_, 6, 2 (September 1965), pp. 40–53.

Sadka, Emma. "Singapore and the Federation: Problems of Merger", _Asian Survey_, 1, 11 (Jan 1962), pp. 17–25.

Smith, T.E. "Malaysian After the Election", _The World Today_, 20 (August 1964), pp. 351–57.

Sopiee, Mohamed Noordin. "The Formation of Malaysia: A Reinterpretation", _Suara Pelajar_, 1, 1 (August 1971), pp. 8–13.

Starner, Frances L. "Malaysia and the North Borneo Territories", _Asian Survey_, 3, 11 (November 1963), pp. 519–30.

————. "Malaysia's First Year", _Asian Survey_, 5, 2 (February 1965), pp. 113–19.

Stenson, M.R. "The Malayan Union and the Historians", _Journal of Southeast Asian History_, 10, 2 (September 1969), pp. 344–54.

Taylor, Don. "Singapore goes it — but not so alone", _New Commonwealth_, 43, 1 (November 1965), pp. 567–69.

Tilman, Robert O. "The Alliance Pattern in Malaysian Politics: Bornean Variations on a Theme", _The South Atlantic Quarterly_, 63, 1 (Winter 1964), pp. 60–74.

————. "Malaysia: The Problems of Federation", _The Western Political Quarterly_, 16, 4 (December 1963), pp. 897–911

Turnbull, C.M. "The Post-War Decade in Malaya: The Settling Dust of Political Controversy", _Journal of the Malaysian Branch of the Royal Asiatic Society_, 60, 1 (June 1987), pp. 7–26.

Van der Kroef, Justus M. "Indonesia, Malaya and the North Borneo Crisis", _Asian Survey_, 3, 4 (April 1963), pp. 173–81.

Vasil, R.K. "The 1964 General Elections in Malaya", _International Studies_, 7, 1 (July 1965), pp. 20–65.

————. "Why Malaysia Failed?", *Quest*, 49 (April/ June 1966), pp. 51–59.

Wang, Gungwu. "The Way Ahead", *Straits Times Annual* (1966), pp. 26–31.

Wong, Ling Ken. "The Malayan Union: A Historical Retrospect", *Journal of Southeast Asian Studies*, 13, 1 (March 1982), pp. 184–91.

Yeo, Kim Wah. "The Anti-Federation Movement in Malaya, 1946–48", *Journal of Southeast Asian Studies*, 4, 1 (March 1973), pp. 31–51.

Theses

Andersen, Robert Allen. "The Separation of Singapore from Malaysia: A Study in Political Involution" (Unpublished PhD dissertation submitted to The American University, 1973).

Bedlington, Stanley Sanders. "The Singapore Malay Community: The Politics of State Integration" (Unpublished PhD dissertation submitted to Cornell University, 1974).

Elinah Abdullah. "Malay Political Activities in Singapore 1945–1959". (Unpublished Academic Exercise submitted to the Department of History, National University of Singapore, 1992).

Foo, Kim Leng. "The 1964 Singapore Riots" (Unpublished Academic Exercise submitted to the Department of History, National University of Singapore, 1980).

Joseph, Abraham. "The Foreign Relations of the PAP, 1961–1965: The International Campaign for Malaysia" (Unpublished Academic Exercise submitted to the Department of History, University of Singapore, 1979).

Lee, Gary. "The Political Career of Ong Eng Guan" (Unpublished Academic Exercise submitted to the Department of History, National University of Singapore, 1987).

Lee, Kah Chuen, "The 1963 Singapore General Elections" (Unpublished Academic Exercise, Department of History, University of Singapore, 1976).

Nam, Tae Yul. "Malaysia and Singapore: The Failure of a Political Experiment" (Unpublished PhD dissertation submitted to Georgetown University, 1975).

Ostrom, Charles Richard. "A Core Interest Analysis of the Formation of Malaysia and the Separation of Singapore" (Unpublished PhD dissertation submitted to the Claremont Graduate School, 1970).

Tan, Soo Kiat, "PAP in the 1964 Malayan General Elections" (Unpublished Academic Exercise submitted to the Department of History, National University of Singapore, 1980).

Wee, Shoo Soon. "The Separation of Singapore from Malaysia: Approaches and Issues" (Unpublished Academic Exercise submitted to the Department of History, National University of Singapore, 1998).

Oral History Interviews

Mohammed Khir Johari, transcript of interview by the Oral History Centre, National Archives of Singapore

Lee Gek Seng, transcript of interview by the Oral History Centre, National Archives of Singapore

INDEX

Abdul Ghafar bin Baba, 41; re-merger possibility, 280

Abdul Hamid bin Haji Jumat, 35, 59

Abdul Khadir bin Talib, 104

Abdul Rahman, Tunku, 5, 6, 22, 23, 70, 83–84, 106, 107, 193, 197, 199, 230, 238, 244, 249, 250, 251; on Malay rights, 240; rights of natives, 243; disengagement, 227, 238, 252, 291: *secret negotiations*, 217–27; electoral pact between PAP and SA, 23; on Grand Opposition, 240; on Singapore's independence, 11; and Lee Kuan Yew, 113, 198, 238, 251, 252, 254, 255; meeting on Federal Budget, 215; post-election meeting, 134–35; on Malaysia, 281; on MSC, 254; on MCA, 126; meeting BS leaders, 212; on merger, 10–11, 13, 22; on PAP, 105, 106, 108, 131, 198, 213, 230, 239, 286; Afro-Asian countries, 76; revitalizing SA, 96; separation, 257, 259, 261–64, 293; on Singapore, 12, 71, 263, 282: *election, 1963*, 11, 206, *and Malaysia*, 14, 16; *racial riots*, 169, 171, 192–95, 208; on SUMNO's defeat, 65–66, 67, 285; on Syed Ja'afar Albar, 194, 279; Truth Mission to Africa, 75, 78, 83

Abdul Rahman bin Talib, 106

Abdul Razak, Tun, 24, 73, 74, 103, 195, 218, 227, 231, 285; on communal politics, 183; on disengagement, 220–21; Federal elections, 1964, 114–15; and Goh Keng Swee, 182–83; and Lee Kuan Yew, 182, 184–85, 243, 249, 250, 254–55, 259; on Malay political domination, 184; on MSC, 255; and PAP, 133, 179, 184, 185; racial remarks, 111; on separation, 257–59; Singapore racial riots, 169, 170, 171, 173, 182, 187, 190, 197

Ahmad bin Abdul Hamid, 137

Ahmad bin Haji Taff, 33, 50, 66, 112, 139, 155

Algeria, on Malaysia–Indonesia dispute, 79

Ali Abu, 144

Ali bin Haji Ahmad, 137, 141, 150, 155, 178

All Malaya Council of Joint Action, 5

Alliance Party, 5, 6, 96, 292; and Barisan Sosialis (BS), 212; Federal elections, 1964, 109, 118, 120, 123; Hong Lim by-election, 256; Malaysian Malaysia, 250; and MSC, 253, 254; pan-Malaysian party, 95; and PAP, 105, 211–213, 239–46, 283: *showdown in Parliament*, 246–50; state elections, 1964, 119

Alliance Party Singapura, 239

Almenoar, Syed Esa, 33, 151, 152, 156, 163, 173, 190, 211, 212

Anglo-Malay relations, pro-Malay policy, 2

Australia: on disengagement, 237; holding the ring, 235; Lee Kuan Yew's visit, 236–38; preserving integrity of Malaysia, 237

Bahnini, Ahmed, 79

Baldwin, Charles F., 65, 66, 70, 89, 92

Balewa, Abubakar Tafawa, 81

Banda, Hastings, 81

Bani, S.T., 52

Barisan Sosialis (BS), 12, 21, 25, 26, 27, 32, 57, 86, 212, and Alliance Party, cooperation, 212; in central government, 71; election, 1963, 30–32, 34–39, 48, 49, 50, 51; Hong Lim by-election, 256; merger, 13, 28; protest march, 58; setback, 30

Barker, E.W., 50, 117, 122, 230, 257; on separation, 258, 259, 260

Belfrej, M. Ahmed, 79

Bell, James D., 89, 107–9, 187, 190, 195, 196; on Lee Kuan Yew, 84

Ben Bella, Ahmed, 79

Bogaars, George, 161, 186

Borneo territories: effect of disengagement on, 222, 223, 224; in Malaysia, 12, 13–15, 16, 20: *opposition*, 16

Bottomley, Arthur, 239

Bottomley, James, 182, 225, 226

Bourdillon, H.T., 3

Bourguiba, Habib, 78

Brahimi, M., 79

Britain, 4: on disengagement, 217–27; Second World War, defeat, 1

Brown, William A., 229